Commerce with the Classics

By his will, Mr. Thomas Spencer Jerome endowed the lectureship that bears his name. It is jointly administered by the University of Michigan and the American Academy in Rome, and the lectures for which it provides are delivered at both institutions. They deal with phases of the history or culture of the Romans or of peoples included in the Roman Empire.

F. E. Adcock, *Roman Political Ideas and Practice*

G. W. Bowersock, *Hellenism in Late Antiquity*

Frank E. Brown, *Cosa: The Making of a Roman Town*

Jacqueline de Romilly, *The Rise and Fall of States According to Greek Authors*

Anthony Grafton, *Commerce with the Classics: Ancient Books and Renaissance Readers*

Claude Nicolet, *Space, Geography, and Politics in the Early Roman Empire*

Massimo Pallottino, *A History of Earliest Italy*

Jaroslav Pelikan, *What Has Athens to Do with Jerusalem?* Timaeus *and* Genesis *in Counterpoint*

Brunilde S. Ridgway, *Roman Copies of Greek Sculpture: The Problem of the Originals*

Lily Ross Taylor, *Roman Voting Assemblies: From the Hannibalic War to the Dictatorship of Caesar*

Mario Torelli, *Typology and Structure of Roman Historical Reliefs*

Paul Zanker, *The Power of Images in the Age of Augustus*

JEROME LECTURES, 20

Commerce with the Classics: Ancient Books and Renaissance Readers

Anthony Grafton

Ann Arbor

THE UNIVERSITY OF MICHIGAN PRESS

Copyright © by the University of Michigan 1997
All rights reserved
Published in the United States of America by
The University of Michigan Press
Manufactured in the United States of America
⊗ Printed on acid-free paper

2001   2000   1999   1998   5   4   3   2

A CIP catalog record for this book is available from the British Library.

Library of Congress Cataloging-in-Publication Data

Grafton, Anthony.
    Commerce with the classics : ancient books and Renaissance readers
/ Anthony Grafton.
        p.   cm. — (Jerome lectures ; 20)
    Includes bibliographical references and index.
    ISBN 0-472-10626-0 (acid-free paper)
    1. Classical literature—Appreciation—Europe—History—16th
century.   2. Books and reading—Europe—History—16th century.
3. Learning and scholarship—History—16th century.   4. Classicism—
Europe.   5. Fifteenth century.   6. Humanists—Europe.
7. Renaissance.   I. Title.   II. Series: Jerome lectures ; 20th ser.
PA3013.G68   1997
880'.09—dc20   96-36751
                                                                  CIP

To the memory of Margaret Gibson

Preface

This book reports on the results of a personal inquiry, one that began more than two decades ago, into the ways in which the intellectuals of early modern Europe read and used Greek and Latin texts. It takes the form not of a survey, which would be both presumptuous and premature, but of a series of essays. Each sets out to show how a particular Renaissance intellectual bought and borrowed, interpreted and applied classical texts. By sticking to the concrete details of biography and library history, by adopting the limited, but focused, point of view of one who travels the high-walled mazes of texts and marginal commentaries on classical texts, and by studying methods and experiences of reading, one reader at a time and in detail, I have tried to convey the flavor and texture, as well as something of the substance, of a culture of the ancient book that lies at the origins of modernity.

My research into primary sources was carried out chiefly in the Firestone Library of Princeton University and at the Biblioteca Apostolica Vaticana, the Bibliothèque Nationale de France, the libraries of the Freie Universität Berlin, and the two houses of the Staatsbibliothek zu Berlin, Stiftung Preußischer Kulturbesitz. Shorter forays into the collections of the Leiden University Library, the Universitätsbibliothek of the Eberhard-Karls-Universität Tübingen, the University of Delaware Library, and the Cambridge University Library also turned up vital material. The Wissenschaftskolleg zu Berlin, which invited me to spend the academic year 1993–94 as a visiting fellow, enabled me to carry out additional research and to complete the text. My special gratitude goes to Ms. Gesine Bottomley, the librarian of the Wissenschaftskolleg, and her staff, who showed astonishing efficiency and ingenuity in obtaining the varied and often recondite materials that I needed.

Ellen Bauerle of the University of Michigan Press benignly supervised the transformation of a series of lectures into a book. Two anonymous readers engaged by the press commented helpfully on a draft of the text. So, at other stages, did my friends Tom Kaufmann, Jill Kraye, Glenn Most, Maurice Olender, David Quint, and Nancy Siraisi, whose erudite and unsparing criticism of earlier drafts resulted in many improvements. Ann Blair, Henk Jan de Jonge, Peter Godman, François Hartog, Bob Lamberton, Carol Quillen, Wilhelm Schmidt-Biggemann, and Noel Swerdlow taught me much about more than one of the subjects treated here. Friedrich Seck expertly guided me through the riches of the Tübingen collections, and P.E. Easterling generously let me use her notes on the manuscripts of George Hermonymus in the Cambridge University Library. Emily Kadens, finally, helped prepare the manuscript for the press.

The chapters of this book draw in various ways on earlier research and publications. Chapter 1 incorporates a much expanded version of a lecture first delivered at the conference on "Alexandrie ou la Mémoire du Savoir" organized by the Bibliothèque de France in June 1993: the original French text appears in *Le pouvoir des bibliothèques,* ed. M. Baratin and C. Jacob (Paris, 1996), 189–203. Parts of chapter 2, which were presented to a memorable conference on Erwin Panofsky at the Institute for Advanced Study in October 1993, appear in *Meaning in the Visual Arts: Views from the Outside,* ed. I. Lavin (Princeton, 1995), 123–30. Chapter 4 builds on earlier research into the reception of Homer in the Renaissance. For a preliminary discussion see "Renaissance Readers of Homer's Ancient Readers," in *Homer's Ancient Readers,* ed. J.J. Keaney and R. Lamberton (Princeton, 1992), 149–72. Chapter 5 uses and revises earlier discussions of Kepler's scholarship first published in *Defenders of the Text* (Cambridge, Mass., and London, 1991), chapter 7, and in "Kepler as a Reader," *Journal of the History of Ideas* 53 (1992): 561–72. In every case, however, I have substantially revised these borrowings from myself.

For comments on the lectures from which each chapter gradually grew I owe thanks to audiences at a workshop on the uses of examples in historiography, organized by François Hartog and me, at the Wissenschaftskolleg zu Berlin (chapter 1); the Institut für Romanistik at the Freie Universität Berlin (chapter 2); the Departments of History and History of Science at Johns Hopkins University, the Institut für Philosophie (II) at the Freie Universität Berlin, the Seminar für Klassische Philologie at the University of Tübingen, the Institutes for History of Medicine and History of Science at the University of Göttingen, and the Potsdam Einstein Forum (chapter 3); the Institute for Reformation History at the University of Geneva (chapter 4); and the participants in a session on humanism and science at the annual meeting of the History of Science Society in Madison, Wisconsin, in 1990 (chapter 5).

The book as a whole exists because the Department of Classics at the University of Michigan invited me to deliver the Thomas Spencer Jerome lectures in 1992 and the Collège de France awarded me a visiting professorship for the same year. The hospitality of Joseph and Françoise Connors in Rome in March 1992, of Marc Fumaroli in Paris in June, and of John D'Arms and Ludwig Koenen in Ann Arbor in October and early November of the same year made my stays in those cities unforgettably pleasant and stimulating. In singling out for thanks Leonard Barkan, Mac Bell, Jean Céard, Roger Chartier, Jean Dupèbe, Charles Fantazzi, Marie-Madeleine de la Garanderie, Nicholas Horsfall, Diane Hughes, Sally Humphreys, Lester Little, Massimo Miglio, John O'Brien, and Silvia Rizzo, I mention only those of my hearers whose acute questions remained most embarrassingly prominent in my memory as I rethought my original formulations. To them and to the many others who offered valuable suggestions, collateral references, and objections, I owe some of the most challenging and stimulating weeks of my life.

Special thanks, finally, must go to those whose kindness enabled me to use Guillaume Budé's notebooks, briefly discussed in chapter 4. These extraordinary documents are preserved in Geneva, in the private library of Jean-Evrard Dominicé, himself a descendant of Guillaume Budé. My colleague at the Wissenschaftskolleg, Thomas Gelzer, put me in contact with M. Olivier Reverdin, who invited me to examine the notebooks in the best possible working conditions during a stay at the Fondation Hardt.

Some of the ideas presented in this book were first formulated amid the spring beauties of the garden of the Villa Aurelia, others during early summer walks across the Seine bridges, others in the sharp, cool air of dark autumn afternoons in Ann Arbor and Berlin. Though these biographical facts add nothing to the solidity of my theses, they greatly enhanced the pleasure with which I carried out this particular piece of work. My thanks, once more, to all my generous friends, for their hospitality and their criticism. I will always cherish both.

Contents

Introduction: From Confucius to Cicero 1

1. Commerce with the Classics 11

2. Leon Battista Alberti: The Writer as Reader 53

3. Giovanni Pico della Mirandola:
Trials and Triumphs of an Omnivore 93

4. How Guillaume Budé Read His Homer 135

5. Johannes Kepler: The New Astronomer Reads Ancient Texts 185

Epilogue 225

A Note on Further Reading 229

Index 233

Plates 239

Commerce with the Classics

Introduction: From Confucius to Cicero

Shortly after 1600, Chinese readers learned that even scholarship, the Confucian art of arts and science of sciences, could be taken to excess: "When a man is proud because he can understand and explain the *Book of Changes*, you listen and say to yourself quietly: if Fu Hsi, in making known 'the order of [the holy sages'] nature and of fate,' had not covered over his meaning with graphs and lines and had not enveloped them in trigrams and hexagrams, this man would have nothing to be proud of."[1] The same text dismissed the man who could comment on books but could not put their precepts into practice as a mere "actor and not a philosopher of life."[2] It urged readers to "set [their] life's mission on cultivating learning."[3] And it warned them that the imperial court, the focus of learned ambition and the locale of much lurid entertainment in Ming China, should not attract the serious man: "The men of this world are like actors on a stage. The commonplace jobs they do are like the dramatic roles actors perform. Emperors, public ministers, grand officials, functionaries, servants, the empress and her attendants are all momentary decoration. The costumes they wear are not their own."[4]

The text that stated these sound principles and many others bore the title *Twenty-Five Sayings*. Written in fluent classical Chinese, it was heavily salted with the internal quotations from classical texts that Chinese students learned both to recognize and to introduce into their own "eight-legged essays" as they moved up the imperial educational ladder. Deftly brandished traditional Chinese references, such as one to the myth of Wei Che and K'uai K'uei, the father against whom Wei Che rebelled "because he

---

1. C. Spalatin, SJ, *Matteo Ricci's Use of Epictetus* (Waegwan, 1975), 45, adapted; the internal quotation comes from the *I-ching,* 2. See H. Goodman and A. Grafton, "Ricci, the Chinese, and the Toolkits of Textualists," *Asia Major,* ser. 3, 3 (1991): 95–148, at 99 n. 6; The sinological segments of what follows are fully documented in that article and are all owed—as are many thanks—to my collaborator, Howard Goodman.

2. Spalatin, *Ricci's Use of Epictetus,* 46.

3. Ibid., 33; see Goodman and Grafton, "Ricci," 101 n. 13.

4. Spalatin, *Ricci's Use of Epictetus,* 42; Goodman and Grafton, "Ricci," 101 n. 16.

believed that his happiness consisted in being master in place of his father," made its local color even brighter.[5] In most respects it looked like a native product of the Chinese mental world.

Yet the text also had disturbing, alien elements: notably a reference to the disciples of a wise mandarin named Saint Francis.[6] Moreover, the presence of these bumps in the smooth lacquer of this piece of chinoiserie should occasion no surprise. For the book was not an original text but an adaptation, and its author—though a mandarin—was hardly Chinese. Matteo Ricci, the Jesuit missionary to whom Jonathan Spence and Jacques Gernet have each devoted brilliant, sharply contrasting books, drew the bulk of his *Twenty-Five Sayings* from Stoic, rather than Confucian, sources—from works written not in Chinese but in Greek.[7] He relied particularly on a moral work that Renaissance humanists had loved for more than a century: the *Enchiridion* of Epictetus, which both Niccolò Perotti and Angelo Poliziano had translated into Latin.[8]

Some of Ricci's *Sayings* literally reproduced Epictetus' teachings, changing only the names. But most precepts needed at least a little preparation and fertilizing before they could bloom in Chinese soil. Ricci's attack on the theatricality of the Chinese court, for example, gave a sharper moralizing point to Epictetus' general description of the world as a theater and life as a play.[9] Ricci's warning against the arrogance that afflicts exegetes changed the direction of Epictetus' original statement. "When a man is proud because he can understand and explain the writings of Chrysippus," Epictetus had told his readers, "say to yourself, if Chrysippus had not written obscurely, this man would have nothing to be proud of."[10] An attack on the unnecessary obscurity of an ancient, canonical text would have sounded immodest coming from a Westerner. It might have sounded even worse if a comment had made clear that the object of this criticism, Chrysippus, had himself written authoritative commentaries on still earlier classics—and thus resembled, as Socrates and Epictetus did not, the literati of traditional China. The sting of the passage was nicely removed, however, when Ricci transformed it into an attack on the pretensions of the *I-ching* commenta-

---

5. Spalatin, *Ricci's Use of Epictetus,* 37–38.

6. Ibid., 33.

7. J. Gernet, *China and the Christian Impact,* trans. J. Lloyd (Cambridge, 1985); J. Spence, *The Memory Palace of Matteo Ricci* (New York, 1984).

8. See *Niccolò Perotti's Version of the Enchiridon of Epictetus,* ed. R.P. Oliver (Urbana, 1954); and *La traduction française du manuel d'Epictète d'André de Rivaudeau au XVIe siècle,* ed. L.P. Zanta (Paris, 1914).

9. Epictetus *Enchiridion* 17.

10. Ibid., 49.

tors of his own day, whose elaborate diagrams would later fascinate Bouvet and Leibniz.

Even giving the apparently straightforward admonition to be a philosopher, rather than an actor, required work on Ricci's part. Like Seneca, Epictetus dismissed passive readers who failed to live by their texts, calling them mere *grammatikoi* not *philosophoi*.[11] In China, the same literati traditionally established texts, drew their vital lessons in commentaries, and used them in practice—or at least claimed to do so—as state functionaries. The distinction could not be made. Ricci's small alteration of the central phrase reflected careful thought about the differences between languages and cultures.

Ricci could produce his version of Epictetus for one reason: like all Jesuits, he had been drilled in the central skills of Renaissance humanism. As a scholar, he knew the techniques of what some teachers already called "historical" exegesis. He could set texts back into their contexts, using his knowledge of earlier and contemporary texts to decode allusions and explicate usages, in the hope of reconstructing what a given work had meant to both its authors and its first readers. As a teacher, he knew the techniques of "accommodation." He could, that is, detect every point where what he took as the original message of a text from a distant time or place challenged the beliefs of his own Christian culture, and he could hide these points effectively from European schoolboys, without an awkward pause for thought, by wrapping them in the decent obscurity of moral chatter or allegorical interpretation. No wonder that he could also dress the Greek and Latin classics in the more elaborate disguise needed by a reading public, like the Chinese one, that lived at an even greater historical and cultural distance from ancient Rome.[12]

When Ricci interpreted Chinese texts for Christian converts in the East or for his superiors at home in the West, he used the same analytical tools that he had applied to the Western classics, to similar effect. He divided the Chinese tradition, just as the humanists had long since divided the Western one, setting the boundary between golden antiquity and modern darkness just after A.D. 1000. The Chinese had ancient classics, of which he thoroughly approved. But they also had modern interpretations, which he rejected as a

---

11. Epictetus *Enchiridion* 49. Cf. Seneca *Ep. mor.* 108.23; for the impact of this passage in the later sixteenth century see A. Grafton, *Defenders of the Text* (Cambridge, Mass., and London, 1991).

12. For the origins of Jesuit humanism see now the splendid survey by J. O'Malley, *The First Jesuits* (Cambridge, Mass., and London, 1993), chap. 6, with references to the main earlier studies. See also G.P. Brizzi et al., *Università, principe, gesuiti* (Rome, 1980); and Brizzi, ed., *La 'Ratio studiorum'* (Rome, 1981).

late perversion of the older, still valid texts. The doctrine of the *t'ai-chi,* for example, he condemned as a Chinese scholasticism that, like its Western equivalent, only distracted the modern reader from the best of ancient metaphysics and morals. Only when Ricci could not avoid it did he insist that a Christian must attack the errors of the ancient Chinese, rather than twist their words to bear a Christian sense.[13]

The hermeneutical and expository skills that Ricci used so adeptly had been developed by humanists from Petrarch to Erasmus and beyond. Erasmus, like his friend and ally Juan Luis Vives, was a brilliant historical reader of the classics and the Bible. He rejected the scholastic culture of the universities. Its proponents were obsessed with classical texts, like the works of Aristotle, that he did not think central to living the good life. Moreover, they misinterpreted even these as coming from a world identical to their own. They were, in short, bad readers. Erasmus, by contrast, insisted that the best way to read a text was to envision as clearly as possible the world that its author had lived in, to work out, detail by detail, the particular character of its style and the way this reflected the author's ideas and beliefs.[14] But he also saw that this indispensable program could have uncomfortable results—especially for a scholar who hoped to combine classical culture with a reformed Christianity. Erasmus stated forcefully in his *Ciceronianus* that to Christians, the Roman world was a foreign country. Religion, institutions, and language itself had changed radically between Cicero's time and his own. Hence, he admitted, even the best of classical texts could not provide all the moral or rhetorical guidance that a Christian scholar needed.[15]

As a teacher, however, Erasmus stood ready to cover up the defects that his scholarship detected in the classical canon. His *De ratione studii,* for example, had as its core an exegesis of the first line of Virgil's second *Eclogue,* "Corydon the shepherd was hot for pretty Alexis"—perhaps the hardest line in Virgil's works for a Christian teacher to explicate. The whole point here, Erasmus told the future teachers whom he saw as his public, was to distract the boys. One should tell them firmly that the poet dealt with friendship, and then digress. Topics readily suggested themselves. The teacher could praise friendship, criticize enmity, quote proverbs ("like likes

---

13. See the text by Ricci published by P. D'Elia, SJ, in *Fonti Ricciane* (Rome, 1942–49), 2: 297–98.

14. Erasmus, *Methodus, Ausgewählte Werke,* ed. H. Holborn and A. Holborn (Munich, 1933; repr., 1964), 150–62.

15. Erasmus, *Dialogus Ciceronianus,* ed. P. Mesnard, *Opera omnia* (Amsterdam, 1971), series 1, vol. 2, esp. 709–10.

like"; "seek a wife who is your equal"), or tell the stories of bad and good friendships: Romulus and Remus, Castor and Pollux, Narcissus and Narcissus. So primed, the teacher could hope that the boys would miss the homoerotic message of a poet who was a Roman, not a Christian.[16]

Halfway around the world and almost a century later, Ricci worked in exactly the same spirit. Where Epictetus' original text did not teach exactly the moral Ricci wanted it to, he adapted it. To make his new text appetizing, he basted it with purist, classical Chinese and stuffed it, like a Christmas goose, with learned references to texts and myths. To ensure that it reached a public, he had it cast and printed in an appropriate literary and calligraphic form. Ricci's Chinese readers encountered a Western text so deftly and completely repackaged that its charm seemed, for the most part, that of the intimately familiar—if not mutton dressed as lamb, then kebabs got up as wind-dried beef.

Ricci's efforts were not isolated. At another border of the expanding Christian world, Catholic missionaries in New Spain and the Andes recorded traditional Meso-American images and their interpretations. They made what had been a fluid, oral tradition into a fixed, classical set of texts, modeled on the encyclopedias of Latin antiquity and the Middle Ages and the heavily annotated Bibles of Nicholas of Lyra. Like the Chinese missionaries, they went to great pains to master and communicate in the languages of the peoples they meant to convert—which they interpreted as a primitive brand of hieroglyphics surprisingly like those of the mandarins.[17] Like the Chinese missionaries, they were both surprised and pleased to find what they took as morals worthy of Plato and Aristotle in the teachings of the Indian sages. Unlike the Jesuits in China, however, the friars in New Spain found in what they saw as the core traditions of Aztecs and Incas a great deal that they could not interpret as anything but diabolical efforts to deceive.[18]

These and other Renaissance intellectuals shared a commitment to a continuous, intensive conversation with ancient texts. This provided the foundation of their efforts to understand other cultures and religions, devise natural and political philosophies, create a personal code of conduct, and cultivate a literary style. From the outset of the Renaissance, as reading the classics became a central preoccupation of intellectuals, first in Italy and

16. See Grafton, *Defenders of the Text,* chap. 1.

17. See G. Cantelli, *Mente, corpo, linguaggio* (Florence, 1986).

18. See, e.g., D. Durán, *Book of the Gods and Rites and the Ancient Calendar,* trans. and ed. F. Horcasitas and D. Heyden (Norman, 1971); S. Gruzinski, *La colonisation de l'imaginaire* (Paris, 1988); and S. MacCormack, *Religion in the Andes* (Princeton, 1991).

then in other areas of Europe, every aspect of reading underwent scrutiny. The humanists debated—and changed—the physical appearance of books and the content of the school canon; they created a new form of public library and argued vigorously about the way texts should be read and discussed within it. Should one read alone and in private or in company? Should one begin with summaries of the main texts in any area or read only the original sources? Should one read the sources in the light of older and newer commentaries, and if so, which? Every humanist teacher felt the need to provide precise instructions for his students on how to read and annotate the classics. But this apparently simple task proved contentious. Some held that readers should mark their books, others that they should copy out extracts into notebooks. Some wanted notes to be brief and schematic, others to be full and informative. Some expected the young aristocrat to read texts on his own, others to work with a tutor who would summarize them and identify their salient points. And the establishment of a hermeneutical method—a method for interpreting classical texts, for explaining their apparent contradictions and errors, and for reconciling their teachings with those of Christianity—naturally proved far more complex and more contentious than these controversial points of technique.

By the seventeenth century, when the educational reformers J.H. Alsted and J.A. Comenius systematically analyzed the virtues and failings of humanist education, they offered systematic answers to every one of these questions. Young readers—said Alsted—should at first study methodical, modern books: though they should read the ancients for their "authority," they should begin with the moderns, and they should avoid all magical, obscene, and pagan texts. Comenius, by contrast, showed more enthusiasm for wide reading in the classics. He urged students to imitate the style and analyze the arguments of their authors, down to the minutest detail. They must perform a full anatomy on each text to discover its fundamental "artificium"; then they must imitate this, translating it into the vernacular, adapting it in Latin, or imitating it in an independent exercise of their own.[19] Less important than the details of their recommendations—fascinating though these are—is that they summarize and respond to two and a half centuries of development in the practice and theory of reading. Like dancing—another activity that moderns consider free and natural but that the intellectuals of early modern Europe saw as a complex and rule-bound pursuit that must be learned and practiced with meticulous care—classical

---

19. For Alsted's rules see H. Zedelmaier, *Bibliotheca universalis und Bibliotheca selecta* (Cologne, Weimar, and Vienna, 1992), 79 n. 218. For Comenius see his *Opera didactica omnia* (Amsterdam, 1657; repr. Prague, 1957), 2: cols. 203–5.

reading formed the object of a large theoretical apparatus. It had an etiquette and an aesthetic, a morality and a method, a market and a set of ideals: in fact, it had several of each. These form the object of this book.

Limitations should be stated. I certainly will not try to survey in one short book all the multiple modes of reading, from memorization to rewriting, with which the members of early modern Europe's many literate cultures fished for meaning in the oceans of manuscript and printed texts from the ancient world and later that were available to them. More than one Italian city harbored everything from learned Byzantine exiles who read the core texts of Greek epic and tragedy, drawing explanations of hard words and strange objects from the rich marginal commentaries that their forebears had compiled a millennium before, to barely literate men and women who memorized and happily distorted in retelling them the stories of Boccaccio and the lives of the desert saints. This vast territory of misreading is still very far from being mapped.[20] Similarly, many individual texts have attracted highly skilled and original readers through the centuries. Reactions to a single demanding work—the *Naturalis Historia* of the elder Pliny, recently the object of an impressive study—changed radically with time and environment. Ancient, medieval, and Renaissance readings of Pliny took a staggering variety of forms, ranging from active rewriting and imitation to sophisticated philological analysis. In reconstructing this complex history, Arno Borst has shed new light on the intellectual development of the West as well as the narrower history of books and readers.[21] Ideally, many similar diachronic studies should complement works devoted to the range of forms of reading that existed simultaneously in a single place and time. I hope only to chart a short course across one small segment of this enormous territory—to catch some Renaissance intellectuals at work on the hard task of making sense of the Greek and Latin classics.

Accordingly, this book deals with the exceptions rather than the rule: with intellectuals who brought sophisticated training and high originality to the task of reading. It does not describe the experiences of the ordinary humanist teacher and his student. The study of reading in the Renaissance makes a particularly opportune case on which to try an interdisciplinary approach—one that combines the methods of the philologist with those of the intellectual historian and the historian of the book. Humanistic philology—a field founded by Georg Voigt and others in the nineteenth century—has now become a well-established, if not a populous, field of scholarship.

20. For a survey see J. Hankins, *Plato in the Italian Renaissance* (Leiden, 1990), introduction.

21. A. Borst, *Das Buch der Naturgeschichte*, 2d ed. (Heidelberg, 1995).

Sabbadini, de Nolhac, and Ullman amassed a treasury of information about the sorts of books that humanists liked to read, steal, and buy and about the ways in which they copied, annotated, and recycled them. They and more recent scholars have reconstructed in detail the libraries and the working habits of many individual readers. The work of Giuseppe Billanovich and Armando Petrucci, Silvia Rizzo and Vincenzo Fera, among others, offers exemplary guidance into the intricacies of Renaissance scholarship.

The historian of reading, however, cannot simply piece together a mosaic of technical details and claim to have recovered the experience of contact with the classics. Roberto Cardini, for example, has recently argued that the traditional approach, for all its importance, does not re-create the humanist's "real library"—that is, identify the books that historians, philosophers, and poets wrestled with, reinterpreted, and rewrote in their own creative work. Only scrutiny of the texts they wrote—and systematic analysis of how they used ancient materials to rear their new structures—can achieve this goal.[22] Cardini's methodological point is well taken, but it amounts to a description of measures already taken rather than a prescription for reform. Historians of Renaissance literature, philosophy, and science have long concentrated on the ways in which writers worked into their own books implied responses to the texts with which they contended. Vladimir Zabughin, Don Cameron Allen, Frances Yates, and D.P. Walker showed long ago how much of the intellectual energy of the Renaissance derived from intellectuals' systematic efforts to adapt and alter ancient texts—not to mention their wrong but fertile assumptions about the dates and origins of particular texts.

To restore the humanists' lost experience of reading in all its life and color, finally, a third form of historical inquiry must also come into play—one that lays less emphasis on the textual contents than on the physical form of classical books in the Renaissance. Paleographers, codicologists, connoisseurs of bookbindings, and historians of printing have shown, in complementary ways, that the fifteenth and sixteenth centuries saw a revolution take place in the aesthetics of book production and consumption as well as in the contents of school curricula and learned libraries. The shape that Renaissance books took had effects on their appeal to buyers and their impact on readers. The physical aspects of reading—the hardest, perhaps, to reconstruct, but vital nonetheless to any effort to produce a three-dimensional vision of this lost world of experience—call as loudly as the intellectual ones for sustained discussion.

---

22. R. Cardini, *Mosaici: Il 'nemico' dell'Alberti* (Rome, 1990).

For the last two generations, many of the most original students of the reception of the classics in the Renaissance have refused to be confined to a single one of the disciplinary pigeonholes just described. Garin, Kristeller, Schmitt, and Baxandall long ago combined the study of the rules and conditions of reading as a craft with that of the creative achievements of individuals who made it an art and those of the scribes and printers who laid its material basis. Younger scholars in many fields have continued their work, and many of them pursue their quarry with equal ease through the ragged underbrush of their marginal notes and across the sunny highlands of their formal treatises.[23] This book sets out not to revise accepted opinion but to summarize and extend an ongoing enterprise. In it I use case studies to suggest that the history of Renaissance thought and scholarship, the history of philosophy and that of philology, and the history of the book are enriched when the scholar accepts that many individuals usually seen only as writers were also readers—and some of them more the latter than the former.

To capture the feel and texture of our protagonists' contact with what they called the classics, we will first learn to see them among the elegant wooden shelves and benches where they spent so many hours leaning over heavy, odoriferous books, writing in margins, and using the skills, and sometimes breaking the rules, they had learned from influential teachers. But "by their fruits shall you know them." We will also read their finished works and establish how they used the treasures for which they hunted with such strenuous and devoted attention. When these lenses are put into a single tube and focused, even familiar intellectual figures may take on a new look. So, perhaps, will the long series of transactions and transformations by which ancient texts were kept alive for generations of modern readers and transmuted by dozens of modern writers. At least it may become apparent that the study of these margins is no marginal enterprise for the historian of Renaissance culture in any of its forms.

---

23. E.g., (in Italy) Cardini himself, L. Cesarini Martinelli, V. de Caprio, M. Miglio, M. Regoliosi, S. Rizzo, V. Fera; (in Germany) the late K. Krautter, P. Godman, F.-R. Haussmann; (in the Netherlands) H.-J. de Jonge, A. Wesseling; (in France) J. Céard, M. Fumaroli, P. Laurens; (in England) M. Davies, L. Deitz, A.C. Dionisotti, L. Jardine, J. Kraye, J. O'Brien; (in the United States) the late J. d'Amico, M.J.B. Allen, A. Ascoli, B.P. Copenhaver, A. Field, J. Gaisser, P. Grendler, J. Hankins, D. Marsh, J. Monfasani, G.W. Pigman, D. Robin. Naturally, this selection is arbitrary and could be greatly extended.

1

Commerce with the Classics

A Book for a Pope

On 13 July 1452 the scribe Ioannes Lamperti de Rodenberg finished copy-ing a manuscript of Lorenzo Valla's Latin translation of Thucydides. In a holograph note at the end, Valla explained both how excellent he found the result and what he saw as its purpose: "I, Lorenzo Valla, corrected this codex of Thucydides, of whom I believe that even the Greeks had no more splendidly written or illuminated text, at the command of Pope Nicholas and working with the very Ioannes who wrote it so well. Therefore I have entered this subscription in my own hand, so that this codex would be the official copy of my translation and could be used to correct other copies."[1] Valla deposited the manuscript in the Vatican Library. There, Nicholas and Valla both hoped, it would serve as an official text—the model for all other copies and a resource for the members of "la corte di Roma," for whom Nicholas destined his collection.

At first sight both the manuscript and the text it proffers seem to realize the humanists' boldest claims. Its readers made contact with two of the keenest intellects that the classical tradition can boast. Thucydides, that most darkly analytical and starkly eloquent of historians, had remained unknown in the Western Middle Ages and the early Renaissance. Some of the best-informed readers in the early fifteenth century, such as Coluccio Salutati—who had parts of book 1 of Diodorus Siculus specially translated by Leonardo Bruni to aid him in his mythological researches—seem not to have read him. A number of Salutati's younger friends, who learned Greek

---

1. MS Vat. lat. 1801, fol. 184 recto: "Hunc Thucydidis codicem, qualis nullus ut opinor unquam apud ipsos grecos vel scriptus vel ornatus est magnificentius, idem ego Laurentius iussu sanctissimi domini nostri domini Nicolai divina providentia pape Quinti, recognovi, cum ipso Ioanne, qui eum tam egregie scripsit. Ideoque hec meo chirographo subscripsi, ut esset hic codex mee translationis archetypus, unde cetera possent exemplaria emendari." For a descrip-tion of the MS see B. Nogara, *Codices Vaticani Latini III: Codices 1461–2059* (Vatican City, 1912), 275–76, but his text of the subscription is imperfect. For a critical text and an impor-tant discussion see S. Rizzo, *Il lessico filologico degli umanisti* (Rome, 1973), 312.

from the Byzantine scholar Manuel Chrysoloras, studied the *Histories* in whole or in part. But the text remained the possession of the tiny group capable of reading the original.[2] To encounter his history, translated in full, for the first time, was surely a great and salutary shock—as if one had come to the top of a roller coaster and then had the full panorama of Athens in prosperity, crisis, and defeat suddenly appear.

Valla, moreover, made the perfect interpreter for his demanding Thucydidean text. A brilliant iconoclast, he demolished the pretensions of medieval lawyers and theologians by showing that they misunderstood their own canonical texts. He destroyed the reputation of a rival humanist, Poggio Bracciolini, by writing a dialogue in which the cook and stable-boy of another humanist, Guarino da Verona, exposed Poggio's errors in Latinity.[3] And he dismantled the papal claim to lordship over the Western empire by proving that it rested on a forged text, the *Donation of Constantine*. In this case rhetoric and hermeneutics combined to produce an unreading, rather than a reading—a searing demonstration that the text could not be what its title claimed, could not even have been written in its supposed century of origin.[4] No one was better equipped by temperament than Valla to appreciate Thucydides' clear-eyed unmasking of the springs of victory and defeat in human affairs.

In technique, moreover, no one was better qualified than Valla to translate Thucydides. An expert Greek scholar, he could cope with what he called Thucydides' notoriously "difficult and rocky" style, even when Cardinal Bessarion, who had promised to help him, proved unable to do so.[5] A

---

2. See B.L. Ullman, *The Humanism of Coluccio Salutati* (Padua, 1963), 227; Salutati, *De laboribus Herculis,* ed. Ullman (Zürich, 1951), 2:569–71. For the early spread of interest in Thucydides in the circle of the Greek scholar Manuel Chrysoloras see U. Klee, *Beiträge zur Thukydides-Rezeption während des 15. und 16. Jahrhunderts in Italien und Deutschland* (Bern, New York, and Paris, 1990), 19–23.

3. On this episode see R. Pfeiffer, "Küchenlatein," *Philologus* 86 (1931): 455–59 = *Ausgewählte Schriften,* ed. W. Bühler (Munich, 1960), 183–87.

4. See J.M. Levine, "Reginald Pecock and Lorenzo Valla on the *Donation of Constantine,*" *Studies in the Renaissance* 20 (1973): 118–43; W. Setz, *Lorenzo Vallas Schrift gegen die Konstantinische Schenkung* (Tübingen, 1975); V. de Caprio, "Retorica e ideologia nella *Declamatio* di Lorenzo Valla sulla *donazione di Costantino,*" *Paragone* 29, no. 338 (1978): 36–56; and G.W. Most, "Rhetorik und Hermeneutik: Zur Konstitution der Neuzeitlichkeit," *Antike und Abendland* 30 (1984): 62–79.

5. Vat. lat. 1801, fol. 1 verso. On the earliest stage in his progress see also his letter to Tortelli of 28 October 1448, *Epistole,* ed. O. Besomi and M. Regoliosi (Padua, 1984), 345: "Nunc me Thucydides exercet, duntaxat in orationibus, nec ullius presidio iuvor. Dominus Nicenus abest, Rinucium experiri non audeo, forsitan aut non satisfacturum mihi aut cum difficu[ltati]bus sententiarum non colluctaturum; Trapezuntium et morosum et mihi nescio quam equum consulere nolo. Ceteri nulli sunt. Co[nsti]tui tamen adire dominum Nicenum, qui

brilliant Latinist, the author of the first systematic modern treatment of Latin syntax and usage, Valla could also devise a fitting Latin dress for his author.[6] But Valla's qualifications went beyond the technical. He had read much and thought hard about history. He knew and quoted, for example, the now famous argument in Aristotle's *Poetica* that "poetry is more akin to philosophy and is a better thing than history; poetry deals with general truths, history with specific events. The latter are, for example, what Alcibiades did or suffered."[7] This passage seemed, at least to an Aristotelian of a somewhat later generation, to prove the superficiality of historical knowledge and the impossibility of constructing an *ars historica*: a systematic and methodical art of historical writing.[8] Valla explained the text as a precise reference to "Thucydides, who records the deeds of Pericles, Lysander, and some other men of his time."[9] And he rebutted Aristotle's argument at length, on grounds to which we will return later in this chapter. Evidently, Valla was a connoisseur of history in general and of Greek history in particular. When he set out to translate Thucydides, he had made a principled decision to do so, one informed by a sense of the pains, as well as the pleasures, of history. His new text, written in classical Latin, not surrounded by a thorny hedge of medieval misinformation, offered the new men of the Curia an orderly Renaissance garden, elegant and symmetrical, sown with the most vivid historical insights.

Valla's manuscript and text were splendid creations. But naturally they did not offer the mid-fifteenth-century reader a crisp, panoramic view of Athens in the late fifth century B.C. The manuscript, in the first place, was a

---

apud Laurentum agit, ut nunc vocant Neptuniam. Primum tamen librum transtuli et secundi partem, in quo si adesses me plurimum iuvares." See also the editors' very helpful commentary, ibid., 323–24, and cf. J. Monfasani, "Bessarion, Valla, Agricola, and Erasmus," *Rinascimento,* ser. 2, 28 (1988): 319–20.

6. On Valla's text (and its Greek *Vorlage*) see *Thucydidis Historiae,* ed. G.B. Alberti (Rome, 1972–), 1:cxix–cxxxii; F. Ferlauto, *Il testo di Tucidide e la traduzione latina di Lorenzo Valla* (Palermo, 1979); and N.G. Wilson, *From Byzantium to Italy* (London, 1992), chap. 9.

7. Aristotle *Poetics* (trans. Grube) 1451 b 5–11.

8. See J. Zabarella, *De natura logicae* (1578), *Opera logica* (Hildesheim, 1966), 100–102; quoted by L. Gardiner Janik, "A Renaissance Quarrel: The Origin of Vico's Anti-Cartesianism," *New Vico Studies,* 1983, 49 n. 14.

9. L. Valla, *Gesta Ferdinandi regis Aragonum,* ed. O. Besomi (Padua, 1973), 3: ". . . tamen detrahunt nobis philosophi quidam, et ii permagni ac pervetusti . . . anteferentes historico poetam, quia dicant illum propius ad philosophiam accedere, quia in generalibus versetur et propositis fictis exemplis in universum precipiat . . . historicum vero tantum narrare qualis unus quispiam aut alter fuerit, veluti Thucydides, qui gesta Periclis, Lysandri aliorumque nonnullorum sui temporis scribit." See the full analysis of Valla's work by G. Ferraù, "La concezione storiografica del Valla: I 'Gesta Ferdinandi regis Aragonum,'" *Lorenzo Valla e l'umanesimo italiano,* ed. O. Besomi and M. Regoliosi (Padua, 1986), 265–310.

physical object—and one which, as Valla himself said, had enormous sensual appeal. Each book of the text began with a fine miniature. A bearded man, wearing a robe (and sometimes a hat or a tabard), holds a book: presumably this man is Thucydides himself. In book 1 he writes on a scroll, in book 4 he reads one, and in book 8 he holds one; in books 2, 3, 5, 6, and 7 he holds a modern codex bound in red. This series of coordinated images gives the impression, no doubt deliberately, that Thucydides has come back to converse directly with his reader. The scribe's writing reinforced the impression of direct access to classical instruction. Firm, stately epigraphic capitals dramatized the titles of the books, while a round, legible, open minuscule, only lightly peppered with abbreviations, made the body of the text smooth classical sailing. A good deal of gold leaf highlighted the book's significance. Valla himself evidently prized—and very likely chose—this design. As we saw, he described the book as "more splendidly written and illuminated" than any Greek codex.

In fact, the book's design has little to do with ancient precedent, everything with up-to-date humanist tastes. Many of its special features were shaped by its modern situation. The book's lack of extensive marginal apparatus, for example, reflects the taste of its future owner. Nicholas V told Vespasiano that he infinitely preferred Traversari's translation of pseudo-Dionysius the Areopagite, which had no glosses, to "the others with the numberless commentaries they contained."[10]

Valla clearly knew that the material qualities of his book would help to endear it to Nicholas. Among the metaphors of conquest in his dedicatory letter appears an even more revealing metaphor of commerce.[11] Valla compares the translator to the merchant: both make precious things universally available. The comparison was highly charged in the 1440s and 1450s. Fraticelli pounded the streets of Italian cities, preaching a doctrine of total renunciation. Bernardino da Siena hung from the ceiling of the Florentine Duomo, denouncing the city's rampant greed and usury. But he and many Dominicans argued that social life required the existence of commerce and commerce that of merchants. Humanists like Leonardo Bruni, for their part, derived from Greek texts on ethics and household management the thesis that only wealth enabled the citizen to practice the virtues of philanthropy and magnificence.[12] Valla clearly knew these debates, in which his enemy

---

10. Vespasiano, *Vite,* ed. A. Greco (Florence, 1970–76), 1:68.

11. On Valla's preface and its context in his work see M. Pade, "The Place of Translation in Valla's Thought," *Classica et Medievalia* 35 (1984): 285–306.

12. See H. Baron, *In Search of Florentine Civic Humanism* (Princeton, N.J., 1988), 1:chaps. vii–ix.

Poggio took an active hand.[13] He occupied a characteristically mocking position, arguing that merchants, by moving goods of all sorts around the world, restored the original golden age, when all things were held in common. Translation did the same for the (naturally more valuable) things of the mind.

Valla thus made clear that he offered his patron a thing of monetary, as well as a text of spiritual, value. Like many of his Italian contemporaries, Valla did not see the desire for gain and that for learning as necessarily contradictory. The same project could please a patron and bring men to the true religion. Without translation, after all, the Latins could have no "commerce"—*commercium*—with God himself. Valla's use of a term that had a traditional religious meaning and a prominent place in the mass only sharpened his metaphor.[14] Valla's critical self-awareness and lack of pretense make it easier to appreciate the extent of the sensual, even erotic appeal that the humanist book undoubtedly often held for both its maker and its intended reader. The vivid dreams of Girolamo Cardano included several scenes in which he saw vivid images of books or script—from more than one of which he derived a piercing feeling of pleasure.[15] What Nicholas dreamed we do not know. But there is every reason to think that he took as much interest in the appearance of books as he did in that of buildings—a subject that, as we will see, interested him deeply.

Reading, of course, requires more than a text and an editor; the reader must also play a part and have a stage on which to play it. Valla prepared his Thucydides for Nicholas V, the pope whose subsidies made possible the infusion of so much of classical Greek prose into the Latin mental world of Quattrocento Italy. Valla revealed again and again his desire to please this singular prelate and to use his scholarly work to cement their relations. This desire animated his dedicatory letter, in which he claimed that Nicholas'

---

13. J. Oppel, "Poggio, San Bernardino of Siena, and the Dialogue *On Avarice,*" *Renaissance Quarterly* 30 (1977): 564–87.

14. Vat. lat. 1801, fol. 1 recto: "Nam quid utilius, quid uberius, quid etiam magis necessarium librorum interpretatione? Ut hec mihi mercatura quedam optimarum artium esse videatur. Magne rei eam comparo cum mercature comparo. Quid enim illa in rebus humanis conducibilius, que omnia ad victum, ad cultum, ad presidium, ad ornamentum, ad delitias denique vite pertinentia comportat: ut nihil usquam desit, omnia denique abundent, et quod in aureo seculo fuisse fertur, sint cunctorum quoddammodo cuncta communia? Idem fit in translatione linguarum, sed tanto preclarius quanto potiora sunt bona mentis corporis bonis. . . . Adeo nullum cum deo nos Latini commercium haberemus nisi Testamentum vetus ex hebreo et novum e greco foret traductum." My thanks to Charles Fantazzi for pointing out to me the ecclesiastical usage of *commercium.*

15. G. Cardano, *Somniorum Synesiorum omnis generis insomnia explicantes libri iiii* (Basel, 1562), bk. 4, chap. 4, 259 (no. 18), 260–61 (nos. 25–26), 262 (no. 29), 276 (no. 54).

support for new translations had enhanced the power of Rome as greatly as the conquest of Asia, Macedonia, or the rest of Greece. It lent fire to Vallas' praise of Nicholas' project, which he described as an effort to translate books from Greek, Hebrew, Chaldean, and Punic into Latin.[16] It found concrete embodiment in the miniatures on the first page, which show Valla holding out his book and looking dutifully upward from the first initial, while Nicholas beams down at him from the top margin. It even inspired one of Valla's marginal notes. He picked out from an otherwise uninspired passage on a Greek embassy to Persia a reference to a Corinthian envoy whose name would delight his patron: "NICOLAUS," says Valla's note, in capital letters as revealing as they are unusual.[17]

Valla's patron demanded more than pleasant coincidences. Nicholas V was a very serious consumer of books, with strongly developed tastes and a personal commitment to the humanist program for direct study of classical texts. Thucydides, even in Valla's Latin, was a tough nut. The reader needed guidance, needed to have the text not only brought over into Latin but also both equipped with explanatory notes where the going became too difficult and set into an interpretative frame that provided perspective and emphasis.

Valla provided the stately arias and choruses of his text with a staccato accompaniment of glosses, sometimes frequent, but often interrupted by rests for several pages at a stretch. These did the donkeywork that glosses always do. Valla cleared up difficulties and offered helpful tips. When Thucydides remarked that it was dark "at the end of the month," for example, Valla explained that "he means a lunar month," of the sort the Greeks had used—one in which new moon, and dark nights, invariably came at the end.[18] When Thucydides mentioned Stagirus (better known as Stagira), Valla noted, "this is the native country of the philosopher Aristotle."[19] More complex glosses pointed out implications that might remain hidden even from a reader who could construe the words of the text. For example, Valla explained that Pericles' praise of the mutability of the Athenian constitution implied a critique of the conservative Spartans, who had

---

16. Here Valla elided the distance between Nicholas' program for translations of the Greek classics and the program of the Egyptian king Ptolemy Philadelphus to translate just about everything—including the Hebrew Bible. See later in this chapter for a more detailed treatment of Renaissance views of Ptolemy's Alexandrian library. Described in glowing terms in more than one accessible text, it glimmered alluringly before the eyes of patrons and intellectuals, just too far away to see clearly.

17. BAV, Vat. lat. 1801, fol. 42 verso, on 2.67.1.

18. Ibid., fol. 30 recto, on 2.4.2: "Mensem lunarem intelligit."

19. Ibid., fol. 89 verso, on 4.88.2: "hec est patria Aristotelis philosophi."

never changed the laws Lycurgus gave them.[20] And he suggested that Thucydides spent so much time on the story of Harmodius and Aristogiton's plot against Hippias, the son of Pisistratus, because he himself was descended from Pisistratus.[21] Pointing hands and monograms formed from the word *NOTA*, finally, called attention to especially sententious bits of speech or narrative.

Valla's glosses are for the most part elementary in content, fragmentary in character, and scattered in distribution. Most important, they are unoriginal. Valla translated most of them word for word from the Greek scholia on Thucydides.[22] Many more scholia, as Marianne Pade has shown, found employment, even though Valla did not explicitly translate them as part of his marginal apparatus. Rather, he incorporated them—occasional errors and all—into the Latin text of his translation.[23] Valla's notes and text thus represent, like Ricci's rewriting of Epictetus, moves in an existing game of updating and interpretation. A personal note emerges rarely, and for the most part only in contexts peculiar to a translator, as when Valla compares a Greek expression peculiar to Thucydides with the Latin equivalent used by his Roman imitator Sallust.[24] In other cases, Valla compiled his final, commented copies of texts with meticulous care: he had an especially keen eye for chronology and context. To prepare his glosses on Quintilian's *Institutio oratoria*, he wrote, he had tried to read "all extant books, especially those that existed before Quintilian's time." Only the purchase and reading of the complete works of Hippocrates, for example, had enabled him to gloss the word παιδομαθεῖς, which Quintilian used once.[25] When examined in the light of Valla's own standards and practices, his Thucydidean glosses disappoint. They seem to reflect surprisingly little thought about what equipment the Quattrocento reader needed to grapple in detail with Thucydides, crux by crux.

The frame into which Valla set the text as a whole, by contrast, was both coherent and innovative. As we saw, he insisted, against Aristotle, that

20. Ibid., fol. 36 recto, on 2.37.1: "Contra lacedemonios quibus lycurgus scripsit leges, emulatus cretenses atque egyptios."

21. Ibid., fol. 130 recto, on 6.54.1: "Ideo tot verbis de hac re loquitur Thucydides, quia ipse a Pisistrato fuit oriundus."

22. E.g., for the notes on 2.4.2, 4.88.2, and 2.37.1 previously quoted; see *Scholia in Thucydidem*, ed. K. Hude (Leipzig, 1927; repr., New York, 1973), ad locc.

23. M. Pade, "Valla's Thucydides: Theory and Practice in a Renaissance Translation," *Classica et Medievalia* 36 (1985): 275–301.

24. E.g., Vat. lat. 1801, fol. 59 recto, on 3.42.1 (φιλεῖ γίγνεσθαι): "mos suus loquendi Thucydidis. ut Salustius eum imitatus: vulgus amat fieri." On Valla's notes and their diffusion see E.B. Fryde, *Humanism and Renaissance Historiography* (London, 1983), 93–98.

25. Valla, *Epistole*, ed. Besomi and Regoliosi, 306.

history was no less philosophical than poetry. His argument was simple. Historians did not simply narrate whatever happened to Lysander or Pericles. Rather, they invented, just as poets did, works of high literature: "Does anyone believe," Valla asked, "that the admirable speeches in the historians are real, and that they were not adapted by those skillful artisans to the persons, times, and events, so that they could teach us eloquence and wisdom?" Historians' speeches, like poems, had artistic unity in conception and execution. Unlike poems, however, they were only partly fictitious, since they accreted around a core of historical fact. The difference was entirely to history's advantage. "The truer history is," Valla contended, "the more powerful it is."[26]

Valla's argument was deft. He converted rhetoric, the art of composing speeches, into hermeneutics, an art of historical reading and reasoning—the art that worked out what sort of speech fitted the needs of a given place, time, and speaker. The whole text of Thucydides became a series of cases in point. A quotation from Quintilian in Valla's dedicatory letter established Thucydides' status as an exemplary writer. Careful headings, in capitals, identified the speeches and speakers in the text. In the Melian dialogue in book 5, for example, headings in red letters set off the Melians from the Athenians throughout. Even the derivative marginal glosses fell most thickly beside the most elaborate rhetorical venture in the work, Pericles' funeral oration for the Athenian dead in book 2. The book that resulted from Valla's efforts, in short, sheds as much light on the needs and interests of a fifteenth-century humanist rhetorician as on those of the original Greek author. It looks more like an anthology of speeches than a narrative. Leonardo Bruni, who had read Thucydides before Valla translated the text, also saw the speeches as especially valuable, and he imitated Pericles' funeral oration in his own set-piece funeral speech of 1428 for Nanni degli Strozzi.[27] This way of reading Thucydides has a certain justification: a recent historian of classical rhetoric has suggested that Thucydides meant his work to serve as a coherent collection of set-piece speeches, each of

---

26. Valla, *Gesta Ferdinandi,* 5: "An est quisquam qui credat admirabiles illas in historiis orationes utique veras fuisse, et non ab eloquenti ac sapienti opifice personis, temporibus, rebus accommodatas, quibus nos eloqui et sapere docerent?" Ibid.: "nimirum tanto robustiorem esse historiam, quanto est verior."

27. H. Baron, *The Crisis of the Early Italian Renaissance* (Princeton, 1966), chap. 18. Bruni used Thucydides in many other ways as well: see Klee, *Beiträge zur Thukydides-Rezeption,* 23–58.

which exhibited the qualities appropriate to its situation and its speaker.[28] But Valla, for all his wit and insight, framed the text in a way that suppressed some of its basic elements—for example, its tragic qualities—as effectively as it emphasized others. The most original, even radical, of Renaissance thinkers wrapped an unconventional Greek text in a Latin toga that made it acceptable by disguising it. Is this what the patrons and first readers of such advanced texts expected of Valla and their other suppliers? We turn now from production to consumption: to the world of the erudite nobles and teachers who read—and paid for—books like Valla's Thucydides.

Into the Library

One natural way to begin watching readers encounter books is to explore the place where the two naturally met: the library. Here, as Roger Chartier has recently shown, the centrifugal and centripetal forces inherent in reading interfere with each other like opposed waves in a tank of water. Librarians arrange books into branches of a coherent system of knowledge; they put related books next to each other; they set limits on the numbers of books one can have, the hours in which one can have them, and the things one can do to them. Readers, by contrast, try to find new connections between apparently unrelated texts and to see more books than the rules allow; they write in the margins and tear out individual pages or steal whole books. Interesting meanings are constructed where the two interact; but their simultaneous presence always implies a struggle.[29]

Of the several humanist libraries that invite and reward inspection, one makes an especially attractive case study: that of the Este family of Ferrara. Many of its original holdings survive in the Biblioteca Estense in Modena. A vivid account of its formative years also survives—one that describes in detail both the literary debates and decisons that guided it and the creative, quarrelsome readers who used it. This forms the central thread of one of the oddest and most colorful texts ever woven by a humanist: the set of curious dialogues *De politia litteraria* that the Milanese humanist Angelo Decembrio dedicated to Pius II in 1462. These describe the intellectual life of the

---

28. T. Cole, *The Origins of Rhetoric in Ancient Greece* (Baltimore, 1991). Cf. also T.P. Wiseman, *Clio's Cosmetics* (Leicester, 1979) and A.J. Woodman, *Rhetoric in Classical Historiography* (London and Sydney, 1988).

29. R. Chartier, *L'ordre du livre* (Paris, 1992).

court of Ferrara in the age of Leonello d'Este, who studied with the great humanist teacher Guarino of Verona during the 1430s and ruled the city, after the death of his father, Niccolò III, from 1441 to 1450.[30] The shifting cast of characters in Decembrio's dialogues includes the court's dominant humanist, Guarino of Verona; Leonello himself; and the young poet Feltrino Boiardo. The settings range from the spectacular Este palaces of Belriguardo and Belfiore, outside the city, to Leonello's private room or *studiolo*. Decembrio's subjects cover the humanist waterfront, from the psychological analysis of Aeneas' behavior toward Helen to the mechanical details of Latin grammar and lexicography. For two reasons, the text has not yet found an editor. First, its Latin style is idiosyncratic, ungrammatical, even difficult to divide into individual sentences. Second, it exists in two recensions, one represented by a famous manuscript in the Vatican Library, the other by two printed editions, both based on a second manuscript stolen from the Vatican during the Sack of 1527.[31] Every page challenges the reader with difficult constructions, obscure references, or simple solecisms. Yet it eminently deserves a critical edition, as one of the richest extant sources for the teaching, the scholarship, and the sociability of the humanists.[32]

---

30. The wider background is laid out by E.G. Gardner, *Dukes and Poets at Ferrara* (London, 1904); W. Gundersheimer, *Ferrara: The Style of a Renaissance Despotism* (Princeton, 1973); and L. Lockwood, *Music in Renaissance Ferrara, 1400–1505* (Cambridge, Mass., 1984). On Decembrio's career see esp. R. Sabbadini, *Classici e umanisti da codici Ambrosiani* (Florence, 1933), 94–103; and *Dizionario biografico degli italiani*, s.v. "Decembrio, Angelo Camillo," by P. Viti. For his manuscripts see P. Scarcia Piacentini, "Angelo Decembrio e la sua scrittura," *Scrittura e civiltà* 4 (1980): 247–77.

31. The manuscript is Vat. lat. 1794; the printed editions appeared at Augsburg in 1540 and in Basel in 1562.

32. Scarcia Piacentini denies that the Vatican manuscript was the one Decembrio prepared for presentation to Pius II, because (among other reasons) it lacks Pius' arms. For a recent and cogent counterargument, arguing that Decembrio intended the manuscript for Pius but left it unfinished after the pope died in August 1464, see E. Fumagalli, *Matteo Maria Boiardo volgarizzatore dell' "Asino d'Oro"* (Padua, 1988), 15–16 n. 24. J. Monfasani and M. Regoliosi both inform me that students working under their supervision have produced more systematic studies of the question: the latter are in course of publication. The most elaborate studies of the content of the *Politia* are M. di Cesare, *Vida's 'Cristiad' and Virgilian Epic* (New York, 1964); A. Biondi, "Angelo Decembrio e la cultura del principe," in *La corte e lo spazio: Ferrara estense*, ed. G. Papagno and A. Quondam (Rome, 1982), 2:637–57; L. Balsamo, "La circolazione del libro a corte," in ibid., 659–81; and C. Ross, "Poetics at the Court of Leonello d'Este: Virgil, the Marvelous, and Feltrino Boiardo in the Competing Discourses of Angelo Decembrio's 'De politia literaria,'" in *La corte di Ferrara e il suo mecenatismo, 1441–1598: The Court of Ferrara and Its Patronage*, ed. M. Pade, L.W. Petersen, and D. Quarta (Copenhagen and Ferrara, 1990), 55–69; A. Tissoni Benvenuti, "Guarino, i suoi libri, e le letture della corte estense," *Le muse e il principe: Arte di corte nel Rinascimento padano* (Milan, 1991), 1: 63–82; A. Chiappini, "La biblioteca dello studiolo," ibid., 155–64. For editions of segments

One central theme links many of the variegated sections of the *Politia:* the question of how a Renaissance prince and his courtiers and scholars should choose and use books.[33] Leonello himself provides such a precise description of the ideal library and its contents that it reads, as he promises, rather like a catalog.[34] An analysis of this text—and of the complementary information preserved in Guarino's rich correspondence, edited by Sabbadini, and in the Este archives, studied by Fava and Bertoni—does not yield simple results.[35] But it does show that large parts of Decembrio's account correspond with the testimony of less artful sources. Taken together, these materials provide some vivid examples of the programs and practices of the humanist library in the decades when princes, patrons, humanists, and librarians were inventing it.

The Este library of the mid–fifteenth century, as Decembrio describes it, not only swarmed with classical texts but embodied classical principles of design. The intellectuals of the Este court had read about and marveled at the scale and splendor of the ancient public libraries. Pier Candido Decembrio—Angelo's older brother—explicitly wrote of Nicholas V in 1451, "He has decided to create a library that, if he has time, will rival even that of Pergamum or the one given by Antony to Cleopatra in both size and elegance."[36] In a passage preserved only in the printed version of the *Politia,*

of the text with important commentary, see M. Baxandall, "A Dialogue on Art from the Court of Leonello d'Este," *Journal of the Warburg and Courtauld Institutes,* 26 (1963): 304–26; Rizzo, *Il lessico filologico,* 200–202; J.P. Perry, "A Fifteenth-Century Dialogue on Literary Taste: Angelo Decembrio's Account of Playwright Ugolino Pisani at the Court of Leonello d'Este," *Renaissance Quarterly,* 39 (1986): 613–43; and B. Curran and A. Grafton, "A Fifteenth-Century Site Report on the Vatican Obelisk," in *Journal of the Warburg and Courtauld Institutes* 58 (1995).

33. In the dedication to Pius II, Decembrio describes his intentions. See BAV, Vat. lat. 1794 (hereafter *Politia*), fol. 6 verso: "Nam et hic non minus de oratorio poeticoque tractatur artificio: in primis enim de omni bibliothecarum seu librorum omnium ornatu instrumentoque, qui apud doctissimos magis necessarii cognitu recensentur [MS: recenscentur] . . ."

34. Ibid., fol. 13 verso: "in catalogi speciem."

35. *Epistolario di Guarino Veronese,* ed. R. Sabbadini (Venice, 1915–19); G. Bertoni, *La biblioteca Estense e la coltura Ferrarese ai tempi del Duca Ercole I (1471–1505)* (Turin, 1903); D. Fava, *La biblioteca Estense nel suo sviluppo storico* (Modena, 1925). Naturally, the text contains certain anachronisms: for example, Decembrio makes Leonello refer to Valla as already hard at work on a translation of Herodotus: this project actually began after Leonello's death, in 1453 (*Politia,* fol. 21 recto).

36. Quoted by L. Gargan, "Gli umanisti e la biblioteca pubblica," in *Le biblioteche nel mondo antico e medievale,* ed. G. Cavallo, (Bari, 1989), 183 n. 40: "Bibliothecam fieri instituit cui, si tempus non defuerit, nec Pergamenae aut Antonianae dono datae quondam Cleopatrae cessurae sunt vel numero vel elegantia." Given the ancient story that Antony gave the library of Pergamum to Cleopatra (Plut. *Ant.* 58.5), I have tried to preserve the ambiguity of Decembrio's Latin in my translation.

Angelo made Guarino denounce the medieval popes "who, in the belief that they were doing a good deed, destroyed many of the finest monuments of the ancients, including their loveliest libraries."[37] Evidently he thought Christian bigotry had polished off the Palatine and Ulpian libraries—where Roman scholars, as he knew from his beloved *Noctes Atticae* of Aulus Gellius, had once applied to see rare manuscripts and argued about the variant readings these provided. To a considerable extent, in fact, Decembrio modeled both the style and the content of the *Politia*—with its extended, polite conversations about rare texts and corrupt passages, carried out in the presence of books and libraries—on those of Gellius.[38] The Este library, which provided the background for so much of Decembrio's book, was clearly meant to appear as a locus classicus: a small corner of the Roman literary world called back to life.

The external evidence of manuscripts confirms the classical origin of the Este library program. The most famous text produced for Leonello is the illustrated manuscript of Caesar that survives in the Biblioteca Estense (α W.1.3). The most revealing point about it, for present purposes, is its closing subscription: "Corrected by Guarino of Verona, with the help of Giovanni Lamola of Bologna, 4 July 1432, at Ferrara."[39] The critical work Guarino and Lamola did in this Caesar is not in fact as distinguished as what they did in other manuscripts.[40] But they represented what they did achieve as the continuation of a classical enterprise: the work of those late antique correctors, or *emendatores,* whose subscriptions appear in manuscripts of Caesar and Livy, to name only two of Decembrio's, and Leonello's, favorite writers.[41] By formulating this message to readers as they did, the Ferrarese humanists asserted their connection to ancient scholarship as well as to the modern court.

At the beginning of the fifteenth century, the Florentine chancellor Coluccio Salutati had lamented the ongoing corruption of classical and vernacular texts. He had also suggested a solution—that the authorities should

37. Decembrio, *Politia,* chap. 55 (Basel, 1562), 428: "qui bene agere putantes, multa veterum praecipua monumenta, ipsas etiam pulcherrimas bibliothecas, absumpserunt."

38. On the study of the *Noctes Atticae* in Guarino's circle in Ferrara see H. Baron, *From Petrarch to Leonardo Bruni* (Chicago and London, 1968), chap. 7.

39. "Emendavit Guarinus Veronensis adiuvante Io. Lamola cive bononiensi anno Christi MCCCCXXXII IIII° nonas Iulias Ferrarie."

40. V. Brown, *The Textual Transmission of Caesar's Gallic War* (Leiden, 1972), 46.

41. E.g., (from Caesar's *Bellum Gallicum*) "Julius Celsus Constantinus v.c. legi"; (from Livy) 'Emendavi Nicomachus Flavianus v.c. ter praef. urbis apud Hennam"; "Victorianus v.c. emendabam domnis Symmachis." See L.D. Reynolds and N.G. Wilson, *Scribes and Scholars,* 3d ed. (Oxford, 1991), 39–43.

revive the ancient library, in which the librarians had been textual critics who corrected and stabilized the texts in their care: "Let public libraries be established, as repositories for all texts, and let scholars of the highest quality be put in charge of them, so they may correct the texts by careful comparison. . . . We find that the greatest men used to do this job, thinking it glorious to add subscriptions to the texts they had revised, as can be seen in ancient codices. That is why in the plays of Terence one commonly finds 'Calliopius recensui' at the end."[42] Salutati thus neatly conflated the work of the ancient scholars who emended manuscripts with the practices of the medieval university book trade, in which entrepreneurs stabilized the texts of required books by maintaining official copies of them, from which segments, or *peciae,* were copied over and over again for customers. Like Salutati, and even more literally, Guarino and Lamola set out to imitate ancient scholars and reconstruct ancient libraries as they tried to create a modern textual criticism.

The enterprise Decembrio described was not idiosyncratic. Valla, as we have seen, also tried to make the copy of his Thucydides that he prepared for the Vatican at the orders of Nicholas V an official copy, a standard for all the rest.[43] To that extent at least the Roman and Ferrarese enterprises moved on parallel tracks (and shared an anachronistic vision of ancient scholarship). More generally, as Armando Petrucci has shown, the founders of the public libraries of the humanist republic of letters looked back with passionate interest at the achievements of their ancient predecessors.[44] The great libraries of Alexandria, Pergamum, and republican and imperial Rome, in particular, fascinated them. They collected every detail they could find (in texts that ranged from the letters of Cicero to the so-called letter of Aristeas) about these lost encyclopedias of ancient knowledge—which, they hoped, could still serve as models of enlightened patronage. From Petrarch on, they marveled at Livy's account of the vast public library of Ptolemy Philadelphus in Alexandria and drooled enviously at what the *Scriptores historiae Augustae* had to say about the vast private library of Serenus

---

42. C. Salutati, *De fato et fortuna,* ed. C. Bianca (Florence, 1985), 49 (2.6): ". . . ut, sicut hactenus aliquando factum fuit, constituantur bibliothece publice, in quas omnium librorum copia congeratur preponanturque viri peritissimi bibliothecis, qui libros diligentissima collatione revideant. . . . Cui rei maximos quondam viros invenimus fuisse prepositos, qui gloriosissimum reputabant se libris subscribere quos revisissent, sicut in antiquis librorum codicibus est videre. Et hoc est quod communiter in Terentii fabulis post omnia reperitur 'Caliopius recensui' . . ." See Rizzo, *Il lessico filologico,* 227–28, 341–44.

43. Vat. lat. 1801; see Rizzo, *Il lessico filologico,* 312.

44. A. Petrucci, "Le biblioteche antiche," in *Letteratura italiana,* vol. 2, *Produzione e consumo,* ed. A. Asor Rosa (Turin, 1983), 527–54.

Sammonicus—even if they also quoted Seneca, at length, about the importance of collecting books for use only, not for ostentation.[45] Imitation took place on every level, down to the minutely technical—as when the Vatican Library followed Roman precedent in dividing its holdings into, among other sections, a Bibliotheca Graeca and a Bibliotheca Latina.

The new libraries, like the books they housed, set out to be classical in more than a general sense. Their owners and librarians read in Plutarch about the grand public library founded by Lucullus, with its porticos and exedrae. They read in the *Scriptores historiae Augustae* about the *armaria* (cases) of the Ulpian Library in Rome, where one of the supposed authors of this text, Flavius Vopiscus, claimed to have read a precious book written on ivory (unfortunately, he was lying). Above all, they read in Gellius and Cicero that Roman libraries had been centers of conversation and debate— the sort of place where Cicero and his brother Quintus discussed the validity of astrology and haruspication and where Gellius and his friends teased out the intricacies of poetic allusions.[46]

Patrons, architects, and librarians did their best to replicate these ancient machines for learning. They used what they took to be the same library furniture that the Romans described—though they had to ignore the inconvenient fact that modern readers of codices needed desks on which to prop them, while ancient readers of rolls had simply held their books in their laps. They emulated the Roman customs of illuminating the library with large windows and of decorating its walls with portraits and busts of the learned. This updated classical ideal persisted. At the end of the sixteenth century the Salone Sistino in the Vatican and the Library of the University of Leiden in Holland, at the intellectual centers respectively of Catholicism and Calvin-

---

45. See Petrarch *De remediis utriusque fortunae* 1.43: *De librorum copia;* for a Latin text, English translation, and extensive commentary on Petrarch's sources see *Four Dialogues for Scholars,* ed. C.H. Rawski (Cleveland, 1967).

46. For a full review of the main texts about Roman libraries and their intimate connection with literary and philosophical life see H. Blanck, *Das Buch in der Antike* (Munich, 1992), chap. 8. This account—like that of P. Fedeli, ""Biblioteche private e pubbliche a Roma e nel mondo romano," in *Le biblioteche,* ed. G. Cavallo, 29–64—seems a bit optimistic in the use of certain sources (notably the *Scriptores historiae Augustae*). Both Blanck and Fedeli, however, give a good sense of the textual information that would have lain at a fifteenth-century humanist's disposal and that would have seemed generally reliable; cf. also E.J. Kenney, "Books and Readers in the Roman World," *Cambridge History of Classical Literature,* vol. 2, *Latin Literature,* ed. E.J. Kenney and W.V. Clausen (Cambridge, 1982), 23–27. The information available in classical literary texts about ancient libraries was first fully assembled in the later sixteenth century by Achilles Statius and Justus Lipsius. See, e.g., S. Zurawksi, "Reflections on the Pitti Friendship Portrait of Rubens: In Praise of Lipsius and in Remembrance of Erasmus," *Sixteenth Century Journal* 23 (1992): 727–53. Most of it, however, came from Latin texts that Petrarch and the fifteenth-century humanists knew well.

ism, still shared the same largely Roman vision of what a library should be, though they expressed it in sharply contrasting styles; they also shared the same anachronisms (most vividly apparent in the fresco of a Roman library in the Salone Sistino, with its benches covered with chained books).

The single overriding model for public libraries, the one that continued to reverberate in the European mind as a sort of metaphor for the enchanted palaces of traditional learning, was of course not the Palatine library or its rivals in imperial Rome but the older and more mysterious library of Alexandria. The earliest detailed account in Latin of the Alexandrian library—the so-called *Scholium Plautinum*—was copied down by Giovanni Andrea de' Bussi, an early librarian of the Vatican, in the margins of a manuscript of Plautus. When Giannozzo Manetti wanted to praise the collecting ambitions of Nicholas V, he used the library of the Ptolemies as his standard for comparison. The idea gained some currency. At Nicholas' death, according to the book dealer Vespasiano, he left behind the largest library since that of the Ptolemies.[47]

As always, however, the house of the ancients proved to have many mansions. Moreover, imitation of ancient models and methods was often—perhaps always—governed by prejudices and assumptions that determined what one thought the ancients had done. Thus Bussi or his informant, translating a Byzantine text about the library of the Ptolemies, introduced into his Latin version the erroneous notion that Callimachus had served as librarian in Alexandria. Perhaps Bussi hoped to find himself an illustrious predecessor: certainly he introduced a long-lasting confusion into the history of the Alexandrian library. He also omitted the equally problematic statement of the original Greek text that Ptolemy had employed foreign experts who knew both their own languages and Greek to translate important works for his library. It seems all too likely that Bussi did so because he deprecated the importance of Byzantine emigrés in the Roman book world of his own time and wished to give no leverage to Levantine rivals.[48]

47. E. Garin, *Il rinascimento italiano* (Florence, 1980), 56–57. For another reference to the ancient precedents of Pisistratus and Ptolemy, forming part of a poetic compliment to Federigo da Montefeltro's library, see G. Zannoni, "Il Cantalicio alla corte di Urbino," *Rendiconti della Reale Accademia dei Lincei, Classe di scienze, morali, storiche e filologiche*, ser. 5, 3, pt. 2 (1894): 503 (reference kindly supplied by D. Hughes).

48. For the text of the *Scholium*, see W.J. Koster, "Scholium Plautinum plene editum," *Mnemosyne*, ser. 4, 14 (1961): 23–37. A color facsimile appears as the frontispiece of E.A. Parsons, *The Alexandrian Library* (Amsterdam, 1952); a detailed description appears in J. Ruysschaert, *Codices Vaticani latini: Codices 11414–11709* (Vatican City, 1959), 104–5. For Bussi's source (Johannes Tzetzes) see *Comicorum Graecorum Fragmenta*, ed. G. Kaibel (Berlin, 1899–), 1:19–20. On the omissions and interpolations in the Latin see Koster's notes in "Scholium Plautinum" and R. Pfeiffer, *A History of Classical Scholarship from the Begin-*

For all its equally classical inspiration, the Ferrarese model of collection and reading evoked by Decembrio differed widely from the project of Nicholas V. Vespasiano described Nicholas as, if not a universal man, at least a universal reader: "There was no Latin writer that he did not know, in any discipline, to such an extent that he knew all the writers, Greek as well as Latin."[49] An expert bibliophile in his own right, Nicholas had drawn up in the 1430s instructions for Cosimo de' Medici to follow in creating an ambitious collection.[50] In building his own library he emulated the grandiosity, as well as the catholicity, of the Ptolemies. "At his death," Vespasiano commented, "it was found by inventory that since the time of Ptolemy, there had never been collected half so great a store of books in every discipline."[51] No more modest project would have slaked what Pier Candido Decembrio described as Nicholas' insatiable thirst for books. Pier Candido's brother Angelo also had a clear sense of Nicholas' plans. He described the libraries of Eugenius IV and Nicholas V above all as huge: "they saw to it that they had, in addition to the sacred scriptures, libraries replete with ancient authors."[52]

By contrast, Leonello and Guarino followed a different vein of ancient commentary, one that insisted on the need to limit one's collection to the

---

nings to the End of the Hellenistic Age (Oxford, 1968), 101. The more normal version of the story—which rested on the letter of Aristeas, either read directly or as abridged and reproduced by Josephus—emphasized the Septuagint. It found much wider circulation. See, e.g., U. Jaitner-Hahner, *Humanismus in Umbrien und Rom: Lilius Tifernas, Kanzler und Gelehrter des Quattrocento* (Baden-Baden, 1993), 1:354 and 2:766; and C. Landino, *Disputationes Camaldulenses*, ed. P. Lohe (Florence, 1980), 53, 191–93. Silvia Rizzo (to whom I owe warm thanks) points out (in a private communication) that the classical scholars who have studied the *Scholium* have taken no interest in the fact that Bussi, a scholar famous in his own right, was the scribe who wrote out the text. See now Rizzo, "Per una tipologia delle tradizioni manoscritte di classici latini in età umanistica," *Formative Stages of Classical Traditions: Latin Texts from Antiquity to the Renaissance*, ed. O. Pecere and M.D. Reeve (Spoleto, 1995), 371–407 at 386–392, which reached me after the present text was written. Yet Ruysschaert (*Codices Vaticani*) identified Bussi long ago, using paleographical evidence, and the nature of Bussi's own scholarly interests and contacts could well help to explain the nature of the text he wrote. This case provides another instance of the unnecessary separation between two different ways of studying the history of reading: one based on textual content, the other on external form.

49. Vespasiano, *Vite,* ed. Greco, 1:46: "Non era iscrittore ignuno nella lingua latina, del quale egli non avessi notitia in ogni facultà, in modo di sapere tutti gli scrittori, così greci come latini."

50. L. Balsamo, *Bibliography: History of a Tradition,* trans. W.A. Pettas (Berkeley, 1990), 18–19.

51. Vespasiano, *Vite,* ed. Greco, 1:63–64.

52. Decembrio, *Politia,* fol. 151 recto: "qui . . . cum sacris quoque scripturis refertissimas veterum auctorum bibliothecas habere curarent. . . . ad bibliothecam replendam magis quam poliendam opportunos."

good and the useful. When Ugolino Pisani tried to present Leonello with an elegant manuscript of his dire Latin comedy about kitchens, for example, he was deliberately and systematically humiliated.[53] Tito Strozzi began his inquisition by asking if Pisani knew the views of Seneca: "'But doesn't Seneca give you some example of how to read and treat books? You look to me like a sort of third Seneca.' 'But no,' replied Pisani, 'he warns us above all to avoid a large number of books, because it distracts the mind.'"[54] Here, as Decembrio's readers knew, he referred to Seneca's characteristically stern warning against bibliophilia: "A large quantity of books distracts the mind. Therefore, since you cannot read all the books you have, it is better to have only as many as you can read."[55] Seneca—who hated ostentation in the buying and adorning of books—set the prevailing aesthetic tone for Decembrio's discussion. The central intellectual question of the *Politia*, like that of Seneca's discussions of bibliophilia, is how to limit a library to the correct, restricted set of classics, arranged in the proper way. The collector, Guarino explains, must adopt a "modus," to ensure "that he does not buy more books than he needs."[56]

In Decembrio's portrayal, Guarino and Leonello assess the riches of the fifteenth-century stationer's shop with the disdainful air of jewelers looking for a few real diamonds amid a heap of paste. They reject the great compendiums of the scholastic world with contempt: "But as to the '*Historiarum maria*' as they call them, those very heavy loads for asses, and the three equally huge Vincents, who wrote histories, rather than historically, and made many grammatical errors, we think that these giants, like so many Polyphemuses and Cyclopes, should not be given room and board in our library."[57] They dismiss the standard texts of the fourteenth-century court library—vernacular translations of the classics and vernacular writers, such as Petrarch and Boccaccio—as medieval and inferior, comparable at best to

---

53. See Perry, "Fifteenth-Century Dialogue."

54. Decembrio, *Politia*, fol. 147 verso: "Sed nunquid a Seneca forte exemplum habes de legendis tractandisque libris? nam mihi tu potius videris tertius Seneca. Immo vero, Parmensis excepit, librorum multitudinem in primis vitandam admonet, quod animos distrahat."

55. Seneca *Epistulae morales* 2.3: "Distringit librorum multitudo. Itaque cum legere non possis quantum habueris, satis est habere quantum legas."

56. Decembrio, *Politia*, fol. 8 verso: "Quid mirum . . . si in comparanda quoque bibliotheca . . . modus idem sit opportunus, ut ne libros plures tibi compares ac opus est."

57. Ibid., fol. 16 verso: "Contra vero historiarum maria, ut aiunt, vastissima quidem asinorum onera, ac eiusdem molis immensae tres Vincentios, qui historias scripserunt magis quam historice, sermonumque improprietate laxius abusi sunt, non utique tantae immensitatis homines quasi polyphemos et cyclopas intra bibliothecam nostram hospitandos arbitramur."

the baroque preciosities of late antique Latin: "We do not dare to admit them into this more refined library that we are seeking to create. They should be given another place, along with the Gualfredi, the Gualteri, and their like, with Cassiodorus and Isidore, glittering with the torch of their imperial style."[58] More solid medieval authors, such as Albertus Magnus and Pietro de' Crescenzi, they damn with faint praise—as informative but unfit, because of their poor style, for a cultivated collection.[59] Even Dante is dismissed; the scholar should read the *Divine Comedy* only with women and children, on long winter nights. Minor Latin classics gain entrance only because the owner can lend them to friends of lower status, "minores amici," without worrying too much about their return.[60] Cicero and Virgil, Sallust and Terence, the classics from whom the best grammarians took their examples, provide all the literary territory that the courtly scholar really needs to explore and settle.[61] Leonello insists more than once that the scholar should not waste much time and attention on those books that seem "more fit to fill a library than to adorn it"—even though one must own some of them.[62] The ideal library thus offers neither an encyclopedia in the style of the Vatican nor a massive historical record of a lost civilization in the manner of Bessarion, who set out to rescue and collect as many of the shattered remains of Greek culture as he could and preserve them in Italy. Rather, it should amount to a modest shelf of canonical texts chosen with meticulous care. Such a collection would embody the same chastely classical aesthetic that led Leonello, elsewhere in the text, to condemn Flemish tapestries for their historical mistakes and anachronisms.[63] Even here, however, as Fumagalli has pointed out, differences of taste appear; Feltrino Boiardo's glorification of Livy and appreciation of Apuleius mark a departure from Guarino's narrower canon of classic texts.[64] The humanist library had centrifugal elements of a sort even before the first reader trod its tiled floor.

The problems that Guarino and his pupil solved by their self-denying ordinances would persist—would, in fact, grow more serious with time. In

---

58. Ibid., fol. 17 verso: "Non tamen eos audemus in hanc politiorem quam nunc struimus bibliothecam admittere. Alius quippe eis locus assignandus est cum Gualfredis, Gualterisque similibus, cum Cassiodoris et Isidoris palatini stili lampade coruscantibus."

59. Ibid., fol. 19 recto.

60. Ibid., fol. 14 verso.

61. Cf. Leonello's comment, ibid., fol. 13 verso: "Neque enim fere praeter hos quattuor alii ab eruditissimis grammaticis testimoniorum gratia proferuntur. Quo bene memineritis in aliorum auctorum lectione non eandem ubique servari proprietatem."

62. Decembrio, *Politia*, fol. 14 verso.

63. Baxandall, "Dialogue on Art," 316–19.

64. Fumagalli, *Matteo Maria Boiardo*, 97–100.

the fifteenth century as in the ancient world, collectors had somehow to con-
struct a filter that would stop the mass of worthless texts from entering their
collections, while offering a place to genuinely valuable ones. The problem,
of course, was where to place the filter and how wide to make its mesh.
Some, like Guarino, made a chaste, selective canon of worthwhile texts their
instrument of selection; but this, as we will see, was inevitably too fine. If
strictly applied it would have kept out far too much. More promising, but
more difficult, was the formulation of a systematic art of reading—an art
whose practitioners could discriminate between the genuine and the spurious, the historical and the fanciful.[65] But here too, as we will see, grave
problems confronted orderly minds. The librarian had to cope not only with
the Latin canon, which was complex enough, but also with the more and
more bizarre and foreign texts and theses that came to light as Greek codices
arrived in Western libraries and were translated into Latin. (These novelties,
of course, Guarino wanted in his library, whatever the interpretative conun-
drums they posed.) Over time, moreover, bizarre but attractive Western
texts, such as the influential but forged histories of Berosus and Manetho,
continued to arrive on the scene; these particular ones may have conquered
a wider market in print than Herodotus or Diodorus.[66] Though the Ferrarese effort to impose order on the dangerous crowd of books proved
short-lived, in other words, the dangers it recognized did not. They provoked many creative responses from Renaissance readers.

A library, of course, is a collection of physical objects as well as a set of
texts. Decembrio describes the material side of the book collector's task in
concrete and revealing detail. Guarino, early in the text, insists that the collection must be ruled by "ordo," "so that you have some books which are
more accessible than others, as they are better and more familiar."[67] Later,
in a powerful speech, Leonello offers what seems to be the earliest detailed
treatment of the qualities that add up to order in the humanist library, public or private:

If you are making diligent inquiry about everything that pertains to
creating a polished library (which is the origin of our term *polity*), you

65. See J. Franklin, *John Bodin and the Sixteenth-Century Revolution in the Methodology
of Law and History* (New York and London, 1963).

66. For recent discussions see A. Grafton, *Defenders of the Text* (Cambridge, Mass., and
London, 1991), chap. 3; V. de Caprio, *La tradizione e la trauma* (Manziana, 1991); and M.
Wifstrand Schiebe, *Annius von Viterbo und die schwedische Historiographie des 16. und 17.
Jahrhunderts* (Uppsala, 1992).

67. Decembrio, *Politia*, fol. 8 verso: "ut alios [MS: alius] aliis ad manum magis, veluti
praestantiores familiaresque magis habeas."

will keep your books free from household dust. Some make a habit of keeping them in chests or a cupboard, taking them out only one by one to read them and replacing them. That is to reserve them within a private and secret library, not a public and household one. They become dusty when, as it were, they travel, and the dust sticks all the harder if the floor tiles of the room are often swept. Wetting these in advance prevents that inconvenience. One must provide for this still more carefully if one has the books tied, and as it were chained, to the desks before the shelves, as is the custom in the libraries of monks. But some introduce glass or cloth windows because of that sort of dirt. These serve to keep off the excess brightness of the invading sun and dust that is raised nearby. Odors stick for a long time in such places, which are rather unpleasant to visitors not accustomed to them, just as happens in the dining halls of priests, which they call refectories. Therefore the entrance should be somewhat closed off, and one should provide for this with some form of sweet odors— though not those that hurt the brain, such as white lilies and cypress planks. But this may be trivial. More harmful and entirely poisonous is the practice of using coals for heat without ventilation. Twigs of rosemary and myrrh or bouquets of roses and violets and sweet apples, especially those called crab apples, delight; so do some bitter things, such as wormwood and rue, which are also sensible remedies against maggots, scorpions, and other insects of that kind. When dried, these last for several years, and their juices, when combined in a glue, prevent bookworms in bindings. This is thought useful not only to books but to clothing and all sorts of household possessions. One should not admit playing kittens and birds in cages. For these reasons it is proper to have your library in the more private part of the house; this sort of special room for a collection is seen, in Pliny, and contains, as he says, the books that are to be reread rather than read: it should be proof against noises not only from the household but also from next door. Inside the library it is appropriate to have as well a sundial or sphere of the universe and a lyre, if you find that pleasant at times (it makes no noise unless we want it to); also decent pictures and carvings that represent the records of gods or heroes. There we often see that many find it pleasant to have an image of Jerome writing in his retreat; this teaches us that solitude, silence, and hard work in reading and writing are appropriate to libraries. . . . Therefore let everything in the library be seen to be polished and elegantly laid out—the paving, the wall, the beams. Indeed, you should not even leave spiderwebs under the desks or smearings from the wax of candles and the smelly and sometimes inconvenient remains of night work, which Pliny calls *vulcanalia*. Not to mention that some who have fallen asleep while reading have burned the book even in the midst of letters.[68]

Leonello's imaginary library—its walls decorated with an image of Saint Jerome writing while his lion sleeps, its ceiling painted with the horoscope of its owner, its tiled floors and wooden benches and cupboards immaculately clean—is as vivid and austere as one of Botticelli's paintings of a saint

---

68. Ibid., fols. 8 verso–9 recto: "Et si omnia diligentius exquiras quae ad poliendam rem librariam attinent (unde nunc ipsam dicimus politiam) a pulvere quoque domestico libros custodies intactos. Vti quidam solent eos in arculis vel armario continere, nec nisi singillatim ad legendum excipientes reponentesque. Quod est intra privatam bibliothecam secretamve non publicam et familiarem reservare. Quibus quidem velut inter itinerandum obsitis etiam pulvis ipse concretior adheret quo saepius cellulae pavimenta deterguntur. Illi incommodo propterea irroratio prior adversatur. In quo sit attentius providendum si seriatim ante ora libros pluteis appensos ac tanquam cathaenatos servos habeas, ut in bibliothecis est monachorum. Caeterum nonnulli vitreas fenestras ob id squaloris genus aut linteaceas obducunt: ut invadentis solis nimius splendor et excitus e proximo pulvis arceatur. Retinenturque diutius talibus in locis odores supervenientibus et inusitatis asperiores: ut est in sacerdotum diversoriis, quae ipsi refectoria appellant. Quamobrem nonnunquam recludendi aditus odorumque suavitate providendum: non qui cerebrum laedant, ut alba lilia tabulaeque cupressi. Sed haec leviora fortasse. Illud vero nocentius et pestiferum penitus si concalefaciendi causa sine spiramento prunas intuleris. Rosmaris autem myrrhique virgulta aut rosarum violarumve manipuli ac dulcia mala praecipue quae cedra nominantur, quin et amara delectant: ut absinthum, ruta lauribaccae: eadem in tineas scorpios et eius generis insecta non absurda remedia. Quorum etiam desiccatio in plerosque perdurat annos et eorum succi conglutinatio in librorum tabulationibus teredinem prohibet. Nec libris solum, sed vesti praecipue omnique domesticae supellectili plurimum conferre creditur. Arceantur ludentes catelli et aviculae caveis suspensae. His autem rationibus bibliothecam in secretiore domus parte habere par est, cuiusmodi apud Plinium minorem atque cubiculum deprehenditur, qua quidem lectitandos magis libros, ut ipse ait, quam legendos includeret [*Ep.* 2.17.8]. Caeterum ut non domestici solum, sed ex proximo strepitus arceantur. Intra bibliothecam insuper horoscopium aut sphaeram cosmicam citharamque habere non dedecet, si ea quandoque delecteris, quae nisi cum volumus nihil instrepit. Honestas quoque picturas caesurasque [caelaturasque?], quae vel deorum vel heroum memoriam repraesentent. Ideoque saepenumero cernere est quibusdam iucondissimam imaginem esse Hieronymi describentis in Eremo: per quam in bibliothecis solitudinem atque silentium et studendi scribendique sedulitatem opportunam advertimus. Aliis et aliorum effigies: denique ut quaedam signa sunt electissima apud Iuvenalem, Euphranoris aut Polycleti dulcia venientibus spectacula [see Juvenal 3.216–20]. Igitur omne perpolitum, pavimentum, parietem, contignationem, diligentique ordine locatum intra bibliothecam conspiciatur. Adeo ne sub pluteis quidem aranearum telas, immo ne pigmentorum etiam liturationes candelarum ac nocturnarum lucubrationum, quae vulcanalia idem Plinius appellat [*Ep.* 3.5.8] vestigia olida ineptaque interdiu reliqueris. Quid dicam qui inter legendum sopore comprehensi librum in mediis etiam litteris cremavere?"

among his books.[69] Revealingly, its classical model is not one of the ancient descriptions of the Alexandrian library but the younger Pliny's brief but appealing evocation of his private collection of his favorite books and Juvenal's description of the rich man's library, with its statues in bronze and marble.[70] The same Roman model reappears in another passage, in which Guarino and Leonello defend the practice of decorating libraries with elaborate classical sculptures.[71]

Decembrio gives precise information on the iconography of Leonello's *studiolo:* "I remember that in the dwelling of Leonello at Ferrara, where he used to spend the winter, separate from his father but in the same palace, I often saw images of Scipio Africanus and Hannibal painted on the wall, addressing one another, as it were, with shared admiration, as in Livy. The Roman was accompanied by a horse and a servant, the Carthaginian by an elephant bearing a seat and a black Ethiopian controlling it. But the generals were there on foot."[72] In the room where only one's favorite classic texts were to be savored, scholarly and precise images of historical characters naturally replaced the chivalrous, armored ancients anachronistically displayed on Flemish tapestries.

Two set pieces about another library offer complementary information. Leonello and his circle leave the palace at one point to visit the suburban house of an older man, Giovanni Gualengo, with the Curia of Eugenius IV and the Florentine ambassadors in attendance. They eat early figs from Giovanni's garden and wash with rose water from a silver vessel. Then they go upstairs to the library—which they find decked out as a celebration of spring, its floor and books strewn with white and purple flowers—and read

---

69. In fact, elsewhere Leonello expressly criticizes the collector who has a splendid set of rooms to house a large set of elegant books that he has not read. Decembrio, *Politia,* fol. 10 verso: "Nam quid tandem picturatae bibliothecae? auratae testudines? decora toreumata? Quid ipsi libri saepissime numerati venustissimique nobis auxilio fuerint nisi eorum frequentissimam quoque familiaritatem habuerimus?" This position seems in keeping with the Senecan morality of the book as a whole. The widely felt tension between the desire for beauty and that for well-prepared, useful texts call for repeated discussion later in this chapter.

70. See Juvenal 3.216–20 and the commentary of E. Courtney (London, 1980), 184 ad loc. Giorgio Valla remarked in his commentary (which he claimed came from one Probus) that the "forulos" mentioned by Juvenal were "loculos librorum sive armaria"; see *Scholia in Iuvenalem vetustiora,* ed. P. Wessner (Leipzig, 1931), 44.

71. See Baxandall, "Dialogue on Art."

72. Decembrio, *Politia,* fol. 33 verso: "Memini siquidem iis aedibus Leonelli Ferrariae, ubi potissimum a genitore separatus quanquam in eodem palatio hibernare solebat, saepenumero vidisse Scipionis Affricani et Hannibalis imagines in pariete picturatas, mutua velut admiratione, ut apud Livium est, sese compellantes, Romanum equo comitatum et famulo, Poenum cum elephante cathedrato et Aethiope nigro gubernante. Caeterum ipsos duces adstare pedestres."

Terence together.[73] In another passage Giovanni himself describes his modest, orderly holdings: "They include all the works of Cicero, especially in moral philosophy, in one volume. I also have a very correct copy of Terence, surrounded in the more difficult passages by the commentaries of Donatus, and I read it regularly. . . . And clearly if you believe me at all, when I look at and study the ranks of my books—for I have put the name of each author on the binding—I feel as if I am looking at the holy graves of those who wrote them."[74]

These charming evocations of *primavera nella biblioteca* refer to real books and collections. Leonello's description of the physical problems of maintaining a library, for example, corresponds exactly to what we know from other sources. Guarino describes himself, in a letter to Leonello, as pathetically trying to work in a small apartment that lacks all the facilities Leonello calls for. The children play and cry; rain streams in when the window is open; but candles must be lit in daytime, and the coal smoke suffocates Guarino, when the window is shut.[75] Leonello's ideal library sets out to preserve not only the books but the scholars who use them. Many of the problems he confronts, such as coal smoke, would remain central for centuries to come.

The two scenes in which Gualengo describes his books are even more realistic. When Gualengo mentions his one-volume Cicero, for example, he refers to a scholar's book, one in which elegance has been sacrificed to compressed script for the sake of convenience and cheapness. He has in mind something like the single codex containing all of Livy, Caesar, Justin, and Sallust that belonged to Decembrio himself.[76] When Gualengo describes his practice of putting authors' names on the spine, he refers to contemporary Ferrarese practice. The first known librarian of the Estensi, Biagio Bussoni, made parchment labels for the bindings of the books in his care.[77] And when Gualengo, in another passage, warns the others never to lend books except to their social inferiors, he clearly refers to the fact that the Este

---

73. Ibid., fol. 49 recto.

74. Ibid., fol. 35 verso: "In iis Ciceronis omnia volumina, praesertim philosophiae moralis, uno in codice. Et Terentium habeo correctissimum, in locis etiam difficilioribus expositionibus Donati circumscriptum, legoque assidue. . . . Et profecto si mihi quicquam creditis, cum saepe voluminum meorum ordines considero evolvoque, nam cuiuslibet autoris sui in tegumento nomen apposui, videor tanquam eorum qui scripsere sanctissima quaedam sepulchra contueri . . ."

75. Guarino, *Epistolario*, ed. Sabbadini, no. 557.

76. Laur. Conv. Soppr. 263; see A. De la Mare, "Florentine Manuscripts of Livy in the Fifteenth Century," in *Livy*, ed. T.A. Dorey (London and Toronto, 1971), 186, 194 n. 62.

77. Fava, *La bibliotheca Estense*, 27.

library regularly lent books—sometimes with disastrous results.[78] Aristocratic users are no unmixed blessing for librarians.

Decembrio's programmatic chapters, in short, reflect the specific attention he had given to the two great difficulties, one external and one internal, that tormented a humanist who wished to maintain high standards of order and elegance in a library. The collector had to establish rigorous control over the quality of the books that he bought or copied. But he also had to control the books themselves. A collection of manuscripts on parchment—as librarians know—gives off a powerful smell and attracts pests and rodents of all sorts. Scholars need light and heat; but books need protection from sun and rain. Finally, of course, books also need to be sheltered from users and borrowers, who seek to take them away or leave them in disorder. These long passages, with their descriptions of public and private library furniture, of methods of keeping order and cleanliness, are the direct ancestor of Gabriel Naudé's *Advis pour dresser une bibliothèque* of 1644, the work often taken as the first detailed manual for librarians.[79]

Even the apparent contradictions within the text are historically revealing. The advice Leonello offers is as confusing as it is specific. Sometimes he describes a large-scale library, with *banchi* and chained books; sometimes a very private collection, held in a single locked press in a *studiolo*. But here too the documents show that Decembrio described the situation in the Ferrara that he knew. For the books of the Estensi, in the time of Niccolò and Leonello, were divided. The official library was housed in two rooms in the palace tower (Buxoni was known as *Ser Biaxio della Torre*). The court eventually employed full-time scribes, illuminators, and binders. But Leonello's books were kept in his *studiolo,* and a constant traffic ran between the two collections, as Leonello and his courtiers borrowed texts that did not figure in his personal collection. The *Politia,* in short, described the practices of the real collections Decembrio and Leonello knew, just as Naudé's *Advis* describes those of the brothers Dupuy, the keepers of the great library assembled by Jacques-Auguste de Thou to serve as a center of historical research. Even more ambitious family libraries—like that of the Medici—

---

78. Decembrio, *Politia,* fol. 37 recto: "Quo quidem tutius est cum inferiore hominum genere minusque superbo rem habere . . ."

79. See G. Naudé, *Advis pour dresser une bibliothèque* (Paris, 1644; repr., Paris, 1990). Cf. C. Jolly, "L'*Advis,* manifeste de la bibliothèque érudite," in ibid.; J. Revel, "L'*Advis pour dresser une bibliothèque,*" in G. Naudé, *Consigli per la formazione di una biblioteca,* trans. and ed. M. Bray (Naples, 1992), vii–xvi; and A. Coron, "'Ut prosint aliis': Jacques-Auguste de Thou et sa bibliothèque," in *Histoire des bibliothèques françaises,* vol. 2, *Les bibliothèques sous l'Ancien Régime,* ed. C. Jolly (Paris, 1988), 101–25.

led a similarly shady existence, only half formalized. Many humanists did their most important work within the flexible—and sometimes permeable— boundaries of such collections.

The Books on the Benches

Decembrio describes the Ferrarese book stock as vividly as the spaces it occupied. He makes Leonello and his friends condemn those who thought they could assess a book's value from its binding. But Decembrio does not suggest that they completely rejected the notion that books should be phys- ically attractive. Leonello argues, in one careful speech, that the collector should maintain a balance: "One part of the perfection of a library that we surely should not omit, generous sirs, is that the books should be as beauti- ful as possible and written by the hand of a very deft scribe. Yet we should not become obsessed with this sort of refinement or with shining bosses or ornaments, miniatures, and bindings—as is said to have happened to Aeneas when he fed on an empty image. It is a well-known proverb that ornaments put on an ordinary sort of horse make it prettier but not bet- ter."[80] Collectors' tastes vary. Some "deck their books in purple, silk, pearls, and gold, for beauty makes many men more eager to read, just as proper ornaments make a soldier more spirited." Others prefer old script and dust, as severe parents care about their children's characters, not their beauty. Others want virtue, talent, and beauty together.[81] The most impor- tant quality of any book is that it be correct.[82] And the ideal library will obviously include both beautiful new texts and reliable old ones.

Leonello—or Decembrio—here takes a position on live issues. Books are physical objects as well as sets of words. Their outward signs tell stories about their inward grace or lack of it. Any Western intellectual of the 1990s can infer volumes from the chaste white cover of a Gallimard monograph or

---

80. Decembrio, *Politia,* fol. 9 verso: "At Leonellus, una haec sane pars est, inquit, O mag- nanimi equites, bibliothecae poliendae non omittenda, ut libri quam pulcherrimi sint et aptis- sima librarii manu descripti. Non tamen omnis in hoc politiae genere, nec in umbilicis nitentibus aut phaleris litterarumque picturis et tabularum tegumentis nostra versatur intentio, ut Aeneae dicitur contigisse cum pictura inani pasceretur [*Aeneid* 1.464]. Sed vulgo ferunt equum qualen- cunque addita phalerarum ornamenta veluti pulchriorem, non meliorem tamen efficere."

81. Ibid., fols. 9 verso–10 recto: "Sunt enim qui libros purpura serico margaritis auroque vestiant. . . . Alios autem contra scripturae vetustas et fuligo demulcet: magis tanquam parentes quidam severi non de filiorum forma vel cultu sed moribus tantum solliciti sunt: alii cum vir- tute simul dignitatem indolis et oris gratiam appetentes."

82. Ibid., fol. 9 verso: "Equidem eam inprimis ego dixerim librorum politiam, ut quam cor- rectissime scripti sint . . ."

the lurid, moulting colors of a Zone Books dust jacket. This was at least as true in the mid–fifteenth century. Historians of the book and paleographers have shown that the humanists demanded, produced, and consumed new kinds of book as well as a new canon of texts. They objected not only philologically to the content of the medieval scholarly book but also aesthetically to its form.

The authoritative books of the medieval scholarly world were produced by monastic scriptoria and the specialized, efficient stationers of the university towns. The most elaborate of these works—glossed copies of the Bible, theological and legal texts—were laid out in two columns and written in a spiky, formal Gothic script. The texts in question occupied a relatively small space in the center of a large page. Around them a thick hedge of official commentary written in a still smaller, less inviting script repelled unlicensed readers. This was, of course, the very mass of medieval glosses that the humanists so disliked. Even smaller-scale high medieval texts—like the portable two-column Paris Bibles, many of which had little or no marginal commentary—seemed ugly and unreadable to Renaissance readers, who saw their modern script and layout as a distortion of their contents.[83]

Petrarch hated "the tiny and compressed characters" that the scribe himself "would be unable to decipher, while the reader ends up buying not just a book but blindness along with it."[84] And he rejected just as indignantly the more flamboyant scripts that were becoming fashionable in his day. These seemed to him "delightful to the eye from a distance but confusing and tiresome when seen close by, as if it were intended not for reading but for some other purpose." Petrarch's tastes ran above all to the splendid courtly manuscripts of his time, such as his own famous manuscript of Virgil; but his criticism of other types of book presaged momentous changes.[85]

In the years around 1400 Coluccio Salutati and Poggio Bracciolini devised a new, rounded, elegant minuscule, which they considered more classical than the Gothic of their own day. Scholars and artists—notably Alberti and Mantegna—learned from Roman inscriptions to draw capital letters in a convincingly symmetrical and grandiose style. Others—above all

---

83. See in general *La production du livre universitaire au moyen âge: Exemplar et pecia,* ed. L.J. Bataillon et al. (Paris, 1988), esp. the articles by H.V. Schooner ("La production du livre par la pecia," 17–37) and R.H. Rouse and M.A. Rouse ("The Book Trade at the University of Paris, ca. 1250–ca. 1350," 41–114).

84. *Seniles* 6.5, quoted by A. Petrucci, "Libro e scrittura in Francesco Petrarca," in *Libri, scrittura e pubblico nel Rinascimento,* ed. A. Petrucci (Bari and Rome, 1979), 5.

85. A. Petrucci, " 'L'antiche e le moderne carte': *imitatio* e *renovatio* nella riforma grafica umanistica," in *Renaissance- und Humanistenhandschriften,* ed. J. Autenrieth with U. Eigler (Munich, 1988), 1–12.

the scholar Niccolò Niccoli and the scribe Bartolomeo Sanvito—invented an elegant cursive, which could be used for less formal purposes, such as the compilation of notebooks, and which fitted more words into less space than the standard, straightforward, humanist script. These new scripts were gradually taught to other scholars and, with difficulty, to professional scribes (whom Poggio, after long experience, described as *faex mundi,* "the excrement of the universe").[86]

The transformation of the classical text only began with the classicizing of its script. Fine binding became a specialty—even an obsession—for producers and consumers alike. Early collectors, such as Federigo of Urbino, favored red velvet with gold clasps. But from the middle of the fifteenth century, as Anthony Hobson has shown, a taste for a different, more austere style took hold. Binders learned how to make and wield delicately patterned stamps. Richly worked leather, more austere than velvet, became the binding preferred by all great collectors, from manuscript hunters, such as Sixtus IV and Matthias Corvinus, to lovers of the printed word, such as Jean Grolier and Jacques Auguste de Thou. They employed famous artists to design intricate traceries for the leather-covered boards that protected their books. Patterns from ancient coins and medals, supplied by antiquarians, such as Felice Feliciano, often gave these a classical patina, and the owner's name or initials or motto, which often figured amid the classicizing ornament, identified the patron whose tastes were on display. The great person's classic book could certainly be told by its cover.[87] And even plain men, paid scholars, considered it tasteless to keep a book in paper wrappers. "I can't stand to read books unless they're bound," Joseph Scaliger commented soon after 1600, as he made a rare exception to read a polemic against him and a friend by the Jesuit Serarius. The catalog of Scaliger's library, made for its sale by auction on 11 March 1609, confirms his statement. Of the almost 250 books designated as containing his marginal notes, not a single one figures in the section of "libri incompacti."[88]

E.H. Gombrich, in short, was characteristically prescient when he

---

86. B.L. Ullman, *The Origin and Development of Humanistic Script* (Rome, 1960); J. Wardrop, *The Script of Humanism* (Oxford, 1963); M. Meiss, "Towards a More Comprehensive Renaissance Paleography," in *The Painter's Choice* (New York, 1976), 151–75; *Libri, scrittura e pubblico nel Rinascimento,* ed. Petrucci; A.C. de la Mare, "New Research on Humanistic Scribes in Florence," in *Miniatura fiorentina del Rinascimento,* ed. A. Garzelli (Florence, 1985), 1:393–476. For Poggio see E. Walser, *Poggius Florentinus* (Leipzig, 1914), 104–10.

87. A. Hobson, *Humanists and Bookbinders* (Cambridge, 1989).

88. See *The Auction Catalogue of the Library of J.J. Scaliger,* ed. H.J. de Jonge (Utrecht, 1977).

pointed out a generation ago that classical books underwent an aesthetic revolution in the Renaissance. But books do not result from parthenogenesis, or revolutions from the cogitations of detached intellectuals. Entrepreneurs and merchants hired and instructed the scribes, typesetters, and illuminators who produced the books. And those who dominated the economics of publishing also had much to do with the identity and physical form of the books that the humanist public read. Even in the age of the manuscript book, entrepreneurs dominated the trade and shaped the experience of most readers of the classics. The *cartolai* who hired scribes and illuminators and provided texts and materials for them to work with also did much to set the proper styles for classic texts. Vespasiano, the brilliant Florentine bookseller who supplied Federigo da Montefeltro with his famous all-manuscript collection, did as much as any scholar to spread the taste for humanist script and title pages glamorously wrapped with intricately knotted, white grapevines.

However, in the age of manuscripts and even in the later one of print, Renaissance consumers did not buy ready-made books like slabs of pizza and consume them standing up. The well-educated reader knew his duty: he must personalize his texts before reading them. Individual choices of format, script, rubrication, and illustration sharply distinguished one library from another. The heavily illustrated classical texts that went into court libraries in northern and southern Italy, in which isolated classic elements did not transform the medieval appearance of landscapes and costumes, differed radically from the chaste texts manufactured for the Medici library and the library of San Marco. In them only the first page normally bore elaborate decoration—often, a spectacular architectural border, classical in style, around which satyrs or putti sport. The Vatican and the great Roman library of Francesco Gonzaga, in this respect and in others, followed a via media.[89] Bindings, which bristled with classical medallions, owners' devices, and elegant mottos, made particularly strong statements about the tastes and values of collectors.[90] In every case, however, one rule holds. The classical text was defined, even before its entrance into a public or an individual library, as both a precious object and a personal possession—the point at

---

89. See esp. de la Mare, 401–6, and J.J.G. Alexander, ed., *The Painted Page* (Munich, 1994). It should be noted that Federigo did own some printed books. For the library of Francesco Gonzaga see D.S. Chambers, *A Renaissance Cardinal and His Worldly Goods: The Will and Inventory of Francesco Gonzaga (1444–83)* (London, 1992).

90. See E. Diehl, *Bookbinding: Its Background and Technique* (New York, 1980); Hobson, *Humanists and Bookbinders,* and J.B. Trapp's review of Hobson, *TLS,* 17 May 1991.

which a cultural and an individual style should intersect. Before most books even entered a humanist library, serious thought and substantial resources had been devoted to their appearance.

The documents confirm the general accuracy of this description. The Caesar that Guarino and Lamola emended for Leonello, for example, was profusely illuminated in a handsome, if old-fashioned, way by Giovanni Falcone and Iacopino d'Arezzo. A letter from Falcone to Guarino, published by Sabbadini, shows that Guarino supervised the illustrations personally. Other manuscripts clearly appealed to the reader's eye as well as to his mind. Guarino's translation of Plutarch's *Sulla* and *Lysander,* for example, begins with an illuminated capital *P*. Inside its loop Guarino himself appears on bended knee, handing a copy of his book to Leonello.[91]

The library that Guarino and his noble pupil created, in other words, clearly reflected not just a negative effort to avoid excesses but a positive one to follow the best tastes of the time. As a very young man, just back from his time in Constantinople, Guarino fetched up in Florence. There he became enmeshed in a battle with one of the creators of the new humanist book, Niccolò Niccoli. In a brilliant piece of invective, Guarino lampooned Niccoli's obsession with the fine points of bookmaking—as opposed to the true details of scholarship. Niccoli, Guarino insisted, wasted his time on trivialities—such as the diphthongs that he insisted on restoring to classical texts and the elegant, legible loops and risers of humanistic script.[92] His attack—like the several others provoked by Niccoli, a spiky personality who treated his mistress, Benvenuta, too much as an intellectual and social equal for the comfort of other humanists—need not be taken literally. All of these diatribes, as Martin Davies has shown, reflect in part an inspiration more rhetorical than factual. One of the classical discoveries that Niccoli greedily collected and generously shared, Cicero's *In Pisonem,* which Poggio had discovered in 1417, ironically provided their model. Niccoli served as a popular victim of what became a favorite form of intellectual aggression, the formal invective. A useful surrogate Piso, he found more than one would-be Cicero taking aim against him with a pleasurably bent nib.[93]

For all their stylized quality, several of these texts converge in detail. They describe Niccoli as someone who cared only for the commercial, not

---

91. Laur. 65, 27, fol. 1 recto. For Leonello's Caesar see the preceding section of this chapter.

92. Guarino, *Epistolario,* ed. Sabbadini, no. 652.

93. See M.C. Davies, "An Emperor without Clothes? Niccolò Niccoli under Attack," *Italia Medioevale e Umanistica* 30 (1987): 95–148.

the aesthetic or intellectual, value of his library.[94] Evidently the beauty of the humanist's books could prove threatening as well as attractive. The very value of a collection of splendid books like Niccoli's might reveal that the motive behind its collection had been commercial, not intellectual.[95] For all their iconoclasm, many humanists still accepted the old principle that knowledge, as a gift of God, cannot be sold. Valla, who happily admitted that a fine book could properly become a fine commodity, stood against convention in that respect as in others.

By the time Guarino came to Ferrara, more than a generation later, his views had not radically altered, but they had softened. At one point in the *Politia*, Guarino's pupils clamor to know what Livy could possible have meant when he made Philip of Macedon demand "a Romanis equum sibi restitui."[96] Decembrio describes the manuscript of Livy that they used as "a book very prettily written in [or by] the Florentine hand, but without completely correct use of diphthongs."[97] In fact, of course, Philip had demanded not "equum," a horse, but "aequum," fair treatment. Another passage shows that the text in question filled three volumes. Leonello's Livy belonged, in short, to a well-known family—the three-decker manuscripts, equipped with elegant title pages and written in humanistic script, that Vespasiano produced for court libraries from Naples to Ferrara. Decembrio acknowledges this fact when he has Guarino say: "The most beautifully made books are normally bought from Tuscany and Florence. They say that there is one Vespasiano there, an excellent bookseller, with expert knowledge of both books and scribes, to whom all of Italy and foreigners as well resort when they want to find elegant books for sale. Though we think he seeks out good exemplars, with the diligence of Leonardo Bruni and Carlo

---

94. See Leonardo Bruni's *oratio* in G. Zippel, "Niccolò Niccoli, Contributo alla storia dell'umanesimo," in *Storia e cultura del Rinascimento italiano,* ed. Zippel (Padua, 1979), 136; and Zippel, "L'invettiva di Lorenzo di Marco Benvenuti contra Niccolò Niccoli," in ibid., 164–65.

95. In fact, Niccoli lent texts in his collection freely to others and meant them to serve, as they eventually did, as a public library for Florence. For the history of his collection, see B.L. Ullman and P.A. Stadter, *The Public Library of Renaissance Florence* (Padua, 1972).

96. Livy 33.13.9 (on Phaineas).

97. Decembrio, *Politia,* fol. 178 verso: "liber venustissime florentina manu descriptus, caeterum non integra cum diphthongorum aptitudine." A manuscript of Livy that belonged to Leonello, its opening page splendidly illuminated by Marco dell'Avogaro in 1449, is now in a private library in France. See H.J. Hermann, *La miniatura estense,* ed. F. Toniolo et al. (Modena, 1994), plate 50 and 249–53, and cf. more generally G. Mariani Canova, "La committenza dei codici miniati alla corte estense al tempo di Leonello e di Borso," *Le muse e il principe,* 1: 87–117.

Marsuppini, nevertheless, as I said, the exemplars read one way, the scribes copy them in another."[98] Guarino's speech reveals much. He now accepted Niccoli's view that the details of a text matter deeply, since they can interfere with its understanding. He thus acknowledged a fact that recent scholars have rediscovered and underlined: that Niccoli read his books with a sharp eye for content as well as form, stripping them down for historical and bibliographical information that could help him in his lifelong effort to reconstruct the canon of Latin literature.[99]

Yet Guarino's speech also reveals that the pursuit of correct texts and that of elegant ones were not always yoked. Even by his new standard, he held, the elegant copies of texts produced by Vespasiano and other stationers who served the luxury trade must fail, for they did not rest on critical scholarship.[100] But a court library necessarily consisted, at least in part, of the elegant folios Vespasiano and others produced—such as the Caesar whose creation Vespasiano himself supervised in Ferrara. This fact was hardly surprising; stationers and their scribes designed these folio manuscripts of the classics to appeal to noble and princely tastes. As Feltrino Boiardo puts it early in the *Politia*, all princes made a habit of ordering fine copies of Livy from Florence.[101] Evidently Guarino's time in Ferrara changed him as well as his pupils. Exposure to life at court made him see the utility of the Florentine elegances of book production that he had once scorned (even as his experience as a teacher made him insist that they should be accompanied by Florentine niceties of scholarship).[102] For as Leonello himself points out, an attractive appearance makes a text more readable—

---

98. Decembrio, *Politia*, fol. 180 recto: "Solent igitur ex Hetruria Florentinaque civitate potissimum libri quam venustissime facti comparari. Feruntque ibi Vespasianum quendam eximium bibliopolam, librorum librariorumque solertissimum, ad quem omnis Italica regio, longinquae etiam nationis homines confluunt: quicunque libros ornatissimos venales optant. Quem licet arbitramur Leonardi Carolique Aretinorum diligentia exemplaria bona conquirere, tamen ut antea dixi, cum alio modo exemplaria sint, alio librariis excribuntur."

99. For Niccoli's methods and habits as a reader, see the excellent survey by Stadter, "Niccolò Niccoli: Winning Back the Knowledge of the Ancients," in *Vestigia: Studi in onore di Giuseppe Billanovich*, ed. R. Avesani et al. (Rome, 1984), 2:747–64, with references to the earlier literature.

100. The accuracy of this judgment cannot be definitively tested even now, since no full assessment of the quality of Vespasianio's texts exists.

101. Decembrio, *Politia*, fol. 9 verso.

102. Cf. the views of his son Battista, who praised a friend for amassing a library full of "libris adeo ornatis et, quos [quod?] praestantius est, adeo emendatis . . . ut plurimos tum vetustatis tum bonitatis causa ad sui spectaculum alliciat." L. Piacente, "Tirocinio ed attività esegetica dell'umanista Battista Guarini," *Giornale italiano di filologia*, n.s., 13 [34] (1982), 70.

just as a fine suit of armor may give its wearer new courage.[103] The new court library meant a genuine fusion of courtly and humanist tastes, not a simple victory for the austerity of the early humanist book. At least some of its manuscripts fused the traditional decorations of the traditional aristocratic book with the classicizing mise-en-scène preferred by the innovative humanist pedagogue. Unfortunately, these elegant superstructures sometimes rested on shaky textual foundations.

Vespasiano's folios had plenty of company on Leonello's shelves. Ferrara offered the collector ample opportunities (and dangers). The city had its own stationers and monastic scriptoria, and patronage of the Este made it one of Italy's centers of lively, lavish manuscript illumination.[104] Books also streamed into its many substantial private libraries, humanistic and legal, Jewish and Christian, from a wide catchment area. One of the greatest humanist collectors, Aurispa, spent the last decades of his life in the Ferrara of the Este. A substantial part of his unique collection—which contained several hundred classical texts, almost all chosen for their contents rather than their luxurious materials—was bought by Borso d'Este in 1461. He gave the books in part to his Carthusian monastery, in part to one of Decembrio's most attractive characters, "that noble and charming student of humane letters, Tito Strozzi."[105]

Decembrio's characters refer to texts of many shapes and sizes—and often, as in the case of Livy, fashionable ones. For at least a century, for example, cultivated Italians had liked to own pocket-size copies of their favorite books, portable texts that they did not have to consult on a lectern but could toss into their rucksacks and consult even while playing the courtier. Leonello describes the pious elders he has seen, "who carried about with them the texts of the Old and New Testaments, bound in a very small volume." He mentions from among his own books a tiny Sallust, "minima forma compactum," and a pocket anthology of verses from the Latin comic poets, "libellus dictorum in Terentio Plautoque notabilium."[106] The last phrase at least describes a book that belonged to the historical Leonello—the "libreto de li fioreti de Terentio de messer Leonello" that the *cartolaio*

---

103. Decembrio, *Politia*, fol. 9 verso: "Nam librorum pulchritudo ad legendum plerosque magis invitat, uti decora militem armamenta animosiorem efficiunt."

104. See, e.g., D. Diringer, *The Illuminated Book: Its History and Production* (New York and Washington, 1967), 338–42.

105. A. Franceschini, *Giovanni Aurispa e la sua biblioteca* (Padua, 1976). Decembrio describes Strozzi as "generoso et lepidissimo studiorum humanitatis cultore Tito Strozza."

106. Decembrio, *Politia,* fol. 22 recto: "qui secum veteris novique testamenti monumenta, quae bibliam dicunt, minimo quidem compacta volumine gestarent"; fols. 42 verso, 12 verso.

Nigrisolo dei Nigrisoli bound in April 1433.[107] The library, in short, contained a full range of fashionable types of book—not quite the tiny canon of prim, austere texts that the scene between Pisani and the courtiers might lead one to expect.

Reeling and Writhing

Readers and patrons also shared a sense of what they should do in a library, and the range of permissible activites included, as it had in Rome, a good deal more than silent scrutiny of texts. Pietro Crinito, in his *De honesta disciplina* of 1504, describes the lively discussions held by Pico, Poliziano, and others in what he called both the library of San Marco and the Florentine academy.[108] His reference is clear. Cicero set the *De divinatione* in the library in his villa in Tusculum, part of which he called the academy (the other part, eclectic as ever, he called the lyceum; the library was actually there). Crinito and his contemporaries imitated art in life, staging their conversations as the Roman scholars had, in the midst of the great book collections.

Decembrio shows the members of Leonello's circle engaged in a variety of rituals that demonstrate their intimate command of the right texts. One day at Belriguardo, a courtier brings Leonello's Sallust to the young prince just as he wakes from his midday nap. He not only hands over the book but delivers a little appreciative speech about Sallust's brevity. Decembrio explains that this was customary: "For it had become the standard practice that one who offered him a book should deliver a short, appropriate discourse at the same time. This reached such a high level of literary elegance or royal license, in the manner of plays, that the most pleasant of actors, Matotus, though illiterate, still recited speeches in Leonello's presence, both by heart and sometimes in Greek."[109] Books thus provided the occasion for formal, ceremonious exchanges—something like that courtly civil conversation of which *The Book of the Courtier* would give the definitive portrait many years later.

Books also gave Leonello's courtiers opportunities for informal duels of

---

107. Bertoni, *La biblioteca Estense,* 103 n. 2.

108. P. Crinito, *De honesta disciplina,* ed. C. Angeleri (Rome, 1955), 3.2.

109. Decembrio, *Politia,* fol. 43 recto: "Nam sic fuerat vicissim institutum, ut cum libro simul quem quis ei legendum obtulisset, oratiunculam ederet ad id opus opportunam. Resque eo iam vel politiae litterariae vel regalis licentiae processerat in scenarum morem, ut histrionum iucondissimus Matotus, quamvis illiteratus, orationes tamen assumeret coram Leonello et corde et nonnumquam graeco sermone recitandas."

wit, in which they fought politely (or at least without doing one another physical harm) for precedence. This was a matter of besetting interest in the Renaissance court, that world in which new men equipped with spurious genealogies and real swords fought to retain their footing on slippery floors that could at any moment turn into quicksand and engulf them.[110] At one point in Decembrio's text, for example, the courtiers play a game of *sortes Livianae*. Feltrino Boiardo clutches all three volumes of Livy in one arm and reads out passages chosen by chance for discussion. The game ends badly for him, however. A devoted admirer of Hannibal, he opens his book at the passage where Hannibal, forced to leave Italy, appears wailing and complaining in a most unheroic way; like Pisani, he is humiliated in public for his literary error.[111] At another point Tito Strozzi tells the tale of how a schoolmaster had challenged Tito and his friends to give him any verse of Virgil's *Bucolics*. He promised to respond by quoting the next two and more from memory. Tito at once said: "Vrbem quam dicunt Romam Meliboee putavi"(1.20), forcing the schoolmaster to reply with the next line, which begins "Stultus ego"—"I was a fool"(1.21).[112]

Decembrio naturally makes Leonello retain mastery in the game, dominating interpretation as he will the state. Twice courtiers challenge the conduct of ancient heroes, criticizing Aeneas for mistreating Helen in *Aeneid* 2 and Caesar for weeping when he saw the corpse of his enemy Pompey (in Petrarch's poem on the event).[113] In each case Leonello draws on the superior real-life experience of the prince to support the excellence of the ancient hero. Great men, he insists, were certainly prey to strong emotion at certain moments. His own father, Niccolò, had expressed his feelings powerfully in the crisis of his life, when he caught his young wife flagrante delicto with his older son and had to put both of them to death.[114]

Books, in short, permeated everyday life in Leonello's world. They offered entertainment in dull moments and helped to deal with crises. They also moved about Ferrara and its suburbs almost as continually as the peripatetic court itself. Leonello carried his Sallust with him when he and his court moved dramatically out of the city to Belriguardo, "riding at night to

---

110. Cf. Leon Battista Alberti's remark, significantly made in Ferrara: "Ferrariensibus ante aedem, <in> qua per Nicolai Estensis tempora maxima iuventutis pars eius urbis deleta est: 'O amici—inquit—quam lubrica erunt proximam per aestatem pavimenta haec, quando sub his tectis multae impluent guttae!' " (R. Fubini and A.N. Gallorini, "L'autobiografia di Leon Battista Alberti: Studio e edizione," *Rinascimento*, n.s., 12 [1972], 21–78, at 76).

111. Decembrio, *Politia*, fol. 57 recto.

112. Ibid., fol. 145 recto–verso.

113. *Rime* 102 ("Cesare, poi che 'l traditor d'Egitto").

114. Decembrio, *Politia*, fols. 30 verso–31 verso, 34 verso–35 recto.

avoid the heat."[115] And he discussed literary questions while lying in bed, hunting, hawking, and sitting under the great laurel at Belriguardo. Early in the sixteenth century, in his eloquent praise of Aldo Manuzio, Erasmus described the "library without walls" that the great printer created.[116] In some sense, the humanist library of Estense Ferrara was already a library without walls—a library constantly connected with the big and little dramas of court life. To be sure, many ancient books had to stay on the shelves— such as Juvenal, who, Leonello comments, "should not be the subject of public discussion but should be read privately," because of his frank attacks on the vices.[117]

Decembrio's accounts of reading practices are what one might expect from the pupils and friends of Guarino. He had trained all his pupils, including Leonello, to master every detail of the texts they studied. The good reader would work through his text sentence by sentence, parsing every verb and solving every difficulty, pronouncing the words as he read to promote both memorization and good digestion of food. Then he must enter the results in systematic notebooks, organized by topics—or at least pay a poor young scholar to do it for him.[118] Naturally, young men who had mastered this disciplined way of reading knew their classical texts as the products of a modern yeshiva know the Talmud. Like the library of a yeshiva, that in Ferrara ideally served as a reinforcement to an oral culture, as the basis for a knowledge that was meant to be demonstrated not in silent reading but in active and ardent debate and writing. Leonello describes how his senior "orator" exulted and wept for sheer joy as he heard his son reciting *Aeneid* 2.[119] Elsewhere in the dialogue, Thomas Rheatinus makes savage fun of a Spaniard who brought his elaborate notebook with him to court so that he could quote appositely from it.[120] These literary evocations of learned conversation that was carried on without reference books at hand correspond well with other documents—for example, a letter from Guarino to Leonello, in which he described, at second hand, a lively discussion about the meaning of the peplum mentioned in book 1 of Virgil's *Aeneid*.[121]

115. Ibid., fol. 42 verso.

116. *Adagia* 2.1.1 ("Festina lente"); *Ausgewählte Schriften*, 7:464–513, at 488–89.

117. Decembrio, *Politia*, fol. 14 recto: "Caeterum ob patentiorem in vicia dicacitatem non publice adeo legendus [sc. Juvenalis], sed in bibliotheca tractandus est."

118. Guarino, *Epistolario*, ed. Sabbadini, no. 679.

119. Decembrio, *Politia*, fol. 11 recto: "uti Poggium nuper audivimus seniorem ex oratoribus nostris exultantem simul et prae gaudio lacrymantem, cum filium secundum Aeneidis librum recitantem audiret."

120. Ibid., fol. 166 recto.

121. L. Capra, "Nuove lettere di Guarino," *Italia Medioevale e Umanistica* 10 (1967): 165–218, at 212–13. Capra makes the connection with Decembrio in his headnote to the letter (210).

Leonello and his friends never resembled their master more than when they took their books out of the library, risking the books' cleanliness and safety to read them in the open air. In another letter to Leonello, Guarino evoked the beauties of making nature into one's study. Escaping the noise and squalor of the family house, he took a river journey to visit a friend. His description of what he saw and did obviously inspired his young pupil:

> I saw both banks, blooming with fertility, with tall, shady trees in every direction, with furrows, vines, and carefully cultivated fields, which offered a sweet spectacle, since nothing can be more attractive than a well-cultivated field. There were also the villages with their closely clustered farmhouses, stretched out far and wide; a sign of peace and blessedness, a matter of envy to neighbors and of glory to the Este, was that everything rang with the songs and dances of the farmers. Sometimes, to feed my mind as well as my ears and eyes, I let my book rest on my knees, while I read, made notes, and copied out extracts. Thus while my mind profited by reading, my eyes drew great pleasure from looking.[122]

Leonello and his friends knew exactly what Guarino meant.

In another and perhaps more important respect, however, the Ferrarese evidence remains provocative rather than definitive. One wants to know what Guarino's pupils and Leonello's friends made of the texts they used. But the evidence of the *Politia* and the associated documents reveals only one side of the coin. The text shows how closely the Ferrarese studied their books, how strongly they believed that they could wring a coherent and instructive sentiment from every line, and how reluctant they were to believe that a great canonical text could have gaps. Leonello discusses at one point the humanist Maffeo Vegio's addition to the *Aeneid* of a thirteenth book that rounds out the plot and arrives, as the original did not, at a happy, moral ending. He tries to show in detail that Virgil's text is complete in itself

---

122. Guarino, *Epistolario*, ed. Sabbadini, no. 557: "Occurrebant oculis virentes utrinque ripae, umbrosae quaquaversum et procerae quidem arbores, arva, vineta, arbusta et agrorum lata planities culta diligenter, quae res dulce afferebant spectaculum, cum agro bene culto nihil possit esse speciosius. Accedebant vici frequentissimis habitati villis, longo latoque porrecti spatio: quodque pacis et beatitudinis inditium, finitimis invidiosum et Estensi regno gloriosum est, agricolarum cantibus et choreis circumsonabant omnia. Tantisper, ut non minus animum quam aures prospectumque pascerem, liber genibus accumbebat, legebam, annotabam, excerpebam. Sic animus cum lectionis fructum con<ciperet, oculus> spectandi amoenitate laetitia fruebatur amplissima."

and needs no description of the funeral of Turnus and the marriage of Lavinia. "After all, by Turnus' own confession, 'Lavinia is your spouse; and let your hatred not continue.' All this, though said as it were in passing, is abundantly clear to the competent."[123]

This attitude seems natural enough in readers schooled by Guarino—and all the more so when one takes into account that he not only trained his pupils to read in a moral, positive way but marked up their texts so they could not avoid reaching the proper conclusions about them. The marginal notes in the Caesar that he prepared for Leonello, as Pade has shown, steer the reader through the *Commentarii,* praising Caesar's actions as clement, benign, and marvelous; labeling the remarks and deeds of his opponents as cruel; and emphasizing the great power of fortune, not to suggest that the cosmos lacks order, but to highlight the virtue that had allowed Caesar to triumph.[124] These tactics marked no exception to Gaurino's normal practices: he had done much the same, as James Hankins has shown in a fascinating study, when he marked up a Latin translation of Plato's *Respublica* so that Francesco Barbaro could strip-mine it for his own treatise on marriage. Guarino's notes on the *Respublica* avoided any confrontation with Plato's philosophical theses on justice and the good, occasionally misrepresented passages he found especially repellent, and they highlighted sententious sayings that Barbaro could lift out of their original contexts for reuse, without regard to the purposes they had originally served.[125]

Even the most striking passages in Decembrio's book—certainly those where Leonello argues that ancient heroes did not violate decorum when they showed violent emotion—reflect no shattering of the rules of the game of moral interpretation. After all, Leonello reflects, even the greatest men are not always pitilessly waging war or bitterly attacking their mortal enemies. "'Men act thus,' Leonello held, 'when they are led by ambition, the desire for glory, greed, or anger. But the same men, when the causes of war and hatred have passed away, know that they too were born men, and that

---

123. Decembrio, *Politia,* fol. 26 recto: "Quippe ipsius Turni confessione tua est Lavinia coniunx: et ulterius ne tende odiis: omnia haec licet per transitum a peritis abunde percipiuntur."

124. M. Pade, "Guarino and Caesar at the Court of the Este," in *La corte di Ferrara,* ed. Pade et al., 71–91, at 76–80.

125. J. Hankins, "A Manuscript of Plato's *Republic* in the Translation of Chrysoloras and Uberto Decembrio with Annotations of Guarino Veronese (Reg. lat. 1131)," in *Supplementum festivum: Studies in Honor of Paul Oskar Kristeller,* ed. Hankins et al. (Binghamton, N.Y., 1987), 149–88, at 162–76, 181–88.

nothing of the natural turn of mind is foreign to them.'"[126] In this case Leonello attacked a respectable late antique authority. Servius, in his great commentary on the *Aeneid,* had condemned Aeneas' conduct in book 2. He described Aeneas' furious desire to kill Helen as both inconsistent with the version of events offered in book 6 and shameful for a hero.[127] But, as Decembrio naturally did not say, Leonello found the moral with which he refuted Servius in a older and still more authoritative source, Terence's *Heauton timorumenos:* "I am a human being: I think nothing human foreign to me."[128] The half-quotation of Terence's phrase, the original of which any schoolboy could have supplied, could actually have come from the Terentian anthology that, according to Decembrio, figured among Leonello's favorite books. His twist on the original wording was perhaps meant to prove that he cited from memory. Leonello's memorized Terentian commonplaces merged with the splendid frontispieces and marginal notes in his books, forming a frame that determined what responses to the ancients were acceptable. As Leonello himself puts it, while describing the feelings that come over him when he hears his favorite Terentian *sententiae,* "I feel as if I am listening not to arguments between slaves or lovers but to an explanation of the nature and ways of thinking of the whole human race."[129] Only this steeping in general principles, concretely stated in the best Latin, gave Leonello a way to assimilate his father's tragic demeanor to the classical rules of conduct that the fictional Aeneas and the real Caesar had obeyed.[130]

---

126. Decembrio, *Politia,* fols. 34 verso–35 recto: "Ergo fingerent exclamarentque sed incassum, Lucanus praecipue longa satis in Caesarem oratione frustratus. Nam quod diceret cum senatus iura libertatemque publicam Caesar calcaret pedibus, cumque tot Romanis civibus generoque bellum et caedes inferret, non plorasse, non poenituisse, sic facere homines arguebat Leonellus, modo ambitione, gloria, cupiditate, iracondia ductos: eosdem modo cum belli odiorumque causae desiissent se scire homines natos, ingeniique naturalis nihil a se alienum."

127. Servius on *Aeneid* 2.592: "Nam et turpe est viro forti, contra feminam irasci: et contrarium est Helenam in domo Priami fuisse, illi rei, quae in sexto dicitur: quia in domo est inventa Deiphobi, postquam ex summa arce vocaverat Graecos." On the problems in question—above all the authenticity of the so-called Helen episode in *Aeneid* 2—see the sharply contrasting treatments of G.P. Goold, "Servius and the Helen Episode," *Harvard Studies in Classical Philology* 74 (1970): 101–68, and G.B. Conte, *Vergilio. Il genere e i suoi confini* (Milan, 1984), 109–19. On the importance of Servius for humanistic commentators on Virgil, see C. Kallendorf, *In Praise of Aeneas* (Hanover and London, 1989), esp. chap. 4; for Guarino's use of Servius see Capra, "Nuove lettere."

128. Ter. *Hau.* 77: "Homo sum. Humani nil a me alienum puto."

129. Decembrio, *Politia,* fol. 12 verso: ". . . non quidem inter servos amatoresve contentiones audire videar, sed de omni hominum genere naturas et rationes explicari."

130. Here too, external evidence matches Decembrio's testimony. Guarino's son Battista describes his father's use of Terentian *sententiae* in his school: see his *De ordine docendi et discendi,* in *Il pensiero pedagogico dello umanesimo,* ed. E. Garin (Florence, 1958), 434–71.

For all its lively qualities, in short, the Ferrarese library remained an intellectual, if not a physical, *hortus conclusus*. The new contact with the ancient world that it promoted and sustained followed rules as clear and restrictive as the aesthetic ones that governed the appearance of its contents. In fact, there is a clear relation between the two sets of principles. The clarity and legibility of the script provided a material counterpart to the moral clarity and legibility of the texts. Though the content and organization of the Este library show the interaction of opposing urges that we expected, the actual contact between books and readers often seems disappointingly predetermined. But the constraints of physical form and interpretative tradition did not hem in the interpretative powers of all those who read texts in Ferrara or elsewhere.

Valla and Thucydides: A Reprise

A second look at Valla's dealings with Thucydides may serve as a coda to this chapter. He too read and used his text in more than one way. Valla certainly understood the dark, even tragic side of the *Histories*. His most striking marginal comment in the manuscript of his translation deals with what remains one of the most powerful and disturbing passages in Thucydides, the analysis of the corruption of political language during civil war that forms the core of his description of the revolution in Corcyra. "Note," Valla wrote, "this neatly fits the corruption of our times as well."[131] Evidently Valla experienced the same shock of recognition that many modern readers have felt on reading this profound analysis of the corruption of political language. He saw that Thucydides offered more than neat, appropriate speeches. Thucydides knew that language, like political behavior and society itself, could fall apart; and he embodied that belief in words that retain their power to frighten, like the Melian dialogue and the last speeches of Nicias. One wonders what Valla made of these passages, which he left unadorned with monograms or explicit comments. He might well have connected them, for example, with the pervasive corruption of ecclesiastical rhetoric at every level, which he exposed in his *Declamation on the Donation of Constantine*.[132] Apparently Valla did not wish such messages to emerge as the dominant ones in his Latin Thucydides. But we will see that

---

131. Vat. lat. 1801, fol. 66 verso, on 3.82.2: "Pulchre et ad nostri temporis corruptelam omnia hec congruunt."

132. See S. Camporeale, "Lorenzo Valla e il 'De falso credita donatione': Retorica, libertà ed ecclesiologia nel '400," *Memorie domenicane*, n.s., 19 (1988): 191–293.

at least one contemporary proved as deft as Valla himself at making the text yield information of a sort that the translator had not highlighted.[133]

Valla himself, moreover, made clear in the course of the polemics provoked by his history of Ferdinand and his criticism of other humanists in Naples that his own apparently radical and innovative practices as a historian in fact owed much to the classical model of Thucydides. Early in the *Gesta Ferdinandi* Valla pointed out that he could not consistently use classical place-names in his Latin, since some names had changed and others had come into being, and he wrote for a modern, not an ancient, world and public. Language, he argued, rested on nothing more or less than custom, and custom changed with time: "Since I am writing for men of the present and the future, I must use not the original names but those widely used in our time and for a long period before it, if I wish all my readers to understand me. I see that this was the general practice of the ancients. For these and other places came repeatedly to be called by different names, and the old language is simply an old custom of speaking."[134] The same point held for other "new things," like the mounted scouts whom Valla insisted on calling "caballerii" or "equerii," rather than "equites." The effort to find a classical term for things that had not existed in the ancient world led only to error and confusion: "Anyone can see that new names must be fitted to new things. This was the custom of the ancients, from whom we have our rules and derive our examples."[135] Valla went so far as to dedicate a long essay to developing this point—a piece that became so long and dense that he eventually excised it from his history and passed it on to his friend Giovanni Tortelli, who included it in his own massive reference work on the Latin language, the *De orthographia*.[136]

Valla had infuriated his Neapolitan rival Bartolomeo Facio, undermining his competence as a Latinist and philologist by asking sharp questions at the public discussions of classical texts that their patron, Alfonso of Aragon, liked to stage. When Valla left Naples, Facio attacked him bitterly in writ-

---

133. See chapter 2.

134. Valla, *Gesta,* ed. Besomi, 10–13, at 11 (1.2.1): "ut necesse habeam, cum presentibus futurisque hominibus scribam, non priscis nominibus uti, sed nostro seculo et iam longa etate usitatis, si ab omnibus legentibus intelligi velim, ut veteres quoque ipsos video factitasse; nam et hec et cetera loca fere diversis subinde vocibus appellata sunt, et vetus sermo nihil aliud est quam vetus loquendi consuetudo."

135. Ibid., 62–63, at 63 (1.14.7): "Quare quis non videt rebus novis esse accommodanda nova nomina, ut veteres, a quibus precepta habemus et exempla sumimus, factitarunt?"

136. Ibid., 194–204; see the more detailed treatment, also by Besomi, "Dai 'Gesta Ferdinandi regis Aragonum' del Valla al 'De orthographia' del Tortelli," *Italia medioevale e umanistica* 9 (1966): 75–121.

ing, both for his supposed departures from classical usage and for the modest digressions on the history of language that remained in his text to justify them. In his discussion of place-names, Facio argued, Valla had confused history with cosmography. In his discussion of the "caballerius" he had simply wandered off into elementary and irrelevant matters: "You seem not to want to write a history but to transmit the rules of the grammarians. Therefore I think this whole disputation about the words *miles* and *eques* particularly bad, as it is superfluous and awkward."[137]

When Valla appealed to "custom" or "usage" to defend his apparent departures from a strictly classical vocabulary, he in fact adapted a classical source, as Vincenzo de Caprio has made clear. Quintilian, in his *Institutio oratoria,* had discussed the role of "consuetudo," custom, in forming a good orator's choice of words. Though wary of the errors with which popular usage swarmed, Quintilian nonetheless admitted that the speaker of real Latin must sometimes follow modern, oral usage rather than the practice of older writers. After all, he asked, "what is the old language but an old custom of speaking?"[138] Valla characteristically put his own twist on his ancient source. He turned Quintilian's question into a statement. He did not fully acknowledge that the Roman orator had hedged this loophole in his classicism with many qualifications. And he did not make clear that a modern Latinist must inevitably find it far harder than did an ancient one to walk the tightrope of "usage" without falling off it into barbarism or vulgarity.

Nonetheless, Valla saw his historical method as classical. And he defended it against Facio, as Mariangela Regoliosi has shown in her exemplary edition of his reply. With assurance and superiority, Valla showed that his apparent departures from classical rules for history in fact rested on the best of ancient authorities.[139] Valla naturally cited Thucydides as his predecedent for discussing problems of language in a historical work. Thu-

---

137. B. Facio, *Invective in Laurentium Vallam,* ed. E.I. Rao (Naples, 1978), 75–76, 81–82, at 82: "Est enim vitiosa digressio brevitati contraria. Videris enim non historiam velle scribere, sed grammaticorum precepta tradere. Itaque totam istam de militis et equitis vocabulo disputationem, ut superfluam atque ineptam vitiosissimam puto. Nec minus hoc loco elegantiam tuam damnandam atque irridendam censeo, cum velis nova et absurdissima formare nomina, quando propriis usitatis atque honestis uti liceat." On this edition see M. Regoliosi, "Per la tradizione delle 'Invective in L. Vallam' di Bartolomeo Facio," *Italia Medioevale e Umanistica* 23 (1980): 389–97.

138. Quintilian *Institutio oratoria* 1.6.43: "Et sane quid est aliud vetus sermo quam vetus loquendi consuetudo?" See de Caprio, *La tradizione e la trauma,* 152–62.

139. L. Valla, *Antidotum in Facium,* ed. M. Regoliosi (Padua, 1981), introduction, liii–lxvii.

cydides, after all, had devoted even more space than Valla to subjects that
Facio would have condemned as irrelevant to history. He had discussed the
cultural development of Greece between Homer's time and his own—providing, perhaps, the inspiration for Valla's analysis of the necessary mutability of culture and language.[140] And he had shown that a historian must
address linguistic problems, at least when they reflected substantial changes
in the order of society. Valla argued that his digression was "neither a disputation nor long but a very short account" and that it dealt "not with a
new word but with a new thing—just as Thucydides did with the word
Greece, that is, *Hellas.*"[141] Valla's model of how to write history, in short,
was Thucydidean—in a complex, carefully considered sense. In Valla's
adherence to this classical model lay the key to his ability to write a work
not confined within the sterilizing norms of so much humanist historiography. The ancient text helped the modern reader to bend, even to break,
what others defined as the restrictive rules of a classical genre. Valla's
library—and the Neapolitan court library in the days when he worked
there—was no *hortus conclusus.*

We stop here, for now: in the center of the Italian Renaissance, in another
of those locations where books of the new kind were most dramatically collected and discussed. Even here the intermediary comes between the ever
receding original text and the hungry reader. But here too, without the intermediary the reader would have no text to consume. Valla's translation of
Thucydides offered sharp new insights into ancient historiography as well as
models for modern speeches; its apparatus contained rigorously established
facts as well as imaginatively fabricated constructions. Both its deceptive
glamor and its solid scholarship, its classicizing frame and its ancient content, are emblematic of the humanists' new world of the book.

---

140. Ibid., 211 (3.1.6).
141. Ibid., 235 (3.4.8): "neque hec disputatio est neque longa, sed perbrevis narratio, neque
tam de novo verbo quam de nova re, sicut Thucydides de vocabulo 'Grecie,' idest, Ἑλλάδος,
fecit."

2

Leon Battista Alberti:
The Writer as Reader

Leon Battista Alberti could leap from a standing start over the head of a man standing next to him, hurl lances and shoot arrows with astonishing force, and throw a coin so high that it rang as it struck the vaulted roof of the church in which he stood. A penetrating observer of society, he could divine men's intentions toward him at a glance and enjoyed interrogating knowledgeable artisans about their skills. A dazzling amateur artist, he could paint or sculpt the likeness of a friend while dictating an essay. A pioneer in the wedding of artistic and scientific practices, he stated the rules of one-point perspective and devised an optical device that provided startling illusions of landscapes, the night sky, and the ocean. Though Alberti loved to look at dignified old men, he wept when he saw spring flowers or autumn fruits, because they made him feel unproductive. He trained himself to bear pain without flinching (he sang to distract himself) and even to tolerate the presence of garlic and honey, which had originally made him vomit. In short, he made his life an art. All this we learn from the so-called *Anonymous Life* (or *Vita Anonyma*) of Alberti, first published in the eighteenth century.[1]

The Alberti of this anonymous account—the universal savant, the brilliant man of action, the cultivator of artistic grace and ease before Castiglione—enthralled Jacob Burckhardt, that passionate lover of the life of the Italian streets and the beauty of the Italian landscapes, both of which had so fascinated his hero. Alberti's character forms the nucleus of the brilliant description of the "universal man" that lights up the second section of

---

1. See the exemplary edition by R. Fubini and A.N. Gallorini, "L'autobiografia di Leon Battista Alberti: Studio e edizione," *Rinascimento*, ser. 2, 12 (1972): 21–78; and the new translation and commentary by R. Watkins, "L.B. Alberti in the Mirror: An Interpretation of the *Vita* with a New Translation," *Italian Quarterly* 30 (1989): 5–30, from which I borrow translations. Cf. also Watkins' older study, "The Authorship of the *Vita Anonyma* of Leon Battista Alberti," *Studies in the Renaissance* 4 (1957); and D. Marsh, "Petrarch and Alberti," in *Renaissance Studies in Honor of Craig Hugh Smyth*, ed. A. Morrogh et al. (Florence, 1985), 363–73.

Burckhardt's *Die Kultur der Renaissance in Italien.* In both the original account and Burckhardt's incomplete retelling, reading plays only a supporting role—and a rather frightening one—in the lively cast of Alberti's tasks and hobbies. For Alberti, in fact, the very experience of textual study—at least when carried out on an empty stomach—proved unhealthy, almost lethal: "As he was reading, the keenness of his eyesight suddenly failed, and he was overcome with dizziness and pain while a roaring and loud ringing filled his ears."[2]

Burckhardt selected carefully as he drew on the *Vita Anonyma* of Alberti (which, as recent scholarship has shown, was probably Alberti's own work, a precocious autobiography written in the late 1430s). In drawing his own pen-portrait, Alberti began by pointing out that he did not find reading either a consistently obsessive interest or a reliably restful pastime: "He had discovered in the study of letters, he used to remark, the truth of the saying that all things grow wearisome to mortal men. For letters sometimes delighted him so much that they seemed like flowering and fragrant blossoms from which hunger or weariness could hardly distract him; yet at other times they would seem to be piling up under his eyes, looking like scorpions, so that the last thing he could do would be to continue looking at books."[3] Alberti, in short, represented himself as a man of universal curiosity, one who studied the physical cosmos of stars and planets, landscape, wind and weather as passionately as the written cosmos of classical literature, and whom reading could exhaust and exasperate. But he never abandoned his books entirely. When the doctors ordered him to cease taxing his memory, he studied physics and mathematics "quod sine literis esse non posset"—"because he could not bear to live without letters." That is, he now read books on mathematics instead of law and history because they called for thought, not memorization. Burckhardt transmuted the passage by omitting the crucial clause. His Alberti did not study a new range of texts but simply "settled . . . on physics and mathematics"—moved, in nineteenth-century fashion, from books to nature.[4] Perhaps Alberti's fear of books and study

2. Fubini and Gallorini, "L'autobiografia," 69: "eo deventum est gravissima valitudine, ut lectitanti sibi oculorum illico acies obortis vertiginibus torminibusque defecisse videretur, fragoresque et longa sibila ad inter aures multo resonarent."

3. Ibid., 68: "Solitus fuerat dicere sese in litteris quoque illud animadvertisse, quod aiunt rerum esse omnium satietatem apud mortales. Sibi enim litteras, quibus tantopere delectaretur, interdum gemmas floridasque atque odoratissimas videri, adeo ut a libris vix posset fame aut somno distrahi: interdum autem litteras ipsas suis sub oculis inglomerari persimiles scorpionibus, ut nihil posset rerum omnium minus quam libros intueri."

4. J. Burckhardt, *Die Kultur der Renaissance in Italien: Ein Versuch, Gesammelte Werke* vol. 3 (Darmstadt, 1955), 95: "legte . . . sich auf Physik und Mathematik."

made him seem especially engaging in the ebbing years of the romantic era, when Burckhardt discovered Italy and the Renaissance. But even the heroic protagonist of the autobiography was more bookish than Burckhardt's version of him.

Burckhardt, in fact, cast Alberti as his exemplary "universal man," a natural forerunner to Leonardo da Vinci, that self-proclaimed "man without letters" who was to Alberti, according to Burckhardt, "as the finisher to the beginner, the master to the dilettante."[5] True, Alberti did more than live; he wrote, and at great length. Burckhardt took extensive notes on several of his texts.[6] But for a long time, Alberti's books seemed also to set their author apart from the literary intellectuals of his time—as a man of the street, the building site, and the countinghouse rather than a library-bound humanist.

Alberti's literary career really began, after all, when he began to write on what he himself described as novel subjects—subjects for which no classical prototype existed.[7] Born in 1404 into a family exiled from Florence, he studied the humanities with Gasparino Barzizza in Padua and tried his hand, unhappily, at Roman law. He then wrote a mordant treatise *De commodis litterarum atque incommodis* (On the advantages and disadvantages of letters). But this recital of the ills that scholars suffer, to which we shall return, had no great impact, even on its author. Alberti's comedy, the *Philodoxeos fabula,* was a successful mystification, taken by some readers as an ancient text. But his first really influential and original work was *De pictura,* his manifesto on perspective and painting. He wrote this just after his return to Florence, in an incandescent burst of enthusiasm triggered by Brunelleschi's Duomo and Masaccio's frescoes. Alberti's little book resembles Baudelaire's "The Painter of Modern Life" in its sharply etched combination of description and prescription. *De pictura* evokes the quintessentially modern, bookless world of the studio and the salon, where amateurs and professionals mingled and exchanged artistic chat, not the quiet contemplative life of the library.

Alberti's most impressive work of the 1430s and early 1440s, *I libri della famiglia,* did not reach print or find attention until the nineteenth century. But when that matchlessly vivid evocation of the life of a high bourgeois

---

5. Ibid., 96: "wie zum Anfänger der Vollender, wie zum Dilettanten der Meister."

6. W. Kaegi, *Jacob Burckhardt: Eine Biographie,* vol. 3, *Die Zeit der klassischen Werke* (Basel and Stuttgart, 1956), 657–58. For Burckhardt's central interest in what he took as the anonymous "Schilderung" of Alberti—and the way in which both this text and Cellini's autobiography, as interpreted by Goethe, shaped his work—see 720–22.

7. On Alberti's life see *Dizionario biografico degli italiani,* s.v. "Alberti, Leon Battista," by C. Grayson.

clan of the Renaissance reappeared, it too seemed the work of one who cared more about the world than about books. Its third book, in particular, with its detailed plans for the management of a successful household, provoked the heaviest guns of German sociology to exchange barrages about the ideology of modern life.[8]

De re aedificatoria, Alberti's manual of architecture, took shape in the 1440s, as his own career as cleric and architectural adviser in the papal Curia prospered. He probably advised Nicholas V when the latter worked up his ambitious plans to rebuild the Borgo, which were not carried out; perhaps he also advised Pius II, who created what remains one of the most enchanting of urban complexes, the planned city of Pienza. Alberti certainly did innovative architectural work for Giovanni Rucellai in Florence and Sigismondo Malatesta in Rimini, and he became a familiar figure at other sophisticated courts, such as that of Leonello d'Este in Ferrara. Though it was never finished, *De re aedificatoria* summed up Alberti's impressive theories about architecture and his matchless knowledge of antiquities. Within a few years after his death in 1472, manuscripts circulated widely; Poliziano's printed edition of 1486 reached a still wider public. Endlessly modernized and endlessly fruitful, *De re aedificatoria* survived into England's Palladian age as part of the connoisseur's library and the architect's working kit. It looks still more modern and less literary than Alberti's other writings on art. This long Latin book was self-evidently the work of someone who knew firsthand about gutters and downspouts, roofs and drains—who had scrambled about the streets and basements of Rome in search of new facts about old buildings.[9]

Finally, Alberti's building projects, from the Rucellai Palace in Florence to the Malatesta Temple in Rimini, reinforced his reputation as a doer. Vasari, who dismissed Alberti as a typically unproductive intellectual, the sort of man who made his name by writing, was one of the few dissenters. On the whole, as a result, historians have often followed Burckhardt, showing themselves reluctant to situate the young Alberti in his original place of employment, as one of the lively but undignified humanists of the papal

---

8. See H. Baron, *In Search of Florentine Civic Humanism* (Princeton, 1988), 1: chap. 10.

9. Alberti's own achievements as an architect and student of ancient architecture remain controversial. In addition to the literature cited in notes 75, 79, and 118, see C.W. Westfall, *In This Most Perfect Paradise* (University Park and London, 1974); F. Borsi, *Leon Battista Alberti: The Complete Works* (New York, 1989); M. Jarzombek, *On Leon Battista Alberti: His Literary and Aesthetic Theories* (Cambridge, Mass., and London, 1989); C. Burroughs, *From Signs to Design* (Cambridge, Mass., and London, 1990); and B. Curran and A. Grafton, "A Fifteenth-Century Site Report on the Vatican Obelisk," *Journal of the Warburg and Courtauld Institutes* 58 (1995), 234–48.

Curia, whose constant quarrels and occasional brawls did so much to lend credence to the old view of the humanists as amoral luftmenschen.[10]

No modern student of Alberti reveals Burckhardt's impact more vividly than Georg Voigt, the historian of the revival of classical antiquity. A detailed sketch of Alberti already formed part of the first edition of his work, which was published a year before Burckhardt's *Kultur der Renaissance*. In later editions, he not only took over some of Burckhardt's phrasing but echoed his interpretation of Alberti's career. He described Alberti as having had too "original a nature" to spend much of his time with the humanists, among whom he stood out as a lonely exception to all norms— an idea hard to reconcile with the facts, which Voigt had already assembled in his first edition, about Alberti's friendly relations with Leonardo Bruni, Leonardo Dati, and other scholars.[11] More recent scholars aimed at a similar destination but reached it by a different tack. In more than one memorable account, Alberti appears not as a reader and scholar but as a uniquely systematic thinker—one whose dominating passion for order, symmetry, and harmony found only a partial expression in his own buildings and attained their full realization in Bramante's Tempietto and Palladio's villas.[12] This Alberti, while a far more productive intellectual than the brilliant dilettante portrayed by Burckhardt and Voigt, remains just as distant from the normal social and cultural type of the humanist.

Since the 1940s, however, a second Alberti has begun to take shape. Cecil Grayson, Giovanni Orlandi, Laura Goggi Carotti, and others have published new editions of many of Alberti's lesser and greater works. In some of these texts—many of which, such as *Momus* and the *Intercenales*, found

---

10. This view of the Curial humanists has long been obsolete. See now R. Fubini, *Umanesimo e secolarizzazione da Petrarca a Valla* (Rome, 1990), esp. chaps. 3 and 5–8.

11. Cf. G. Voigt, *Die Wiederbelebung des classischen Alterthums oder das erste Jahrhundert des Humanismus* (Berlin, 1859), 190–91, with the fourth edition (1893; repr., Berlin, 1960), 1:370–76. For use of Burckhardt see e.g., the fourth edition, 372: "Im 24. Jahre legte er sich dann vorzugsweise auf Mathematik und Physik." For efforts to show that Alberti was no humanist see esp. the fourth edition, 375–76: "Dass wir Alberti nicht mitten im Treiben der Humanisten finden . . . erklärt sich schon aus der Originalität seiner Natur und seines Strebens . . . Sein Leben und Schaffen verlief nicht auf der Bahn der humanistischen Gesellschaft, er steht in beidem als ein einsamer Sonderling da." These sentences bracket Voigt's description of ample countervailing evidence, reproduced in text and footnote from the original edition (191), but slightly altered in phrasing. In the first edition, he had said: "Mit den Humanisten . . . stand er friedlich und freundschaftlich"; in the second, "Mit Bruni und Poggio . . . stand er friedlich und freundschaftlich."

12. See above all the classic work of R. Wittkower, *Architectural Principles in the Age of Humanism* (London, 1952); A. di Tommaso, "Nature and the Aesthetic Social Theory of Leon Battista Alberti," *Medievalia et humanistica*, n.s., 3 (1972): 31–49; and J. Kelly Gadol, *Leon Battista Alberti: Universal Man of the Early Renaissance* (Chicago, 1969).

few readers in the critical years around 1500, when printed editions froze the moving cultural life of fifteenth-century Italy into images at once permanent and deceptive—Alberti mobilized formidable learning to portray a frightening world. A crude Stonehenge, populated by lurid, gesticulating goblins, replaced the orderly, Euclidean cosmos of *De pictura, De statua,* and *De re aedificatoria.* The new (and newly accessible) material showed that Alberti took a serious interest in the philosophy of the Epicureans and the cynicism of Lucian. More important, it reinvigorated the study of the canonical texts. Few scholars now set out to scale Alberti's monumental or even his minor works equipped with simple categories and brief labels.

Students of humanistic philology and intellectual historians—above all Eugenio Garin, Riccardo Fubini, David Marsh, Lucia Cesarini Martinelli, and Roberto Cardini—have demonstrated that Alberti's thought and language are dense with paradoxes and sometimes riven by contradictions. He described the orderly cosmos of patrons, builders, and citizens in *De re aedificatoria* and the hideous chaos of masked and mendacious rulers and courtiers in *Momus* with equal force. He wrote the life of an ancient martyr, who resisted the temptations of the world, and the speech of Momus, who praised the sturdy beggar's life as the best of all, as well as the discourses of uncle Giannozzo, who dedicated himself to business with a tenacity and rigor worthy of a medieval saint. The new Alberti seems at least as fascinating a thinker as, and far more challenging than, the old one. Moreover, the study of his language has proved as rewarding as that of his ideas. It has become clear that Alberti picked his Latin words and phrases with a watchmaker's delicate precision from a wide range of sources, some of them newly discovered. The systematic weaving of a dense web of direct and indirect allusions—the forging of a direct bond between reading and writing—has turned out to be one of his central strategies as a writer. Alberti's works, in short, are cast in a style as densely worked with meaningful details as the surfaces of the traditional Florentine paintings that he considered too busy to be the highest form of art. Like the paintings, too, they reveal their maker's complex relation to ancient and medieval traditions.

Even Alberti's professedly practical works on the arts now look very different than they did two or three generations ago. Nineteenth-century scholars like Janitschek emphasized the "popular" Italian *Della pittura* rather than the Latin *De pictura.*[13] More recent studies, by contrast, have shown that the more learned Latin texts lay at the heart of Alberti's enterprise. He

---

13. See Alberti's *Kleinere kunsttheoretische Schriften,* ed. H. Janitschek (1877; repr., Osnabrück, 1970).

modeled his manual for painters on such classical prototypes as the rhetorical works of Cicero and Quintilian.[14] He also stuffed the work to bursting with classical references and allusions.[15] Naturally enough, he found his chief audience in courts and humanist schools, where such evidence of erudition was the common coin of intellectual exchange. Each new interpretation of *De pictura*—and every year brings forth a number of them—now routinely rests on an identification of Alberti's major structural source or sources (unfortunately, no two of these seem to agree with one another).[16] The great example of the Renaissance's discovery of the world and of man has become the object—and is portrayed as the protagonist—of an unending paper chase.

Alberti was no Vespasiano, no enthusiast for pretty books and obsessive collectors. From the start of his career he nourished no illusions, and allowed his readers to nourish none, about the difficulties and asperities of the life of the professional reader. In *De commodis litterarum atque incommodis*, for example, the disadvantages of the scholar's life take up far more space and are described far more memorably than the advantages.[17] Alberti evokes every imaginable defect of reading, both as a career and as an intellectual activity. The need for books, he pointed out, could reach literally as well as financially monstrous extremes. The lawyer, for example, must buy "huge letters, enormous codices, huge—my God, how huge—bundles" and install them in a specially built room. This room must have all the appurtenances of serious reading: "a vast amount of baggage in book form and equipment and elaborately constructed libraries."[18] In particular, the lawyer must have a book wheel, so that he could turn the vast codices of his glossed *Corpus iuris*. These displays looked impressive; Bartolomeo Scala,

---

14. The best account of Alberti's position in the Renaissance revival of classical rhetoric remains M. Baxandall's classic *Giotto and the Orators* (repr., Oxford, 1986). See also the classic articles of C.E. Gilbert, "Antique Frameworks for Renaissance Art Theory: Alberti and Pino," *Marsyas* 3 (1943–45); and J.R. Spencer, "Ut rhetorica pictura," *Journal of the Warburg and Courtauld Institutes* 20 (1957): 26–44.

15. See the landmark edition of *De pictura* and *De statua* with translation and notes by C. Grayson, *On Painting and On Sculpture* (London, 1972), from which I borrow translations throughout.

16. For good recent specimens of this literature see M. Jarzombek, "The Structural Problematic of Leon Battista Alberti's *De pictura*," *Renaissance Studies* 4 (1990): 273–85; and J.M. Greenstein, "Alberti on *Historia*: A Renaissance View of the Structure of Significance in Narrative Painting," *Viator* 21 (1990): 273–99.

17. L.B. Alberti, *De commodis litterarum atque incommodis*, ed. L. Goggi Carotti (Florence, 1976).

18. Ibid., 89: "grandes littere, amplissimi codices, sarcine, proh superi, immanes." Ibid., 90: ". . . iurisperiti cum suis omnibus impedimentis librorum machinisque atque architecturis bibliothecarum."

later the chancellor of Florence, also described the stately rows of books and mobile library furniture with which the Roman lawyers of his day intimidated and inspired their clients.[19] But Alberti ridiculed them as ineffectual. The owner of such a library could make more money, he says, displaying his books for a fee in the marketplace than using them in the practice of law in the courtroom.[20] When he sets out to use his texts in a case, he will find himself staying up all night, nodding over his book, eyes red with fatigue and stomach aching with hunger—only to lose his reputation in his quest for profit, as he tries to stand up to the great men of the city, wielding pitiful glosses as his only weapon.[21]

The lawyers are hardly the only readers to cut a feeble figure in Alberti's account. Doctors and humanists prove equally wretched; for the reader, it emerges, is not a free man working peacefully in his study but a slave to the physical embodiments of his erudition. The scribes who sell him books continually besiege him for payment. The books themselves are equally demanding. If the scholar thinks of buying clothes, his library reproaches him: "You owe us this money; I forbid it." If he thinks of taking exercise or practicing music, his books complain: "You're taking this time away from us."[22] He spends the flower of his youth locked up "amid papers and dead sheep [parchments]."[23] When a scholar tries by marrying a young woman to escape the poverty to which he is doomed, her mother will ridicule him as half-dead and unkempt, her brothers will dismiss him as boring and repulsive, and she herself will spurn him, since young women prefer to be amused by something other than the only thing the scholar has to offer, "the sayings of the philosophers."[24] When he tries to play a role in public affairs, finally, he will only make a fool of himself. Questions of state require not knowl-

---

19. B. Scala, "Dialogus de legibus et iudiciis," ed. L. Borglia, *La bibliofilia* 42 (1940): 252–82.

20. Alberti, *De commodis,* ed. Goggi Carotti, 89–90: "quas qui ordine similique apparatu in tabernam apud forum exposuerit, quo iurisconsulti domi pompam apertam atque dispositam ostentant, certe illic plures, procul dubio longe plures ille pecunias si pretio ad rem visendam intromittat accipiet quam iurisperiti cum suis omnibus impedimentis librorum machinisque atque architectaris bibliothecarum sint soliti capere."

21. Ibid., 90: "Cras, inquit, causam te orare oportebit, modica tum porrigit cliens, plura in crastinum pollicetur. Tu quicquid porrigitur accipis, totam deinde noctem inter libros ad nidorem lucerne pedibus manibusque algentibus somnescis, queritans, pervolvens machinas et libros omnes atque te ipsum cura, somno, inedia frigoreque conficiens. Ergo prodis ad causam rauca voce, obtorto collo, rubentibus atque gementibus ocellis . . ."

22. Ibid., 61: "Nonne si vestes cupiveris, inquiet bibliotheca, Has mihi pecunias debes, veto? Si venationem, si musicam, dimicandive artem, aut palestram ipse prosequare, nonne inquient littere: Tu nobis has operas surripis, tibi nos famam et nomen non referemus?"

23. Ibid., 62: "inter chartas et mortuas pecudes (ut sic libros nuncupem) . . ."

24. Ibid., 94.

edge of letters but experience in affairs: "I think it is well established," Alberti remarks, "that there is rarely need for public discussion of the heavens and the planets, never of the nature of the gods, or the generation and powers of the mind."[25] The scholar's heaped-up intellectual capital looms threateningly over him, inducing paralysis rather than stimulus.

Worst of all, the scholar condemns his mind, as well as his body, to a doomed, lifelong struggle with his obsession. Knowledge, the object of his quest, inevitably eludes him as Daphne did Apollo, perpetually receding: "Letters include innumerable things worth knowing, and it is hard to express how much the desire to learn them oppresses the student's mind. He falls on a difficult scholarly disputation or discovers something elegant, worthwhile, full of learning; then he doesn't sleep, eat, or rest; he feels no pleasure at all; he is possessed by an obsessive desire to master the thing entirely. But it takes great effort to learn it, great care to keep it, great concern to preserve it."[26]

Few could survive this exhaustive regimen. Like a Florentine patrician assessing the resources of Giangaleazzo Visconti—or a modern assistant professor calculating his or her probability of getting tenure—Alberti even drew up a quantitative analysis of the life chances of the scholar. Imagine a thousand young men starting out on a literary career. At best three hundred of them will reach forty, the normal age of maturity and financial independence. Only one hundred of these will persist in their studies. Only ten of that one hundred will have the memory and intellect to do distinguished work, and only three of that ten will actually survive the pressure and misery to become productive scholars. The world of the book looks depressing indeed.[27]

And yet, Alberti did not design this grisly introduction to the horrors of the life of learning as a simple attack on erudition. It ends with a passionate defense of the value of the classics, which provide not transitory goods like

25. Ibid., 107: "Mihi tamen non persuadeo rem publicam in magistratibus exposcere copiam litterarum magis quam rerum experientiam longo usu et tractatione perfectam. Verum brevissime hunc locum transeundum censeo; nam constare arbitror ut raro de celo aut planetis, utque nunquam de deorum natura, de animorum procreatione et vi apud rem publicam consulatur."

26. Ibid., 64: "Habentur enim in litteris innumerabilia cognitu dignissima, neque facile dici potest quam earum studiosum ingenium ediscendi cupiditas premat. Incidit in difficilem doctissimorum disceptationem aut rem comperit elegantem, dignam, plenam eruditionum: studiosus non dormit, non comedit, non quiescit, nullam penitus voluptatem sentit; stat mordax cura rem totam recognoscere atque tenere. Ea quidem magno labore apprehenditur, multa solertia detinetur, grandi sollicitudine servatur."

27. Ibid., 78–82.

wealth and power but eternal ones like knowledge of the past and prudence for the future. Along the way it includes—as its excellent recent editor, Laura Goggi Carotti, has shown—a great deal of new learning of Alberti's own. In 1421 a manuscript of Cicero's *Brutus* was discovered at Lodi. Gasparino Barzizza, Alberti's teacher, was one of the several humanists who immediately had copies made of the original, which was written in a difficult script (it is now lost). One of these copies came into Alberti's hands before 1429. Now preserved in the Biblioteca Marciana in Venice, it contains his autograph notes on his personal and family life—including a famous one that dates the completion of his book *De pictura*.[28] Even as Alberti deplored the miseries of the humanistic lifestyle, in short, he was leading it. He collected books; he made them his confidants; and he used them, exhaustively. The *Brutus* provided basic facts, striking quotations, and even a curious trick of style—the use of *sic* to introduce the infinitive— for the *De commodis litterarum atque incommodis*.[29] The very text in which Alberti denounced the ills of reading, in short, recorded the results of his studies. Like Giovanni Pontano—a later humanist, better known as a scholar, whose deft marginal notes on Plautus transmuted themselves gradually into an elegant, Plautine Latinity—Alberti nourished his original writing on attentive classical reading.[30] His satire on the foibles of scholarship paradoxically made a scholarly contribution of its own. And Alberti was literally the last person on whom an irony like this one could have been lost.

Alberti, in fact, mastered every tool in the humanist reader's kit during his time with Barzizza and after. Consider what may seem an unlikely case in point: his one hagiographical text, the *Vita Sancti Potiti*, which he wrote at a patron's request. The bulk of this narrative takes the form of the sort of saint's life that Valla and Erasmus notoriously disliked. Potitus (now known as Potinus) refuses to be tempted or intimidated by the pagan emperor Antoninus, whose daughter he has freed from possession by a demon. He persists in his faith even when burned, eaten by beasts, boiled in oil, and deprived of his tongue and eyes; and he goes on preaching the one God even after his tongue is cut out. Alberti's skepticism has seemed patent to many readers.

Alberti submitted this work, as he did the books on the family, to his friend Leonardo Dati, his chosen literary adviser. He seems to have worried

---

28. Lat. XI, 67 (=3859), ex Nani; see Alberti, *De commodis,* ed. Goggi Carotti, 8 and n. 4.

29. Alberti, *De commodis,* ed. Goggi Carotti, 39–40 n. 9.

30. R. Cappelletto, *La 'Lectura Plauti' del Pontano* (Urbino, 1988). Goggi Carotti suggests that content summaries in the margin of the Marcianus reflect Alberti's efforts at digestion of the *Brutus*.

that he might be thought to have invented something, and he admitted that Potitus' life had been "carelessly passed on." But in his letter to Dati Alberti provided the best possible defense for his excursion into hagiography. He gave a careful account of his sources in the approved humanist style. Reading "in the most widely accepted ancient writers," he told Dati, he had discovered that Potitus was a problematic figure.[31] Tatian, an early Christian writer of great authority, had described him as one of those who, like Marcion, saw the universe as governed by two powers, not by one.[32] Further reading in Eusebius' *Historia ecclesiastica* cleared matters up. The letters of certain martyrs of Lyons, quoted by Eusebius, vividly described the courage of a young Christian named Ponticus.[33] Alberti checked the chronology of his life; it matched that of Potitus, for "those letters were written in the time of Antoninus," when Potitus had suffered and preached. "Therefore," Alberti concluded, "I feel little concern for the judgment of those who think the history is invented. For either there is an error in the name, and thanks to the negligence of the scribes they say Ponticus in place of Potitus; or he had two names, Ponticus Potitus. In any case it is clear that there was a young man who became a holy martyr in his fifteenth year."[34]

The object of the exercise is problematic. But Alberti's techniques, which include the collation of witnesses, the setting of testimonies into their proper chronological order, and the denunciation (and explaining away) of scribal error, matched those of the most erudite humanists of his time. A high-powered, eight-cylinder humanist, Alberti worked as smoothly when he needed to collate manuscripts or criticize divergent sources as when he set out to look for the remains of a fallen obelisk or excavate an Etruscan tomb.[35] Though in later years he stayed away from hagiography, he kept up his interest both in Eusebius and in historical criticism. When he described the descendants of Protogenes as the first builders of houses, for example, he did so on the basis of material supplied by "Eusebius, that fine student of antiq-

31. *Opuscoli inediti di Leon Battista Alberti: 'Musca', 'Vita S. Potiti'*, ed. C. Grayson (Florence, 1954), 86: "negligenter traditam"; "apud veteres approbatissimos."

32. Actually Tatian's pupil Rhodo ap. Euseb. *Eccl. hist.* 5.13.3.

33. Ibid. 5.1.53–54.

34. Alberti, *Opuscoli,* ed. Grayson, 87: "Habeo igitur hunc Ponticum, cuius etas, res geste, cum Antonini temporibus pulchre conveniant. Ille enim epistole Antonini temporibus scripte sunt. Idcirco eorum iudicium minus timeo qui fictam esse hystoriam arbitrentur. Vel enim sit error in nomine librariorum negligentia Ponticum pro Potito dixerint vel binomius Ponticus Potitus fuerit, constat tamen fuisse adoloscentem qui quinto et decimo anno martir sanctissimus fuerit."

35. For Alberti's expertise as an archaeologist see C. Dionisotti, review of *Pirro Ligorio's Roman Antiquities*, by C. Mitchell and E. Landowsky, *Rivista storica italiana* 75 (1963): 890–901; and R. Weiss, *The Renaissance Discovery of Classical Antiquity* (Oxford, 1988).

uities, from ancient sources."[36] Eusebius, this time in the *Praeparatio evangelica*, had not given this information on his own authority but cited it from the ancient Phoenician history of Sanchuniathon, translated into Greek by Philo of Byblos.[37] Source criticism abided; it showed that one should trust Eusebius because he cited even older witnesses.

Alberti knew the techniques of humanist philology well enough to enjoy playing with them—always a sign, as Michael Baxandall has pointed out, that one has mastered a difficult skill and likes to display the acquisition in public.[38] Guarino of Verona translated Lucian's mock encomium on the fly into Latin and sent it to Alberti, who was suffering from a fever. The text amused him so much that he immediately sat up and dictated a mock encomium of his own, the *Musca*.[39] Alberti praised everything about the fly. The fly is heroic (he can attack and defeat far larger animals, such as bulls and elephants); he is pious (whenever the ancients sacrificed animals to the gods, the flies were the very first to attend); he and his female companions wear the same fine classical dress as their ancestors and show the same musical talent. Above all, however, Alberti praises the fly's erudition and antiquity. Flies are insatiably curious; in fact, they know the answers to questions that have tormented scholars for centuries. Flies know what Circe fed her suitors to turn them into pigs, what flaws appeared in Helen's *nates* and what beauties in Ganymede's *occulta*.[40] So much for exactly the sorts of historical and mythological questions most beloved of the humanist commentators who, like oysters gone mad and operating in reverse, secreted glosses around Ovid and Juvenal—and whose ancient predecessors had been satirized by Seneca.[41]

Even textual criticism, the humanist science of sciences, came in for mockery at Alberti's hands. The flies, he explains, stood at the origins of ancient science: they had taught Pythagoras his new mathematics. A simple feat of conjectural emendation proved the point. The texts said that after Pythagoras proved his theorem, he sacrificed "musis" (to the Muses). Surely the ignorant scribes had, as usual, substituted an easy reading for a hard one. In reality, Pythagoras must have offered his hecatomb of oxen "mus-

---

36. Alberti *De re aedificatoria* 2.4, in *L'archittetura*, ed. and trans. G. Orlandi, annotated by P. Portoghesi (Milan, 1966), 1:111: "Eusebius Pamphilus elegans antiquitatum perscrutator ex veterum testimoniis."

37. Eusebius *Praeparatio evangelica* 1.10.10.

38. M. Baxandall, *Painting and Experience in Fifteenth-Century Italy*, 2d ed. (Oxford, 1988), chap. 2.

39. Alberti, *Opuscoli*, ed. Grayson, 45.

40. Ibid., 54.

41. Seneca *Ep. mor.* 88.6–8.

cis" (to the flies).[42] The parody is so detailed that it amounts to an act of homage.

Despite Alberti's close and intricate involvement in the worlds of book hunters and humanist scribes, textual critics and exegetes, he offered few explicit comments about exactly how he read the books he liked so much. Some elementary points are easily established. Alberti was fascinated, as we have seen, by the shapes of letters—so much so that they turned into scorpions before his eyes when he read while overtired. Not surprisingly, he took a hand in fomenting the "aesthetic revolution" that created new forms of books and writing in the fifteenth century. The inscription on the Holy Sepulchre that he built for Rucellai in Florence is one of the earliest to be carved in Roman epigraphic capitals, and the first in a geometrically constructed alphabet. These symmetrical and imposing letters soon imposed themselves on *cartolai* as well as architects.[43] Thus Alberti had a part in creating the Florentine version of the humanist book marketed so effectively by Vespasiano and others. Rather like his Holy Sepulchre, this too was a pastiche of classical and medieval elements, which he no doubt appreciated fully.[44]

Alberti used his classical books in fashionable ways: for example, as diaries to which he could confide for the record such memorable events as the death of a crowd of pilgrims, crushed on or pushed off the Ponte S. Angelo during the Jubilee year of 1450.[45] He also took a deep interest in one of the most fashionable (and luxurious) books of his time, Ptolemy's *Geographia*. In his *Descriptio urbis Romae* and *Ludi matematici* Alberti offered a method of his own devising for plotting rigorously the locations of all the buildings in a city. This he evidently worked up after examining Ptolemy's maps and working out their relation to his lists of longitudes and latitudes. But Alberti found more than technical inspiration in the text. In his praise of flies Alberti referred to the generosity with which they had contributed to the cartographers: "they say that Ptolemy the mathematician drew his picture of the world from them; for they say that the Ganges, the Danube, the

42. Alberti, *Opuscoli,* ed. Grayson, 57: "Illud preterea facile assentior ac mihi fit quidem verisimile, quod fama in primis fertur, Pythagoram non, ut ineruditi librarii exscribunt, musis, sed muscis echatomben, muscis inquam, echatomben, sacrificium fecisse . . ."

43. See C. Sperling, "Leon Battista Alberti's Inscription on the Holy Sepulchre in the Capella Rucellai, San Pancrazio, Florence," *Journal of the Warburg and Courtauld Institutes* 52 (1989): 221–28; and more generally, E.H. Gombrich, "From the Revival of Letters to the Reform of the Arts," in *The Heritage of Apelles* (Ithaca, N.Y., 1976), 93–110.

44. For a recent account see J. Hankins in *Rome Reborn* (New Haven and London, 1993).

45. Alberti, *Opera inedita et pauca separatim impressa,* ed. G. Mancini (Florence, 1890), 308, from a Marciana MS of Cicero's *De senectute, De amicitia,* and *Paradoxa* (Lat. VI, 205, ex Nani).

Nile, and the Po are splendidly depicted on the wings of flies, showing the mountains from which they flow to the sea and the peoples whom they flood." Some, Alberti continues, claim that Ptolemy's maps included the pyramids of Egypt and the temple of Eleusis, but he admits that he has not been able to find these sites, though he has identified the Caspian Sea and the Sea of Azov.[46] Comic in tone, this passage still has a solid core of fact. It locates Alberti in a recognizable humanist world of the book—one in which Ptolemy's *Geographia* commanded attention for its splendor and wealth of information. Humanists and navigators alike had a powerful appetite for what Alberti called, in a passage he later deleted from the *Musca,* maps "beautifully depicted in triangles, rectangles and hexagons, with intersecting parallels drawn perpendicular to one another."[47] This is perhaps the earliest description of Ptolemy's maps to refer explicitly to their outlines and their coordinate system as well as, more generally, to their beauty. It shows that Alberti's bibliophilic tastes were as conventional as his expression of them was unconventionally sharp and precise.

On the whole, however, Alberti showed no special desire for luxury, or even for aesthetic consistency, in his books. The Vatican and Bodleian manuscripts, which apparently represent Alberti's own efforts to codify his major works, are written in a messy combination of humanist scripts and an old-fashioned chancery hand, respectively.[48] Unlike Vespasiano, moreover, Alberti rejoiced at the invention of the printing press and at its potential to replace handmade books with mechanically reproduced ones. He tells us that he and Leonardo Dati walked one day in the Vatican gardens, where they "passionately approved of the German inventor who has recently managed, by certain impressions of letters, to make it possible for no more than three men to produce more than two hundred copies of a given original text in one hundred days."[49] Otherwise the form of writing that interested him

---

46. Alberti, *Opuscoli,* ed. Grayson, 57: ". . . quin et mundi picturam Ptholomeum mathematicum illinc aiunt desumpsisse, namque ferunt alis muscarum Gangem, Histrum, Nilum, Eridanum et eiusmodi, quibus a montibus in mare perfluat quasve inundet gentes pulchre expictas exstare. Sunt et qui affirment illic Egyptias pyramides Eleusinumque templum conspici. Tantas me res fateor non illic satis recognovisse. Caspium mare Meotimque paludem atque Elicona crispantibus sub radio undis me interdum despectasse illic non infitior."

47. This is a marginal addition, later deleted, in Riccardiana 767, fol. 46: "quas triangulis tetrangulis exangulis horsum isthorsumque mutuo in transversum ductis parallelis perquam belle pictissimas videmus" (Alberti, *Opuscoli,* ed. Grayson, 57).

48. Biblioteca Apostolica Vaticana MS Ottob. lat. 1424; Bodleian Library MS Canonic. misc. 172.

49. Alberti, *De cifra,* in *Opera inedita,* ed. Mancini, 310: "Cum essem apud Datum in hortis pontificis maximi ad Vaticanum et nostro pro more inter nos sermones haberentur de rebus quae ad studia literarum pertinerent, incidit ut vehementer probaremus Germanum inven-

most was what he took as the symbolic writing of the Egyptians, the hiero-glyphs, which he saw as ideal for public inscriptions.[50] If Alberti really designed the sails that scud across the facade of Santa Maria Novella and the top of the Rucellai loggia (symbolizing the views of his patron Giovanni Rucellai about the power of fortune) and the winged eye that decorates the Washington medallion that bears his portrait, they may also be his most visually distinctive communications to posterity. But they tell us little about his responses to ordinary books.

Alberti's beliefs and practices as a reader are not easy to identify. Some of them, like some of his tastes, were conventional. Often he read classical texts to pieces, treating them as a pork butcher treats a carcass—as some-thing to be rendered down and repackaged in a neat, confining form. Com-plex ancient philosophical positions shrank down to single sentences that Alberti could deploy more or less ad lib, without reference to original con-texts or subtle discriminations. He used individual tags over and over again and sometimes assembled groups of them with what seems a magpie's zest for brightly colored objects rather than a beaver's interest in rearing a solid structure.

In book 2 of *Della famiglia,* for example, Alberti makes his fictional per-sona Battista quote an eloquent moral precept from the greatest of Greek philosophers: "Plato, in a letter to Archytas of Tarentum, declared that men were born to serve their fellow men."[51] This sounds impressive. Alberti uses a novel source to celebrate the civic life, lived in the marketplace and the law courts, to which he devoted some of the most eloquent passages of *Della famiglia.* But the glitter dims considerably when one realizes that, as Goggi Carotti has shown, Alberti derived this tag not from a Greek text but from a standard Latin one, Cicero's *De officiis;* that he quoted it in at least four other works; and, above all, that he used it, in *Della famiglia,* in the course of an argument designed not to bring into focus but to blur all distinctions among the ancient schools and sages. Lionardo first quotes Anaxagoras: man was born to contemplate. Then come the Stoics: Chrysippus taught that all creatures on earth should serve man, but man should serve other

---

torem, qui per haec tempora pressionibus quibusdam characterum efficeret ut diebus centum plus ducenta volumina librorum opera hominum non plus trium exscripta redderet, dato ab exemplari; unica enim pressione, integram exscriptam reddit paginam maioris chartae."

50. See *De re aedificatoria* 8.4, in *L'architettura,* ed. Orlandi, 2:696–97.

51. Alberti, *Opere volgari,* ed. C. Grayson (Bari, 1960–73), 1:132, referring to Cicero *De officiis* 1.22: "Platone scrivendo ad Archita tarentino dice gli uomini essere nati per cagione degli uomini." I use the translation of R.N. Watkins, *The Family in Renaissance Florence* (Columbia, S.C., 1969), 134.

men. Plato says much the same.[52] According to Battista, moreover, he has some unexpected company: "Protagoras, another ancient philosopher, seems to some interpreters to have said essentially the same when he declared that man is the mean and measure of all things."[53] All these thinkers, Battista claims, converge on a single basic point: "man should live not in idleness and repose but in works and deeds."[54] Alberti thus yokes Stoicism, Platonism, and the positions of the Sophists. He makes a believer in Providence, an evoker of cosmic harmony, and a radical underminer of all absolute truths sing in tune. Alberti clearly knew that his juxtaposition of Plato and Protagoras would seem implausible. But he defended it merely by citing unnamed authorities, "alcuni," who had read Protagoras as agreeing with the philosophers.[55]

In reducing his texts, literally, to a least common denominator that enabled him to equate them, Alberti manipulated his classics in the most drearily normal humanist fashion: he hurled all his quotations into one basket. True, humanist standards of quotation were tolerant, even lax. But Alberti seems to go beyond the norm here—a suspicion confirmed by the fact that Leonardo Dati, the friend who read an early draft of the full text, warned Alberti that his most serious error lay in his vague system of referring to ancient authorities: "Your second mistake, which we consider more serious [than Alberti's then inadequate grasp of the Tuscan dialect], is that you have quoted the examples and opinions of other authors without mentioning their names, almost as if you had not read their works or were inventing the quotations and leaving a blank."[56] If Alberti really wrote down his supposed quotations without naming their authors, he may have regarded them as decorations rather than authorities, a literary crust no more weighty, on the whole, than those that modern editorial writers, using

---

52. Alberti, *Opere volgari*, ed. Grayson, 1:131–32. Cicero already connects Plato and the Stoics, though he does not mention Chrysippus by name, in *De officiis* 1.22. Alberti's eclectic use of sources is thus, to some degree, an extension of Cicero's already eclectic procedure. See also Alberti, *De commodis*, ed. Goggi Carotti, 10–11 n. 8.

53. Alberti, *Opere volgari*, ed. Grayson, 1:132: "Dalla quale sentenza Protagora, quell'altro antico filosofo, fu, quanto ad alcuni suol parere, non alieno, el quale affirmava l'uomo essere modo e misura di tutte le cose" (trans. Watkins, *Family*, 134). His probable source is Aristotle *Metaphysica* K 6.1062b.13 = DK 80a.19.

54. Alberti, *Opere volgari*, ed. Grayson, 1:132: "Ma sarebbe lungo seguire in questa materia tutti e' detti de' filosafi antichi, e molto più lungo sarebbe agiugnervi le molte sentenze de' nostri passati teologi. Per ora questi m'occorsono a mente, a' quali, come vedi, tutti piace nell'uomo non ozio e cessazione, ma operazione e azione" (trans. Watkins, *Family*, 134).

55. Ibid., putting the ascription in a subordinate clause: "quanto ad alcuni suol parere."

56. Quoted in Borsi, *Alberti*, 260, from L. Dati, *Epistolae*, ed. L. Mehus (Florence, 1743), 19; cf. Alberti, *Opere volgari*, ed. Grayson, 1:380.

Bartlett's *Familiar Quotations,* set atop their comments to give them an
unearned appearance of learning. He certainly did not worry overmuch
about the original contexts from which he had ripped these sentiments.

So far, it is hard to detect anything very novel or very individual in
Alberti's use of ancient texts. Even his best-known defense of the need to
read the best texts and read them well, the description of humanist education in book 1 of *Della famiglia,* says little about the actual process of reading. Alberti makes Lionardo insist that reading combines pleasure with
profit, that it teaches the classic skills of the orator, prudence and persuasion: "There is no labor so rewarding, if we should call it labor at all rather
than pleasure or recreation of mind and soul, as the reading and study of
many substantial works. You come out of it filled with significant examples,
abounding in aphorisms, rich in persuasive points, strong in arguments and
reasons. Then you can make yourself listened to. You are eagerly heard
among other citizens. They admire, praise, and love you."[57] Lionardo further specifies what boys should read: not the medieval texts, the *Cartula* and
the *Graecismus,* but the late antique Latin commentaries and textbooks by
Servius and Priscian and the original works of Sallust, Livy, and Cicero. But
when it comes to method, he contents himself with a simple metaphor: "The
intellect, they say, is like a drinking vessel [*uno vaso*]; if you first fill it with
bad stuff it always retains something of the taste. This is why one should
avoid crude and rough writers. One should follow the finest and most polished, keep them ever at hand, never tire of rereading them, recite them
aloud frequently, and commit them to memory."[58] Reading, in short, seems
simple and unidirectional. If a boy follows a sound regimen and reads the
right things in the right way, he becomes not an active digester but a passive
recipient. The texts endow the plain pottery of his mind with the fine odor
and taste of antiquity.

Alberti drew this strikingly simple image of reading, with its assumption
that doctrines shape the reader's mind as easily and rapidly as liquid impreg-

---

57. Alberti, *Opere volgari,* ed. Grayson, 1:70: "Niuna è si premiata fatica, se fatica si
chiama più tosto che spasso e ricreamento d'animo e d'intelletto, quanto quella di leggere e
rivedere buone cose assai. Tu n'esci abundante d'essempli, copioso di sentenze, ricco di per-
suasioni, forte d'argumenti e ragioni; fai ascoltarti, stai tra i cittadini udito volentieri, miranoti,
lodanoti, amanoti" (trans. Watkins, *Family,* 81–82).

58. Ibid., 1:71: "Allo intelletto si dice interviene non altrimenti che a uno vaso: se da prima
tu forse vi metti cattivo liquore, empre da poi ne serba in sé sapore. Però si vogliono fuggire
tutti questi scrittori crudi e rozzi, seguire que'dolcissimi suavissimi, averli in mano, non restare
mai di rileggerli, recitarli spesso, mandarli a memoria" (trans. Watkins, *Family,* 83).

nates porous clay, from one of Horace's *Epistulae*.[59] No process could seem simpler; and no humanist could seem less aware of the problems necessarily involved in teaching the young sons of Italian Catholic merchants the morals and metaphors of ancient Romans. Alberti modeled this passage on Plutarch's work on the education of children, translated into Latin by Guarino, which was well known to a wide audience even before Alberti wrote. In resorting to Horace, Alberti glossed Plutarch's similar statement that powerful influences shape the flexible mind and character of the young as rapidly and definitively as a hot seal shapes wax.[60] Like his sources—and rather like the modern American pedagogues who have gone to war over the school and university curriculum—Alberti seems more concerned to find powerful imagery with which to evoke the rewards and perils of reading than to investigate the actual nature of a complex intellectual activity.[61]

Alberti's interpretative practices as a writer, however, are more intricate and interesting than his precepts for the reader. They make it possible to localize in space and time his reponses to texts, or some of them at least, and to gain considerable insight into his working methods. Consider one tiny sample, drawn from a prominent place: the preface of *De re aedificatoria*. "Of course," Alberti remarks there, "Thucydides did well to praise the ancients who had the vision to adorn their cities with such a rich variety of buildings as to give the impression of having far greater power than they really had."[62] The text Alberti refers to unemotionally, as a standard work,

---

59. Horace *Ep.* 1.2.67–70:

> nunc adbibe puro
> pectore verba puer, nunc te melioribus offer.
> quo semel est imbuta recens servabit odorem
> testa diu.

Cf. 54:

> sincerum est nisi vas, quodcumque infundis, acescit.

A century later, Denys Lambin compared this passage with Plato's description of dyers in book 4 of the *Republic:* here too it is a question of the purity of the existing fabric and the immediacy and completeness of the effect of adding color (*Q. Horatii Flacci Sermonum seu satyrarum seu eclogarum libri duo: Epistolarum libri totidem* [Paris, 1557], 214–15).

60. Plutarch *De liberis educandis* 3e–f.

61. Cf. Plutarch's much more detailed and differentiated account in *Quomodo adolescens poetas audire debeat*.

62. Alberti *De re aedificatoria* prologue, in *L'architettura,* ed. Orlandi, 1:13: "Praeclare igitur apud Tuchididem prudentia veterum comprobatur, qui ita urbem omni aedificiorum genere parassent ut longe quam erant potentiores viderentur." Translation from *On the Art of Building in Ten Books,* trans. J. Rykwert, N. Leach, and R. Tavernor (Cambridge, Mass., 1988), 5.

was really a great novelty. It became widely available to the public for the first time at a precisely identifiable place and time: at Rome, in the summer of 1452, when Valla published his Latin version and deposited an official copy of it in the Vatican.[63] In fact, in *De re aedificatoria* Alberti cited a slew of Greek texts that first reached the Latin-reading public in the very years when he was at work, the middle decades of the mid–fifteenth century, most of them as the result of the direct patronage of Eugenius IV and Nicholas V. Alberti's novel Greek sources included Diodorus (translated by Poggio and P.C. Decembrio), Eusebius (translated by George of Trebizond), Plato's *Laws* (translated by George) and Theophrastus (translated by Theodore Gaza).

The histories of Herodotus interested Alberti particularly—a revealing fact, since Herodotus' reappearance is also precisely dated. Like Thucydides, Herodotus was translated into Latin by Valla. The work took place in 1453 and 1454, after Alberti had supposedly completed his own book. The chronological moral seems clear: Alberti continued to do research on classical architecture and urbanism well after 1452. More interesting is the historical one. As a member of the Curia, Alberti very likely read his translated Greek texts in the library for which most of them were originally destined: that of the Vatican itself. He must have been one of the first systematic users of the inventories that led the reader to the books themselves. And he must have spent many hours sitting at the *banchi* to which these were chained, prospecting what were already the inexhaustible lodes of a collection that looked like the concrete embodiment of the frightening imaginary library described in *De commodis litterarum atque incommodis*.

Further details, physical and textual, make the scene still more vivid. Around Alberti as he sat ran dark wood panels, adorned with splendid marquetry panels representing that favorite subject of mid-fifteenth-century artists, piles of books represented in perspective. These now decorate the small room adjacent to the Salone Sistino, above the present Vatican Library. And Alberti's pursuits must have been as bookish as his scenery. His systematic use of architectural and urban details from Thucydides, Herodotus, Diodorus, and others in *De re aedificatoria* must in fact have required an immense preliminary effort of systematic reading, carried out with pen in hand. For Alberti was turning the texts into something rich and strange. Valla, as we saw, regarded Greek historical works above all as anthologies of orations finely adjusted to their original contexts. But in his polemical works he also suggested, to the more intelligent among his read-

---

63. Vat. lat. 1801, for which see chapter 1.

ers, that the historians offered instruction about the development of Greek society and culture. Alberti took the hint. He used the Greeks not as authoritative models but as historical sources—as repositories of data, much of which their authors recorded only in passing, about the building practices of the ancients. A detailed recent study has followed Alberti's admirer and colleague Flavio Biondo as he did the research for and composed his *Italia illustrata*. The process began with systematic, pointed reading; in Biondo's case, elaborate marginalia trace some of the stages of his progress through the ancient and medieval chronicles in the Vatican. Only after Biondo had shredded the originals in this meticulous way could he recycle the results as a coherent work of his own. Both Alberti and Biondo thus turned the apparent dross of insignificant historical detail into the raw materials of their brilliantly innovative recreations of the built and settled world of Roman—or, more precisely, Italian—antiquity.[64]

Alberti's systematic reduction of classical texts into historical sources matters a great deal. It provides a firm—and relatively late—date for the composition of *De re aedificatoria,* which can hardly have reached its current state of near completion until sometime after 1450–52, the date traditionally assigned for its entry into the public domain.[65] It establishes the considerable extent of his investment in the normal procedures of textual scholarship—which clearly occupied him almost as seriously as the object-oriented archaeology that he more glamorously practiced. And it explains why Poliziano, the most erudite Italian Hellenist of the fifteenth century,

64. See the detailed study by O. Clavuot, *Biondos Italia Illustrata: Summa oder Neuschöpfung?* (Tübingen, 1990). Cf. also the important work of R. Cappelletto, in *Ricuperi Ammianei da Biondo Flavio* (Rome, 1983) and "Nuovi ritrovamenti: Passi nuovi di Ammiano Marcellino in Biondo Flavio," *Atene e Roma,* n.s., 30 (1985): 66–71: Cappelletto has used Biondo's careful work as a compiler to restore otherwise lost fragments of Ammianus Marcellinus. On Biondo's method see also R. Weiss, *The Renaissance Discovery of Classical Antiquity,* new ed. (Oxford, 1988); D.M. Robathan, "Flavio Biondo's *Roma instaurata,*" *Medievalia et humanistica,* n.s., 1 (1970): 203–16; A. Mazzocco, "Some Philological Aspects of Flavio Biondo's *Roma Triumphans,*" *Humanistica Lovaniensia* 28 (1979): 1–26; and Mazzocco, "Flavio Biondo and the Antiquarian Tradition," in *Acta Conventus Neolatini Bononiensis,* ed. R.J. Schoeck (Binghamton, 1985), 124–36.

65. Here I disagree, hesitantly, with the widely accepted arguments of C. Grayson, "The Composition of L.B. Alberti's *Decem libri de re aedificatoria,*" *Münchener Jarbuch der bildenden Kunst,* ser. 3, 11 (1960): 152–61. A nineteenth-century scholar who noticed that Alberti used Gaza's Theophrastus tried to draw from that fact a *terminus post quem* for *De re aedificatoria* (O. Hoffmann, *Studien zu Albertis zehn Büchern "De re aedificatoria"* [Frankenberg i.S., 1883]); Garin remarked on Alberti's heavy, early use of Plato's *Leges* (*Rinascite e rivoluzioni* [Bari, 1975], 184). But no one, not even Grayson, seems to have seen that Alberti's massive use of Greek materials, which he treats as a matter of course, presupposes the library situation of the mid-1450s—and makes it most unlikely that he had finished the substance of the work by 1452, when he supposedly showed it to Nicholas.

praised Alberti not only for his technical expertise but also for his literary erudition.[66]

Alberti, however, often worked with his texts in a highly idiosyncratic way—one that hardly resembles Biondo's meticulous efforts to collate texts and explain or eliminate difficulties. For example, the passage in Thucydides that Alberti quoted in his prologue does not say quite what he suggested. Thucydides points out that it is hard to judge a city's power from its physical remains. If Sparta were wiped out, no one could guess the power it had once had. But if Athens were wiped out, one would think it twice as powerful as it had been. Therefore, "we must not be entirely credulous or regard the appearance of cities rather than their strength."[67] Alberti has subverted the source that inspired his remark. Where Thucydides warned that architectural splendors could obscure the truth, Alberti made him praise their ability to project a deceptive image.

This case is not isolated. For as Eugenio Garin pointed out long ago in an article as short as it was brilliant, Alberti very often cited or responded to his texts in ways that fundamentally altered the apparent meaning of the ancient original.[68] In *De natura deorum* Cicero praised man for his ability to exploit the earth, to find the hidden veins of gold and iron and make use of them.[69] In *Theogenius* Alberti repeats the description but reverses the evaluation: nature, he says, has filled her depths and desert places with hidden riches, and man robs her, dragging trees from their natural place in the mountains to make them float on the ocean as parts of ships, and pulling marble from its natural place underground to adorn buildings. Cicero praised the human mind, unique in nature, which could penetrate the heavens: "Soli enim ex animantibus nos astrorum ortus, obitus cursusque cognovimus" (We alone, of all the animals, have come to know the risings of the stars, their settings and their paths). Alberti again reversed Cicero's verdict: "Gli altri animali contenti di quello che li si condice: l'uomo solo sempre investigando cose nuove sé stesso infesta" (The other animals are content with what is useful for them: man alone continually investigates new things, and harms himself by doing so).[70] Cicero saw the world and its ani-

---

66. Poliziano, dedicatory letter to *De re aedificatoria*, in *L'architettura*, ed. Orlandi, 1:3: "Nullae quippe hunc hominem latuerunt quamlibet remotae litterae, quamlibet reconditae disciplinae."

67. Thucydides 1.10.2–3.

68. E. Garin, "Fonti albertiane," *Rivista critica di storia della filosofia* 29 (1974): 90–91; developed in his fundamental "Studi su L.B. Alberti," *Rinascite e rivoluzioni*, 133–96.

69. Cicero *De natura deorum* 2.60–61, 150–54.

70. Ibid., 2.153; Alberti, *Theogenius*, quoted by Garin, "Studi su Alberti," 149.

mals as made for man. Alberti, in *Momus,* insisted that the human race had
no reason to assume that the good things of the world had been created only
for its use.[71] Garin rightly uses these passages in his mordant, memorable
portrait of an Alberti as horrified by man's attacks on nature as he was
delighted by nature's beauties—and as he was impressed, in the different
context of *De re aedificatoria,* by man's abilities at "cutting through rock
. . . tunneling through mountains . . . filling in valleys, . . . restraining the
waters of the sea and lakes and . . . draining marshes, . . . altering the course
and dredging the mouths of rivers."[72] His work has done much to inspire
recent revisions of the traditional portrait of Alberti.[73]

For our purposes, however, these juxtapositions serve a different end.
They suggest the outlines, still faint, of a deliberate strategy in reading: an
aggressive one, in which the reader seeks not so much authorities for his
positions as objects for his criticism. The act of reading, as embodied in literary texts like Alberti's, amounts to a critical dialogue with the ancient
world—one in which the ancients haunt the modern texts, like vampires,
and the modern author seeks to prove his originality both by how efficiently
he summons them and by how firmly he then drives a stake through their
hearts. Often the author carries off a tour de force by using material from
one ancient to attack or revise another. Book 6 of *De re aedificatoria,* to
take the most obvious example, begins with a powerful expression of dis-
satisfaction with the large-scale ancient work on the same subject by Vitruvius. Alberti says that his ancient predecessor's text was so corrupt, so illiterate, and so inaccessible "that as far as we are concerned he might just as
well not have written at all, rather than write something that we cannot
understand."[74] The body of the book carries on, as Krautheimer and others
have shown, a sharp, if implicit, debate.[75] When Alberti insists in book 6
and elsewhere that an architect need not be a universal savant, he attacks

---

71. Cicero, *De natura deorum* 2.158; cf. Garin, "Studi su Alberti," 149.

72. Alberti *De re aedificatoria* prologue, in *L'architettura* ed. Orlandi, 1:9 (trans. Rykwert
et al., *Art of Building,* 3). Cf. however his cautions at *De re aedificatoria* 2.2.

73. See M. Tafuri, " 'Cives esse non licere.' The Rome of Nicholas V and Leon Battista
Alberti: Elements Toward a Historical Revision," *Harvard Architectural Review* 6 (1987):
60–75; and Jarzombek, *Alberti.*

74. Alberti *De re aedificatoria* 6.1, in *L'architettura,* ed. Orlandi, 2:441 (trans. Rykwert et
al., *Art of Building,* 154).

75. R. Krautheimer, "Alberti and Vitruvius," in *Studies in Early Christian, Mediaeval, and
Renaissance Art* (New York, 1969), 323–32. See also C.W. Westfall, "Society, Beauty, and the
Humanist Architect in Alberti's *De re aedificatoria,*" *Studies in the Renaissance* 16 (1969):
61–79; and H. Mehlmann, *Ästhetische Theorie der Renaissance: L.B. Alberti* (Bonn, 1981),
88–95.

Vitruvius' encyclopedic program.[76] When he makes the history of human building begin with the dividing of living spaces by function and the raising of a roof, he reverses the story told by Vitruvius, which starts with the discovery of fire.[77] The modern writer makes architecture the crown of human artifice; the ancient one made it part of nature. Even when Alberti insists, apparently innocently, in book 6 and elsewhere, on the systematic and orderly nature of his writing, he implicitly rebukes his predecessor's disorderly profusion of facts and topics.[78] Concepts drawn from Cicero and Quintilian came into play in a characteristically original fashion; they enabled Alberti radically to reshape the Vitruvian material to which he gave his contemporaries access. For a century and more, many readers' and commentators' responses to Vitruvius showed that they still read him through the veil Alberti wove.[79]

Della famiglia offers similar reversals of ancient precedent. The whole of book 4, for example, treats friendship, a subject dear both to Cicero and to the Roman poets who wrote so much about their relations with one another and with prominent patrons. Alberti's characters analyze human relationships as a game of manipulation, which one plays to connect and endear oneself to the powerful. One of them, Adovardo, explicitly insists that the ancient philosophers have nothing useful to say about the subject. He is clearly attacking Cicero, whose *De amicitia,* the standard Roman work on

---

76. Alberti *De re aedificatoria* 9.10.

77. Ibid., 1.2; cf. Vitruvius 2.1.1.

78. Alberti *De re aedificatoria* 6.1. See also A. Tönnesmann, *Pienza* (Munich, 1990), 93–95.

79. O. Onians, "Alberti and *Philarete:* A Study in Their Sources," *Journal of the Warburg and Courtauld Institutes* 34 (1971): 96–114; P.N. Pagliara, "Vitruvio da testo a canone," *Memoria dell'antico nell'arte italiana,* vol. 3, *Dalla tradizione all'archeologia,* ed. S. Settis (Turin, 1986), 16–19. Vitruvius was not the only technical work to be studied, in the Renaissance, chiefly through a modern reworking that combined summaries of the original with criticism and extensive discussion of other—sometimes more recent—texts. The German astronomer Johannes Regiomontanus, an acquaintance of Alberti's, produced a particularly influential specimen of this genus. The *Epitome* of Ptolemy's *Almagest* that he composed, working from a partial draft by his teacher Georg Peurbach, offered essential help in mastering Ptolemaic astronomy, not only to his own well-informed patron Cardinal Bessarion, but also to all Renaissance astronomers, down to Copernicus and beyond. On the context and development of the *Epitome* see A. Rigo, "Bessarione, Giovanni Regiomontano e i loro studi su Tolomeo a Venezia e Roma (1462–1464)," *Studi Veneziani,* n.s., 21 (1991): 49–110. Unrivaled as an analysis of the work's technical content and importance is N. Swerdlow, "The Derivation and First Draft of Copernicus's Planetary Theory: A Translation of the *Commentariolus* with Commentary," *Proceedings of the American Philosophical Society* 117 (1973): 423–512 (not cited by Rigo). See also N. Swerdlow and O. Neugebauer, *Mathematical Astronomy in Copernicus's De Revolutionibus* (New York, Berlin, Heidelberg, and Tokyo, 1984), esp. 48–54.

the subject, described friendship as an ideal communion of souls rather than a pragmatic series of efforts at networking. Alberti's work again implicitly overturned its classical predecessor—even though he cited plenty of classical texts and tags in doing so.[80]

He does the same even more strikingly in another famous passage—the speech in which Uncle Giannozzo, in book 3, tells his young relatives that time is at once immensely valuable and entirely within the control of the individual. All one need do, he explains, is to plan each day systematically at dawn, review its events at nightfall, and ensure that one has seen to every pressing task. Doing so will give one power over time: "In the morning I plan my whole day, during the day I follow my plan, and in the evening, before I retire, I think over again what I have done during the day. Then, if I was careless in performing some task, and can repair the damage immediately, I do so; for I would sooner lose sleep than lose time, that is, than let the right moment for doing something slip by."[81] This prescription for a secularized examination of conscience has been cited more often, perhaps, than any other passage in Alberti's work. Hans Baron recognized, with characteristic insight, that Alberti here reworked Seneca. But he did not quite capture the nature of Alberti's response to the original.[82] In *De ira* Seneca describes how Sextius "when the day was over and he had retired to his nightly rest . . . would put these questions to his soul: 'What bad habit have you cured to-day? What fault have you resisted? In what respect are you better?' Anger will cease and become more controllable if it finds that it must appear before a judge every day. . . . I avail myself of this privilege, and every day I plead my cause before the bar of self. When the light has been removed from sight, and my wife, long aware of my habit, has become silent, I scan the whole of my day and retrace all my deeds and words. I conceal nothing from myself, I omit nothing."[83] The ancient moralist argued

---

80. For a somewhat different view see D. Marsh's helpful treatment in *The Quattrocento Dialogue* (Cambridge, Mass., and London, 1980), chap. 5.

81. Alberti, *Opere volgari*, ed. Grayson, 1:176–77, at 177: "La mattina ordino me a tutto il dì, il giorno seguo quanto mi si richiede, e poi la sera inanzi che io mi riposi ricolgo in me quanto feci il dì. Ivi, se fui in cosa alcuna negligente, alla quale testé possa rimediarvi, subito vi supplisco: e prima voglio perdere il sonno che il tempo, cioè la stagione delle faccende" (trans. Watkins, *Family*, 172).

82. Baron, *Florentine Civic Humanism*, 1: chap. 10. Cf. R. Glasser, *Studien zur Geschichte des französischen Zeitbegriffs* (Munich, 1936), 108.

83. Seneca *De ira* (trans. J.W. Basore) 3.36.1–3. For the use of time in classical moral philosophy see above all P. Hadot, *Philosophie als Lebensform*, trans. I. Hadot and C. Marsch (Berlin, 1991), chap. 5, though the point of view I offer here differs somewhat from Hadot's in detail.

that time was partly in man's power—but only past time, and that only because it could be subjected to a consistent and unhurried moral scrutiny.[84] The modern writer argues that rational calculation can control the future. The ancient insisted that worldly and practical desires were the thieves of time.[85] The modern treats the successful use of time for practical ends as the chief goal of self-discipline. Nowhere did Alberti show more sharply that the disciplines of classical moral philosophy could not shape the daily life of a modern mercantile society than in Giannozzo's purportedly uncultured discourse—where any humanist reader would recognize the pervasive but negative classical influence.

None of Alberti's works, however, reveals his tactics more crisply than *De pictura*. Though that work is not directed against a single ancient text, it challenges the major ancient writer in the same field. Alberti boasts that "it is of little concern to us to discover the first painters or the inventors of the art, since we are not writing a history of painting like Pliny but treating of the art in an entirely new way. On this subject there exist today none of the writings of the ancients, as far as I have seen."[86] So much for the model ancient account of the development of painting that inspired Ghiberti and so many other artists to envision their pursuit as one with a history—not a craft whose rules were stable and permanent, but a liberal art continually improved by rational human action.[87] Alberti deftly upends or reorients numerous other ancient authorities in passing. At the very end, for example, he uses Cicero's explanation for the imperfect quality of earlier oratory—"Nothing can be simultaneously invented and brought to perfection"—to excuse the faults of his own current work on painting.[88]

Two specimens of Alberti's tactics call for more extended comment. Both form central parts of his effort to define and analyze painting. Both have received extensive discussion in the past. And both become far easier to understand when seen in the light of Alberti's normal relation to the books he knew best. Alberti himself defines the first specimen as fanciful: "I used to tell my friends that the inventor of painting, according to the poets, was

---

84. Seneca *De brevitate vitae* 10.2–6.

85. Ibid. 11.1–13.7.

86. Alberti *De pictura* 2.26, in *Opere volgari*, ed. Grayson, 3:47: "Sed non multum interest aut primos pictores aut picturae inventores tenuisse, quando quidem non historiam picturae ut Plinius sed artem novissime recenseamus, de qua hac aetate nulla scriptorum veterum monumenta quae ipse viderim extant."

87. E.H. Gombrich, *Norm and Form* (London, 1966).

88. Alberti *De pictura* 3.63, in *Opere volgari*, ed. Grayson, 3:107: "Simul enim ortum atque perfectum nihil esse aiunt." He refers to Cicero *Brutus* 18.71: "Nihil est enim simul et inventum et perfectum."

Narcissus, who was turned into a flower; for, as painting is the flower of all the arts, so the tale of Narcissus fits our purpose perfectly. What is painting but the act of embracing by means of art the surface of the pool?"[89] This passage has naturally stirred up a good deal of discussion and speculation. Is it a dark joke about the moral dangers involved in any project of representing the world? Or a proud assertion of the painter's power to make the evanescent permanent? Historians of art have more than once juxtaposed Alberti's joke with Plotinus' version of the story of Narcissus. As they point out, the neoplatonist took the myth as an allegorical account of the man who clings to beautiful bodies and sinks with them into a dark abyss where there is no intellect. But they have thus located Alberti in the wrong library, that of the Medici, and several decades too late, after Ficino had rendered the bitterly difficult text of the *Enneads* into Latin. The Alberti of the 1430s probably had no access to the original, direct or indirect. He would have found Plotinus' Greek excruciatingly hard, and even if he had read a Latin version like the partial one in the *Theologia Aristotelis,* he would not necessarily have connected it with the story of Narcissus (whose case Plotinus described without ever naming the protagonist).[90]

This result is unsurprising and should cause no discouragement. The analyses we have undertaken so far suggest that chasing recondite sources and obscure lemmas through modern encyclopedias and collections of sources is not the most natural way to learn what Alberti had in mind, here or elsewhere. Allusion, after all, loses impact if the author cannot assume that readers will know the text to which he or she refers. Alberti's allusions, as we have studied them, usually follow this rule. They refer either to standard components of the Latin canon or to new texts widely discussed and disseminated—such as the Ciceronian *Brutus* and the humanist translations from Greek that Alberti fielded in so rapid and agile a way. The first ports of call for would-be decoders lie within the range of texts that Alberti and his readers would have shared. In setting the course for any given project, moreover, the scholar should bear in mind that the advanced humanists' range of references changed rapidly from year to year and was certainly much smaller in the 1430s than in the 1450s. Normally—especially in Alberti's earlier works—a passage as readily identified as the ones we have

---

89. Alberti *De pictura* 2.26, in *Opere volgari,* ed. Grayson, 3:47: "Quae cum ita sint, consuevi inter familiares dicere picturae inventorem fuisse, poetarum sententia, Narcissum illum qui sit in florem versus, nam cum sit omnium artium flos pictura, tum de Narcisso omnis fabula pulchre ad rem ipsam perapta erit. Quid est enim aliud pingere quam arte superficiem illam fontis amplecti?"

90. This point was already made by E. Panofsky, *Idea: A Concept in Art Theory,* trans. J.J.S. Peake (Columbia, S.C., 1968), 209 n.

examined will turn out to refer to a text that he had read in a characteristically inventive way.

In fact Narcissus plays a starring role in a central curriculum text. Alberti gives a useful hint: he says that he tells his tale "according to the poets" [*poetarum sententia*]. Ovid, in the *Metamorphoses*, had told the story of Narcissus as a lesson about the danger of representation and the vanity of self-love. The pool that reflects Narcissus' image is "deceptive"; Narcissus' efforts to embrace the boy he sees in it naturally fail. The tears he sheds disturb and dim the image of himself that he mistakes for another person. He dies in despair.[91]

Alberti, in referring to Narcissus, ventures a simple and characteristic paradox: the painter can use *ars,* technical skill, to do what Narcissus had failed to do with love. Narcissus had confused a two-dimensional reflection with three-dimensional reality; the modern painter—like those ancients whose painting contests Pliny vividly described—could reproduce the outlines of a three-dimensional scene on a two-dimensional wall or panel. The painter could thus produce a permanently deceptive surface. But the painter achieved this effect by cold, hard calculation rather than the chance interaction of air, water, and light. Alberti notes, for example, that the painter finds it very hard "to paint something which does not continually present the same aspect." However, by setting a veil or grid, stretched on a frame, between himself and his subject, the painter can reduce the scene before him to stable outlines, "because it always presents the same surfaces unchanged."[92] Only by emulating the obsessiveness with which Narcissus loved his reflection, in short, will painters master the whole range of techniques and texts that, Alberti argued in *De pictura,* enabled them to claim to practice a liberal art rather than a craft. The myth, transformed by Alberti's conceit, encapsulated his artistic program.

Another story, that of Zeuxis and the girls of Croton, played an even more prominent role in Alberti's aesthetics. Alberti tells it thus:

The idea of beauty, which the most expert have difficulty in discerning, eludes the ignorant. Zeuxis, the most eminent, learned and skilled

---

91. Ovid *Metamorphoses* 3.427–29:

inrita fallaci quotiens dedit oscula fonti!
in medias quotiens, visum captantia collum
bracchia mersit aquas, nec se deprendit in illis!

92. Alberti *De pictura* 2.31, in *Opere volgari*, ed. Grayson, 3:55: "Et nosti quam sit impossibile aliquid pingendo recte imitari quod non perpetuo eandem pingenti faciem servet"; (earlier on same page) "Habet enim haec veli intercisio profecto commoda in se non pauca, primo quod easdem semper immotas superficies referat . . ."

painter of all, when about to paint a panel to be publicly dedicated in the temple of Lucina at Croton, did not set about his work trusting rashly in his own talent as all painters do now; but, because he believed that all the things he desired to achieve beauty not only could not be found by his own intuition, but were not to be discovered even in nature in one body alone, he chose from all the youth of the city five outstandingly beautiful virgins, so that he might represent in his painting whatever feature of feminine beauty was most praiseworthy in each of them. He acted wisely, for to painters with no model before them to follow, who strive by the light of their own talent alone to capture the qualities of beauty, it easily happens that they do not by their efforts achieve the beauty they seek or ought to create; they simply fall into bad habits of painting, which they have great difficulty in relinquishing even if they wish.[93]

Alberti's version of the story became a classic commonplace of artistic literature and studio chatter, passed on for centuries and steadily losing content and definition—rather like a bar of soap used by a whole football team as they take a shower. Writers on beauty, like Firenzuola, cited it to justify their endless catalogs of the ideal standard for each bit of the female anatomy, those verbal vivisections that provided a prose counterpart to the descriptions of lovers in Petrarchan poetry. Writers on art cited it to widely different effect: sometimes in the sense in which Alberti took it here, as proof of the vital importance of direct study of nature; sometimes in the sense in which Alberti took it in *De statua*, as proof that the artist's idea of beauty is better than any individual human.[94]

Close examination of the passage and its sources reveals that Alberti has once again performed a meticulous job of hermeneutical surgery. He drew the story from two absolutely standard works: Cicero's *De inventione* and

---

93. Alberti *De pictura* 3.56, in *Opere volgari*, ed. Grayson, 3:97–99: "Fugit enim imperitos ea pulchritudinis idea quam peritissimi vix discernunt. Zeuxis, praestantissimus et omnium doctissimus et peritissimus pictor, facturus tabulam quam in templo Lucinae apud Crotoniates publice dicaret, non suo confisus ingenio temere, ut fere omnes hac aetate pictores, ad pingendum accessit, sed quod putabat omnia quae ad venustatem quaereret, ea non modo proprio ingenio non posse, sed ne a natura quidem petita uno posse in corpore reperiri, idcirco ex omni eius urbis iuventute delegit virgines quinque forma praestantiores, ut quod in quaque esset formae muliebris laudatissimum, id in pictura referret. Prudenter is quidem, nam pictoribus nullo proposito exemplari quod imitentur, ubi ingenio tantum pulchritudinis laudes captare enituntur, facile evenit ut eo labore non quam debent aut quaerunt pulchritudinem assequantur, sed plane in malos, quos vel volentes vix possunt dimittere, pingendi usus dilabantur."

94. See the classic study of Panofsky, *Idea*.

Pliny's *Naturalis Historia*.[95] And he made clear, to the sharp-eyed humanist reader, that he used both. Alberti locates the story in Croton, as Cicero did (Pliny put it in Agrigento); but he describes the temple for which Zeuxis worked as that of Lucina, as he thought Pliny did (Pliny really placed it in the temple of Hera Lacinia). The passage thus amounts to an elegant pastiche, as Nicoletta Maraschio showed in a very attentive examination of it twenty years ago.[96] As Maraschio also pointed out, the procedure clearly fits the texts Alberti exploited. Cicero told the story of Zeuxis as justification for his own eclectic use of several sources in *De inventione;* just as Zeuxis had used several models' bodies, Cicero would use several model texts. Pliny, of course, represented his own work as a virtual library of extracts from older sources. Alberti, defending his own eclectic use of sources, deftly wove together two ancient eclectics' vivid defenses of their similar practices.

Alberti, however, not only combines the two Latin models; he systematically abridges and alters them. Cicero's story is far longer and quirkier than Pliny's or Alberti's. Zeuxis, he says, asked the Crotoniates to show him their five most beautiful maidens. They replied by taking him directly to the *palaestra,* the wrestlers' gymnasium, and showing him many handsome boys (as Cicero remarks, in those days the Crotoniates were great athletes). They then told him the good news: the boys he saw wrestling had equally beautiful sisters. Unfortunately, bad news followed immediately: Zeuxis had to infer their *dignitas* from that of the boys. Undaunted, Zeuxis begged the Crotoniates to let him see the five most beautiful virgins for just so long as he needed to transform the truth about them into a *mutum . . . simulacrum*. At last they agreed, and by a public decree they gave him the power to choose his models. The point of the story is evidently double. It affords an argument for eclecticism in writing. But it is also a teacher's joke, inserted by Cicero to liven up the beginning of a textbook. It seems to imply a Roman's negative look at Greek love of naked athletic practice (and of boys). It also shows the Roman's clear, uneasy awareness that to paint a nude, the painter needed a naked model—and that respectable women and their parents would find this requirement of his art, with its suggestions of erotic involvement and social inversion, unacceptable.[97] Cicero's story, in

95. Cicero *De inventione* 2.1; Pliny *Naturalis Historia* 35.64.

96. N. Maraschio, "Aspetti del bilinguismo albertiano nel '*De pictura*,'" *Rinascimento*, ser. 2, 12 (1972): 193–228.

97. Pliny's shorter text was much blunter on the point at issue. Zeuxis, he said, "inspected the Agrigentine virgins, naked, and chose five" [ut . . . inspexerit virgines eorum nudas et quinque elegerit] (*NH* 35.64).

other words, had an erotic edge as well as a literary moral. Victorinus, the late antique commentator on Cicero, saw this point clearly. A typical schoolmaster, he tried to distract his students, not to inform them, by describing Zeuxis—against the clear intent of Cicero's text—as a specialist in painting the faces, the *vultus,* of women.[98]

Alberti's version scrupulously avoids the sexy suggestiveness of the original. The gymnasium and the Crotoniate boys have disappeared. Paradoxically, he has changed places with his source. Cicero, who used the painter and his models only as an analogy for the rhetorician and his books, described the episode in sharply vivid physical terms. Alberti, who actually meant to tell painters how to paint and patrons what to buy, insisted on the ethereal and intellectual nature of the same story. The decision was clearly deliberate. In *De statua,* after all, Alberti used the same story to very different effect, citing it to justify his own measurement of many beautiful bodies in the hope of determining the best actual proportions.[99] Alberti not only borrowed Cicero's and Pliny's material, in short, he rewrote it to fit an ethical and aesthetic program that involved the exaltation of the visual arts and the simultaneous suppression of their erotic qualities. Because he did so using sources that most of his readers knew, he could feel confident that they would understand and emulate his practices, making a similarly modern and eclectic use of classical materials.[100]

Alberti enjoyed one special advantage in this case. He and his readers intimately knew the Petrarchan tradition of praising one's beloved, in verse, by itemizing the parts of her body and comparing them, in turn, to the most splendid features of the natural world: all eyes became suns, all breasts

---

98. Victorinus on *De inventione* 2.1: "Omnis praefatio quasi similitudo est ad id, quod dicturi sumus. . . . Si partibus conductis tota conveniunt, pulchra semper et praecipua dicetur esse praefatio. . . . Cum multa dicendi genera sint, ut inter picturas multas Helena, ita inter ceteras dictiones eminet semper oratoria, et ut Zeuxis in femineis pingendis vultibus summus, ita in orationibus Tullius." Amusingly similar tactics can be found in the humanist commentary on *De inventione* by Nascimbene de' Nascimbeni (Venice, 1563), based on a course in rhetoric given at Ragusa. Nascimbene limpidly explains Cicero's purpose in citing the story (69 recto) and tells the amusing story of how Zeuxis' habit of charging admission to see his statue resulted in its being called *Helena meretrix* (69 verso). But when it comes to the problematic passages, he skips off into the empyrean. When the Crotoniates tell Zeuxis that he can judge the *dignitas* of the girls from that of their brothers, for example, Nascimbene writes: "Hic observandum est, dignitatem de mulieribus quoque dici. Nam Cic. in primo de off. duo pulchritudinis genera facit, quorum alterum dignitatis, alterum venustatis nomine appellat. Dignitas virilis est pulchritudo: venustas vero muliebris (69 verso)." The grammatical observation neatly distracts the audience from the problematic subject matter.

99. Alberti *De statua* 12, in *On Painting and On Sculpture,* ed. Grayson, 132–35.

100. For an excellent account of another case of what appears to be deliberate misreading see Grayson's *On Painting and On Sculpture,* 20–21, 24.

globes, in this updated, more systematic form of Ovidian taxonomy. For a long time, Petrarchan poets insisted, with evident sincerity, that these detailed descriptions had no erotic content—and therefore implied no derogation to the honor of the woman described. The Petrarchan tradition acted as a sort of screen—rather like Alberti's perspective veil—that enabled him to make productive, modern use of classical materials that would have caused problems if looked at directly.[101] It is no wonder that Alberti's reuse of Cicero proved acceptable to so many readers who shared his own direct knowledge of the text: once again he had brilliantly fused the classical with the modern, the Greek and Latin with the Tuscan.

It may seem curious that Alberti, who read the classics with such dedication, applied them with such arbitrariness. However, his rewritings of his sources fell within the norms of a certain kind of humanist practice. As a boy he had studied with Barzizza, who taught his pupils to show their respect for and independence from classical sources at the same time. "Imitation," he explained, "is understood or carried out in four ways, by addition, subtraction, transferral, and transformation"—never by straight copying.[102] Quoting a (corrupt) text of Seneca's letter 84.8, he warned that "Seneca tells Lucilius that imitation must not be an echo [a misreading for *ex quo*]; that is, when we want to imitate, we must not simply take the text as it appears in the book we want to imitate but must change the words and sentences so that they do not appear to be the same words that are in the book."[103] Simple verbal changes could make a single sentence new: "If Cicero says, 'Scite hoc inquit Brutus,' I will add, 'Scite enim ac eleganter hoc inquit ille vir noster Brutus.' See how it seems to have a different form."[104] A still more effective method was simply to invert the classical text one used: "if Cicero, whom we wish to imitate, praised someone to

---

101. For the conventions of description in Petrarchism see the classic works of H. Pyritz, *Paul Flemings Liebeslyrik* (Göttingen, 1963); and L. Forster, *The Icy Fire* (Cambridge, 1969). My argument here is indebted to C. Ginzburg, *The Cheese and the Worms*, trans. J. Tedeschi and A. Tedeschi (Baltimore and London, 1980), 21–51.

102. G.W. Pigman, "Barzizza's Treatise on Imitation," *Bibliothèque d'Humanisme et Renaissance* 44 (1982): 341–52, at 349: "Imitatio sumitur vel fit quattuor modis, videlicet, addendo, subtrahendo, transferendo, et immutando."

103. Ibid., 349–50: "Nota de imitatione per alium modum et maxime secundum Senecam. Dicit Seneca ad Lucilium quod imitatio non debet esse echo, id est, quando volumus imitari, non debemus accipere recte litteram sicut stat in illo libro in quo volumus imitari, sed debemus mutare verba et sententias ita quod non videantur esse illa eadem verba quae sunt in ipso libro."

104. Ibid., 351: "Si ponatur quod Cicero dixerit, 'Scite hoc inquit Brutus,' addam et dicam, 'Scite enim ac eleganter hoc inquit ille vir noster Brutus.' Ecce quomodo videtur habere diversam formam a prima."

the skies, we could blast him to the depths."[105] Naturally, the results of this systematic reshuffling sometimes showed little of the classic elegance they supposedly exemplified.

Mature humanists practiced richer forms of the aggressive imitation or emulation they had learned as schoolboys, as G.M. Pigman and Thomas Greene have shown.[106] And often their reuses of classical texts reveal how perceptively they read the works that they transformed. Leonardo Bruni, for example, found under Livy's triumphant telling of the early history of Rome a counterhistory, that of the defeat of the Etruscans, and wove the relevant passages into the first, politically charged book of his *Historiae Florentini populi.* This glorified not early Rome but something even earlier: the independent Italian cities that Rome had crushed.[107] Maffeo Vegio, the Roman cleric who wrote a thirteenth book for the *Aeneid,* often appears in accounts of Renaissance classicism as a truly transcendent nitwit. He certainly helped to spoil the *Aeneid* for generations of schoolboys, by grafting onto the real, grim text, with its inexorably harsh ending and defiant lack of closure, the pastel-colored tale of how Aeneas buried Turnus, married Lavinia, ruled his peoples, and finally ascended to heaven, to become a star. Yet Vegio knew what he was doing. He saw, under the august surface of Virgil's text, the same tensions that have bothered and stimulated readers in recent times: the harm done by Aeneas in his travels, the innocents who suffered, the strange ending, so much less humane than that of the *Iliad,* in which Aeneas savagely kills Turnus, and the latter's death scream is the last sound heard. Vegio rewrote the poem, in short, because he understood it so well: after the death scream came a series of elegantly crafted model speeches. Like Valla, in short, Vegio made a difficult and alien text into a worked example of the best rhetorical practices. His book 13 fully deserved to become part of Renaissance manuscripts and editions of the *Aeneid,* and it did so, almost as regularly as the other 12.[108]

To establish that Alberti's procedures fell within tolerances—as the roofer says when your new chimney leaks—is not to explain why he chose them or how he used them in individual cases. And here any argument must

---

105. Ibid., 350: ". . . ut si Cicero quem imitari vellemus eximie laudaret aliquem, possemus illum maxime vituperare."

106. See G.W. Pigman, "Versions of Imitation in the Renaissance," *Renaissance Quarterly* 33 (1980): 1–32; and T.M. Greene, *The Light in Troy* (New Haven and London, 1982).

107. H. Baron, *The Crisis of the Early Italian Renaissance,* 2d ed. (Princeton, 1966), 424–25.

108. For the text see B. Schneider, *Das Aeneissupplement des Maffeo Vegio* (Weinheim, 1985), on which see C. Kallendorf's review in *Renaissance Quarterly* 49 (1987): 95–96. For Vegio's rhetorical interpretation of Virgil see Kallendorf, *In Praise of Aeneas* (Hanover and London, 1989), chap. 5.

remain very tentative—since, as Roberto Cardini points out in his challenging study of Alberti's *Intercenales,* close study of Alberti as an active reader remains, for the most part, to be carried out.[109] Yet two points can be made. The first is that Alberti deliberately chose his tactics. In fact, he described them explicitly. Consider another text—the *Disputationes Camaldulenses* of the influential Florentine teacher Cristoforo Landino, perhaps the most delightful Virgilian allegory before Freud's *Psychopathology of Everyday Life.* Alberti appears as the main speaker. Though some of the doctrines he presents derive from Ficino, much of the terminology he wields and some of the exegesis he offers are undoubtedly his own. For example, the Alberti of the *Disputationes* makes a careful, elaborate distinction between what he presents as Virgil's normally consistent Platonism, which separated the created world from the divine, and the Stoic doctrine of the famous "spiritus intus alit" passage in *Aeneid* 6, which treats the whole world as permeated by the divine mind.[110] Alberti himself had already made the same careful distinction between Platonic and Stoic doctrines in the *Momus,* where his protagonist encounters philosophers engaging in violent argument (one eventually bites Momus' beard off) on exactly the same range of doctrines.[111] Both Landino and Alberti drew their philosophical material from the same source: Cicero's *De natura deorum.* Like Cicero, the Alberti of the

---

109. R. Cardini, *Mosaici: Il 'nemico' dell'Alberti* (Rome, 1990).

110. C. Landino, *Disputationes Camaldulenses*, ed. P. Lohe (Florence, 1980), 257–58: "Id igitur, quod Maro ait . . . huiuscemodi est, ut Stoicorum de diis opinionem referat. Longum esset, si nunc omnium antiquorum philosophorum de diis inmortalibus sententias referam; quae quidem tam diversae tamque inter se adversae sunt, ut totidem paene reperiantur, quot sunt eorum qui scripserunt capita. Non enim singulae solum familiae singulas sententias excogitarunt, sed saepe inter se eiusdem sectae viri vehementer de re ipsa dissentiunt. Verum ut reliqua ad praesens missa faciam et ad ea, quae praesenti inquisitioni consentanea sunt, deveniam, plerique Stoicorum, sed praesertim eorum princeps Zeno universum mundi globum mentem et ratione et summa sapientia praeditam habere crediderunt eamque esse ignem quendam purissimum ac tenuissimum ac, veluti animi nostri per sui corporis particulas omnes diffunduntur, ita illum per omnia mundi membra veluti genitale semen, unde cuncta procreantur, penetrare. . . . Virgilius igitur, quanvis in reliquis a Platone suo nunquam discedat, tamen, cum vidisset Chrysippum in eo, quem de natura deorum scripsit, libro Orphei, Musaei, Hesiodi atque Homeri fabellas ita interpretari, ut idem priscos olim poetas sensisse conetur ostendere, quod multis postea annis Stoici senserunt, statuit hac in re, ne ab iis poetis, quorum similis esse cupiebat, dissimilis putaretur, et ipse Porticum fulcire ac Stoicis adhaerere. Nam Platonis longe alia sententia est. Ponit enim deum penitus incorporeum atque extra omnem materiam omnemque mundum in ipso caeli dorso existentem."

111. L.B. Alberti, *Momo o del principe*, ed. and trans. R. Consolo (Genoa, 1986), 48: "Alii praesidem moderatoremque rerum unum esse aliquem arguebant: alii paria paribus, et inmortalium numerum mortalium numero respondere suadebant: alii mentem quandam omni terrae crassitudine, omni corruptibilium mortaliumque rerum contagione et commercio vacuam liberamque, divinarum et humanarum esse rerum alumnam principemque demonstrabant; alii vim quandam infusam rebus, qua universa moveantur, cuiusve quasi radii quidam sint hominum animi, Deum putandam asserebant . . ."

dialogue describes how Chrysippus made "ancient poets, who had not the faintest idea about these theories," into Stoics.[112] Unlike Cicero, he evidently favors the appropriation, since he drops Cicero's critical remark while retaining his chronological discussion of the development of theology. Other speakers too sometimes express genuine Albertian doctrine. Landino makes Lorenzo de' Medici exclaim with pleasure at Dante's deliberate misinterpretation of Virgil, which he sees as exemplary. Landino, he says, has always taught him that true imitation requires one to resemble the writer one imitates "in such a way that the resemblance is barely perceptible, and only to the learned."[113] Here too Landino's personae speak for Alberti. In the preface to *Momus*, Alberti had argued that artful writing necessarily took the form of presenting familiar matter in a novel way—that is, in creative reuse of earlier texts.[114] When Alberti read his texts for their potential misuse, in other words, he expected his readers to see what he had done (and perhaps to invert him as he had inverted Vitruvius and Cicero).[115]

The second point, more tentative still, is that Alberti's general attitude toward the past may shed more light on his particular practices as a reader. Like many other humanists, Alberti cherished a real ambivalence toward the ancients. On the one hand, he insisted that one must look to the Romans for

---

112. Cicero *De natura deorum* 1.30–41. At 1.41 Cicero describes how Chrysippus imposed his views on "veterrimi poetae, qui haec ne suspicati quidem sunt." For an important recent discussion of this and related passages see A.A. Long, "Stoic Readings of Homer," in *Homer's Ancient Readers,* ed. R. Lamberton and J.J. Keaney (Princeton, 1992), 41–66.

113. Landino, *Disputationes*, ed. Lohe, 254 (Lorenzo speaking): "Ego a prima paene pueritia ex utriusque parentis instituto adeo familiare universum opus Florentini poetae mihi reddidi, ut pauci omnino sint in eo loci, quos ego, si quando illi huiuscemodi oblectamenti genus requirerent, non facile ad verbum exprimerem. Sed quid poteram puer ex tam divino vate praeter mera verba percipere? Nunc autem, cum universum rei argumentum mente percurro, summa admiratione eius viri ingenium prosequor. Nam cum in opere suo texendo pauca omnino fila de Vergiliana tela mutuari videatur, tamen inde omnia paene sint. Quam ob rem nunc id demum intelligo, quod nos ex Ciceronis praecepto saepenumero Landinus admonere solet esse in aliquo imitando diligentem omnino rationem adhibendam; neque enim id agendum, ut idem simus, qui sunt ii, quos imitamur, sed eorum ita similes, ut ipsa similitudo vix illa quidem neque nisi a doctis intelligatur."

114. Alberti, *Momo,* ed. Consolo, 24: ". . . ut scriptoris officium deputem nihil sibi ad scribendum desumere, quod ipsum non sit iis qui legerint incognitum atque incogitatum? Quae cum ita sint, non me tamen fugit quam difficillimum ac prope impossibile sit aliquid adducere in medium quod ipsum non a plerisque ex tam infinito scriptorum numero tractatum deprehensumque exstiterit. Vetus proverbium: nihil dictum quin prius dictum. Quare sic statuo, fore ut ex raro hominum genere putandus sit, quisquis ille fuerit, qui res novas, inauditas et praeter omnium opinionem et spem in medium attulerit. Proximus huic erit is, qui cognitas et communes fortassis res novo quodam et insperato scribendi genere tractarit . . ."

115. For a still more explicit description of these procedures, see *Profugiorum ab aerumna libri iii,* in *Opere volgari,* ed. Grayson, 2:160–62, which is brilliantly discussed by Cardini, *Mosaici,* 4–5.

the best models of architecture, the best treatises on education, and the best examples of prudent behavior. On the other, Alberti persistently argued that modern achievements had a value and a power all their own. And sometimes he simply elided the distance between his Florence and Cicero's Rome.[116] Throughout *Della famiglia,* for example, he tried to identify the customs of the *antichi* (ancients) in Rome with those of the Albertis in medieval Florence. He praised the latter not only for their wealth, adventurousness, and business sense but for their erudition and eloquence, as if they had been fourteenth-century Ciceronians.[117] As the designer of the Malatesta Temple and the Rucellai Palace facade, finally, Alberti created three-dimensional physical links between the modern and the classical worlds—freely adapting and misusing ancient forms as he did so.[118]

Alberti's classicism, in other words, was anything but absolute. In one of his most famous texts—the letter to Brunelleschi that serves as the preface for the Italian text of *De pictura*—he brilliantly makes the case for modern life:

I used both to marvel and to regret that so many excellent and divine arts and sciences, which we know from their works and from historical accounts were possessed in great abundance by the talented men of antiquity, have now disappeared and are almost entirely lost. Painters, sculptors, architects, musicians, geometers, rhetoricians, augurs, and suchlike distinguished and remarkable intellects are very rarely to be found these days, and [those found] are of little merit. Consequently I believed what I heard many say, that Nature, mistress of all things, had grown old and weary and was no longer producing intellects, any more than giants, on a vast and wonderful scale such as she did in what one might call her youthful and more glorious days. But after I came back here to this most beautiful of cities from the long exile in which we Albertis have grown old, I recognized in many, but above all in you, Filippo, and in our great friend the sculptor Donatello and in

116. Recent work on *De pictura,* for example, has tended to stress continuities with the Middle Ages as well as the classical elements in the work. See, e.g., Jarzombek, "Structural Problematic"; Greenstein, "Alberti on *Historia*"; and J.A. Aiken, "Truth in Images: From the Technical Drawings of Ibn al-Razzaz al-Jazari, Campanus of Novara, and Giovanni de' Dondi to the Perspective Projection of Leon Battista Alberti," *Viator* 25 (1994): 325–59.

117. Cf. T. Kuehn, *Law, Family, and Women* (Chicago and London, 1991), chap. 6; and C. Klapisch-Zuber, *Women, Family, and Ritual in Renaissance Italy,* trans. L. Cochrane (Chicago and London, 1985), chap. 11.

118. Cf. Tönnesmann, *Pienza,* and C. Smith, *Architecture in the Culture of Early Humanism* (New York, 1992), for complementary discussions.

the others, Nencio [Ghiberti], Luca [Della Robbia], and Masaccio, a genius for every laudable enterprise in no way inferior to any of the ancients who gained fame in these arts. I then realized that the ability to achieve the highest distinction in any meritorious activity lies in our own industry and diligence no less than in the favors of Nature and of the times. I admit that for the ancients, who had many precedents to learn from and to imitate, it was less difficult to master these noble arts which for us today prove arduous; but it follows that our fame should be all the greater if, without preceptors and without any model to imitate, we discover arts and sciences hitherto unheard of and unseen. What man, however hard of heart or jealous, would not praise Filippo the architect when he sees here such an enormous construction towering above the skies, vast enough to cover the entire Tuscan population with its shadow, and done without the aid of beams or elaborate wooden supports? Surely such a feat of engineering, if I am not mistaken, that people did not believe possible these days and was probably equally unknown and unimaginable among the ancients.[119]

It seems highly appropriate that a modern architect won Alberti's warmest enthusiasm. In some ways, after all, Alberti read his ancient texts exactly as any modern architect who works in a classical mode reads both texts and buildings.

Even among the humanists, however, Alberti was not simply idiosyncratic in taking this approach to the ancients. Even the peerless classicist Lorenzo Valla felt some of the same mixed emotions. Valla, as we have seen, insisted on the "sacramental" character of classical Latin, and he reviled Poggio and others for writing an impure prose, even as he insisted that the classical vocabulary was far more extensive than they realized. But he also insisted that some modern inventions, such as the escapement clock, or *horologium*, had no classical precedents, and that modern terms for them must find inclusion in the Latin lexicon.[120] Bruni made the tension between the desire for classical perfection and the right of the modern to make his work new a central theme of his *Dialogi*.[121] Perhaps, then, Alberti's favored method of reading expressed, in a consistent if not a straightforward way, the very attitudes that led him to produce his major pieces of writing. By

119. Alberti, *Opere volgari*, ed. Grayson, 3:7–8.

120. See chapter 1.

121. See D. Quint, "Humanism and Modernity: A Reconsideration of Bruni's *Dialogus*," *Renaissance Quarterly* 38 (1985): 423–45.

reversing his texts he could insist simultaneously on his continuous reference to classical authority and his absolute commitment to modernity and independence—as he did when he insisted that in using Italian, rather than Latin, to address his own contemporaries, he actually followed the best classical precedent, since Cicero had also written for the readers of his own time, and that though he had invented modern architectural terms, he still wrote pure Latin.[122]

Alberti's letter to Brunelleschi, as E.H. Gombrich, Christine Smith, and many others have shown, swarms with allusions.[123] Lucretius' analysis of the exhaustion of nature's powers, Pliny's praise of the abilities of Vergilius Romanus, Manuel Chrysoloras' comparison of old and new Rome—all may have struck sparks from Alberti here. But one more text, not previously referred to in precisely this context, may be still more relevant. In a famous letter to Guglielmo da Cremona, the Paduan doctor and astronomer Giovanni Dondi dall' Orologio insisted on the superiority of ancients to moderns. "Justice, courage, temperance, and prudence really dwelt more profoundly," he claimed, in the souls of the Romans than in those of the moderns.[124] Their minds were "robust and strong," while those of the moderns are "not only weak and feeble . . . but none at all." Dondi cited as evidence not only the ancient texts, whose "authority and majesty are so great that no one can fail to trust them,"[125] but material objects: "Of the artistic products of ancient genius, few survive. But those that do remain anywhere are eagerly sought and seen and highly prized by those who feel strongly about such things: and if you compare them with those of today, it will soon become obvious that their authors were by nature more powerful in genius and more learned in the mastery of their art. I am speaking about ancient

---

122. Alberti *I libri della famiglia,* "Proemio del libro terzo," in *Opere volgari,* ed. Grayson, 1:155: "Benché stimo niuno dotto negarà quanto a me pare qui da credere, che tutti gli antichi scrittori scrivessero in modo che da tutti e'suoi molto voleano essere intesi"; *De re aedificatoria* 6.1, in *L'architettura,* ed. Orlandi, 2:441 (on the "difficultates . . . nominum inveniendorum"), 445: "Et, ni fallor, quae scripsimus, ita scripsimus, ut esse Latina non neges . . ." (an echo of Valla?).

123. See Smith (*Architecture in Early Humanism*), who gives full references to the older literature.

124. I use the edition and translation by N.W. Gilbert, "A Letter of Giovanni Dondi dall'Orologio to Fra' Guglielmo Centueri: A Fourteenth-Century Episode in the Quarrel of the Ancients and the Moderns," *Viator* 8 (1977): 299–346. Here the Latin text is at 333: ". . . iustitiam fortitudinem temperantiam atque prudentiam altius profecto illorum animis insedisse"; for English translation see 341.

125. Ibid., 333: "scripture . . . quarum quibusdam tanta est auctoritas atque maiestas ut eisdem fides negari non possit"; for English translation see 341.

buildings and statues and sculptures."[126] Even Petrarch, the greatest modern writer, could not compare with the ancients: "Our minds are of inferior quality."[127] Artisans—so Dondi, who was one himself, insisted—agreed on this point with the scholars. A modern marble sculptor, tantalizingly unidentified, assured Dondi that his ancient predecessors had not only imitated but beaten nature; their statues lacked nothing but breath itself.[128]

Dondi's letter itself reversed an ancient authority—Seneca, whose philosophical letters, as Neal Gilbert has shown, provided the principal ancient model for the collection of open letters in which this text appears.[129] Seneca dealt more than once with the development of human culture. He found some evidence for progress in the realm of thought. Philosophy and law, like the vices that had made them necessary, had developed in the course of human history, and these Seneca esteemed.[130] But in the material realm he saw only degeneration. Primitives, who had done without the appurtenances of modern society, had lived a far more virtuous life than moderns. Seneca unequivocally condemned the greed and gluttony that accompanied a life spent not in natural shelters but in houses, not in the forest but under pitched roofs. Against Posidonius, he insisted that the "towering tenements" of his day were the result not of philosophy put into practice but of corruption rendered universal: "Believe me, that was a happy time, before there were architects."[131] Dondi—who became famous for making the astronomical instrument that showed the positions of the sun, moon, and planets, which gave him his nickname—accepted Seneca's view that culture had degenerated, but he overturned Seneca's condemnation of material culture. High architecture and the liberal arts, like high philosophy, formed part of a whole in the ancient world, one that moderns could never hope to match. Alberti, in overturning Dondi's verdict on the modern world, accepted his reversal of Seneca as well as his original insistence that architecture, like philosophy, showed the intellect at its highest. He thus used—and criticized—a classical authority and an authoritative classicist at one

---

126. Ibid. 336: "De artificiis ingeniorum veterum quamquam pauca supersint, si qua tamen manent alicubi, ab his qui ea in re sentiunt cupide queruntur et videntur magnique penduntur et si illis hodierna contuleris, non latebit auctores eorum fuisse ex natura ingenio potiores et artis magisterio doctiores. Edificia dico vetera et statuas sculpturasque cum aliis modi huius . . ."; for English translation see 344.

127. Ibid., 336: "Sic est profecto. Nostra ingenia inferioris sunt note"; for English translation see 344.

128. Ibid., 336 (Latin); for English translation see 345.

129. Ibid., 317–21.

130. Seneca *Epistulae morales* 90.6; cf. 86.

131. Ibid., 90.7–10: "Mihi crede, felix illud saeculum ante architectos fuit."

and the same time, and he did so in a way that, as Dondi's letter shows, would have been clear at the time to a literate, well-informed artist as well as to a scholar.

Alberti did not share Valla's dedication to the craft of philological reading. His vocation lay more in the exploration of ancient sites than in the exploitation of ancient codices. But he also lacked the conscious commitment to traditions of evaluation and interpretation that hemmed in many humanist readers. He read the ancients deliberately and systematically, exploring the world of his texts with a precise sense of what he needed. Where other humanists often resembled lepidopterists seeking perfect specimens to capture and display, Alberti resembled a biochemist seeking genetic material to manipulate and reshape. And his work was fruitful. His interpretations, like nested Russian dolls skillfully turned and painted and transformed from the original rough stock, are as original and distinctive as his buildings. Above all, they are free.

Alberti, for example, stayed calm even when he read what many of his contemporaries found the most inspiring and terrifying of ancient texts— the Hermetic *Asclepius*. Ficino and Bruno were moved by its evocation of the perfection of the universe, excited by its description of how the Egyptians had captured demonic spirits in their statues, and both saddened and exalted by its lament for the future destruction of Egypt. Alberti responded to this mixture of practical magic and theoretical eschatology in a characteristic way—with parody. In *Momus* Alberti's Jupiter, like the Hermetic creator, wishes to make a wholly orderly universe; but he fails. Alberti's gods, like those of the *Asclepius,* enter statues. But they do so of their own will, not as the result of human incantations, and more or less by accident. Furthermore, the statues themselves soon undergo gross mutilation, when a great wind knocks them down. The gods arrange the damaged images in a row and depart before mortals can discover them at a disadvantage.[132] The

---

132. Cf. *Momo,* ed. Consolo, 236–46, 272–74; and *Asclepius* 13–14, 24–26. Di Grado and Consolo (*Momus,* 11 n. 47, 236 n. 8) note the parodic relation between Alberti's statue episode and that in the *Asclepius,* but they do not analyze the wider relationship between the two texts. Garin's argument that Alberti used the *Corpus Hermeticum* as well seems to me as yet unproven, despite the parallels adduced by di Grado and Consolo. Alberti's method of free combination and radical reworking sometimes makes it unnervingly difficult to determine where he found a given fact or drew the inspiration for a particular metaphor—a problem that makes the reconstruction of the actual circumstances in which he read all the more urgent. See the useful case study by S. Salomone, "Fonti greche nel '*De equo animante*' di Leon Battista Alberti," *Rinascimento,* ser. 2, 26 (1986): 241–50; and the magisterial treatment of Alberti's style by L. Cesarini Martinelli, "Metafore teatrali in Leon Battista Alberti," *Rinascimento,* ser. 2, 29 (1989): 3–51.

powers of an ancient barbarian wisdom, which had so impressed the neo-platonists of the imperial age, evoked from Alberti only bitter laughter. Lucian's mockery suited him better than the awe-filled rhetoric of the *Corpus Hermeticum.* Even this most severely independent of humanists found a central intellectual tool—as well as sources to rearrange and adapt—in his favorite ancient texts; yet he went beyond even Lucian in his willingness to bring the gods down to earth.[133] Other humanists would find the appeal of ancient magic more compelling—and would, as we will see, have to pay a high intellectual and personal price to win the freedom of interpretation that Alberti took for granted.

---

133. See the excellent analysis by D. Marsh, "Alberti's *Momus:* Sources and Contexts," *Acta conventus neo-latini Hafniensis,* ed. R. Schnur (Binghamton, N.Y., 1994), 623–32.

3

Giovanni Pico della Mirandola: Trials and Triumphs of an Omnivore

Early in 1487 Pico della Mirandola suffered one of the worst fates that could befall a scholar in Renaissance Rome. He lost his right to use the Vatican Library—something that normally happened only to those scholars who were so ill bred that they quarreled with other readers, failed to put their books back in place, or climbed over the *banchi* to which the books were chained instead of walking around them as they should.[1] Unfortunately, Pico would soon suffer worse indignities. He had come to Rome to hold a public disputation on nine hundred theses, which Eucharius Silber printed.[2] The ceremony was to begin with a powerful polemical statement, the *Oratio de hominis dignitate*. Then Pico would take on every opponent he could attract in a debate that would cover all schools of philosophy, all areas of knowledge, and all corners of the universe.[3] Though only twenty-three years old, Pico intended to transform philosophy. He thought he could prove that every great thinker, past or present, had arrived at one of the dozens of vital truths that he hoped to fit together, like pieces of a vast jigsaw puzzle, into a single philosophical system. He would show that the Jewish Cabalists and the sages of ancient Persia and Egypt, Zoroaster and Hermes Trismegistus, had grasped and taught the basic truths of Christianity; that all men were free to rise by study and contemplation to unity with their

---

1. The posted reasons for loss of privileges were recorded by C. Bellièvre, *Souvenirs de voyages en Italie et en Orient, Notes historiques, Pièces de vers*, ed. C. Perrat (Geneva, 1956), 4: "EDICTUM S. D. N. Ne quis in Bibliotheca cum altero contentiose loquatur et obstrepat neve de loco ad locum iturus scamna transcendat et pedibus conterat. Utque libros claudat et in locum percommode reponat ubi que [qui?] volet perlegerit. Secus qui faxit foras cum ignominia mittetur atque hujusce loci aditu deinceps arcebitur."

2. For the text of Pico's theses see his *Opera omnia* (Basel, 1572; repr., as *Opera omnia*, ed. E. Garin, Turin, 1971), 1:63–113. The newer edition by B. Kieszkowski (Geneva, 1973) is not entirely reliable.

3. Pico was not the first Renaissance intellectual to emulate Hippias; see J. Monfasani's amusing study of the career of *Fernando of Cordova: A Biographical and Intellectual Profile*, Transactions of the American Philosophical Society 82, pt. 6 (1992). He describes his protagonist as "[p]art charlatan, part *Wunderkind*, and part learned scholastic."

Creator; and that a healthy, virtuous form of magic could help them do so. Pico was so eager to see his theses debated that he offered to pay the expenses of anyone who came to Rome to take part.

The papal Curia of the 1480s was not scandalized by learning that philosophers seemed to disagree. Debates between the great sages made a favorite subject for painters and artisans even before the *School of Athens* provided the canonical image of one.[4] Pico's public reference to recondite Near Eastern books and languages also had predecents. On Good Friday 1481 the Jewish convert Flavius Guillelmus Ramundus Mithridates preached before the pope and the cardinals that "misteria omnia passionis Iesu Christi" had been predicted by the Jews who wrote the "older Talmud." He quoted the relevant texts at length in the original languages, which no one in the audience could understand. Yet Flavius' speech, according to the papal master of ceremonies, "pleased everyone, even though it was two hours long, both because of its varied contents and because of the sound of the Hebrew and Arabic words, which he pronounced like a native. Everyone, especially the pope and the cardinals, praised him to the skies."[5]

The popes and cardinals were also used to dramatic claims that the pagan sages of the ancient Near East had anticipated elements of the Christian revelation. On Palm Sunday 1484, Giovanni Mercurio da Correggio appeared in Rome, wearing a black silk toga, scarlet boots, and a crown of thorns. The crown was capped by a silver ornament in the shape of the crescent moon, on which Giovanni had written a strange text: "Hic est puer meus Pimander, quem ego elegi." Pimander is the chief speaker in the first dialogue of the *Corpus Hermeticum,* the strange revelation in dialogue form of the mysteries of Egyptian theology that Marsilio Ficino translated into Latin for Cosimo de' Medici. The dialogues in the *Corpus,* though they contain fragments of Egyptian belief and ritual, were actually written in Greek in the second and third centuries A.D. Giovanni, like Ficino, Pico, and many others, took them as a genuine Egyptian account of the creation of the world and the path to salvation—a pagan equivalent, ancient and profound, to the Bible.[6] Through the streets of Rome he marched, according to the account

---

4. A. Cutler, "The *Disputà* Plate in the J. Paul Getty Museum and Its Cinquecento Context," *J. Paul Getty Museum Journal* 18 (1990).

5. See Flavius Mithridates, *Sermo de passione Domini,* ed. C. Wirszubski (Jerusalem, 1963); and C. Wirszubski, *Pico della Mirandola's Encounter with Jewish Mysticism* (Cambridge, Mass., and London, 1989).

6. For these texts and their impact see G. Fowden, *The Egyptian Hermes* (repr., Princeton, 1993); P.O. Kristeller, *Supplementum Ficinianum* (Florence, 1937); F.A. Yates, *Giordano Bruno and the Hermetic Tradition* (Chicago, 1964); and E. Garin, *Ermetismo del Rinascimento* (Rome, 1988); *Hermetica,* ed. and trans. B.P. Copenhaver (Cambridge, 1992).

by Ludovico Lazzarelli, passing out slips of paper on which he identified himself as "the angel of wisdom and Pimander." He preached to great crowds in the Campo de' Fiori and on the piazza before Saint Peter's. The pope's own guards made way for him as he entered Saint Peter's. He prayed at the great altar before leaving unmolested for his home in Bologna.[7]

In circumstances like these, it seems strange that anyone worried about a mere Latin disputation—especially one based on Jewish texts that Mithridates himself translated for Pico and on the *Corpus Hermeticum*, which Giovanni da Correggio had brandished in the streets. But the pope and his theologians were losing their tolerance. The world shook around them. In the heavens, the great conjunction of Saturn and Jupiter, which had taken place in 1484, portended great changes in society and religion. On earth, the system of Italian states that had taken shape after the Peace of Lodi a generation before was spinning out of control. A savage civil war had just raged in the kingdom of Naples, reaching the outskirts of Rome. Within the city, mobs and the private armies that mustered in every cardinal's palace rampaged unchecked by papal authority. Meanwhile even worse enemies threatened all human societies. The *Malleus maleficarum*, commissioned in 1484 and published just as Pico went through his ordeal, unveiled magic as pervasive and dangerous—not the age-old craft of the cunning men and women who found lost objects and charmed off warts in every village, but an organized conspiracy against God and the Church, leading hundreds of souls astray and depriving dozens of men of their penises.[8]

Pico himself, finally, was not an obscure scholar but a prince, a very rich man, and already eminent in the world of letters. He could neither be ignored nor tolerated. Seven of his nine hundred propositions were condemned, and another six were declared suspect.[9] He failed to defend himself adequately. Stung by criticism, barred from the bibliophile's paradise from which he had borrowed great medieval works on astrology and natural magic, Pico despaired. He fled to France—toward Paris, where he had studied scholastic logic and theology in 1485. Arrested near Lyon, he could have

---

7. See L. Lazzarelli, "Epistola Enoch," ed. M. Brini, in *Testi umanistici su l'Ermetismo*, ed. E. Garin et al. (Rome, 1955); and a brilliant account in D. Weinstein, *Savonarola and Florence* (Princeton, 1970), 199–200. The fundamental studies are those of P.O. Kristeller, collected in his *Studies in Renaissance Thought and Letters* (Rome, 1956). A far more pessimistic account, based on a new source, is provided by D. Ruderman, "Giovanni Mercurio da Correggio's Appearance as Seen Through the Eyes of an Italian Jew," *Renaissance Quarterly* 28 (1975): 309–22.

8. See, e.g., the recent summary of E. Labouvie, *Zauberei und Hexenwerk* (Frankfurt a.M., 1991), 17–34.

9. Pico, *Opera*, 1:62; cf. his *Apologia*, in *Opera*, 1:114–240.

suffered the worst punishment of all if Lorenzo de' Medici had not intervened and brought him to Florence. There he spent the last years of his life, frantically at work on a whole series of scholarly and philosophical projects.[10]

This crisis, the most dramatic one of Pico's life, was not an isolated rough patch in an otherwise smooth fabric. In fact, it identifies the two axes on which his entire existence spun itself out: an obsessive search for danger and an insatiable hunger for learning. Pico deliberately confronted risks of every kind, intellectual and personal. Born in 1463 into a rich, noble family, he chose the life of an intellectual instead of that of a soldier of fortune or a canon lawyer (the gentler path his mother had wished him to follow). Moving constantly, he studied the humanities in Ferrara. Though the erudite Latin culture of Guarino and Leonello no longer dominated Ferrarese intellectual life, the great teacher's son, Battista Guarino, introduced him to the standard classical authors and methods of interpretation. He mastered the Latin Averroist tradition at Padua and Pavia. By the time he was twenty-one years old, in 1484, he knew the greatest Venetian scholar of the day, Ermolao Barbaro, and belonged to the central intellectual circle of Laurentian Florence, that of Ficino, Poliziano, and Lorenzo himself. But within two years, in 1486, he risked discredit and death when he kidnapped Margherita, the wife of a tax gatherer from the Medici family. Pico's retinue died resisting their pursuers, and he himself was imprisoned. Only the indulgence of Ficino—who wrote a long apologia to the effect that gods and heroes like Pico could not be judged by normal standards of conduct—and Lorenzo, who ordered his release, saved him.

Even after Pico had more or less settled in Florence, he led an adventurous spiritual life. In 1489 he persuaded Lorenzo to invite Savonarola to Florence—a fateful decision indeed. Under Savonarola's influence he dreamed and meditated, and as he lay dying in 1494 he enjoyed the respite provided by a visit from the Virgin Mary.[11] Even after death Pico moved about: he appeared to the Carmelite poet Battista Mantuanus in a dream, stuttering badly—a sign that he had left his philosophy incomplete. The two conversed about the value of the bits of coral and engraved amulets that Italian parents hung about the necks of children to protect them. Then Pico—still restless—disappeared.[12]

---

10. For a fine general account of Pico's life and thought see P.O. Kristeller, *Eight Philosophers of the Italian Renaissance* (Stanford, 1964), chap. 4; cf. also B.P. Copenhaver and C.B. Schmitt, *Renaissance Philosophy* (Oxford and New York, 1992), 163–76.

11. See G.F. Pico's *Vita* of his uncle, in Pico, *Opera*, 1:[*7] recto–verso.

12. Baptista Mantuanus to G.F. Pico, 3.1.1495, in Pico, *Opera*, 1:387–88.

Pico read as obsessively as he wandered. In fact, he defined the vocation of the intellectual in terms of reading. In the *Oratio* written to precede his great Roman debate, he described the Greek philosophers as scholars who had anticipated his search for universal erudition: "All the ancients observed this principle: that they studied every sort of writer and passed over no text unread, so far as they could. Aristotle, in particular, did this; and accordingly Plato called him *anagnostes*, that is, 'reader.'"[13] Pico's use of this example seems more than a little forced. Plato notoriously preferred living teachers to dead books, and the anecdote clearly reveals a sense of the difference between his methods and those of his greatest and most rebellious pupil. But Pico found another classical authority to bolster his pursuit of universal erudition: "But I have set out to pass through all the masters of philosophy, while swearing by none."[14] Here he quoted Horace (*Ep.* 1.1.14)—the very passage, in fact, that would become the motto of the seventeenth-century Royal Society of London. The line that Francis Bacon's followers took as their pledge to trust no book, to accept no written authority, Pico used as a charter for his effort to master every written authority in the world. He thus provided a model of eclectic philosophy that would inspire imitation for centuries to come.[15] As this chapter will show, however, the syncretistic method for which Pico argued in his *Oratio* was only one of the styles of interpretation he regularly employed. Some of his boldest experiments in reading texts rested on very different premises.

Pico's insatiable love of old books and desire to explore new ones gave him common ground with other intellectuals. Ficino, for example, recalled with delight what seemed to him his fated encounter with Pico. He connected their first meeting with two of his own most influential projects: "Just when I published Plato in Latin, the heroic soul of Cosimo [de' Medici, who had subsidized the great project] somehow stimulated the heroic mind of Giovanni Pico, so that he came to Florence, though even he himself did not quite know how it happened. He was in fact born in the very year when I started work on Plato [1463]. He came to Florence on the very day and almost at the very hour when I published the Plato, and after our first greeting he asked me about Plato. I replied to him: 'Our Plato crossed our threshold today.' Pico congratulated me on this and then—with words

---

13. G. Pico della Mirandola, *Discorso sulla dignità dell'uomo*, ed. G. Tognon, trans. E. Garin (Brescia, 1987), 38: "Fuit enim cum ab antiquis omnibus hoc observatum, ut omne scriptorum genus evolventes, nullas quas possent commentationes illectas preterirent, tum maxime ab Aristotele, qui eam ob causam ἀναγνώστης, idest lector, a Platone nuncupabatur."

14. Ibid.: "At ego ita me institui, ut in nullius verba iuratus, me per omnes philosophiae magistros funderem."

15. W. Schmidt-Biggemann, *Theodizee und Tatsachen* (Frankfurt, 1988), 203–22.

that neither he nor I can recall—did not induce but spurred me to translate Plotinus."[16] Literary projects, in short, could create social relationships, and social relationships could breed new intellectual enterprises in their turn. Books also served Pico, more conventionally, as a sort of ideal currency, exchange of which cemented and maintained relations with distant friends. Pico's correspondence shows him actively engaged with other scholars and collectors across Italy. He lends, borrows, offers information about titles that he lacks, and sometimes, embarrassingly, confesses that he cannot lay his hands on a particular work that someone else has lent him. Nowhere does the iconoclastic philosopher seem more like a normal humanist of the early fifteenth century than in the book notes that fill so many of his letters.[17]

But reading was more than a shared hobby. It provided, especially in Pico's later life, a consuming occupation, one that kept him away from the social life an aristocrat would normally enjoy and even the friends whom he loved best. When jousts were held in Florence, the low-born and timorous Poliziano attended them and reported at length to the noble Pico, who had remained sequestered with his books.[18] Moreover, Pico did not always read in comfort and seclusion or arrive at interpretations that created common ground with others; the love of books and the love of risks often went together. From the start of his career as an intellectual, Pico felt a powerful impulse to challenge intellectual as well as spiritual and legal authorities. Though fond of Ficino, he sharply disagreed with him on the interpretation of Plato. His earliest substantial work, a commentary on Girolamo Benivieni's *Canzone d'amore,* so sharply challenged what he described as Ficino's obvious errors that several passages were suppressed in the posthumous first edition of the text.[19] His mature works *De ente et uno* and *Disputationes adversus astrologiam divinatricem* mounted fundamental chal-

---

16. Ficino, dedicatory letter to Plotinus, in Ficino, *Opera* (Basel, 1576), 1537 = *Opera omnia,* ed. M. Sancipriano (Turin, 1959), 2:537: "Quo enim tempore Platonem Latinis dedi legendum, heroicus ille Cosmi animus heroicam Ioannis Pici Mirandulae mentem nescio quomodo instigavit, ut Florentiam, et ipse quasi nesciens quomodo, perveniret. Hic sane quo anno Platonem aggressus fueram natus, deinde quo die et ferme qua hora Platonem edidi Florentiam veniens, me statim post primam salutationem de Platone rogat. Huic equidem, Plato noster, inquam, hodie liminibus nostris est egressus. Tunc ille et hoc ipso vehementer congratulatus est, et mox nescio quibus verbis, ac ille nescit quibus, ad Plotinum interpretandum me non adduxit quidem, sed potius concitavit."

17. The largest collection of Pico's correspondence remains that in *Opera,* 1:340–410; many (but not all) letters published later are gathered in *Opera,* 2:245–469.

18. A. Poliziano *Ep.* 12.6, in *Opera* (Basel, 1553, repr., as *Opera Omnia,* ed. I. Maïer, Turin, 1971), 1:167–68.

19. See Pico, *De hominis dignitate, Heptaplus, De ente et uno, e scritti vari,* ed. E. Garin (Florence, 1942), 10–18.

lenges to the Platonic scholarship and astrological medicine of his friend and benefactor. And his exploration of Jewish biblical commentaries led him onto very thin ice. Pico's declaration that the Cabala offered the clearest possible confirmation of the doctrine of the Trinity snapped the camel's back of papal patience in 1487.

A vast and distinguished literature, including classical analyses by Ernst Cassirer, Eugenio Garin, Paul Oskar Kristeller, D.P. Walker, and F.A. Yates and much detailed work by younger scholars, offers guidance through the recesses of Pico's central philosophical texts.[20] His system, its development, and the changes in and consistency of his thought have been explored in intricate detail. I have neither the intention nor the ability to add to this rich heritage of analysis. Rather, I wish to take up the complementary hints offered by some of the greatest authorities on both Renaissance philosophy and the history of the book in the age of humanism. Garin, Kristeller, and Petrucci have all suggested that Pico's philosophical project had a particularly close relation to his scholarship and his bibliophilia.[21] Like some scholastics and many humanists, Pico studded his work with explicit and implicit references to his sources. More unusual, he argued explicitly for the unity of truth, insisting that each thinker had attained a particular insight denied to others. In his *Theses* he drew on every imaginable text, from the oldest Greek philosophers and supposedly older forgeries like the *Hermetica* to the most recent works of scholastic philosophy. In the *Oratio*, finally, he described with the eye for detail of a Florentine cloth merchant the complementary colors and textures of the thinkers he wanted to weave into a single syncretic tapestry: "And to begin with our own Latins, who were the last to be reached by philosophy, there is in John Scot something lively and loose, in Thomas something solid and well thought out, in Giles something terse and precise, in Francis something subtle and acute. . . . Among the Arabs there is in Averroës something firm and stable, in Avempace . . . , in Alfarabi something profound and well considered, in Avicenna something divine and Platonic. In general, the Greeks have a philosophy that is brilliant

---

20. For a well-informed and in part well-argued, but highly polemical, review of the literature, with many of whose conclusions I strongly disagree, see W.G. Craven, *Giovanni Pico della Mirandola: Symbol of His Age* (Geneva, 1981).

21. See three remarkable studies: E. Garin, *Giovanni Pico della Mirandola: Vita e dottrina* (Florence, 1937); P.O. Kristeller, "Giovanni Pico della Mirandola and His Sources," in *L'opera e il pensiero di Giovanni Pico della Mirandola* (Florence, 1965), 1:34–133; and A. Petrucci, "Le biblioteche antiche," in *Letteratura italiana*, vol. 2, *Produzione e consumo*, ed. A. Asor Rosa (Turin, 1983), 527–54 at 551–53. See also P. Viti's *Catalogo* of the Biblioteca Laurenziana exhibition on *Pico, Poliziano e l'umanesimo di fine Quattrocento* (Florence, 1994), which surveys and synthesizes a vast amount of material on these scholars and their hours in libraries.

and pure: rich and eloquent in Simplicius, elegant and concise in Themistius, solid and learned in Alexander, thought out with profundity in Theophrastus, plain and attractive in Ammonius."[22] Pico's brief and epigrammatic characterizations do not reveal much about how he read any single book. But they vividly exemplify his conviction that the true philosopher must literally be a universal reader, since every text had a unique set of virtues that complemented those of all the rest.

In the fifteenth century, however, the universal reader had to be a universal book hunter—a haunter of dark shops, a patron of elegant scribes, and a habitué of established collections. Only substantial private means and direct access to all reaches of the book trade could enable a single person to attain mastery of the encyclopedia. Pico admitted this more than once. According to Pietro Crinito, when Poliziano and many others praised Pico's brilliance and learning, he replied: "There is no reason for you to flatter me or my brains. Look rather at how very hard I have worked. . . . And look, at the same time, at my stock in trade, my treasury of books." "And he showed us," Crinito continued, "his rich and finely laid-out library, stuffed with books of every kind."[23] Pico, in other words, regarded the money, time, and effort he had expended on assembling his library as no small part of his achievement. We commit no injustice, then, in attending to Pico the bibliophile as well as to Pico the philosopher—even though in doing so we must indelicately take account of the material, as well as the intellectual, capital that he assembled.

Pico began to build up his own collection quite early in life. In August 1481, when he was only eighteen years old, Giovanni Mascarini of Ferrara

---

22. Pico, *Discorso,* ed. Tognon, 38–40: "Atque ut a nostris, ad quos postremo philosophia pervenit, nunc exordiar, est in Ioanne Scoto vegetum quiddam atque discussum, in Thoma solidum et equabile, in Egidio tersum et exactum, in Francisco acre et acutum, in Alberto priscum, amplum et grande, in Henrico, ut mihi visum est, semper sublime et venerandum. Est apud Arabes, in Averroe firmum et inconcusum, in Avempace, in Alpharabio grave et meditatum, in Avicenna divinum atque Platonicum. Est apud Graecos in universum quidem nitida, in primis et casta philosophia; apud Simplicium locuplex et copiosa, apud Themistium elegans et compendiaria, apud Alexandrum constans et docta, apud Theophrastum graviter elaborata, apud Ammonium enodis et gratiosa."

23. P. Crinito *De honesta disciplina* 2.2 (Florence, 1504), sig. [a vii recto] = ed. C. Angeleri (Rome, 1955), 84: "Factum est ut Picum Mirandulanum nuper audirem de philosophia docte atque egregie disserentem. Ibique cum Angelus Politianus et alii complures eius ingenium atque multiplicem eruditionem laudarent ac mirabundi extollerent: 'Non est'—inquit Picus—'ut hac in re mihi aut ingenio meo [1504 nunc] velitis blandiri. Quin respicite potius ad labores et vigilias nostras, ac tum facile intelligetis gratulandum potius assiduis vigiliis atque lucubrationibus, quam nostro ingenio plaudendum. Et simul aspicite (inquit) supellectilem nostram atque librorum thesauros.' Ostendebat autem egregie instructam atque copiosam bibliothecam, librisque affatim omnigenis refertam."

finished making a copy of Pliny's *Naturalis Historia* for him. This elegant humanistic manuscript, now preserved in the Biblioteca Marciana, bears the mark of the refined collector on its front page. The text is surrounded by a splendid architectural border, a classicizing fantasy inhabited not only by the normal graceful putti but also, a little incongruously, like Pliny's own text, by satyrs. In its large initial *L* sits Pliny himself, robed and venerable, hard at work with book, compass, and astrolabe.[24] Another copy of Pliny— a printed one, now preserved at Trinity College at Cambridge—bears a fine, if less showy, set of marginal illuminations by the "Pico Master," whose hand Lillian Armstrong has traced in many other Venetian incunabula.[25] These books, so systematically adorned, physically embodied the young Pico's glowingly optimistic vision of the realm of books. So did the library at Mirandola, where he read them. There frescoes by Cosimo Tura laid out a richly encyclopedic vision of the *Theologia poetica*. This was populated not only by the Greek poets but also by the sibyls and Zoroaster, the latter dressed "in a foreign and varied outfit—that is, a Persian-Median one."[26] The appearance of this last, exotic figure may confirm Robert Klein's conjecture that Pico himself provided Tura's iconographical program.[27] In any event it was certainly a rich man's library—as Tommaso Campanella ruefully pointed out, when he contrasted his own poverty and lack of books of masters with Pico's ability to amass all the materials he needed (true, Campanella thought that Pico's obsession with the books of men had blinded him to the wonders of nature, the book of God).[28]

---

24. Biblioteca Marciana, MS lat. VI, 245 (= 2976), fol. 3 recto; illustration in J.J.G. Alexander, ed., *The Painted Page* (Munich, 1994), fig. 28.

25. L. Armstrong, "Il Maestro di Pico: Un miniatore veneziano del tardo Quattrocento," *Saggi e memorie di storia dell'arte* 17 (1990): 7–39; Armstrong, "The Impact of Printing on Miniaturists in Venice after 1469," in *Printing the Written Word*, ed. S. Hindman (Ithaca, N.Y., and London, 1991), 174–202; Armstrong, "The Hand-Illuminated Printed Book," in *The Painted Page*, ed. Alexander, 205–6.

26. L.G. Giraldi, *Historiae poetarum tam Graecorum quam Latinorum dialogi decem, Operum quae extant omnium tomus secundus* (Basel, 1580), 59: "In hac parte fuit Zoroastris imago, qui peregrino ac vario quodam habitu indutus erat, hoc est, Persomede . . ."

27. R. Klein, "La Bibliothèque de la Mirandole et le 'Concert Champêtre' de Giorgione," in *La forme et l'intelligible* (Paris, 1970), 193–203.

28. T. Campanella to A. Querengo, 8.7.1607, in *Opere di Giordano Bruno e di Tommaso Campanella*, ed. A. Guzzo and R. Amerio (Milan and Naples, 1956), 971–72: "Io, signor mio, non ebbi mai li favori e grazie singulari di Pico, che fu nobilissimo e ricchissimo ed ebbe libri a copia e maestri assai. . . . Ecco dunque il diverso filosofar mio da quel di Pico; ed io imparo più dall'anatomia d'una formica o d'una erba . . . che non da tutti li libri che sono scritti dal principio di secoli sin a mò. . . . Veramente Pico fu ingegno nobile e dotto; ma filosofo più sopra le parole altrui che nella natura . . ." In his turn Campanella would be criticized by Mersenne for attending too much to speculation and too little to nature. Paradoxically, Mersenne's profession that he disliked those he called "chartaceos Philosophos, quoniam nunquam ex naturae

By the time Pico died, in November 1494, he owned more than 1,100 books. As Pearl Kibre showed in her valuable study of his library, his collection ranked with the largest private ones of his time, like that of Cardinal Bessarion. Two inventories, neither complete, survive; both have been published. Together they give something of the measure of Pico's extraordinary range of interests and knowledge—a range that, as Kristeller suggests, should inspire awe in anyone who inhabits the narrow comfort of the modern academic disciplines. He really owned—and, as we shall see, really read—all the texts he praised in his *Oratio;* Platonists and Aristotelians, the oracles of Zoroaster and the revelations of Hermes, and Jewish biblical commentators and Arab astrologers jostled on his shelves as they did in his mind.[29] Pico's collection, with its 157 volumes in Greek and 124 in Hebrew, Aramaic, and Arabic, stands out even when compared with the richest private libraries of the time. The very valuable collection of the medical humanist Nicolò Leoniceno, recently studied by Daniela Mugnai Carrara, contained 345 volumes, 117 of them in Greek; ordinary scholarly libraries, as Mugnai Carrara also shows, ran to a mere 50 or so volumes.[30] By contrast Pico's library resembles that of a prince more than that of a normal scholar.

Of the financial and institutional history of Pico's collection we know little. One of the inventories, drawn up in 1498, shows that the books were generally divided by their subject matter into cases (*armaria*): works on medicine, commentaries on Aristotle, classical and humanistic texts, Greek texts, and oriental texts each had a separate location. This method closely resembles that followed at the Vatican in the same period. Librarians there also grouped books by *banchi* and *armaria,* and written inventories gave general guidance to these. Given the size of Pico's collection, it seems likely that he, like the popes, had professional help in acquiring and arranging it. A letter to him from Giovanni Antonio Flaminio suggests as much. The young man, almost visibly cringing and wringing his hands, writes: "I hear that you have a codex of Virgil of venerable antiquity. Now I am not so shameless or abandoned as to dare to ask you to send it to me. For I know

inspectione, sed solis libris sapere volunt," is reminiscent of Campanella's verdict on Pico. See *Correspondance du P. Marin Mersenne,* ed. C. de Waard, (Paris, 1945–88), 8:722 and 722–23 n. 6.

29. For the two lists of Pico's books see, respectively, F. Calori Cesis, *Giovanni Pico della Mirandola* (Mirandola, 1897); and P. Kibre, *The Library of Pico della Mirandola* (New York, 1936). On the post mortem fate of his library see G. Mercati, *Codici latini Pico Grimani Pio e di altra biblioteca ignota del secolo xvi esistenti nell'Ottoboniana* (Vatican City, 1938).

30. D. Mugnai Carrara, *La biblioteca di Nicolò Leoniceno* (Florence, 1991).

that those fortunate enough to obtain such goods do not willingly let them pass their thresholds. But I will dare to ask the next best thing: that you have your librarian inspect some passages in the first book of the *Aeneid*, to see how they read in your exemplar. They are as follows. . . ."[31] Pico offered another correspondent, Giorgio Valla, a complete inventory of his library (a service that the Vatican librarians also performed for favored readers), and he sent a list of his Greek books to Poliziano. By contrast Pico's old friend Battista Guarino, when asked for an inventory of his books, replied that he simply could not undertake so "wearisome and useless" a task, even though Pico asked for the list so he might better determine what his friend needed. Perhaps the poorer man found the request to do a menial job offensive, coming as it did from a richer benefactor.[32] At all events, Pico's ability to provide these time-consuming services suggests that he had a librarian in his service.

To those Pico regarded as colleagues in inquiry, like Ficino and Valla, he was willing to be more generous than Flaminio's letter suggests. He offered to let both men use all his books as their own: to Valla he wrote that "I will send you, if you would like, a full catalog of both my Greek and my Latin library. And then, if you ask, I will send you the whole library too."[33] Sharing information, of course, posed less of a problem than sharing books; Filippo Beroaldo, for example, thanked Pico lavishly for using his manuscript to confirm Beroaldo's reading of a passage in Propertius.[34] Evidently, then,

---

31. G.A. Flaminio, *Epistolae familiares* (Bologna, 1744), 135: "Audio te Virgilianum habere venerandae vetustatis codicem: sed non sum adeo exhausto pudore, neque ita frontem perfricui, ut audeam rogare, ut ad me illum mittas. Scio enim quod non libenter egredi limen sinant, quibus felici sorte bona eiusmodi contigere: quod proximum est, poscere audebo, ut a tuo bibliothecario aliquot in primo Aeneidos libro inspici iubeas, quomodo in tuo codice legantur."

32. B. Guarini to Pico, 5.12.1489, in Pico, *Opera*, 1:404: "Quod librorum meorum indicem petis, id mihi laboriosum est et inutile, satis erit si pro tempore postulatis meis inservies. Nunc Martianum Capellam et Senecae quaestiones naturales opto, si modo emaculati sint codices, nam qui apud nos sunt opera Sybillae indigent: eos si impressos emere possim gratius mihi erit, sin minus non longo postliminio tui ad te redibunt."

33. Pico to Valla, 8 May [1492], in J.L. Heiberg, *Beiträge zur Geschichte Georg Valla's und seiner Bibliothek*, XVI. Beiheft zum Centrallblatt für Bibliothekswesen (Leipzig, 1896), 61: "Mittam ego ad te, si id optaris, et Graecae et Latinae bibliothecae meae absolutum indicem. Mittam ipsam, si petieris, deinde universam bibliothecam."

34. Beroaldo is quoted in Pico, *Opera*, 1:410: ". . . hic [Picus] post severiora studia in Propertii lectione tanquam amoenissimo diversorio requiescere consuevit, et mihi hunc locum ita legenti adstipulatur, ostenditque in suo codice Susa scriptum esse, non Hetrusca." The passage in question is Propertius 2.13.1; a witness that offers the reading in question, and others cited by Beroaldus without mentioning Pico, is Staatsbibliothek zu Berlin, Haus 1, Diez B Sant. 57. *Sussa* appears as a marginal gloss on fol. 25 verso; *hetrusca* is the reading in the text. See J.L. Butrica, *The Manuscript Tradition of Propertius* (Toronto, Buffalo, and London, 1984),

Pico accepted the ideal of the humanist collector at his best. He treated his library as quasi-public, something to be shared with a larger community of those he regarded as learned and intelligent—and capable of providing quid pro quo, as he evidently hoped Valla could when he asked him for the *Hieroglyphica* of Horapollo "sive Aegyptiorum sacras sculpturas," the Hymns of Callimachus, the "Sphere of Ptolemy," and *glosemata in Platonem*, among other texts.[35] It was in much the same spirit that Poliziano and other humanist collectors inscribed their books as belonging to them "and their friends"—*et amicorum* or καὶ τῶν φίλων. The serious humanist's library not only mapped the intellectual territory he knew best but provided in its notes of acquisition and marginal annotations a record of the social and intellectual networks that sustained him.[36]

Certainly Pico used up much of his enormous patrimony on his books. He explicitly said that his cabalistic texts cost him a great deal.[37] Exactly how much money he spent as a collector, however, his letters and the other surviving documents do not tell us. But they reveal his willingness to expend something more precious than money: his own time. When Pico could not buy what he needed, he copied out or annotated whole texts in his own hand.[38] He also wrote out himself the drafts of his own works. The combination of books he finally possessed—handsome, custom-made humanistic manuscripts; printed books; and workaday manuscripts on paper of his own creation—comprised a typical large scholarly library of the time; it would still have been reasonably normal a century later.[39]

155–56, 208–9. This dainty, prettily illuminated manuscript was written, like Pico's Pliny, in Ferrara in 1481; it has long formed part of a set with two other manuscripts of the same tiny, portable format, which bear the same arms and similar decorations in the Ferrarese style, a Catullus (Staatsbibliothek zu Berlin, Haus 1, Diez B Sant. 56) and a Tibullus (Staatsbibliothek zu Berlin, Haus 2, Diez B Sant. 58). The scribe who wrote the latter was one of the two scribes who wrote the Propertius. See U. Winter, *Die europäischen Handschriften der Bibliothek Diez* (Leipzig, 1986), 62–65. The three may well be a coherent piece of Pico's library: his pocket-size collection of light reading.

35. Heiberg, *Beiträge zur Geschichte Georg Valla's*, 61; see also the brief discussion by G. Forlini, "Una lettera di Giovanni Pico all'umanista piacentino Giorgio Valla," *Atti e Memorie della deputazione di storia patria per le antiche provincie Modenesi*, ser. 9, 4–5 (1964–65): 315–18.

36. E. Ph. Goldschmidt, *Hieronymus Münzer und seine Bibliothek* (London, 1938).

37. Pico, *Discorso*, ed. Tognon, 56: "Hos ego libros non mediocri impensa mihi cum comparassem . . ."

38. For a case in point see Biblioteca Apostolica Vaticana, MS Ottob. lat. 607. On this see C. Wirszubski, "Giovanni Pico's Book of Job," *Journal of the Warburg and Courtauld Institutes* 32 (1969), 171–99; and H. Reinhardt, *Freiheit zu Gott* (Weinheim, 1989), 152–58.

39. A. Grafton, "L'umanista come lettore," in *Storia della lettura*, ed. G. Cavallo and R. Chartier (Rome and Bari, 1995), 199–242.

Over time, Pico's tastes and standards as a copyist seem to have changed in one revealing way. When very young, according to his nephew, Pico wrote "pulcherrimos literarum characteres" (very prettily formed letters). As he grew older, however, his passion to set his ideas down as quickly as possible grew, and he wrote so rapidly that his scripts became notoriously hard to decipher.[40] In 1485 Elia del Medigo, replying to a letter on philosophical questions, complained that "I find it harder to read your blessed letters than to answer them."[41] By the end of his life the change in Pico's taste had become manifest. A scribal copy of his late *De ente et uno,* for example, presented the text in a large, symmetrical humanist script, with many titles and marginal summaries in the text to direct the reader. But when Pico decided to fill a lacuna and to add a long note on debates among recent Platonists, he scrawled the new material almost illegibly.[42] The substantive need to master and record every possibly relevant bit of textual detail outweighed aesthetic considerations. Gradually, it seems, Pico came to regard the books he himself wrote as instrumental rather than ornamental. This turn in his practice as a scribe was eventually mirrored by his practice as a reader.

Further evidence shows that Pico frequented the official libraries of his day, public and princely, as well as his own and other private collections. The first loan registers of the Vatican show him borrowing—and returning—Henry Bate and Roger Bacon, along with the chains that held the books to the benches (a subtle reminder that the books in question must be given back).[43] In Florence conditions were even better. Leoniceno reported that Lorenzo hoped to bankrupt himself providing rare books for Pico and Poliziano to work on (and he certainly did send Janus Lascaris on long and expensive fishing expeditions through Italy and Greece itself, on the trail of Greek texts). The Medici family library, whose rarities Poliziano described

---

40. G.F. Pico, *Vita,* in Pico, *Opera,* 1:*5 recto; cf. Pico, *De hominis dignitate,* ed. Garin, 52–54.

41. Pico, *De hominis dignitate,* ed. Garin, 67–72, at 67: "è a me più difficile de leggiere le vostre lettere benedette che non è a dare le risposte."

42. Staatsbibliothek zu Berlin, Haus 1, MS Hamilton 438, fols. 27 recto (lacuna) and 7 recto (addition). On Pico's additions to the text see E. Garin in *Giornale Critico di filosofia italiana* 36 (1957), 130; and Garin, *La cultura filosofica del rinascimento italiano* (Florence, 1961), 278–79. For the MS itself see H. Boese, *Die lateinischen Handschriften der Sammlung Hamilton zu Berlin* (Wiesbaden, 1966), 209–10.

43. M. Bertola, *I primi due registri di prestito della Biblioteca Apostolica Vaticana* (Vatican City, 1942), 79–80. Pico's last borrowing, which he evidently returned at once, having lost his privileges, was the *Speculum naturalium* of Henry Bate.

with fierce pride, was thus formed in part to serve Pico's projects.[44] The San
Marco library also lay open to him, offering rare texts and pleasant sur-
roundings for intellectual debate. Pietro Crinito vividly portrays Pico and
others disputing, joking, and laying out their heartfelt beliefs: "Pico and
Poliziano conversed in the library of San Marco about certain heretics and
their methods and opinions and about the extraordinary learning shown by
Augustine in examining, refuting, and expunging their mistakes."[45] The
conversation soon turned from the theological to the technical, as the two
men tried to determine the identity of certain priests called Sarabaitae whom
Augustine had mentioned. On another occasion, to which I will return later
in this chapter, Pico argued with Savonarola in the same library about the
value of the classics; on yet another, he gave Crinito his opinions on the
prose style of the Latin classics.[46] The exiled prince thus led a comfortable,
bookish existence, one in which benches loaded with well-chosen books
provided the setting for social as well as intellectual life.

Pico, finally, looked as widely for aids in reading as he did for the texts
themselves. He traveled the margins of his texts as indefatigably as he did
the roads of Italy, reading and recording commentaries ancient and modern.
Whenever it proved necessary, he drew on expert advice. Elia del Medigo
introduced Pico to the Averroistic tradition of commentary on Aristotle,
which assumed that "The sayings of Aristotle and Averroës are of such a
character that they do not include a single syllable which lacks a clear
justification."[47] Ficino provided Pico with his own neoplatonic commentaries on Plato and some of their late antique sources. Flavius Mithridates—
the same man who gave the Good Friday sermon in the Vatican a few years
before Pico arrived in Rome—worked with Pico for years, teaching him ori-

44. N. Leoniceno to A. Poliziano, n.d.; Poliziano *Ep.* 2.7, in *Opera*, 1:21: "Audivi, te re-
ferente, vocem illam praeclaram ex Laurentii ore prodiisse, optare tanta sibi abs te ac Pico nostro ad libros emendos praestari incitamenta, ut tandem deficientibus sumptibus, totam supellectilem oppignerare cogatur." See the full accounts in V. Branca, *Poliziano e l'umanesimo
della parola* (Turin, 1983), chap. 7 and S. Gentile, "Pico e la biblioteca Medicea privata," in
Viti, *Catalogo,* 85–101.

45. Crinito *De honesta disciplina* 3.15 (1504), sigs. C verso–C2 recto, at C verso = ed.
Angeleri, 118–19, at 118: "Sermo habitus est in Marciana bibliotheca a Pico Mirandula et Poli-
tiano de quibusdam haereticis eorumque disciplinis atque opinionibus, tum de Augustini egre-
gia et singulari doctrina in examinandis, refellendis atque eiiciendis illorum erroribus, qui
Christianorum mentes, veluti proserpens hedera, facile implicant. Inter alia vero complura
quaesitum est quinam forent Sarabaytae sacerdotes, quoniam in Augustini epistola mentio de
his obiter facta sit."

46. Ibid., 3.2 (1504), sigs. [bv recto–bvi recto] = ed. Angeleri, 104–5; 8.3 (1504), sigs. [eviii]
verso–f recto = ed. Angeleri, 199–200.

47. Pico, *De hominis dignitate*, ed. Garin, 67: "i dicti d'Aristotele et d'Averois sono di tal
sorta che non è in quelli pure una sillaba sença chagione e documento."

ental languages and translating Jewish biblical commentaries and Talmudic passages for him. Some of the results of their work remain, in the form of a group of closely written manuscripts in the Vatican, brilliantly studied by Wirszubski. These studies provided Pico and his readers with the first details of the Cabala ever to become available in a Western language. He paid well for them, evidently providing Flavius not only with cash but with a *na'ar yafeh* (beautiful boy) to ensure his continued collaboration.

The treasures of Pico's library included pyrites as well as gold, and those who provided his books and methods were not equally honest brokers for the ancient wisdom. In a famous letter to Ficino, Pico declared that he was happy to return the latter's copy of the Koran in Latin, since he had learned Hebrew in a month of hard work and was now at work on Arabic and Chaldean; he could read Muhammad in the original. He had been inspired, he explained, by the acquisition of certain books in both languages that "came into my hands not by chance but by God's decision and by that of a divinity that favors my studies." The Chaldean books, in particular, sounded enticing: they included the oracles of Zoroaster and Melchior, with the whole mystical theology of the ancient priests of Babylon—bizarre and unidentifiable texts that Pico quoted, to the bafflement of all modern editors until recent times, in the *Oratio de hominis dignitate*. Like all serious collectors, in short, Pico believed that the acquisition of specially important books had a providential quality. The serious reader would let his library guide his research—at least when it contained *thesauri* (treasures) rather than mere *libri*.[48] In a second letter of November 1486, addressed to an unidentified scholar, Pico explained that his teacher Mithridates would not let him provide even an alphabet for the mysterious Chaldean language: "For he was unwilling to teach me the Chaldean language on any account unless I first swore a formal oath not to teach it to anyone else. Girolamo Benivieni can confirm this to you. He was present by chance when Mithridates was teaching me, and Mithridates flew into a rage and threw the man out."[49]

---

48. Pico, *Opera*, 1:367: "Animarunt autem me, atque adeo agentem alia vi compulerunt ad Arabum literas Chaldaeorumque perdiscendas, libri quidam utriusque linguae, qui profecto non temere aut fortuito, sed Dei consilio et meis studiis bene faventis numinis, ad meas manus pervenerunt. Audi inscriptiones, vadimonium deseres: Chaldaici hi libri sunt, si libri sunt, et non thesauri."

49. Ibid., 1:385–86: "Alphabetum Chaldaicum quod petis, nec a Mithridate impetrasses, nihil per illum licet ut a me impetrare possis, a quo posses omnia. Nam ille docere me Chaldaicam linguam nulla voluit ratione nisi adiuratum prius, et quidem conceptis verbis, ne illam cuiquam traderem: facere fidem huius rei tibi potest noster Hieronymus Benivenius, qui cum adesset forte dum me ille docebat, furens Mithridates hominem eliminavit."

Mithridates had good reason not to let Pico reveal his secret lessons. What he taught was neither the language of ancient Babylon nor the one usually called Chaldean in early modern Europe—Aramaic, the language of the Talmud and the biblical Targumim. Rather, as Wirszubski has shown, Mithridates taught Pico an imaginary language of his own invention: a mixture of Hebrew and Aramaic that he wrote, and taught Pico to write, in Ethiopian script. The Chaldean texts presumably also came from Mithridates' private stock. One fears that his desire for profits, rather than divine benevolence, brought them into Pico's eager hands.

On the whole, however, Pico's reading was an enormous success. He did learn Hebrew, some Arabic, and a great deal of Greek. He mastered the whole ancient corpus, especially that of philosophy and science, never ceasing to work and always keeping an open mind. In his twenties, for example, he saw the Aristotelian natural philosophy of the universities as the key to understanding the physical world. Franz Burchard, who answered Pico's famous letter to Barbaro two generations later, complained that Pico and the scholastic philosophers he defended had apparently ignored the profoundity of Greek mathematics and natural science.[50] By 1493–94, when Pico worked on his attack on the astrologers, he had realized that Aristotle and his many commentators could not instruct him about the heavens. The science of their stars and their movements was necessarily quantitative, and one could learn it only from the astronomers of Greece and Islam. Accordingly Pico worked his way through Ptolemy's *Almagest,* Proclus' *Hypotyposis,* and a vast amount of less rewarding technical material, from astrological treatises to astronomical tables. As we shall see, he studied these hard texts critically as well as comprehensively.

Similarly, the Jews with whom Pico discussed textual questions did not confine themselves to misrepresenting the Talmud. They covered a wide range of theological and cosmological questions, on which Pico had much to teach, as well as to learn from, the Cabalists. He evidently provided Jewish friends with rich information about the works of Porphyry and others, previously inaccessible to them. Pico thus had an impact of his own on Jewish, as well as Christian, Cabala. But Jews also taught this Christian fellow traveler some basic lessons about historical criticism. They showed him that the Hebrew *Yosippon* was a late reworking, not the original source, of the real Greek writings of Josephus—a fact that would be forgotten at once, only to be recovered independently by Joseph Scaliger and others more than

---

50. For the Latin text of Burchard's reply to Pico, see *Corpus Reformatorum,* 9, cols. 687–703; cf. E. Rummel, *The Humanist-Scholastic Debate in the Renaissance and Reformation* (Cambridge, Mass., 1995), 147–51.

a century later. This example of Jewish criticism, not that of Christian humanist scholarship, seems to have inspired Pico when he questioned the authenticity of the *Testimonium Flavianum,* a passage about Jesus supposedly preserved by (but actually interpolated into) Josephus.[51] In this case too it took scholars more than a century to regain Pico's level of critical insight.

Even in his twenties, Pico brought an impressive range of skills and questions to the interpretation of texts. One of his earliest letters, to Lorenzo de' Medici, is an exercise in comparative criticism in the humanist style. Pico compares Lorenzo's Italian poems to those of the "two famous Florentine poets," Dante and Petrarch; he argues that Lorenzo surpasses both of his models. Naturally, this evaluation may reflect Pico's desire to pass a courtly compliment. But the bulk of his letter offers a detailed analysis of Lorenzo's style that would do credit to any humanist analyzing a classical text, and many of his comments are just as well as witty (for example, his nasty but perceptive remark that he found some of Petrarch's verse as devoid of content as "Epicuri . . . vacuum").[52] Evidently Pico, like Valla and other humanists, treated content and style as of equal importance in the evaluation of poetic texts. Beroaldo's testimony shows that he did not hesitate to study and emend these texts even as he read them for pleasure.

In his famous letter to Ermolao Barbaro, however, Pico took exactly the opposite point of view, defending the scholastic philosophers against the charge that their barbarous style disqualified them as thinkers. In this extended polemic, written only a year after the letter to Lorenzo, Pico brilliantly used arguments and metaphors from the Platonic tradition to defend the hideous Latin of the medieval Aristotelians. The ancients, by his account, deliberately expressed their ideas in enigmatic or mythical form to keep them secret from "idiotas homines"—exactly the argument that

---

51. Pico, *Opera,* 1:385: "Quod petis de Iosepho, scias iustum Iosephum apud Hebraeos non reperiri, sed Iosephi epitoma, id est, breviarium quoddam, in quo et multa sunt commentitia, et quae de decem tribubus ibi leguntur, quae post babylonicam captivitatem postliminio non redierunt, ea esse notha et adulterina ex Hebraeis mihi plures confessi sunt, quapropter illorum Iosepho nulla omnino fides adhibenda. In Iosepho Graeco scio esse quaedam quae de Christo et fidem [fidelem?] et honorificam faciant mentionem, sed eadem esse penitus cum his quae in Latinis codicibus leguntur, non assererem nisi exemplar Graecum, cuius hic mihi nulla est copia, recens legerem." For what Pico had to offer his Jewish interlocutors see M. Idel, "The Magical and Neoplatonic Interpretations of the Kabbalah in the Renaissance," in *Jewish Thought in the Sixteenth Century,* ed. B.D. Cooperman (Cambridge, Mass., 1983), 186–242, also published in *Essential Articles on Jewish Culture in Renaissance and Baroque Italy,* ed. D.B. Ruderman (New York and London, 1992), 107–69; and A.M. Lesley, "Proverbs, Figures, and Riddles: The *Dialogues of Love* as a Hebrew Humanist Composition," in *The Midrashic Imagination: Jewish Exegesis, Thought, and History,* ed. M. Fishbane (Albany, 1993), 204–25.

52. For text and translation see *Prosatori latini del Quattrocento,* ed. E. Garin (Milan and Naples, 1952), 796–805.

Proclus used in his commentary on the *Respublica* to defend Homer from Plato's criticisms. Similarly, Pico explained, the modern philosophers have deliberately and rightly hidden their views from the people: "We have not written for the ordinary public, but for you and others like you."[53] Plato's *Symposium* supplied the model of interpretation that Pico offered for such texts, one that took the form not of an argument but of an image: "Shall I give you an image of our sort of speech? It is the very same as that of the Sileni described by Alcibiades. For their images looked rough, foul, and contemptible, but inside they were full of gems, of a rare and precious stock. Thus if you look at the outside, you will see a beast; if you look inwards, you will recognize a god."[54] Pico here transformed Alcibiades' vision of his teacher, Socrates, with his ugly face and splendid soul, into a metaphor for the most important kind of writing. In doing so he denigrated style to the level of a mere appearance and exalted content to the level of the ideal. To defend what the humanists described as the ugly and the trivial writings of the scholastics, Pico appropriated a central argument of the late antique neoplatonists. They had tried to penetrate the troubling surface of Homer's epics, which Plato had condemned, in the hope of finding a powerful and acceptable message beneath it. They had interpreted the apparently raw emotions and immoral actions of Homer's gods as clues to the higher meaning of the passages in question: the uglier the manifest content of a given passage, the more sublime its hidden, higher sense. Pico neatly transformed Proclus' defense of ethically unacceptable behavior into a defense of grammatically unacceptable language. This side of his hermeneutics proved influential. Twenty years later, Erasmus incorporated Pico's vision of insightful reading into his *Adagia*, where he used it to describe the proper way to read and find the deep, rich sense of the simple, apparently inelegant texts of the New Testament.[55] In this revised form Pico's vision reached and influenced a vast reading public. What interests us now, however, is the sharp contrast between this vision of reading—exalted in tone and disdainful of verbal detail—and the rhetorical one of Pico's letter to Lorenzo. Like

---

53. For text and translation see ibid., 804–23, here 812: "Vulgo non scripsimus, sed tibi et tui similibus. Nec aliter quam prisci suis aenigmatis et fabularum involucris arcebant idiotas homines a mysteriis, et nos consuevimus absterrere illos a nostris dapibus, quas non polluere non possent, amariori paulum cortice verborum."

54. Ibid., 812: "Sed vis effingam ideam sermonis nostri? Ea est ipsissima, quae Silenorum nostri Alcibiadis. Erant enim horum simulacra hispido ore, tetro et aspernabili, sed intus plena gemmarum, supellectilis rarae et pretiosae. Ita extrinsecus si aspexeris, feram videas, si introspexeris numen agnoscas."

55. Erasmus *Adagia* 3.3.1, in Erasmus, *Opera omnia*, ed. J. Leclerc (Leiden, 1703–6), 2: cols. 770c–782c. Cf. E. Wind, *Pagan Mysteries in the Renaissance*, 2d ed. (London, 1968).

Erasmus—who praised and practiced both grammatical and allegorical interpretations—Pico could choose his tools as the text and the occasion seemed to dictate.

In what remained of Pico's short, frenetic life after 1487, he produced several powerful new interpretations of ancient texts—the *Heptaplus,* a sevenfold commentary on the Creation story in Genesis; the fragmentary but fascinating commentaries on the Psalms; and the *De ente et uno,* with its brilliant, unsuccessful effort to reduce Plato's *Parmenides* to a dialectical exercise.[56] But none of these rivals in scale or originality the great book that he left unfinished: the attack on divinatory astrology that was published, from a difficult and partly illegible manuscript, now lost, two years after Pico died (in 1494, as the astrologers had predicted).[57] It is not surprising that this text has received far less attention than Pico's other works. The *Disputationes* deals with a complex and unattractive subject in an unremittingly technical and rigorous way. The range of sources Pico deploys is frighteningly broad. His style is often rough: the book lacks transitions, citations, and a conclusion, as well as shorter passages. Pico's nephew Gianfrancesco and Giovanni Mainardi, who prepared the text for publication, found the task very hard and sometimes had to divine, rather than just reproduce, Pico's views.[58] Still, scholars as diverse as Cassirer, Garin, Walker, and Zambelli have found in the *Disputationes* a work of great originality and interest. The subject of astrology forced Pico to mobilize the whole range of weapons and tactics with which he attacked any serious subject. The opinions of his friends, the interpretations of commentators on Plato, Aristotle, and Ptolemy, and the theses of dozens of astrologers and their critics mingled and fused with Pico's own vision of the world to create something at least as original as it is difficult.[59]

---

56. For contrasting treatments see the classic study of R. Klibansky, "Plato's *Parmenides* in the Middle Ages and the Renaissance," *Mediaeval and Renaissance Studies* 1 (1943): 281–330; and M.J.B. Allen, *Icastes: Marsilio Ficino's Interpretation of Plato's Sophist* (Berkeley, Los Angeles, and Oxford, 1989). See also Allen, "The Second Ficino-Pico Controversy: Parmenidean Poetry, Eristic, and the One," in *Marsilio Ficino e il ritorno di Platone,* ed. G.C. Garfagnini (Florence, 1986), 417–55.

57. G. Pico della Mirandola, *Disputationes adversus astrologiam divinatricem,* ed. E. Garin (Florence, 1946–52).

58. See P. Zambelli, *L'ambigua natura della magia* (Milan, 1991), 81, 87–89. Such pathetic editorial professions about authors' manuscripts rapidly became a topos of early print culture—and often have a fictional, or at least a highly creative, component. See L. Jardine, *Erasmus, Man of Letters* (Princeton, 1993), chaps. 3–4; and S. Lerer, *Chaucer and His Readers* (Princeton, 1993).

59. See E. Cassirer, *The Individual and the Cosmos in Renaissance Philosophy,* trans. M. Domandi (New York and Evanston, 1963), 115–20; E. Garin, *Lo zodiaco della vita,* 2d ed. (Bari, 1982); and D.P. Walker, *Spiritual and Demonic Magic from Ficino to Campanella* (London, 1958).

Large segments of Pico's text rest on foundations taken directly from older writers. Ancient writers with great authority (but little knowledge of astrology)—Cicero, Gellius, and Augustine—attacked what they saw as inconsistencies and errors in astrological theory and practice. Most of their arguments—like Augustine's famous one about twins—did not reflect what astrologers really thought and did.[60] Nonetheless Pico embroidered on such traditional complaints as the one that astrologers, to work scientifically, would have to know the exact instant of their client's birth (or even conception). Late medieval philosophers, above all Henry of Hesse and Nicole Oresme, had mounted a more sophisticated attack. They cited, among other arguments, the fact that specific astrological configurations recurred only after intervals of thousands of years; hence it would take hundreds of thousands of years to create a real science based on these configurations—if indeed they proved to be congruent to one another at all.[61] Pico rehearsed this and other objections with respect and interest.

In a sense, however, the sharpest critical tools Pico had came to him from within the tradition of classical astrology. Ptolemy, the greatest ancient astronomer, also wrote the most critical and profound treatment of ancient astrology. He admitted that astrology, which dealt not only with the perfect, unchanging heavens but also with their influence on imperfect and chaotic matter, must be far more incomplete and imprecise than astronomy, which dealt only with the skies. And he condemned many specific astrological doctrines of his day as foolish. Pico praised Ptolemy as the wisest of that pack of fools, the astrologers. To refute the "Egyptian" doctrine that each degree of the zodiac, or *monomoeria,* had a special power, Pico simply cited Ptolemy's verdict that "These matters . . . have only plausible and not natural, but, rather, unfounded arguments in their favour."[62] His own theory that the stars influenced the earth not in precise and limited ways, through the conjunctions and oppositions of individual planets, but by the general, beneficent influence of the sun and moon probably represents an effort to correct Ptolemy by taking the hints he himself offered.[63] Pico offered his readers not a denial of all astrology but an astrology pruned of superstition.

60. A full account of ancient discussions of astrology is given by A. Bouché-Leclercq, *L'astrologie grecque* (Paris, 1899; repr. Brussels, 1963), chap. 16; the arguments of both critics and defenders are helpfully analyzed by A.A. Long in "Astrology: Arguments for and Against," in *Science and Speculation,* ed. J. Barnes et al. (Cambridge and Paris, 1982), 165–93.

61. Cf. the argument of Favorinus in Gellius at *Noctes atticae* 14.1.14–18.

62. Ptolemy *Tetrabiblos* (trans. Robbins) 1.22 cited by Pico, *Disputationes,* ed. Garin, 2:128 (6.16).

63. For Ptolemy see Long, "Astrology," 178–83; for Pico see Walker, *Spiritual and Demonic Magic.*

An austere and classical art would replace the Gothic clutter of later medieval astrology.

The stars haunted the intellectuals of Medicean Florence. Ficino believed that Saturn persecuted him and other gifted men of melancholy temperament. He timed the publication of his version of Plato to an astrologically propitious year, 1484;[64] he even blamed his failures to visit Pico on the fact that Saturn was in the lower, retrograde arc of its epicycle and thus pushed him back when he tried to walk to Pico's house.[65] Ficino also wrote at length on the art of making talismans and composing music that could draw down the beneficent influence of other planets. Paolo Toscanelli cast the horoscope of Florence itself; Pico found two such horoscopes—set on what he took as two different dates, one year apart—among Toscanelli's papers.[66] Even the luminous Leon Battista Alberti, who hated magic and superstition, believed that one should begin buildings at astrologically correct times—a powerful example that Pico's opponent, the Sienese astrologer Luca Bellanti, cited against him.[67] Colorful horoscopes bloomed on the ceilings of churches and the walls of palaces, and Lorenzo himself followed Alberti, not Pico, when he took astrological advice in choosing the time to begin his country house. Like modern economists, Renaissance astrologers provided the only assurance their clients could have about the future: predictions based on what resembled quantitative, rigorous scientific laws. Again like the economists, they were always wrong and still drew higher salaries than anyone else after their mistakes were exposed. It seems a pity that Pico did not live to 1524, when every astrologer in Europe wrongly predicted that a universal deluge would take place in that very year, following a great conjunction of the planets in the watery sign of Pisces—and not one foresaw the Peasants' Revolt of 1525. He could have shared his amusement with Martin Luther and Francesco Guicciardini—two of the rare Renaissance intellectuals who, like Pico, regarded astrology with informed contempt as well as amazed fascination.[68]

---

64. J. Hankins, *Plato in the Italian Renaissance* (Leiden, 1990), 1:302–4.

65. See R. Klibansky, E. Panofsky, and F. Saxl, *Saturne et la Mélancholie*, trans. F. Durand-Bogaert et al. (Paris, 1989), 405–32.

66. Pico, *Disputationes*, ed. Garin, 2:310 (9.6).

67. Alberti *De re aedificatoria* 2.13. See L. Bellanti, *Astrologiae defensio contra Ioannem Picum Mirandulanum*, in *De astrologica veritate liber quaestionum* (Basel, 1554), 171.

68. For Guicciardini see *I Guicciardini e le scienze occulte*, ed. R. Castagnola (Florence, 1990); for Luther see R. Barnes, *Prophecy and Gnosis* (Stanford, 1988). On the flood of 1524 see P. Zambelli, "Fine del mondo o inizio della propaganda? Astrologia, filosofia della storia e propaganda politico-religiosa nel dibattito sulla congiunzione del 1524," in *Scienze, credenze occulte, livelli di cultura* (Florence, 1982), 291–368; for an interesting discussion of the different ways in which the prediction was appropriated and contested see O. Niccoli, *Prophecy and*

Pico's attack on astrology, in short, was genuinely iconoclastic. But its philosophical sections were not drastically innovative. In rehearsing the inconsistencies of astrology, he drew on classical, late antique, and medieval sources (notably Cicero and Augustine). In insisting that the human soul could not be constrained by material objects, he merely stated an implication of the doctrine of complete human freedom that he had framed in the 1480s—a doctrine that was, as he himself had then failed to see, incompatible with any belief in astrological determination. In principle, Ficino and many other astrologers would have agreed: almost all admitted that a wise man should be able to rule the stars. When Pico framed his general attack on astrology in terms of the failure of the art to pass the twin tests of *ratio* and *experientia,* reason and experience, finally, he followed well-established Aristotelian lines, as Brian Vickers has recently shown in detail.[69]

The last two books of the *Disputationes,* however, and those earlier sections that lead up to them directly, are very innovative indeed. Here, as Garin pointed out long ago, Pico undertook something radically new—something without a counterpart in the long history of attacks on the astrologers' pretensions. He wrote a critical history of their art—one that undermined several deeply rooted and widely shared assumptions, not only about astrology, but about the whole history of human culture.[70] One of the first histories of any art to be written in the Renaissance, Pico's analysis was considerably more original in form, more precise in analysis, and more solid

People in Renaissance Italy, trans. L.G. Cochrane (Princeton, 1990), chap. 6; cf. more generally *"Astrologi hallucinati": Stars and the End of the World in Luther's Time*, ed. P. Zambelli (Berlin and New York, 1986). A. Warburg, *Heidnisch-antike Weissagung in Wort und Bild zu Luthers Zeiten*, SB Heidelberg, Phil.-hist. Klasse, 1919 (Heidelberg, 1920), remains fundamental.

69. B. Vickers, "Critical Reactions to the Occult Sciences during the Renaissance," in *The Scientific Enterprise: The Bar-Hillel Colloquium,* ed. E. Ullmann-Margalit (Dordrecht, 1992), 43–92.

70. The fullest treatments known to me—G. Zanier, "Struttura e significato delle 'Disputationes' pichiane," *Giornale critico della filosofia italiana* 1 (1981): 51–86; and the old but still fascinating diploma thesis of E. Weil, *Pic de la Mirandole et la critique de l'astrologie,* recently printed with his *La philosophie de Pietro Pomponazzi* (Paris, 1985)—do not do full justice to Pico as a philologist. The novelty of his reading emerges better from the brief but insightful remarks of H. de Lubac, *Pic de la Mirandole* (Paris, 1974)—better still from P. Rossi, "Considerazioni sul declino dell'astrologia agli inizi dell'età moderna," in *L'opera e il pensiero di Giovanni Pico della Mirandola,* 2:315–31; and E. Garin, *Lo zodiaco della vita,* 2d ed. (Rome and Bari, 1982), 100–102. Craven makes important critical points about the work of Cassirer and others, but his treatment—which ignores all technical matters—remains superficial. When he says that "only the most indulgent eye could see" Pico's work "as a significant step towards the historicizing of knowledge," (149) he reveals an attitude every bit as anachronistic as those of the earlier scholars whom he criticizes.

in substance than such better-known predecessors as the polemical histories of art and architecture written by Alberti and Ghiberti.

Since the Hellenistic period, astrology had claimed an ancient and distinguished lineage. Astrologers were called Chaldaei—"Chaldeans" or "Babylonians." Such men, though they normally spoke Greek, claimed to practice an ancient Near Eastern art—one created on the ziggurats of ancient Babylon by sages of immeasurable learning and wisdom. They represented this art as incredibly old: Cicero made fun of the Chaldaei in his day, who claimed to have studied the stars for some 470,000 years.[71] In the Renaissance, the claims Cicero ridiculed found far more acceptance than the arguments with which he attacked them. Everyone knew that astrology was both Eastern and venerable.

Philosophers as well as astrologers purveyed genealogies of wisdom in the fifteenth century. But these supported, rather than undermined, the astrologers' boasts. Diogenes Laertius had begun his history of philosophy with an attack on the view—evidently a popular one—that the barbarians had created philosophy. Almost all Renaissance philosophers felt compelled to take a position on the problem. Pletho, the sage from Mistra who created so deep an impression on the Italians he met in 1438–39, brought with him to Italy not only the so-called *Oracula Chaldaica* and his commentary on it but also a larger historical argument. The best philosophy was that professed in ancient times by Plato. And that philosophy, Pletho explained, "was not original with [Plato] but was derived from Zoroaster via the Pythagoreans . . . that Plato shared this doctrine is shown by the oracles of Zoroaster that are still extant, which agree completely with Plato's teachings." Zoroaster, in turn, had written his oracles five thousand years before the Trojan War and thus more than six thousand years before the beginning of the Christian Era. The Platonic tradition, in short, was in its origins not Greek but barbarian—and therefore, paradoxically, all the more profound.[72] Ficino, who early in his career began to meditate on the barbarian origins of wisdom, admired the *Corpus Hermeticum* and knew from Plato's *Timaeus* and *Critias* that the Egyptians had claimed great antiquity for their teachings. But he also found the age and profundity of Zoroaster's teachings impressive. Eventually he placed Zoroaster, Hermes, and Orpheus at the

---

71. *De divinatione* 2.97; on the prevalence and importance of such claims cf. Bouché-Leclercq, *L'astrologie grecque*, 38–39.

72. For the texts of Pletho's discussions of the Persian tradition see J. Bidez and F. Cumont, *Les mages hellénisés* (Paris, 1938; repr., 1973), 2:251–59; cf. M.V. Anastos, "Pletho's Calendar and Liturgy," *Dumbarton Oaks Papers* 4 (1948): 279–89.

beginnings of three traditions of the "prisca gentilium theologia," one each for the three continents of Asia, Africa, and Europe.[73]

Two points are crucial. First, Ficino and others assumed that the Egyptian and Babylonian wisdom they celebrated included at least some of the astrological doctrines that fascinated them. Ficino's *Libri de vita,* for example, jumble together astrological images and practices, the *Corpus Hermeticum* and the *Oracula Chaldaica,* and the genuine extant texts of such neoplatonists as Porphyry and Iamblichus. He treated all of these *disiecta membra* as the organic parts of a single, living tradition that had begun in the time of Moses or before, in Egypt, Mesopotamia, and Persia. Alberti had scoffed at the animated statues of the Hermetic *Asclepius.* These images, into which the Egyptians had drawn down by their "illicia" celestial *daemones,* were to Ficino proof of the efficacy of ancient Near Eastern magic; they formed part of the filter through which he read the dialogues of Plato.[74]

Second, Pico evidently subscribed, through the first part of his career, to

---

73. Sometimes Ficino simply followed patristic precedent and identified his Near Eastern sages with Hebrew patriarchs; see the interesting passage in his *Théologie Platonicienne de l'immortalité des Ames,* ed. R. Marcel (Paris, 1964–70), 3:183 (18.1), where he explains of Hermes Trismegistus' views on the Creation that "Neque mirum videri debet hunc talia cognovisse, si homo idem Mercurius fuit atque Moyses, quod Artapanus historicus coniecturis multis ostendit [ap. Eus. *PE* 9.37]." Sometimes he attributed a clearly separate revelation to certain pagan sages. See generally D.P. Walker, *The Ancient Theology* (London, 1972). M.J.B. Allen, "Marsilio Ficino, Hermes Trismegistus, and the *Corpus Hermeticum,*" in *New Perspectives on Renaissance Thought. Essays in the History of Science, Education, and Philosophy in Memory of Charles B. Schmitt,* ed. J. Henry and S. Hutton (London, 1990), 38–47, argues that between 1463 and 1469 Ficino substituted Zoroaster for Hermes at the start of his genealogy of wisdom, perhaps after encountering Pletho's views. For a critique of Allen's thesis see Zambelli, *L'ambigua natura della magia.* I follow here Allen, "Ficino"; and Hankins, *Plato,* 2:460–64.

74. For Ficino's views on these statues see especially his *Three Books on Life,* ed. and trans. C.V. Kaske and J.R. Clark (Binghamton, 1989), 388, with the editors' important textual and exegetical notes. He does say (not quite accurately) that Iamblichus had criticized the Egyptians for worshiping the statues; like other features of the passage, this reveals the uneasiness that mingled with fascination in Ficino's view of the *prisca philosophia.* For another conflation of Near Eastern and Greek discussions of idol magic, which makes the priority of the Eastern sages clear, see Ficino's commentary on the *Cratylus,* in *Opera,* 1309 = *Opera omnia,* ed. Sancipriano, 2:305: "Et quemadmodum ab initio docuit Mercurius Trismegistus, ac diu postea Plotinus et Iamblichus, statuis quibusdam ordine certo compositis, daemones quodammodo includuntur." A delicate effort to explicate Ficino's attitudes toward such practices—especially his effort to show that Hermes shared his disapproval of them—is made by B.P. Copenhaver in a fascinating essay, "Lorenzo de' Medici, Marsilio Ficino, and the Domesticated Hermes," in *Lorenzo il Magnifico e il suo mondo,* ed. G.C. Garfagnini (Florence, 1994), 225–57. On the presuppositions that underlay such genealogies of wisdom see W. Schmidt-Biggemann, "Philosophia perennis im Spätmittelalter: Eine Skizze," in *Innovation und Originalität [Fortuna vitrea, 9],* ed. W. Haug and B. Wachinger (Tübingen, 1993), 14–34. On Pico's relations with Ficino, see esp. S. Gentile, "Pico e Ficino," in Viti, *Catalogo,* 127–47.

this whole complex of beliefs. In the *Oratio*, for example, he celebrated the "secretiorem philosophiam et barbarorum mysteria" of Iamblichus and the "prisca theologia" of Hermes. He made clear that the Greeks derived their wisdom from the profound philosophy of the barbarous East. "Everyone," he says at one point, "who knows himself, knows everything in himself, as Zoroaster wrote first, and then Plato in the *Alcibiades*"; the chronology suggests the dependence of the Greek sage on the Persian.[75] "All wisdom," he says elsewhere, "passed from the barbarians to the Greeks, and from the Greeks to us."[76] Furthermore, Pico identified the barbarian wisdom that passed westward in antiquity with astrology as well as theology and philosophy. Defending the practice of disputation, Pico insisted that the true philosopher must be ready to argue for his positions, to fight honorably "in hac quasi litteraria palestra." The Greeks had indicated this by representing Pallas as armed, the Hebrews by making iron the symbol of wisdom: "And perhaps that is why the Chaldeans held that at the birth of one who must become a philosopher, Mars should be in trine with [120° away from] Mercury, as though removing those meetings and conflicts would render philosophy entirely somnolent and comatose."[77] In juxtaposing his expert use of the technical vocabulary of astrology with his evocation of Chaldean wisdom, Pico showed that in 1486 he still probably revolved within Ficino's sphere.[78]

Eight years later everything had changed. In the *Disputationes* Pico returned to the study of Zoroaster, of ancient wisdom, and of the culture of the ancient Near East. But he treated all of them with disdain. True, the Chaldean astrologers claimed that they had studied the stars for millennia. But the technical evidence in Ptolemy's *Almagest* refuted them:

> When Hipparchus and Ptolemy, the founders of astronomy, produce the observations of the ancients to lay the foundation of their doctrine, they produce none older than those [made] in Babylon and Egypt

---

75. Pico, *Discorso*, ed. Tognon, 24: "Qui enim se cognoscit, in se omnia cognoscit, ut Zoroaster prius, deinde Plato in Alcibiade scripserunt."

76. Ibid., 40: "Quando omnis sapientia a Barbaris ad Graecos, a Graecis ad nos manavit."

77. Ibid., 34: "Quo forte fit ut et Caldei in eius genesi qui philosophus sit futurus, illud desiderent, ut Mars et Mercurium triquetro aspectu conspiciat, quasi, si hos congressus, haec bella substuleris, somniculosa et dormitans futura sit omnis philosophia."

78. As F. Roulier points out in his excellent analysis of Pico's opinions about astrology, here and elsewhere Pico is formally noncommittal. See *Jean Pic de la Mirandole (1463–1494), humaniste, philosophe et théologien* (Geneva, 1989), 298–320. But he also refrains from criticism and seems clearly to see the opinions he recites as those of Eastern sages whose other forms of wisdom he praises.

under King Nabuchodonosor [Nabonassar; accession date 26 February 747 B.C.]. Hipparchus flourished in around the six-hundredth year after his reign; from him to our time no more than about sixteen hundred years have passed. Their claim to have observations from so many centuries is therefore false and mendacious.[79]

Nineteenth- and twentieth-century studies of the cuneiform records, which show that scientific astronomy did not arise in Babylon until the middle centuries of the first millennium B.C., confirm Pico's precise chronology for the rise of science and support his crisp reconstruction of Ptolemy's lost sources.[80] The modern admirers of ancient wisdom dated Zoroaster thousands of years before the beginning of Greek history. But the reliable historian Pompeius Trogus began his account of human history with Ninus. Ninus fought Zoroaster, and yet he lived only a few years before the biblical patriarch Abraham, after the Flood and well within the normal, biblical account of the past: "This shows that those who write that Zoroaster flourished five thousand years before the Trojan War are fabulists."[81] Pico, in short, cut through the origin myths that had bewitched Platonists from late antiquity to his own day, and he reduced the barbarian sages to ordinary humans living within historical time. Their astrology was as recent as it was fallacious.

Pletho and Ficino had insisted on the oriental birth of Platonic wisdom because they revered the mysterious East. Pico admitted that one who wished to understand astrology had to understand the Eastern cultures that it sprang from. But his attitude was the opposite of admiring. The Egyptians and Chaldeans, he explained, had been ignorant and superstitious. True, they had been very pious, and their religious rites and doctrines had attracted such Greeks as Plato and Eudoxus to study with them. But they had not understood natural philosophy at all.[82]

---

79. Pico, *Disputationes*, ed. Garin, 2:476 (11.2): "Hipparchus et Ptolemaeus, principes astronomiae, ubi pro dogmate statuendo veterum observationes afferunt, nullas afferunt ipsi vetustiores his quae sub rege Nabuchodonosor apud Aegyptios Babyloniosve fuere, post cuius regnum sexcentesimo fere anno floruit Hipparchus, a quo ad nostra haec usque tempora anni non plus mille sexcentis aut circiter fluxerunt. Mendaciter igitur et fabulose tot saeculorum habere se iactant observationes; eas vero quas habent necessario esse falsas, ita facile demonstratur."

80. See O. Neugebauer, *A History of Ancient Mathematical Astronomy* (New York, 1975).

81. Pico, *Disputationes*, ed. Garin, 2:474–76 (11.2): "Unde fabulosi deprehenduntur qui Zoroastrem scribunt quinque milibus annorum ante troianum bellum claruisse."

82. Ibid., e.g., 2:492 (12.2): "Fuerunt igitur Aegyptii atque Chaldaei, quantum equidem assequor coniectura, parum facto ad sapientiam ingenio"; 2:498–505 (12.3).

Pico accepted that the Near Easterners had been adept at one set of arts: the mathematical ones. But their mastery of this one, limited set of intellectual tools had actually done more harm than good. It had deceived them into thinking they possessed in mathematics the key to all the secrets of the universe—a fallacy that all experts in one science tend to commit:

> All those who have immersed themselves in a single discipline tend to be eager to use it to explain everything. This is less from ambition, so that they may appear to know everything, than because they think it true. What happens to them resembles what happens to those who travel through a snowstorm. Everything else seems white to them, since the *habitus* of whiteness, once absorbed into the eyes, transforms everything into itself. Thus to those who love passionately, anything they come across reminds them either of their beloved's face or of some quality of hers. The lover's entire imaginative faculty is dominated by a single image. The theologian who is only a theologian refers everything to divine causes; the doctor to the *habitus* of the body; the natural philosopher to the natural principles of the universe; the mathematician to figures and numbers, as the Pythagoreans always did. Thus, since the Chaldeans worked so hard at measuring the motions of the heavenly bodies and observing the paths of the stars and occupied their intellects with nothing more than that, they saw everything as the stars; that is, they found it natural to explain everything by the stars. The same may be taken to hold equally for the Egyptians.[83]

Astrology did come down from the Near East. But this origin proved its puerility, not its profundity. It was merely one of the many superstitions that had insinuated themselves into the credulous minds of the genuinely barbarous sages of Babylon and Egypt; the great Greek philosophers, from

---

83. Ibid., 2:498–500 (12.3): "Solent quicumque in aliquam disciplinam se totos ingurgitarunt, omnia ad illam referre quam libentissime, non tam propter ambitionem, ut scire per illam omnia videantur, quam quod ita illis videtur, quibus scilicet usu venit, quod per nives iter agentibus, nam cetera quoque illis alba videri solent, candoris habitu in oculos iam recepto, reliqua in se transformante. Sic amantibus perdite quicquid occurrat amatae aut faciem aut omnino aliquid refert, sub dictionem unius imaginis tota imaginaria amantis facultate redacta. Qui theologus est, nec aliud quam theologus, ad divinas causas omnia refert; medicus ad habitum corporis; physicus ad naturalia rerum principia; mathematicus ad figuras et numeros, quod Pythagorici factitabant. Hac ratione, cum essent veteres Chaldaeorum in caelestium motibus metiendis et stellarum cursibus observandis iugiter assidui, nec aliud quicquam eorum magis ingenio detinerent, omnia illis erant stellae. Hoc est, ad stellas libenter omnia referebant, id quod de Aegyptiis dictum pariter intelligatur."

Plato and Aristotle down to Porphyry and Plotinus, had rightly ignored it. By putting the vaunted "prisca philosophia" back into its historical context, in short, one could understand not only that the Near Eastern inventors of astrology had gone wrong but why they had done so. And one could see that real wisdom came not from a revelation at the beginning of history but from the progressive efforts of ordinary people in each period; knowledge grew as time passed. One of the great myths of the fifteenth century, that of the golden age of original wisdom in the ancient East, died its first death in Pico's pages.[84] It proved, in later years, to have many lives.

Pico's reading of the evidence about ancient astrology reversed not only the verdict that most of his contemporaries arrived at but the arguments by which they did so—and which he himself had once accepted. Where Pico had once dreamed of continuity, he now insisted on change. Where he had once believed that all profound thinkers arrived at the same set of truths, if not the same individual doctrines, he now assumed that astronomers and astrologers had worked within specific historical circumstances, which shaped and limited their achievements. In theory, man the astronomer was free. In practice, however, he was in chains: in the chains of his political, social, and biographical circumstances, which defined the form his theories would take and might make him rational or superstitious, logical or illogical. The iron cage of history replaced the crystalline cage of astrology.

Pico expressed this insight—the fundamental one of humanist scholarship—repeatedly and explicitly in the course of his work. At one point he even gave it a form as graphic as—and more original than—the image of Silenus that he had used to the opposite effect in his letter to Barbaro. The astrologers attributed Aristotle's achievements to the stars that accompanied his birth. However, they looked at once too low and too high for the circumstances that shaped Aristotle. In so far as Aristotle outdid all his contemporaries, he owed his preeminence to divine gifts, gifts over which the elements and things composed of them could have no control: "Aristotle's lot was not a better star but a better mind. And the mind, which is not cor-

---

84. See Roulier, *Pic de la Mirandole*, 105–6. But he is probably wrong to say that Pico rejected the authenticity of the *Corpus Hermeticum*. The passage in question deals with the recherché Near Eastern authorities cited in astrological works—and the Hermes mentioned is presumably the one traditionally listed as the author of many of these, rather than the Hermes of the *Corpus*. See Pico, *Disputationes*, ed. Garin, 2:482 (11.2): "Hinc Aesculapios et Hermetes et Nechepsos et Petosiris, vana omnino nomina, quasi nebulas lectoribus spargunt . . ." Aesculapius, Hermes, Nechepso, and Petosiris all figure among the astrological authorities invoked by Firmicus Maternus—probably the source and the context that Pico had in mind (see, e.g., *Mathesis* 4 prooem. 5, 5.1.36, 8.5.1).

poreal, he obtained not from a star but from God."[85] But so far as external circumstances shaped what Aristotle did, they were historical and local: "among the causes was the learning of his teacher and the happy condition of the time in which he was born. They were well supplied with monuments of the ancients, though incomplete ones, so that they did not face the effort of having to invent the liberal arts from scratch, and did not lack the material with which they could bring them to perfection."[86] Aristotle had needed the historical Athens to work in as well as a divine *ingenium* to think with.

The case of Aristotle was merely one instance of a general rule. After all, Pico explained, circumstances mold all of us, sometimes in intricate and unpredictable ways. He offered a case in point. An acquaintance of Pico's was unable to enjoy sexual intercourse unless his partner flogged him with a rod soaked in vinegar, so viciously that blood spurted from his wounds. One day Pico asked him how he could be so perverse as to desire pain. The friend replied that the explanation was simple. As a boy, he had been raised with others who traded sexual favors for the right to hurt those they gratified; the association between pleasure and pain ingrained in him then had never departed.[87] Evidently, then, even the strangest of human characteristics were acquired ones; a fortiori, more normal attributes could be explained in the same way. The pathological case of the masochist paradoxically explained the more normal history of "the master of those who

---

85. Pico, *Disputationes*, ed. Garin, 1:410 (3.27): "At profecit plus longe quam coetanei et quam discipuli: sortitus erat, non astrum melius, sed ingenium melium [!]; nec ingenium ab astro, siquidem incorporale, sed a Deo, sicut corpus a patre, non a caelo." This argument is fully analyzed—but also pulled out of context—in A.J. Parel, *The Machiavellian Cosmos* (New Haven and London, 1992), 20–21; more precise is Reinhardt, *Freiheit zu Gott*, 130–32.

86. Pico, *Disputationes*, ed. Garin, 1:410 (3.27): "fuit in causa doctrina praeceptoris et felicitas saeculi in quo editus, veterum pleni monumentis, sed non exactis, ne et labor non adesset inchoandi et perficiendi bonas artes materia non deesset."

87. Ibid., 1:412: "Vivit adhuc homo mihi notus, prodigiosae libidinis et inauditae: nam ad Venerem numquam accenditur nisi vapulet, et tamen scelus id ita cogitat, saevientes ita plagas desiderat, ut increpet verberantem, si cum eo lentius egerit, haud compos plene voti nisi eruperit sanguis, et innocentis artus hominis nocentissimi violentior scutica disseruerit. Efflagitat ille miser hanc operam summis precibus ab ea semper femina quam adivit, praebetque flagellum, pridie sibi ad id officii aceti infusione duratum, et supplex a meretrice verberari postulat, a qua quanto caeditur durius eo ferventius incalescit et pari passu ad voluptatem doloremque contendit, unus inventus homo qui corporeas delicias inter cruciatum inveniat. Is, cum non alioquin pessimus sit, morbum suum agnoscit et odit, quoniamque mihi familiaris multis iam retro annis, quid pateretur libere patefecit; a quo diligenter tam insolitae pestis causam cum sciscitarer, 'a puero,' inquit, 'sic assuevi.' Et me rursus consuetudinis causam interrogante, educatum se cum pueris scelestissimis, inter quos convenisset hac caedendi licentia, quasi pretio quodam, mutuum sibi vendere flagitiosa alternatione pudorem. Hoc ego factum, licet grave auribus liberalibus, ideo non suppressi, ut cognosceremus evidentia ipsa quantum illis affectibus valeat consuetudo . . ."

know." The eerie, anonymous figure of Pico's friend, forced by circumstance to enjoy being whipped, became the symbol of all men, shaped by history and environment—and a notable counterpart to Machiavelli's famous representation of Fortune as a woman. Evidently Pico had recast his view of human dignity—which is not to say that he had abandoned it. Human achievement, he saw at the end of his life, must be won by working within time and history, not by escaping from them into a mystical contact with a pure, primeval wisdom.

Sources Pico could not have known, most of which have become available only in the last two centuries, modify his picture in many ways. For example, they suggest that he miscast the historical relation between astrological superstition and astronomical science. Celestial divination existed in Babylon long before systematic observation of the planets began. The mathematical astronomy of the Babylonians, indeed, may well have been created precisely to make more precise divination possible. Even the evidence Pico knew, moreover, did not always support his theses. The prominent Greek philosophers who did not mention horoscopic astrology, Plato and Aristotle, did so for the very simple reason that it had not yet come into being in their time. At times, moreover, Pico played down texts that raised serious problems for his theses—as when he emphasized Porphyry's account of Plotinus' distaste for astrology (*Vita Plotini* 15) rather than the ambiguous text of Plotinus' own *Enneads* (2.3), which attacked the astrologers but also seemed to give an astrological reading of the *Timaeus*.[88] Still, even now Pico's work is of more than historical interest. A triumph of philology as well as philosophy, it retains its power to stimulate anyone interested in the origins of ancient science or the history of the millenial struggle between the assertion of human autonomy and the belief in the power of the stars.

Pico's history of astrology provoked intense reactions. Ficino, for example, found it profoundly disturbing. In a long, embarrassed letter to Poliziano, he tried to show that his own previous work, which had conflated alien wisdom and Greek philosophy, "Egyptian" astrology and Platonic love, did not necessarily contradict Pico's analysis. In *De vita* he had drawn on sources not strictly but eclectically, as befitted a medical man who could reasonably hope to find effective remedies anywhere.[89] He insisted that he had never meant to say that the Platonists approved of astrological amulets, and that in his commentary on Plotinus, where he strictly followed his

---

88. This point is developed by Zanier, in "Struttura e significato delle 'Disputationes.'"
89. Poliziano *Ep.* 9.12, in *Opera*, 1:134: "Sed in libro de Vita, ubi profiteor Medicinam ac remedia vitae utcunque et qualiacunque possum undique diligenter exquiro: neque despicio prorsus imagines illas, neque omnes respuo regulas."

author's doctrine, he had ridiculed them.[90] The tone as well as the content of the letter reveals Ficino's recognition that Pico had adopted a new way of reading—one that could not be reconciled with the more eclectic approach they had once shared. Bellanti, for his part, wriggled on Pico's philological hook. He insisted that it did not matter if astrology lacked an ancient, Eastern past; the achievements of recent astronomers and astrologers like Bianchini, Regiomontanus, and Paul of Middleburg sufficed to put the subject on a scientific basis. He thus accepted Pico's progressive vision of knowledge for the sake of argument—only to deny it in the next breath, insisting that he had seen "a good many quite ancient instruments, which made it possible to find the motions, eclipses, and true positions of the planets with remarkable ease. Therefore I take no interest in futile authorities."[91] The contradictions in Bellanti's arguments dramatize the uneasiness that Pico's critique inspired in him. Still other astrologers, like Agrippa, took Pico's information and ignored his arguments. The medical philologist Mainardi clearly saw the connection between Pico's attack on astrology and his own historical and critical approach to classical scientific texts.[92]

A full century later Pico's theses still fascinated two of the greatest intellectuals in Europe. His redating of the ancient astronomical tradition aroused the interest and won the assent of such diverse intellectuals as Jean Bodin, Henry Savile, and Joannes Goropius Becanus. Joseph Scaliger accepted and amplified Pico's views in his commentary on Manilius, where he too denigrated the sages of ancient Egypt and praised the philosophers and scientists of Greece. Johannes Kepler accepted only parts of Pico's

90. Ibid.: "Quod autem in principio libri tertii dicere videor imagines ab antiquioribus Platonicis in coelo dispositas esse, non id equidem volo. Non enim consilium ibi meum est, Platonicos affirmare coelestium imaginum assertores. . . . Narro autem illic dispositiones signorum imaginumque non quales apud Platonicos, sed quales apud Astrologos observaverim"; "Caeteri quidem Platonici coelestes imagines, quas describunt astronomi, pro opportunitate commemorant, neque reprobant eas, neque rursus comprobare student: Plotinus autem talia extra controversiam ridet. Ego quoque in Commentariis meis in eum tanquam interpres aeque derideo . . ." For Ficino's interpretation of Plotinus see his *Opera omnia*, 1609–26 = *Opera omnia*, ed. Sancipriano, 2:609–26).

91. Bellanti, *Astrologiae defensio*, 218: "Postremo dicitur non esse opus tanta antiquitate, ut refert Picus, si diligentes fuerint observatores, ut iudicium habere possimus. Ut autem vera loca habeantur, iam apertum est motus stellarum inventos fuisse, ut experientia testatur: licet, ut dictum est, aliquo additionis opus sit, facile est mediocriter introductis assequi: quare fabulas obiectas nihil faciunt periti. Mitto Alfonsum, Blanchinum, Ioannem de Regio monte, adversus opinionem istam, Magistrum Paulum Referendum Fori Sempronii Episc., in utraque astrologiae parte excellentem et in omni disciplinarum genere, qui nostris temporibus veritatem astrologicam cognovere. Ego autem vidi instrumenta complura antiqua satis, quibus mira facilitate planetarum motus, eclypses, vera loca cognosci poterant: quare vanas auctoritates nihil facio."

92. Zambelli, *L'ambigua natura della magia*, chap. 4.

work, but said that Pico stimulated him far more than the defenders of astrology, with whom he sided. Kepler even considered editing Pico's book with a commentary of his own, and he accepted Pico's thesis about the late origins of the exact sciences.[93]

Pico, in short, changed his stance as a reader; the credulous syncretist of the *Oratio* became a discriminating historical critic in the *Disputationes*. In earlier years, precise chronology had hardly interested Pico. Computing the interval between the Creation and the coming of Christ in the *Heptaplus*, he used as his date for the latter not the beginning of the Dionysian era, or even a date for the Crucifixion, but the fall of the Second Temple in A.D. 70 ("this," he said, "was after Christ's death . . . but I am not aiming at real precision").[94] Curiously, he still ended up with a total of 3,508 years for the period in question—more than 250 years lower than the traditional Jewish computation, and still farther from the shortest Christian ones. In the *Disputationes*, by contrast, he showed expert command of the problems of biblical chronology. He elegantly dissected the schematic astrological chronologies of the ninth-century astronomer Albumasar, which had reached a large European public, in Latin translation, in the twelfth century and after, and of the late medieval cardinal and scholar Pierre d'Ailly.[95] He also laid out for the first time the basic data that remained the foundation of technical chronology in the age of Funck and Scaliger.[96]

Anyone concerned seriously with astronomy and astrology had to develop some interest in dates and intervals. Nicole Oresme, for example, pointed out in his attack on astrology that the Ptolemy who wrote the *Almagest* had lived far too late to have been, as traditionally thought, one of the Ptolemies who ruled Egypt. He also reiterated Livy's demonstration that Pythagoras could not have taught Numa.[97] But he claimed no originality for these arguments and did not extend them to anything like Pico's level of sys-

---

93. A. Grafton, *Joseph Scaliger*, vol. 1 (Oxford, 1983), chap. 7; Grafton, *Defenders of the Text* (Cambridge, Mass., 1991), chap. 7.

94. Pico *Heptaplus* 7.4, in *Opera*, 1:52 (on the fall of the Temple he says "quae fuit post Christi mortem . . . neque enim reseco ad vivum"), 54.

95. For later medieval astrology see now L. Smoller's study of Pierre d'Ailly, *History, Prophecy, and the Stars* (Princeton, 1994), with a good bibliography of earlier work.

96. Pico, *Disputationes*, ed. Garin, 1:520–623 (5). Pico planned a special work *De vera temporum supputatione* (ibid., 1:536 (5.2), 1:568 (5.7)). On Pico's development as a chronologer, see E. Hirsch, *Die Theologie des Andreas Osiander* (Göttingen, 1919), 128–35; for the later impact of his work see A. Grafton, *Joseph Scaliger*, vol. 2 (Oxford, 1993).

97. N. Oresme, "Tractatus contra astrologos," in *Studien zu den astrologischen Schriften des Heinrich von Langenstein*, ed. H. Pruckner (Leipzig, 1933), 243–44.

tem and order.[98] When he sought to discredit the example of Zoroaster, for example, Oresme pointed out not that he had lived later than the astrologers thought but simply that he had come to a bad end.[99] He made no effort to discriminate between sources—even between classical texts and medieval compilations. Certainly he did not try to identify, date, and assess Ptolemy's astronomical sources. The change in Pico's approach, in other words, did not come about simply because he read his way into a new subject matter that demanded, and rewarded, precision.

Pico's rereading of ancient astrology may well have begun with a close study of a single classical text that had been familiar in the West for centuries and that Pico himself had known for years. In book 10 of the *Metaphysica*, Aristotle attacks the Pythagoreans, who had argued that reality was really made up of numbers. They committed a simple fallacy: becoming expert in mathematics, they had assumed that their science provided the key to the universe as a whole:

> At the same time, however, and even earlier the so-called Pythagoreans applied themselves to mathematics, and were the first to develop this science; and through studying it they came to believe that its principles are the principles of everything. And since numbers are by nature first among these principles, and they fancied that they could detect in numbers, to a greater extent than in fire and earth and water, many analogues of what is and comes into being . . . and since they saw further that the properties and ratios of the musical scales are based on numbers . . . they assumed the elements of numbers to be the elements of everything, and the whole universe to be a proportion or number. . . . For example, since the decad is considered to be a complete thing and to comprise the whole essential nature of the numerical system, they assert that the bodies which revolve in the heavens are ten; and there being only nine that are visible, they make the "antichthon" the tenth.[100]

A wrong assumption, deriving from an obsession with one discipline, led the Pythagoreans to misunderstand the natural world. They invented celestial

---

98. On Ptolemy Oresme says that "ille, qui transtulit quadripartitum, ostendit, qualiter iste philosophus fuerit per multos annos post Ptholomeos reges" ("Tractatus contra astrologos," 243); on Numa, similarly, he quotes Livy directly (ibid., 244).

99. Oresme, "Tractatus contra astrologos," 240–41.

100. Aristotle *Metaphysica* (trans. Tredennick) 1.5.985b–986a. On Pico's growing commitment to Aristotle see Roulier, *Pic de la Mirandole,* 110–11.

bodies that the laws of number seemed to them to require, though they could not be observed. Aristotle had to rebut their errors—as he had to rebut those of the pre-Socratics and of Plato himself. Aristotle's account treats the study of nature as progressive. He reduces a prominent group of older sages, the Pythagoreans, to fumblers who fell victim to an elementary fallacy. And he suggests that rigorous philosophers must begin by drawing up a critical history of their predecessors' ideas.

Pico cited this passage several times in the *Disputationes*. For example, he compared the astrological historians of his own time, who tried to make every great event fall in the year of a great conjunction of Jupiter and Saturn, to "those ancients described by Aristotle, who when they had once decided that everything was distributed in accordance with the number ten but had not found more than nine spheres in the universe, said that there must be another earth, so that their number ten would be filled out."[101] Aristotle, then, gave Pico a model of how to treat the development of a complex area of thought as a story of progress rather than one of degeneration—to offer a history of forward motion brought about by thought and debate in place of a history of the gradual degradation of a primal wisdom. Paradoxically, a text known and studied throughout the High Middle Ages underlay one of the most original pieces of humanist scholarship carried out in the Renaissance. Pico's early scholastic training served him long and well. Aristotle gave him the lever that enabled him to wrench texts and contexts violently from their accustomed places—so far as to deny the original existence, at least as far as natural philosophy was concerned, of a perfect ancient wisdom that philology or allegory could recover.[102]

Aristotle, however, offered no model for the elaborate research and precise interpretations of texts with which Pico sustained his arguments. Aristotle's histories were short and polemical: they served as prefaces to the systematic arguments that supported his own philosophy. Pico, by contrast, incorporated detailed philological investigations into his work. For these too, however, he had a model—a personal one. From the mid-1480s, he had known, loved, and shared refined interests with Angelo Poliziano. When Poliziano incorporated the first edition and translation of one of

---

101. Pico, *Disputationes*, ed. Garin 1:536 (5.2): "Quemadmodum illi veteres, quos tradit Aristoteles, qui cum semel statuissent omnia esse denario numero distributa, nec tamen in universo plus novem sphaeris invenirent, dixerunt necessario aliam esse terram, ut denarius eorum numerus impleretur . . ."

102. Cf. W. Schmidt-Biggemann, *Geschichte als absoluter Begriff* (Frankfurt a.M., 1991), 15–21. Roulier (in *Pic de la Mirandole*) argues that Pico generally moved, in his later years, toward Aristotelian positions.

Callimachus' hymns into his *Miscellanea*, he claimed that he did so only at Pico's urging.[103] The reference was not merely formal. Pico had in fact given an allegorical reading of the same work, the *Lavacra Palladis*, in his commentary on Benivieni, some years before. He, not Poliziano, was thus the first Western scholar to cite Callimachus from firsthand knowledge, and his taste for Hellenistic poetry was clearly a shared one.[104] Pico gave Poliziano the benefit of his knowledge of Hebrew.[105] The two both had Aristotelian preferences in philosophy. And they both enjoyed teasing Ficino about astrology and other matters.[106]

Poliziano was not only a delightful Italian poet but also the most original and consistently rigorous historical thinker of the later fifteenth century. He traced many histories in his *Miscellanea* of 1489 and after: the histories of textual traditions, which he reconstructed with a rigor not seen again until the eighteenth century; the histories of poetic motifs and myths; and the histories of technical terms in philosophy. Again and again—especially in the case of the manuscripts, where local libraries presented him with coherent textual histories, fully attested—he arranged all the evidence chronologically and removed from consideration all witnesses that were entirely dependent on other extant texts or manuscripts.[107] He became, in other words, one of the creators of modern historical source criticism (though he was also much more than that).

The methods of Poliziano's late scholarship have much in common with those of Pico's late attack on the astrologers. For example, Poliziano's sharp

103. Poliziano *Misc.* 1.80, in *Opera,* 1:288: "Hactenus autem super hoc poetae loco scripseramus, cum nobis Picus noster Mirandula, quasi Cynthius alter in illo ipso, quo iam haec imprimenda fuerant articulo, aurem vellit et admonuit, ut elegiam quoque ipsam Callimachi . . . subiiceremus." See *Callimachus,* ed. R. Pfeiffer (Oxford, 1949–53), 2:lxviii–lxix. On the early study of Callimachus see now G. Benedetto, *Il sogno e l'invettiva* (Florence, 1993), 47–50 and passim.

104. Pico *Commento* 3.4, in *De hominis dignitate,* ed. Garin, 529 (cf. *Opera,* 1:746): "Questo significa la fabula di Tiresia da Callimaco decantata, che per avere visto Pallade nuda, che non significa altro che quella ideale bellezza dalla quale procede ogni sapienzia sincera e non vestita o coperta dalla materia, subito divenne cieco, e dalla medesima Pallade fu fatto profeta, sicchè quella che gli chiuse li occhi corporali li aperse li occhi dello intelletto, co' quali non meno le future cose che le presenti vedere poteva." See also Heiberg, *Beiträge zur Geschichte Georg Valla's,* 61.

105. Poliziano *Misc.* 1.14, in *Opera,* 1:238. For Pico's impact on Poliziano see further Branca, *Poliziano e l'umanesimo,* 248–49 and P. Viti, "Pico e Poliziano," in Viti, *Catalogo,* 103–25.

106. See Poliziano *Ep.* 9.13, in *Opera,* 1:135; cf. E. Garin, *La cultura filosofica del Rinascimento italiano* (Florence, 1971), 259 n. 2.

107. See now V. Fera, "Problemi e percorsi della ricezione umanistica," in *Lo Spazio letterario della Roma antica,* ed. G. Cavallo et al. (Rome, 1990), 3:522–28.

distinction between the fashionable *symbola* of Pythagoras and what he considered real philosophy resembles Pico's distinction between the superstitious trivia of Nechepso and the profound astrology of Ptolemy. And it stands in sharp contrast to Pico's earlier, uncritical use of the *symbola* in his *Oratio* and *Conclusiones*.[108] Pico had every opportunity to learn Poliziano's techniques of historical criticism from their creator. In 1491, they made a joint voyage of discovery through the libraries of the Veneto, in the course of which the two men carefully examined bookcases full of manuscripts and Poliziano took remarkable, systematic notes.[109] Between libraries they passed the time with talk of the scholia they had collated in Florence.[110] By then—if not before—they had become colleagues in philology. It was presumably no accident that Pico dedicated to Poliziano the *De ente et uno*, his own effort to show, from close textual analysis, that Plato's *Parmenides* was different in kind from his other dialogues. This work begins with an evocation of the two men's close collaboration, in the form of a prologue addressed to Poliziano. Here Pico describes how Poliziano and Lorenzo had recently discussed the apparent disagreement of Plato and Aristotle: Pico offers Poliziano—and Aristotle—his support, arguing that the disagreement is only apparent, not fundamental.[111] The presentation—with its suggestion that the three men inhabited a high new domain of knowledge and disputation, and that anyone who hoped to debate with them on even terms must somehow gain access to the rare and difficult materials all of them had at their disposal—reflected a genuine intellectual debt.

Poliziano and Pico sometimes discussed problems of textual interpretation in a sharply historical way. One day someone asked Poliziano for the original Greek equivalent of the Latin theological term *synderesis*. He had never seen the word in any Greek text. Like Sherlock Holmes, Poliziano knew exactly what to do when a problem baffled him; he consulted a higher

---

108. See A. Poliziano, *Lamia*, ed. A. Wesseling (Leiden, 1986), 4, 31–37.

109. See Fera, "Problemi e percorsi," 524–25; Branca, *Poliziano e l'umanesimo*, chap. 9; Flaminio, *Epistolae familiares*, 131–32.

110. See G. Pesenti, "Diario odeporico-bibliografico inedito del Poliziano," *Memorie del R. Istituto Lombardo di scienze e lettere*, cl. di lettere, scienze morali e storiche, 23 (ser. 3, 14) (1916): 229–39 (repr., in Poliziano, *Opera*, 2:155–65), e.g., 230 (156): "1491 Die 3 Junii a hore 17. Partimo el conte Iohanni Pico della Mirandola et io da Firenze. . . . Picus dixit se invenisse Florentiae in bibliotheca sanctae crucis Aristotelis Μετὰ τὰ φυσικὰ latine, ubi erat hoc scriptum in principio. . . . Et hoc ait Picus videri a graeco versum. Similiter se in graeco libro ex bibliotheca sancti Marci recolit, sed tamen pauciora, invenisse. Hoc videndum diligenter."

111. Pico, *Opera*, 1:241: "Narrabas mihi superioribus diebus, quae tecum de ente et uno Laurentius Medices egerat, cum adversus Aristotelem, cuius tu Ethica hoc anno publice enarras, Platonicorum innixus rationibus disputaret . . ."

authority.[112] He took his unnamed friend to see Pico, and they asked him a single, historical question: "Who was the first of the theologians to distinguish between *conscientia* and *synderesis*?"[113] Pico answered at once that Alexander of Hales had done so, and that he had found the idea and the term in Jerome's commentary on Ezekiel. A quick trip to the Medici library at Fiesole showed that Jerome had really used the Greek word *suneidesis,* and further investigations in the libraries of San Marco and Santo Spirito turned up the same reading. *Synderesis* turned out to be a *vox nihili* created by Latin theologians who knew no Greek.

Pico discussed mathematical and astronomical problems as well as philosophical and philological ones with Poliziano. In his first *Miscellanea* of 1489, Poliziano described how the two of them had been amused by a curious argument advanced by a Greek commentator on Genesis, Severianus, who had tried to show that the moon must have been full when it was created, on the fourth day; otherwise it could not have carried out God's commandments. By reaching this state prematurely it had in effect stolen eleven days from the sun (since it should not have become full until fifteen days had passed). That in turn explained the difference of eleven days, or lunar epact, by which the lunar year of 354 days was shorter than the solar one of 365. Each year, the moon had to pay for its initial jump to prominence—"a comment," Pico and Poliziano concluded, "more witty than veracious."[114] Poliziano lent Pico a Greek astrological manuscript of the fourteenth century, now in the Laurenziana. A note reveals that it was still in Pico's hands when he died.[115] And the texts that Poliziano examined in the course of their trip to the Veneto notoriously included the manuscript of the astrological poem of Manilius that belonged to Pietro Leoni—as students of the textual tradition of Manilius have long known.[116]

---

112. For Poliziano's assessment of Pico as a thinker see *Misc.* 1.90, in *Opera,* 1:301; and the *Coronis,* in *Opera,* 1:310.

113. Poliziano *Misc.* 2.7 in *Miscellaneorum centuria secunda,* ed. V. Branca and M. Pastore Stocchi, editio minor (Florence, 1978), 14: "Tum placuit adire ambos ad Picum Mirandulam, qui tum forte ibi aderat, ac rogare eum ostendere nobis (nam ego tum auctores istos nondum attigeram) quinam primus e theologis istis differentiam istiusmodi prodiderit sindereseos et conscientiae."

114. Poliziano *Misc.* 1.94, in *Opera,* 1:305–6. Poliziano comments, "lepidiore tamen, puto, quam veriore commento."

115. Laur. 28.14, fol. 2 recto: "Olim Angeli Politiani. Repertus inter libros comitis Johannis Mirandulani." I. Maïer, *Les manuscrits d'Ange Politien* (Geneva, 1965), 331. See also Viti, "Pico e Poliziano," in Viti, *Catalogo,* 103–25. The traffic ran both ways. In August 1485 Pico had lent Poliziano a codex of Porphyry *De abstinentia,* from which Poliziano took notes, now in BN Paris, MS grec 3069, fols. 122 recto–127 verso; see Maïer, *Les manuscrits d'Ange Politien,* 228.

116. See Branca, *Poliziano e l'umanesimo,* 138; M.D. Reeve, "Manilius," in *Texts and Transmission,* ed. L.D. Reynolds (Oxford, 1983), 235–38; A. Maranini, "Nel laboratorio

Most important, because least circumstantial, is one more fact: Poliziano actually supplied Pico with recherché evidence about Greek ideas on celestial influence. Hesiod's *Opera et dies* concludes with a long passage on the days of the lunar month. The poet identifies some days as holy; others as propitious for shearing sheep, reaping fruit, weaving cloth, or begetting children; still others as dangerous.[117] Alberti, who loved Hesiod, included a few of these precepts in his little Italian treatise on the *Villa*.[118] Poliziano, who used the old scholia ascribed to Proclus as well as the original text, described the whole matter at length in his *Rusticus*.[119] While Pico was at work on his treatise against the astrologers, Poliziano wrote him a long letter about Hesiod. He began by asking Pico if Hesiod's doctrines derived "a naturae causis, an a vulgi magis credulitate" [from natural causes or the credulity of the people]. He then provided a long account, in prose, of everything Hesiod and the scholia had to say about propitious and impropitious days.[120] Pico incorporated Poliziano's material, day by ominous day, into book 3, chapter 14, of the *Disputationes*.[121] The connection seems clear; Pico derived at least part of his iconoclastic historical approach from the close friend with whom he avidly exchanged ideas and information.

Nonetheless, Poliziano did not shape every detail of Pico's method. Though both men approved of Hesiod's observations, for example, they explained them in different ways. Poliziano offered numerological reasons for the value of the days: the first of the month, he suggested, was holy because unity is the principle of all numbers and because every beginning, as Plato had taught, is holy.[122] The material he deployed—and its underlying

---

filologico degli Umanisti e nell'officina moderna: Storia e problemi della tradizione di MANIL. 5, 126," *Schede umanistiche* 1 (1988): 7–71; and Maranini, *Filologia fantastica* (Bologna, 1994), 207–10 and passim.

117. On these beliefs see in general A. Grafton and N. Swerdlow, "Calendar Dates and Ominous Days in Ancient Historiography," *Journal of the Warburg and Courtauld Institutes* 51 (1988): 14–42.

118. L.B. Alberti, *Opere volgari*, ed. C. Grayson (Bari, 1960–73), 1:359–63. He also discusses ominous days in *De re aedificatoria* 2.4.

119. Poliziano's notes on the scholia to the *Opera et dies* are in the Bayerische Staatsbibliothek, cgm 182, fols. 59 verso–71 recto. For significant days see 69 recto–71 recto. Cf. also Poliziano, *Commento inedito alle Georgiche di Virgilio*, ed. C. Castani Musicò (Florence, 1990), 67.

120. Poliziano *Ep.* 12.7, in *Opera*, 1:168–70.

121. Pico, *Disputationes*, ed. Garin, 1:296–305.

122. Poliziano, *Opera*, 1:168: "Ac ne tibi gravioribus et quasi sanctioribus literis occupato requirendi relegendique Rustici poetae onus imponam, breviter hac epistola complectar et quid ille prodiderit, et quas ego vel rationes vel causas, partim de Procli caeterorumque lectione, partim vero de mea coniectura posse videar afferre. Summa igitur est Hesiodi partitio, dies ut alios admittat vel ad inspiciendum, vel ad efficiendum, rursus ut alios velut emortuos praetereat.

assumption that an ancient poet had foreseen the doctrines of a later philosopher—came directly from the scholia, learned references to Plato and the *Orphica* and all.[123] Pico, by contrast, explained Hesiod's advice as based on empirical evidence. The moon really affected life on earth; and the details of its influence as it waxed and waned had been observed through centuries by ordinary men and women. Hesiod summarized these observations, offering his readers not the foolish astrology of the learned but the wise astrology of the people, "lunaris astrologia, a medicis, ab agricolis, a nautis utiliter et naturaliter observata."[124] Clearly Pico always thought for himself. Close friendship did not imply intellectual dependence. In this case Pico, who read Hesiod as genuinely in touch with the land and the experience of country people, showed more historical insight, more concern with context and development, and more originality of thought than Poliziano, who drew his neoplatonic reading from the scholia. Yet it also seems clear that Poliziano helped Pico and shaped his work, honing to a new sharpness the grammatical and historical skills that had formed part of his tool kit, as we have seen, for many years.

Finally, however, it remains possible that the emotional inspiration for Pico's change of heart lay outside the library—and outside the learned traditions of philosophy and philology. Scholars have often suggested that Pico's general view of ancient traditions changed radically when he came under the influence of Savonarola, with whom he spent much time in the last five years of his life. Pico listened eagerly to the messages of the prophet who would soon dominate the city and help to destroy the Medicean regime. And Savonarola sharply distinguished pagan sages from Christian ones, even attacking Augustine for seeing Platonism and Christianity as similar. "And I say this," he explained in this sermons on Exodus, "because some want to make Plato entirely Christian. We should make Plato Plato, and Aristotle Aristotle, and not make them Christians, because they are not."[125] Savonarola did not have the philological equipment to provide

---

Tres tamen Iovis appellat, ut primum diem mensis, quartumque, et septimum. Primum puto, quoniam princeps unitas numerorum, principiumque omne divinum (sicuti Plato docet), ex quo mensis apud Orpheum μονόκερος μόσχος dicitur. Quartum vero quoniam in eo rationes omnes musicae continentur."

123. Σ *Opera et dies* 769–71; see, e.g., *Scholia vetera in Hesiodi Opera et dies,* ed. A. Pertusi (Milan, 1955), 235–37.

124. Pico, *Disputationes,* ed. Garin, 1:298.

125. G. Savonarola, *Prediche sopra l'Esodo,* ed. P.G. Ricci (Rome, 1955–56), 2:290–92, at 291. See E. Garin, "Gian Francesco Pico della Mirandola: Savonarolan Apologetics and the Critique of Ancient Thought," in *Christianity and the Renaissance,* ed. T. Verdon and J. Henderson (Syracuse, N.Y., 1990), 523–32. Savonarola insisted that Plato differed from a Christian as sharply as sin from virtue, and his doctrines from Christian ones as shadows from light:

Pico's arguments; indeed, he epitomized them in a work of his own. And, on the one occasion when we know that Pico and Savonarola discussed the wisdom of the ancients, in the library of San Marco, Pico explicitly defended the tradition of ancient wisdom: "There have at all times in human history been some outstanding men, like Moses, Pythagoras, Mercury, Zoroaster, and Solon, who all, with complete consensus, believed in and affirmed [the basic truths of Christianity, such as the omnipotence of God and the immortality of the soul]."[126] Savonarola, we are told, embraced Pico and praised his learned defense of the ancient sages of the East. If Crinito's testimony deserves credence, then Pico had not yet drawn his final conclusions when this debate—which Crinito does not date—took place.[127] But it seems more than likely that Savonarola's pressure led Pico to reexamine his earlier, syncretic method. If so, then wild eschatological enthusiasm helped to inspire hard intellectual work—as it would again, more than once in the history of early modern Europe.

The case of Pico's *Disputationes* offers a rich model for the larger history of reading in the Renaissance. Confronting ancient authorities was for him an intense and complex act, at once individual and collaborative, private and public. It began with the collecting of a vast number of texts and involved learning and combining several well-developed styles of response to the written word. It required the advice of friends, the assistance of commentaries, and the exhaustive study of the original texts. Often, it followed a course that a modern historian might not expect. Conditioned to see philosophy as far more rigorous than philology, scholars assume that Ficino or Savonarola could have influenced a great philosopher like Pico, but they fail to realize that a brilliant philologist like Poliziano could have had a far deeper effect. More unexpectedly, Pico's case shows that serious philological reading was interactive. Literary scholars have long known that ancient texts shaped modern writers' attitudes even as the moderns wrote new works that reinterpreted the ancients. Evidently the same was true for

---

"E questo dico perchè alcuni vogliono fare tutto Platone cristiano. Si vuol fare che Platone sia Platone, Aristotile Aristotile, e non che siano cristiani, perchè non sono." Cf. G.C. Garfagnini, "Pico e Savonarola," in Viti, *Catalogo,* 149–57.

126. Crinito *De honesta disciplina* 3.2 (1504), sigs. [bv recto– bvi recto], at [bv verso] = ed. Angeleri, 104–5, at 104: "Sed principes—inquit—in omni mortalium vita extiterunt aliquot et iudicio et rerum cognitione maximi, ut Moses, Pythagoras, Mercurius, Zoroastres, Solon, qui omnes pari consensu non modo haec crediderunt, sed maxime affirmarunt." On 105 Pico is made to describe Egyptian and Jewish wisdom as the source of that of *omnis antiquitas* and to praise Hermes Trismegistus, Plato, and Zoroaster.

127. For the interpretation of this passage, which remains problematic in more than one respect, see Walker, *The Ancient Theology;* and Roulier, *Pic de la Mirandole,* 314.

philologists—at least those with Pico's commitment to the study of big questions and provocative texts. Plato and Aristotle, as well as their commentators in late Antiquity and more recent times, offered hints and tools for their own interpretation. Reading them really was—as Machiavelli would suggest in his famous letter to Francesco Vettori—a conversation, not a monologue.

The contextual form of reading that Pico eventually discovered—the systematic humanistic effort to put a text back into the world it came from—brought valuable results, but at a high price. It freed Pico and a few of his readers from ancient myths and atavistic fears; it gave them a crisp, usable criterion for distinguishing jewels from paste in the densely written, difficult manuscripts of Greek literature and philosophy. But it required them to impose on the poor, barbarous denizens of the ancient Near East a system of causality as schematic and rigid as the older one of the astrologers. To prove that astrology was of low value, Pico had to show that the whole world it came from deserved only contempt from the modern intellectual. He had to assume, to argue from "conjecture," not from textual evidence, that the idolatry and superstition of the Chaldeans and Egyptians had enslaved them, had made it impossible for them to be free intellectuals in the manner of a Greek like Aristotle. Human liberty, apparently, belonged only to the Greeks—a notion that would recur all too often in later centuries. This thesis, of course, is no more solid, no more historical, and no better supported by sources than the one it replaced. Sadly, the subsequent experience of the nineteenth century's historical revolution has shown that scholars who invoke a reconstructed context to explain a text always risk making the evidence they do not have dominate the interpretation of the evidence before them. Thus historical philology becomes as fruitful a source of wild speculation as any form of allegory one cares to name. Yet the danger is unavoidable. Scholars cannot avoid the task of creating a context for the texts they study, an activity as essential as it is perilous. The hallmark of Pico's sophistication as a reader, in short, is perhaps his confrontation with the insoluble dilemmas of historicism.

In the end, however, Pico's way of reading stands out less for its technical sophistication, great though that was, than for its public engagement. Pico read to intervene in and transform the practices and paranoias of his society. Like Valla, he saw himself as a public intellectual; like Freud, he saw himself as one whose powers of interpretation could liberate his contemporaries. By attacking classic texts in a new way, he also attacked entrenched interests and powerful corporations. His hours in libraries ranked with the riskiest ones of his short, dangerous life. In particular, Pico's late hours in public libraries mattered deeply. Here he confronted a full run of sources on astrology rather than the books that had caught his eye in shops or which agents had brought to his attention. Here he worked with Poliziano, the scholar who more than any other of his contemporaries made it a matter of principle to keep precise records of the dates, places, and objects of his own readings and to offer these to his public. Here, above all, Pico came to see the connection between the minute details of scholarly work and the corruption or preservation of high culture. Poliziano carried out his fanatically precise philology with a public end in view. He intended to direct a powerful cleansing stream through the Augean stables of contemporary classical editing and commentary. The *Miscellanea* marked only the first broadside in what he saw as a necessarily protracted campaign. Pico, similarly, intended to confront what he saw as the seven enemies of the Church. Even though he did not live to carry out that plan, his research resulted in his most effective intervention in the public domain of knowledge and debate. He directly challenged the astrologers who played lucrative roles at every Italian court and in every Italian city, who advised the Este and Sforza on the details of their personal and political lives and told the Florentine Republic the propitious moment for each new general to receive his baton of command. In doing so he knowingly provoked his opponents, not only to attack his theories but also to issue predictions of his own death. This was a brave, even a rash, act. Most of Pico's contemporaries accepted, as he once had, the power of the stars to inflict harm. Any full account of Pico's thought must include not only the brave philosophical system that he constructed in the *Oratio* but also the profound—and sometimes profoundly troubling—historical interpretations that he gradually learned to weave into the margins of other writers' books.[128]

---

128. For a different assessment of Pico's ways as a reader see Roulier, *Pic de la Mirandole*, 637–40.

4

How Guillaume Budé Read His Homer

Sometime in the last five years of the fifteenth century, a French lawyer in early middle age began to read the *Iliad*. His first encounter with Homer in the original yielded few dramatic results. The text, which he approached in the attractive outward form presented by the first edition of 1488, reads:

Μῆνιν ἄειδε θεὰ πηληϊάδεω ἀχιλῆος
οὐλομένην ἣ μυρί' ἀχαιοῖς ἄλγε' ἔθηκεν
πολλὰς δ' ἰφθίμους ψυχὰς ἄϊδι προΐαψεν
ἡρώων, αὐτοὺς δ' ἑλώρια τεῦχε κύνεσσιν
οἰωνοῖσι τὲ πᾶσι, διὸς δ' ἐτελείετο βουλὴ

[Of the anger sing, goddess, of Peleus' son Achilles,
the destructive anger that brought so many woes on the Achaeans,
and sent many brave souls to Hades
of heroes, and of them made spoils for dogs
and birds of all sorts; and the will of Zeus was reaching fulfillment.]

Guillaume Budé, the jurist in question, placed a sign, a backward diagonal with a dot after it, by the words in the text that needed explication. Then he added explanations, between the lines and in the margins:

[μῆνιν (wrath)] χόλον ἐπίμονον, ἀπὸ τοῦ μένειν (lasting anger, from the [verb] μένειν [remain])

[θεὰ (goddess)] ἡ καλλιόπη (Calliope [the muse of epic])

[οὐλομένην (destructive)] ὀλεθρίαν (destructive)

[ἔθηκεν (brought)] εἰργάσατο (produced)

135

[ἰφθίμους (brave)] ἰσχυρὰς, γενναίας, [ἰσχυρογνώμους corrected to] ἰσχυροψύχους (brave, virtuous, brave-souled)

[προΐαψεν (sent)] πρὸ τῆς εἰμαρμένης ἔπεμψε (sent before their fate)

[ἑλώρια (spoils)] ἑλκύσματα, σπαράσματα. ἕλωρ γὰρ τὸ θήραμα καὶ τῶν κυνῶν ἕλκυσμα (torn bodies, fragmentary body parts, for *helor* means prey and bodies torn by dogs)

[διὸς δ' ἐτελείετο βουλὴ (and the will of Zeus was reaching fulfillment)] Γνώμη (will)

εἰμαρμένη ὡς τινες ἐξεδέξαντο. οἱ δὲ φασι κατὰ τὴν ἀριστάρχου καὶ ἀριστοφάνους δόξαν, τῆς θέτιδος εἶναι βουλήν. ἣν ἐν τοῖς ἑξῆς φησὶ λιτανεύουσαν τὸν δία, ἐκδικῆσαι τὴν τοῦ παιδὸς ἀτιμίαν (fate, as some have taken it. Some say, following the view of Aristarchus and Aristophanes, that the will in question belonged to Thetis. In what follows, he says, she begs Zeus to avenge the dishonoring of her son.)[1]

Synonyms, expansions, many words for body parts, and one reference to the discussions of the Homeric commentators of Hellenistic Alexandria—these seem a poor harvest for the first five lines of a great poem. As will become clear, moreover, the notes are not only thin but derivative: like Lorenzo Valla when he read Thucydides, Budé when he read Homer turned for help to simple, accessible Greek sources. This document of the French Renaissance—which now, oddly, reposes in New Jersey, in the Princeton University Library—seems an unpromising source for the cultural historian. These dry bones do not wish to rise and dance.

And yet the encounter proved to be far more momentous than one might expect. Budé—along with his friends and rivals Erasmus, More, and Vives—led the cohort of north European intellectuals who set out in the decades after 1500 to create new forms of scholarship, education, and intellectual authority. Naturally, northern humanists differed from one another on many points: patriotism, pride, and disgreements on principle often spoiled their relations with one another. Principled debates about both the ancient canon and the modern world eventually divided men who had begun as friends and allies. Nonetheless many agreed on the necessity of challenging the dominant cultures of the north: the encyclopedic Latin eru-

---

1. Homer, *Opera* (Florence, 1488), Princeton University Library ExI 2681.1488 copy 2, I, fol. Ai recto.

dition of the monasteries, the densely sophisticated philosophy and theology of the universities, and the elegantly anachronistic chivalry of the courts. Like the Italian humanists of the fourteenth and fifteenth centuries, to whom they looked back as cultural, if not moral, models, the northerners tried to show that only the humanistic approach to authoritative texts could extract their true meanings. Their rivals, who failed to realize this, had often distorted beyond recognition the very authorities on which they relied. Pseudo-Thomas, the commentator on Boethius' *De consolatione philosophiae,* does not now seem to have much in common with *Amadis de Gaule*—and neither of them, in turn, with the authorities of the late medieval university. To the northern humanists, however, all of them showed symptoms of the same cultural disease. When Thomas identified Alcibiades as a beautiful woman, he made the same mistake—and misrepresented his classical object in the same way—as the illuminator of a romance did when he dressed classic heroes in the fashions of the Burgundian court and made them carry out deeds attested by no ancient source, or as a biblical commentator did when he turned stones into fish and adjectives into proper names. When the northern humanists proposed that schoolboys, princes, priests, and friars put their texts back into their historical contexts, they called for nothing less than a cleansing of the whole house of culture, a restoration of antiquity (which, of course, they too saw in a partly anachronistic light).[2]

Like the Italians, Erasmus and his friends argued that only a sound education based on the best classical literary, philosophical, and historical works could prepare a young man for an active life in church or state. Like the Italians, they worked to win support and preferment at courts, believing that the patronage of one rich and generous ruler could do more to establish the validity of their views than could a host of treatises. And like the Italians, they set out to build institutional bases for their project by creating new colleges where humanistic studies would form the center of the curriculum. Unlike earlier Italians, however, they grew up intimately acquainted with a new means for attaining public position in the republic of letters: the printing press, which could multiply one's words—and give currency to others' praise of them—more rapidly than any form of literary machinery previously known. Preferment and publication went together in

---

2. See the revisionist account of J.H. Overfield, *Humanism and Scholasticism in Late Medieval Germany* (Princeton, 1984); and the well-informed recent survey by E. Rummel, *The Humanist-Scholastic Debate in the Renaissance and Reformation* (Cambridge, Mass., and London, 1995).

their plans—as did the radical improvement of the world around them, which they hoped to rid of poverty, warfare, and superstition.[3]

The center of their battle line directed itself against what all of them saw as the primary bastion of the old culture: the universities in which arts instruction, based on long and detailed study of formal argumentation, led up to the higher studies of law, medicine, and theology. Each of these faculties offered entrance to a learned profession. Each rested its claim to authority on the ancient text or set of texts that its practitioners mastered. But each used these texts, both in systematic university courses and in particular responses to individual cases and problems, in a resolutely unhistorical way; and each pressed the arts faculty, which had as one central task the provision of preparatory instruction for the higher faculties, to emphasize students' grounding in systematic argumentation far more than their mastery of Latin grammar and rhetoric. Erasmus and Johannes Reuchlin criticized the theologians, showing that their central text—the Latin Vulgate—often did not accurately represent the sense of the Hebrew and Greek originals.[4] Thomas Linacre joined a host of Italian medical humanists in making the same point about the Latin set texts in which medical students confronted Galen and his later interpreters. All of them agreed that an arts course based on grammar, rhetoric, and a reformed and simplified dialectic, a course that concentrated on direct study of the best classical texts, would make a better preparation for public life than the abstract, philosophical grammar and rigorous, repellent dialectic of the late medieval schools. In parts of northern Europe university faculties became the locus of a struggle, carefully scripted and produced on the public stage of print, for control over the curriculum—and, in a larger sense, of European high culture.[5]

---

3. For Erasmus as the impresario of print see above all A. Hayum, "Dürer's Portrait of Erasmus and the *Ars Typographorum*," *Renaissance Quarterly* 38 (1985): 650–87; and L. Jardine, *Erasmus, Man of Letters* (Princeton, 1993). For recent surveys of secondary literature on northern humanism see the remarkable articles by J. IJsewijn, E.F. Rice, Jr., and others collected in *Renaissance Humanism: Foundations, Forms, and Legacy,* vol. 2, ed. A. Rabil, Jr. (Philadelphia, 1988).

4. See W. Schwarz, *Principles and Problems of Biblical Translation* (Cambridge, 1955); J.H. Bentley, *Humanists and Holy Writ* (Princeton, 1983); H.J. de Jonge, "Novum Testamentum a nobis versum: The Essence of Erasmus' Edition of the New Testament," *Journal of Theological Studies* 35 (1984): 394–413; de Jonge, "The Character of Erasmus' Translation of the New Testament," *Journal of Medieval and Renaissance Studies* 14 (1984): 81–87; and de Jonge, "The Date and Purpose of Erasmus' *Castigatio novi testamenti*: A Note on the Origins of the *Novum Instrumentum,*" in *The Uses of Greek and Latin,* ed. A.C. Dionisotti et al. (London, 1988), 97–110.

5. See, e.g., the classic case study of T. Heath, "Logical Grammar, Grammatical Logic, and Humanism in Three German Universities," *Studies in the Renaissance* 18 (1971): 9–64; and, for more recent literature and a new interpretation, Jardine, *Erasmus.*

The struggle reached a dramatic climax in the mid-1510s, when a bitter controversy broke out between Johannes Reuchlin, a committed Christian proponent of Judaic studies and cabbalistic Bible interpretation, and those who wished to condemn the Talmud and the Cabala. Reuchlin mustered the testimonials of prominent scholars and published them under the title *Clarorum virorum epistolae* (Letters of Famous Men). Two younger humanists, Ulrich von Hutten and Crotus Rubeanus, assembled a scathing set of parody letters, which they attributed to Reuchlin's enemies, and published these as *Epistolae obscurorum virorum* (Letters of Obscure Men). In point of fact, the divisions between those who favored Reuchlin's brand of Hebraic studies and those who opposed them did not correspond precisely with the division between humanists and scholastics. Older humanists generally found Hutten and Rubeanus not enlightened but outrageous, and Erasmus himself did not approve of Reuchlin's efforts to use and defend the traditions of Jewish scholarship, which seemed to him to threaten a revival of Judaism itself. The Reuchlin affair was not the simple, clear-cut clash of the sons of light with the sons of darkness that nineteenth-century historians and many more recent ones have portrayed.[6] Nonethless, the young man made their texts into sharp statements, purportedly from the point of view of the reactionaries, about just how deep the fissures ran between styles of interpretation. Friar Conrad Dollenkopf, for example, writes as follows to Ortwin Gratius:

I already know by heart all the fables of Ovid in his *Metamorphoses,* and can expound them in four senses: that is, of course, naturally, literally, historically, and spiritually—and that is more than the secular poets [humanists] can do. Just now I asked one of these fellows the origin of *Mavors.* He offered a conjecture, but it was false. So I corrected him and told him that *Mavors* was derived from *mares vorans,* being a man-eater—and he was put to confusion. I next demanded of him the allegorical meaning of the Nine Muses. Again he was at fault. Then I told him that the Nine Muses signify the seven choirs of angels. Third, I asked him the origin of *Mercurius.* But he did not know, and I showed him that *Mercurius* is so called because he is "mercatorum curius"; for he is the god of merchants, and curious about them. You will see that nowadays these poets only study their art literally, and do

---

6. See Overfield, *Humanism and Scholasticism;* see also W.J. Gundersheimer, "Erasmus, Humanism, and the Christian Cabala," *Journal of the Warburg and Courtauld Institutes* 26 (1963): 38–52; and F.A. Yates, *Giordano Bruno and the Hermetic Tradition* (Chicago and London, 1964).

not comprehend allegorizing and spiritual expositions: as the Apostle says, "The natural man does not receive the things of the spirit of God."[7]

For all the differences of taste and tone that separated Rubeanus and Hutten from Erasmus, their parody of scholastic inability to read old texts corresponded closely with both his satire on scholastic exegesis in *Moriae encomium* (The Praise of Folly) and his systematic criticism of it in his treatises on how to read the Scriptures. The battle between an old scholarship and the new took place in the inviting fields of hermeneutics as well as the spiny thickets of dialectic.

Budé—a rich man, a professional lawyer, and an amateur of falconry, descended from a long-established family of French jurists—held a special position as he rode this *nouvelle vague*. Trained in Roman law at Orléans, the possessor of impressive public offices, he was one of the relatively few humanists of the early sixteenth century—Thomas More was another—who knew firsthand, as a practical matter of documents filed and dossiers emptied, the expanding state apparatus of the time. He turned to the humanities late, in the 1490s. Thereafter his life was a divided one, which included periods of devotion to his books, spurts of perpetual motion in the French court, and intervals of gentlemanly leisure and villa building in the country. The double intellectual job that he took on was highly appropriate to his formation and position: he set out both to show that the new methods of the humanists could revolutionize accepted views about Roman laws and institutions and to win the direct financial support of the French crown for the new scholarship.[8]

Though Budé took up scholarship late, his academic bank balance rapidly recorded impressive entries. His *Annotationes in Pandectas* of 1508 offered the first full-scale humanistic commentary on the *Digest*. This elaborate, often controversial, work appropriated and debated the conclusions of the erudite Italian humanists of the last generation. It presented—or seemed to present—a frontal attack on the traditional legal scholarship of the schools, with their easily parodied insistence that "I prefer to have the glossator rather than the text on my side. For if I cite the text, the advocates

---

7. *Epistolae obscurorum virorum*, ed. F.G. Stokes (London, 1909), 73 (1.28); translated ibid., 343 (adapted).

8. The most recent study of Budé's family background and career is D.O. McNeil, *Guillaume Budé and Humanism in the Reign of Francis I* (Geneva, 1975). For further bibliography see *Contemporaries of Erasmus*, ed. P.G. Bietenholz and T.B. Deutscher (Toronto, Buffalo, and London, 1985–87), s.v. "Guillaume Budé," by M.-M. de la Garanderie.

of the other side and the judges too will say: 'Do you believe that the gloss did not see the text just as you did, and didn't understand it as well as you?'"[9] Budé used the most recent scholarship of Italian humanism to demonstrate the importance of reading the whole text of the *Digest*, including the sections in Greek, and of doing so in the light of other classic texts. His treatise *De asse*, written some years later, assembled textual and material evidence in staggering detail to establish the nature of Roman coinage, object by object. Other collectors, a breed that flourished in palaces and mansions, simply accumulated coins, forging what they could not buy and spinning fantasies about what they could not know. Sometimes they innocently invented the noblest of ancient origins for Renaissance coins and medals. Budé, who soberly weighed and measured, used his scale and calipers to reveal to his astonished contemporaries that Demosthenes was perfectly right when he refused to pay the courtesan Laïs forty sesterces. Forty ancient sesterces amounted to 1,750 modern livres—far too high a price to pay for a pleasure of which the Athenian orator would soon repent.[10]

Budé's career as a scholarly entrepreneur also proved successful, though more slowly. He ran into many obstacles, major and minor. Erasmus—for whom he tried to arrange a star appointment in France—preferred independence in Basel and elsewhere. Francis I, his chief patron, had little personal contact with humanist scholarship and proved infinitely distractable. Nonetheless Budé's long campaign of propaganda and persuasion eventually had results. Francis created, at the end of the 1520s, the Royal Professorships of Latin, Greek, and Hebrew that would become the Collège de France—an independent institution that stood (and sometimes still stands) in sharp opposition to the science and scholarship of the Sorbonne.

Even when Budé did not write, he continued to burnish his scholarly

---

9. R. Fulgosio, quoted by L. Delaruelle, *Guillaume Budé: Les origines, les débuts, les idées maîtresses* (Paris, 1907), 97 n. 1: "Volo pro me potius glossatorem quam textum. Nam si allego textum, dicunt advocati diversae partis et etiam iudices: Credis tu quod glossa non ita viderit illum textum sicut tu, et non ita bene intellexerit sicut tu?"

10. The study of Budé's intellectual life remains in an early phase. L. Delaruelle's informative book of almost a century ago remains standard, though it badly needs replacement (in some respects—as in its accounts of the Parisian scene during Budé's youth and of the scholarship of Erasmus—it was unsatisfactory at the time of its appearance). See L. Febvre, "Guillaume Budé et les origines de l'humanisme français, à propos d'ouvrages récents," *Revue de synthèse historique* 15 (1907): 255–77. A detailed study of Budé's legal scholarship forms part of D.J. Osler's unpublished Ph.D. dissertation, "The Textual Criticism of the Digest in the Sixteenth Century" (Cambridge University, 1984). On *De asse* see R. Cooper, "Collectors of Coins and Numismatic Scholarship in Early Renaissance France," in *Medals and Coins from Budé to Mommsen*, ed. M.J. Crawford, C.R. Ligota, and J.B. Trapp (London, 1990), 5–23 at 12–14.

skills. By the end of the 1520s he had become the master Hellenist of his generation. Though frequently discouraged by the difficulty of the task and distracted by his large and lively family, he compiled and published, in 1529, the first full-scale analysis of Greek prose usage based on direct study of the whole range of accessible ancient sources: the *Commentarii linguae Graecae*.[11] With this work he laid up a rich store of observations, which the grammarians of his time recycled as their own, much as their late ancient and Byzantine predecessors had recycled earlier scholia and grammatical works.[12] He founded the great Parisian tradition of Hellenic lexicography that would be continued, in later centuries, by characters as distinct as the erudite, textually omnivorous, decorous DuCange and the brilliant, sexually predatory German exile Hase. And he established himself, even more than Erasmus, as his generation's most meticulous connoisseur of the Greek language and its literature. Through the first half of the 1530s, as French believers in the new culture reached a high peak of enthusiasm, only to plunge into the repression and terror that followed the Protestant demonstration known as the Day of Placards in 1534, Budé devoted himself to writing on the necessity of literary studies and the problems involved in being both a Hellenist and a Christian. In these works—above all the *De transitu Hellenismi ad Christianismum* of 1535—he used his mastery of Greek both to argue the case for classical culture and to establish, from a Christian point of view, its necessary limitations. In doing so he refined, in essays of great subtlety and complexity, theses that he had first put forward in his early works on the *Pandects* and the *as*.

Budé's reading of Homer took place early in his career. It left a deep imprint in his intellectual and literary style, shaping his efforts to define the uses of ancient culture in a modern world. And it is richly documented. When studied in the light of Budé's career, his writings, and his sources, the dry bones in his Homer in Princeton show a suprising amount of life.

Authentication comes before analysis. Anyone acquainted with humanist books and modern libraries might well be excused a certain skepticism about the Princeton copy of Homer. Printed books with marginal annotations, after all, fall into a black hole among the bright constellations of the

---

11. Budé mentioned this project, in response to a letter from Erasmus, as early as 14 December 1522. See *Opus epistolarum Des. Erasmi Roterodami,* ed. P.S. Allen, H.M. Allen, and H.W. Garrod (Oxford, 1906–58), ep. 1328, 5:153, responding to ep. 1233, 4:579–80. See also his letter of 22 April 1527, in *Opus epistolarum,* ep. 1812, 7:35, responding to ep. 1794, 6:477–78.

12. D. Donnet, "La 'Syntaxis' de Jean Varennius et les 'Commentarii' de Guillaume Budé," *Humanistica Lovaniensia* 22 (1973): 103–35.

modern philological disciplines. Their texts belong to bibliographers, but their handwritten content does not. Paleographers and textual critics have generally contented themselves, reasonably enough, with exploring the oceans of complete manuscripts that fill the libraries of Europe. Only a few of them have begun to chart and navigate the crooked streams of annotation that flow by so many printed texts.[13] Few great European or American libraries offer their visitors elaborate, reliable catalogs of their annotated books.[14] No substantial reference work provides generally accepted standards for describing and cataloging them. Worse still, library practices and bibliophilic prejudices render much of the evidence mute. Tight bindings and cropped margins make many important sets of marginal notes impossible to study in full. In earlier days chemical washing restored the overwritten margins of many a large-paper incunabulum to elegant sterility; incomplete cataloging suppresses the existence of others even in the present. Some overeager book dealers and buyers have sinned by *suggestio falsi;* anyone who knows the large American libraries also knows their genial habit, in the last years of the nineteenth century, of assigning every book annotated in Latin by a German to Melanchthon. Others have fallen into *suppressio veri:* for example, librarians in Leiden omitted any reference in their handwritten catalog of annotated books to the copy of Manilius (Heidelberg, 1590), in which an irate Joseph Scaliger expressed his opinion of the editorial work of Franciscus Junius (he lined out whole pages and scrawled "cacas" in the margins).[15] The ambitions of the former and the decorum of the latter have been equally harmful. In these circumstances, anyone could be assailed by doubt when confronted by the claim that a large American library possesses an annotated book of great historical interest—even when its two volumes bear the telltale words HOMERVS BVDAE and HOMER BVD on their handsome seventeenth-century calf bindings. Binders, too, could make mistakes.

Yet the credentials of Budé's Homer seem very strong. To be sure, it was

13. For some informative case studies see the essays collected in *Manuscripts in the Fifty Years after the Invention of Printing,* ed. J.B. Trapp (London, 1983); and *De captu lectoris,* ed. W. Milde and W. Schuder (Berlin and New York, 1988).

14. Exceptions include Cambridge University Library, which has a printed catalog of *Adversaria,* and the British Library and Bibliothèque Nationale, some of whose annotated books are entered under the names of their owners in the printed general catalogs; the Bibliothèque Nationale also maintains a public *fichier des possesseurs* in the Réserve. The Bodleian and Leiden University Libraries have manuscript catalogs, available to those clever enough to ask for the right information. Much information about these and other formal and informal catalogs of annotated books appears in P.O. Kristeller's *Iter italicum* (Leiden, 1963–).

15. Leiden University Library 758e4.

lost from modern scholarly view until the Milton scholar James Holly Hanford discovered it and published a first analysis of the evidence.[16] But it had been studied in a more erudite time: early in the eighteenth century Boivin described it in detail, and Villoison cited this description when compiling his 1788 edition of the Venice scholia to Homer.[17] Boivin was sure that the notes were Budé's, and his confidence was not misplaced, even though some of his evidence was not strong.[18] The arms of the Budé family appear three times in the two volumes in Princeton. The handwriting of many, though not all, of the notes clearly matches that of Budé's holograph letters and that of the annotations in many other books from his library now in Paris, Leiden, Berlin, and Cambridge. Particularly distinctive is the Greek phi that Budé often used, which resembles a crossbow.[19] The notes themselves march through the entirety of the *Iliad* and *Odyssey*. They show expert knowledge of central Greek lexica and grammatical works—the tools of the lexicographer's trade, which only a handful of northern Europeans could wield with dexterity around 1500. And they omit all mention of contemporary works on which slightly later readers of Homer regularly drew—for example, Erasmus' *Adagia,* which offered many elucidations of and parallels for Homeric lines that became proverbial.[20] As we shall see, finally, sev-

---

16. J.H. Hanford, "An Old Master Restored: The Homeric Commentary of Guillaume Budé at Princeton," *Princeton University Library Chronicle* 18 (1956): 1–10.

17. J. Boivin, "Notice d'un exemplaire d'Homère de la Bibliothèque de Budé," in *Histoire de l'Académie royale des Inscriptions et Belles-Lettres* 5 (Paris, 1729): 354–60; *Homeri Ilias ad veteris codicis Veneti fidem recensita,* ed. J.B.G. d'Ansse de Villoison (Venice, 1788), xv n.

18. His decipherment of the string of initials Q.f.f.& a D. o. m. G. & L. B. as "Quod felix, faustum et acceptum Deo optimo maximo. Gulielmus et Ludovicus Budaeus" seems more ingenious than solid—especially as the handwriting is nothing like Guillaume's.

19. See *Repertorium der griechischen Kopisten 800–1600,* vol. 2, *Handschriften aus Bibliotheken Frankreichs* (Vienna, 1989), part B: *Paläographische Charakteristika,* by H. Hunger, 48; part C: *Tafeln,* 68. My thanks to D. Harlfinger and N.G. Wilson, the latter of whom examined the notes and related materials with me. Readily available facsimiles include two of Budé's letter to Janus Lascaris, BN Paris, MS Dupuy 490, fols. 3–4: one in L. Delaruelle, *Répertoire analytique et chronologique de la correspondance de Guillaume Budé* (Toulouse, 1907), facing 240; the other in *La correspondance d'Erasme et de Guillaume Budé,* ed. and trans. M.-M. de la Garanderie (Paris, 1967), facing 9. Both clearly show his peculiar phi. Pages from printed books with annotations by Budé are reproduced in E.A. Loew and E.K. Rand, *A Sixth-Century Fragment of the Letters of Pliny the Younger* (Washington, D.C., 1922), and (less clearly) in Hanford, "An Old Master Restored," and in G. Budé, *L'étude des lettres,* ed. and trans. M.-M. de la Garanderie (Paris, 1988). I have not been able to establish the identity of the second annotator in the Princeton Homer, and I confine my analysis here to annotations that clearly stem from Budé.

20. See, e.g., BN Paris Rés Yb 151, a Louvain 1535 edition of the *Iliad* and *Odyssey* with elaborate manuscript notes, which belonged to one Christophorus Comes a Manderscheit; here one finds many references to Erasmus, which suggest not only what given texts meant but also how they could be applied in one's own writing (e.g., I, sig. [Civ] verso on *Iliad* 2.25: "Non

eral of the interpretations sketched out in a phrase or two in the margins of this Homer reappear, much elaborated, in Budé's published works. There seems no reason to doubt, accordingly, that one can tell this book by its cover. The strata of its annotation, when separated with sufficient delicacy, turn out to represent a great Hellenist's progress through the greatest—and one of the hardest—epic journeys that a reader can undertake.

How then did Budé come to Homer? In Italy, one could arrive reasonably directly, even if Greek instruction remained less regular, and far more elementary, than Latin. A boastful young man from Padua, Girolamo Amaseo, who studied Greek with Varino Favarino Camerte in Florence in 1493, described the scope and rhythm of instruction with all the condescending clarity one could wish:

> For twenty days I have been hearing Homer without a text of my own. I cling to the other students in the school. I understand Aristophanes so well that those who have listened for six months are not embarassed to consult me, so that I can interpret the lesson we have heard and clarify it, translating word for word. This is how Varino sets out to instruct us. First he gives the meaning of the text, elegantly and in a few clear words; after this first translation he finds the inflection of the verbs and nouns, if it is fairly hard; he also provides the etymologies and the other figures. Then he goes through the same text again, and to prevent our forgetting what he had said, he confirms and tests us. Just after the lesson one of our number explains it. We have to give declensions, and we do not mind. All studies, after all, have their infancy. In the morning he lectures on the *Odyssey,* covering thirty verses; after lunch Aristophanes, only twenty verses; at the twenty-second hour the *Iliad,* forty verses. There are sixteen of us students, including the poet Naldi, who is fifty . . . but others are in their forties, others in their thirties, others still younger, while others are youths.[21]

---

decet principem solidam dormire noctem. Eras. in adagiis"). This reader, or his teacher, was no novice, since he also used the "scolia," Eustathius, and Porphyry's *Quaestiones Homericae.* The *Adagia* also appear, along with direct references to Plato's *Symposium* and Demetrius' *On Style,* in BN Paris Rés. Yb 3–4, a copy of the 1488 edition ascribed to Janus Lascaris. The absence of Erasmus in Budé's volume, accordingly, suggests that the notes there were made well before that text appeared in its first full-scale, Hellenizing edition in 1508.

21. The text is edited and annotated in G. Pozzi, "Da Padova a Firenze nel 1493," *Italia medioevale e umanistica* 9 (1966): 193: "Iam autem viginti dies sunt transacti quibus in audiendo Homero sine libro tempus consumo, adhaerens in ludo aliis auditoribus; Aristophanem sic percipio ut qui iam sex menses audierunt se ad me conferre non erubescant: ut interpreter

Though the presence of pupils of many different ages suggests that Greek remained something of a luxury option, the nature of the instruction could not have been more regular. Careful, word-for-word explanation, parsing and paraphrasing, and plenty of repetition—these exercises, then as now, rapidly gave the new student of Greek the fluency that makes reading Homer so accessible a pleasure.[22]

For Budé, in barbarous Paris, no such pleasant roads lay open. In a famous, splenetic letter to Cuthbert Tunstall, written many years after the event, he recalled his introductory Greek lessons with a biting precision that shows how little he had forgotten about how little he at first managed to learn:

> at once I got hold of a certain old Greek, or rather he got hold of me, for I paid him a massive tax. He knew Greek letters up to the point, or a little beyond it, where the spoken language is in accord with the learned one. It would take me more than three pages to give a full account of the ways in which he tortured me, teaching me what I would soon have to unlearn—except that he seemed to me to read very well and to pronounce Greek as scribes customarily do. At the time, to be sure, as I had heard he was the only Greek in France, I thought he was also very learned in Greek. He, as he showed off his Homer to me and mentioned other outstanding authors, naming each man by name, understood that I was burning with mad desire. In addition, I made another mistake: I thought that his ignorance was deliberate playful-

---

et auditam lectionem verbum e verbo transferens enucleem. Hanc autem curam Guarinus ipse in nobis instruendis impendit: primo sententiam lectionis paucis et dilucide eleganterque colligit, post interpretationem primam verborum et nominum inflexionem, si duriuscula est, reperit, etimologiam non tacet et figuras reliquas; secundo eam ipsam lectionem percurrit et, ne quae prius dixerat obliviscamur, confirmat examinatque nos omnis et, post ipsam statim lectionem, aliquis e numero nostrum eam exponit: cogimur declinare, nec displicet (omnia enim studia suam habent infanciam). Legit mane Odysseam, versus autem triginta; post prandium Aristophanem, versus saltem viginti; vicesima secunda hora Iliadem, versus quadraginta. Discipuli autem sedecim audimus, inter quos poeta Naldius, quinquagenarius . . . alii autem quadragenarii, alii triginta annorum, alii iuniores, alii ephebi."

22. For corroboration cf. Andronicus Callistus' lecture on the beginning of the *Iliad*, quite different from Budé's approach in content, but recognizably similar, if more elementary, in method. See I. Maïer, *Ange Politien: La formation d'un poète-humaniste* (Geneva, 1970), for a sample. Still more systematic were Poliziano's lectures on Homer, which drew on a very wide range of older and contemporary grammatical sources and offered a wealth of information on etymology, morphology, and vocabulary. A specimen of his commentary on the *Odyssey* is edited and analyzed by L. Cesarini Martinelli, "Grammatiche greche e bizantine nello scrittoio del Poliziano," in *Dotti bizantini e libri greci nell'Italia del secolo xv*, ed. M. Cortesi and E.V. Maltese (Naples, 1992), 257–90.

ness, so that he could keep me longer as his tributary and as it were in
his grip, given his greed.[23]

The Greek in question was the scribe and tutor George Hermonymus,
Spartan by origin, who served as an intermittently effective facilitator for
Greek studies in northern Europe during the last three decades of the
fifteenth century. Obviously his formal lessons disappointed. In another
respect, however, he proved more helpful. The aspiring student of Greek in
late fifteenth-century Paris had to begin by assembling equipment. The
members of the class into which Budé was born—the Parisian *bourgeoisie
de savoir,* the nobles of the long robe who occupied important posts in the
royal administration and the sovereign courts—were specialists at this.
Knowledge was their business, and in their large libraries and in the dark,
handsome studies that provided the private space at the centers of their city
houses and country villas, they studied, and made their sons study, the Latin
texts that contained the keys to the kingdom of social power. The Parisian
libraries that belonged to such men expanded rapidly in the years around
1500. The catalytic power of print naturally helped to accelerate their
growth, and jurists' libraries could never have reached their standard size of
five hundred to fifteen hundred books without printers' stocks to draw
from. But manuscripts, from splendidly illuminated genealogies to
romances and breviaries, also flowed in, to mingle on the shelves (and, later,
in inventories) with printed books. Cultivated readers amalgamated books
of both sorts, personalizing even printed texts with the illuminations and
notes that their wide margins and occasional blank spaces invited. Miniatures with family arms, inscriptions recording the dates and circumstances
of purchases, and marginal notes made any book, whatever its origin, a
unique record of a given intellectual experience. Some French collectors followed the example of the Italians and bought with an eye not only to their
own family but also to the needs and interests of a wider learned commu-

---

23. Budé, *Opera omnia* (Basel, 1557; repr., Farnborough, 1966), 1:362: "statim Graecum
quendam nactus sum senem, aut ille me potius, illi enim vectigal magnum attuli, qui literas
Graecas hactenus, aut paulo plus noverat, quatenus sermoni literato cum vernaculo convenit:
hic quibus me modis torserit, mox dediscenda docendo, nisi quod et legere optime mihi et pro-
nunciare videbatur e more literatorum, non bene tribus chartis scriberem, cum interim ipse ut
unum eum esse Graecum in Francia audiebam, sic esse doctissimum Graece existimarem, et ille
ostentans mihi Homerum aliosque autores insignioreis nuncupans, ἐξονομακλήδην ὀνομάζων
ἄνδρα ἕκαστον, flagrare me studio insano intelligeret. Accedebat illud erroris, quod quae erat
in eo ignorantia, ego ludificationem esse putabam, quo diutius ille me stipendiarium ac pene
nexum prae aviditate haberet."

nity. Bookbindings, which often followed the Italian tradition we have already encountered, describing a given book as belonging to the owner "et amicorum," dramatized the extent to which such libraries were seen as part of a collectors' permanent contribution to the world of letters.[24] Budé's world was, in short, also that of Jean Grolier.

Budé knew this culture of primitive literary accumulation intimately: in fact, he was born into it. In a famous text he described how he had come to learning late, "stimulated to do so only by the example of my father, who in his great intelligence praised learning and was a passionate buyer of books."[25] Jean Budé, Guillaume's father, amassed a stately collection of manuscripts and printed books in the 1480s. Many of them bore his arms; many also had an inscription that proclaimed his standing and patronage of learning and dated, perhaps, his formal acquisition of the work in question: "This book belongs to Jean Budé, conseiller du roi and audiencier de France. Done [or 'entered': *actum*] on the last day of April 1487."[26] Jean's collection was not innovative: the works of Ambrose, Augustine, and Cassiodorus, a monastic world chronicle, and Geoffrey of Monmouth jostled Aeneas Silvius Piccolomini's *History of Bohemia*, while a large number of medical texts reflected his efforts to deal with the deterioration of his health. But the example was an impressive one. Like his father, Guillaume came to know the world and the customs of the Parisian book-trade intimately—

---

24. R. Doucet, *Les bibliothèques parisiennes au xvie siècle* (Paris, 1956); A. Charon-Parent, "Les grandes collections du xvie siècle," in *Histoire des bibliothèques françaises: Les bibliothèques sous l'Ancien Régime, 1530–1789*, ed. C. Jolly (Paris, 1988), 85–99; S. Charton-Le Clech, *Chancellerie et culture au xvie siècle: Les notaires et secrétaires du roi de 1515 à 1547* (Toulouse, 1993).

25. Quoted by Delaruelle, *Budé*, 62–63 and 63 n. 2: "excitante me tantum patris exemplo doctrinae laudatoris, ut erat hominis ingenium, et librorum emacissimi."

26. From Jean Budé's copy of Jo. Matheus de Gradibus' *Pratica* (Milan 1481), now in the Arsenal; first published by H. Omont, "Nouveaux manuscrits grecs copiés à Paris par Georges Hermonyme," *Bulletin de la Société de l'Histoire de Paris* 13 (1886): 112–13; on the word *actum*, which remains puzzling, see the careful discussion of an interesting unstudied volume from Jean Budé's library in E.K. Schreiber, *Catalogue Thirty* (New York, 1994), no. 10, 13–16. For Jean's library see in general Omont, "Notice sur la collection de manuscrits de Jean et de Guillaume Budé," *Bulletin de la Société de l'Histoire de Paris* 12 (1885): 100–13, with the additions and corrections of J. Martin-Demézil, "Un manuscrit de la bibliothèque de Jean Budé," *Bibliothèque de l'Ecole des Chartes* 99 (1938): 220–22; E. Droz, "Livres imprimés de la bibliothèque de Jean Budé," *Humanisme et Renaissance* 6 (1939): 288–93; and M.-C. Garand, "Les copistes de Jean Budé (1430–1502)," *Bulletin de l'Institut de Recherche et d'Histoire des Textes* 15 (1967–68): 293–331. Jean Budé's habit of annotating his purchases was not, in turn, an innovation but something of a family tradition, extending back to the time of Guillaume's great-grandfather, Jean I Budé. See G. Ouy, "Histoire 'visible' et histoire 'cachée' d'un manuscrit," *Le moyen âge* 64 (1958): 115–38, at 124.

even though he insisted to Erasmus that he rarely spent an afternoon browsing in the Paris bookshops.[27]

Latin compendiums and patrology, of course, were available through many channels, Greek texts by contrast through relatively few. Budé's closest intellectual predecessor in Paris was the jurist David Chambellan, who went so far in his zeal for humane letters as to cite both a verse of Homer (*Odyssey* 1.3) and a line of the Hebrew Bible (Ecclesiastes 9.4) in a 1499 formal plea to the Parlement of Paris.[28] And Chambellan's books record the history of his Greek studies and the vital role played by Hermonymus. A Greek psalter, signed by Chambellan in Greek, bears a short attestation: "I had this Greek psalter made at Paris, before I married, by one George Hermonymus, a Greek by nation. And in those days I worked very hard at Greek, that is, in A.D. 1478. David Chambellan."[29] The four Gospels fill in the details. Here Chambellan not only identified his scribe but explained his own eventual loss of cultural ambitions (in the normal way, by his acquisition of a family): "I had these holy gospels written and fitted out at Paris through the year before I married, by one George Hermonymus, a Greek scholar. In those days I had a tremendous desire for skill in Greek. This was interrupted by concern for my wedding, but after my marriage I often, as it were secretly, studied both Greek and Hebrew letters. God is my witness that I learned the Hebrew letters without a teacher and could read them, but I did not master the nature of this language well enough. But God is strong to provide a teacher, for I am ready to be taught by anybody. D. Chambellan."[30] The second book bore several other tokens of its place in the owner's

---

27. *Opus epistolarum Des. Erasmi Roterodami*, ep. 522, 2:444: "Heri animi causa (id quod raro soleo) tabernis bibliopolarum obeundis pomeridianas aliquot horas consumere statueram." On Budé's afternoon at the bookshops see E.Ph. Goldschmidt, *Medieval Texts and Their First Appearance in Print* (London, 1943), 72–73.

28. R. Delachenal, *Histoire des avocats au Parlement de Paris 1300–1600* (Paris, 1885), 248 nn. 1–2. His quotations are as follows: "De quo posset verificari versus Homeri, Odissa prima: Pollon d'antropon eiden astea kay noon egnon"; "Est autem vetus proverbium apud Ebreos, ut refert concionator xi: c.le.celeb.ai.a eu.tob.a.rerie.hameth [Ki lechelev chai hu tov min haaryeh hamet]. Hoc est, catulus vivus potencior est leone mortuo."

29. BN Paris MS grec 45, fol. 357 recto: "Hoc psalterium grecum feci scribi Parisius, antequam duxissem uxorem per quendam Georgium Hermonimum, natione Grecum. Et magnam illis diebus dabam operam litteris grecis, anno videlicet Domini millesimo CCCCLXXVIIIo. David Chambellan"; first published by H. Omont, "Georges Hermonyme de Sparte, maître de Grec à Paris et copiste de manuscrits," *Mémoires de la Société de l'Histoire de Paris* 12 (1885): 74.

30. BN Paris MS grec 98, fol. 1 recto: "Hec sacrosancta evangelia greca scribi et aptari feci Parisius per annum antequam ducerem uxorem per quendam Georgium Hermonimum, virum litteratum Grecum. Quo tempore mirabiliter optabam peritiam litterarum grecarum, quam interrupit solicitudo nuptiarum, tamen post matrimonium frequenter, quasi furtim, tam grecas quam ebreas litteras legi. Testis est michi Deus quod ebreas sine preceptore didisci [*sic*] litteras,

life and library: Chambellan's arms, twice; also, at the end of Matthew's Gospel, the portrait of a woman with long golden hair, richly dressed and elegantly gloved, with the note "Magdalena, whose image is here, was betrothed to me at the time of this picture, that is, around 1 November A.D. 1479."[31] Sentiment and scholarship melded richly in Chambellan's books, which served him at first as tools for study, later as objects for nostalgia, and still later, perhaps, as the stimulus for his citation of Homer in the Parlement.

Hermonymus apparently gave the clients who bought books from him more efficient service than he did his pupils. A letter to the young Reuchlin, written in the same period, shows him happily selling both custom-made and manufactured items: "I am sending you Theodore [Gaza's] introduction to Greek grammar. The lexicon however, belongs not to me but to a friend; the price will be six *scuta*. The fables [of Aesop?] that you saw in my room are not for sale. But I have a manuscript, written by me, that will be at your pleasure. If the dictionary were in my power, I would make it available to you, as I did in the grammar."[32]

It is not surprising, then, that Budé continued to give Hermonymus a good deal of business. The Greek manuscripts Hermonymus wrote for Guillaume include more than one copy of the Gospels and Epistles; pseudo-Dionysius the Areopagite; Thucydides; and Plato's *Leges*. As in his Homer, so in many of these texts Budé's arms advertise his ownership, while his notes reveal the effort that he expended, as a reader, to make the texts spiritually as well as materially his own.[33] The collection of Greek texts that he assembled included relatively few rarities but many texts that did not reach print until later in his career; in 1528, he told Sadoleto, who had asked for

---

et competenter legi, non tamen sufficienter proprietatem ejusdem lingue novi, sed potens est Dominus ministrare doctorem, paratus sum enim a quocunque doceri. D. Chambellan" (Omont, "Georges Hermonyme," 75).

31. BN Paris MS grec 98, fol. 95 verso: "Magdalena, cujus est hec ymago, tempore picture erat michi desponsata, videlicet circa kalendas novembris, anno Domini 1479" (Omont, "Georges Hermonyme," 76).

32. Omont, "Georges Hermonyme," 88–89, dated 8 February 1478: "Mitto ad te introductionem grammatices Theodori. De λεξικῷ, autem, meum non est, sed amici cuiusdam, precium erit scuta sex. Fabulae quas in camera mea vidisti non sunt venales. habeo tamen manu mea scriptas, quae erunt ad beneplacitum tuum. Si dictionarium esset in potestate mea, facerem tibi placitum, quemadmodum et in grammatica feci."

33. Gospels and Epistles: Cambridge University Library Ll.ii.13; BN Paris MS grec 59; BN Paris MSS grec 108–111. Ps-Dionysius: BN Paris MS grec 447. Thucydides: BN Paris MS grec 1638. Plato's *Leges:* Leiden University Library MS Voss. gr. fol. 74. See Omont's articles on Hermonymus, cited nn. 26 and 29. The best study of Budé's library is the splendid Bibliothèque Nationale exhibition catalog of 1968, *Guillaume Budé,* by M. Gasnault and Mme. Veyrin-Forrer.

a list of his Greek holdings, that the request made him ashamed, since he owned "no particularly remarkable books . . . beyond those that are to be found everywhere in the printers' shops."[34] It was a remarkably precocious working collection, no less and no more.

Hermonymus may not have been Budé's only source. As he looked back from the distance of the 1520s, he thought that the Greek books printed in Italy—for example, his Homer, edited in Florence by Chalcondyles, and the Aldine texts—rather than the manuscripts Hermonymus provided had really made the difference. Budé insisted that by buying and reading these, alone and without a tutor, he had made himself a competent Hellenist: "Finally, when a few years of intercourse with Italy had improved the condition of literature here as well, and books in both languages had gradually begun to arrive here, I set out to make good the loss I had suffered by spending so much time in ignorance." Only by unremitting individual effort—and by profiting from Hermonymus' services as a scribe, after he had abandoned trying to use him as a teacher—did Budé overcome the formidable difficulties that confronted him: "I spared no expense in buying books and no effort in studying them, forcing myself to work an hour and a half each day, with no breaks. First I reached the point where I began to unlearn what I had learned badly. These beginnings of study presented me with a great deal of work. For I had learned nothing but the letters, and those badly—and not to listen to that Greek tutor anymore when he taught, though he continued to visit me often, offering to sell books to me, eager buyer that I was, and writing all those that he had once mentioned."[35] Budé's printed Homer may well have come via the scribe. It certainly reveals as vividly as Chambellan's books the taste of a collector.

---

34. Quoted by Omont, "Notice sur la collection," 102, from a letter written in 1528, in Budé *Opera*, 1:395: "Quod librorum meorum Graecorum indicem mitti ad te postulas, ea de causa quam in literis tuis ascripsisti, rubore me suffusum esse scito: quippe qui nullos alios libros duntaxat memorandos habeam, praeter eos qui in chalcotyporum officinis hactenus passim pervagati sunt, ne huiusmodi quidem omnes. Manu scriptos satis multos olim domi habui, sed depositos et creditos. Quare contentus eris inopiae excusatione pro indice quem postulabas." In fact, his collection did have some rare items, at least in Latin; see Delaruelle, *Budé*, 225–27, on his MS of Pliny, BN Paris MS lat. 6797 (Sillig's *d*).

35. Budé, *Opera*, 1:362: "Tandem literis apud nostros quoque paucis annis illustratis Italiae commercio, librisque sensim utriusque linguae huc advectis, cum ego sarcire damnum contenderem aetatulae transactae per inscitiam, nec pecuniae in coemundis magno libris, nec labori in ediscendis parcerem, quotidianas etiam sesquioperas a me plane exigerem omni vacatione adempta, eo primum perveni, ut dediscere instituerem, quae male edoctus eram, quae mihi discendi primordia negocia multa exhibuerunt. Nihil enim didiceram πλὴν γραμμάτων, καὶ ταῦτα μέντοι κακὰ κακῶς: deinde ut ultra praeceptori illi Graeco ne auscultarem praelegenti, etiam si ad me ventitabat, libros empturienti venditans ac scriptitans quanti semel indicasset."

Like his father, Budé appreciated the physical qualities of books—especially those he gave or lent to high personages, such as the manuscript of "officia ciceronis in membranis" that he gave to the countess of Nassau, who had invited him to converse with her in August 1535.[36] The copy of the *Commentarii linguae Graecae* that he offered to François I has on its title page two splendid dragons holding up a shield with three fleurs-de-lis, the whole wreathed in bands and Greek mottos. The initial capital delta of the dedicatory letter and the border of the page that bears it spill over with microscopically precise, vibrant renditions of flowers, leaves, berries, a butterfly, and a peacock holding a snake.[37] He also took care of his own carefully edited and annotated working copies of his own books; it was a major favor when he allowed the Vitruvian scholar Philander to borrow his copy of *De transitu Hellenismi ad Christianismum,* "manu mea emendatum," for Cardinal Farnese.[38] The presence of Budé's arms, elegantly illuminated, the fine paper, and the care with which Budé entered his own notes show how much his copy of Homer mattered to him.

Budé's annotations run through both texts, only gradually thinning out in the *Odyssey.* In a way characteristic of many northern humanists, he made his printed Homer into something as personal as any entirely handwritten text.[39] Like many readers of manuscripts before him, he used visual signs—horizontal lines and backward diagonals with dots, wavy lines, delicate pointing hands with lacy cuffs, even a human face or two—to plot a way through the text as a whole.[40] Such signs recorded his interest in particular passages and exhibited the same lively amateur facility at sketching, the same pleasure in the deft wielding of the pen, that characterize the archi-

---

36. See the note from the last of Budé's seven notebooks, still preserved in the library of his descendant Jean-Evrard Dominicé in Geneva, in Delaruelle, *Budé,* 276: I cite them in the same order as Delaruelle did, in his full description of them. My thanks, once again, to M. le professeur O. Reverdin, through whose kindness I was able to examine these long-unstudied manuscripts.

37. BN Paris Impr. Vélins 523 (this is volume 1 of the *Commentarii*). See also the presentation copy of *De philologia* that he had prepared for Henri, duc d'Orléans, and Charles, duc d'Angoulême; BN Paris Impr. Vélins 1146.

38. See the note from the last of Budé's Genevan notebooks, in Delaruelle, *Budé,* 273.

39. See the rich parallel material collected and analyzed by J.B. Trapp in his Panizzi lectures of 1990, published in *Erasmus, Colet, and More: The Early Tudor Humanists and Their Books* (London, 1991).

40. On the visual side of annotation in an earlier age, cf. Vespasiano on Nicholas V, *Vite,* ed. A. Greco (Florence, 1970–76), 1:45: "Aveva pochi libri ch'egli non istudiassi e postillassi di sua mano, ch'era bellissimo scrittore di lettera tra l'antica e la moderna; in su quali libri faceva la memoria quando voleva trovare nulla." (He had few books that he did not study and annotate in his own hand. He wrote a lovely script, one somewhere between the old style and the modern; and in his books, where he could find no notes, he made some of his own.)

tectural diagrams and sketches he entered in the margin of his copy of Vitruvius.[41] But they also did more. Like colored pebbles dropped on the way through a maze, they recorded the reader's path for him (and perhaps for his immediate posterity). The annotator superimposed on the immense, pathless, heavily inhabited city of the Homeric text a set of routes as schematic, but also as easily traveled, as the map of the London Underground. The endless, swarming details of the text were thus captured in a coherent mnemonic system—a survival, deep into the age of printed books, of a central practice of the reader of manuscripts.[42] But the marks—which Budé also used in many other sorts of text, including his working copies of his own books—were obviously meant to offer more than summaries. In their clarity and distinct forms, they must have amounted to a code—or a shorthand—for Budé's responses to the text. They distinguished the severe black type of each almost-identical page from that of the rest by characterizing its particular qualities, offering a map of meaning as well as of action.

Unfortunately, Budé's code has proved relatively hard to crack. By contrast, the most systematic of Renaissance annotators, the English Ramist Gabriel Harvey, used a much more accessible set of symbols. He put the astrological sign of Mars beside battles, that for a conjunction beside diplomatic negotiations; and he used the letters *JC* (for *jurisconsultus*) to call attention to nice points of law. Like the fine italic script in which he couched many of his notes, Harvey's code of abbreviations was meant to record, rather than conceal, his judgments. In Budé's notes pointing hands clearly call attention to memorable passages—as in his Thucydides, where a particularly elegant set of fingers points to Cleon's remark that a city is better off with bad laws that are inviolable than with good ones that are ignored.[43] Beyond this, however, his system remains inscrutable in detail. Very likely he meant it to be used, almost like a family *livre de raison* (a secret diary and account book), only by his sons and the younger scholars whom he befriended, rather than by the larger public at which Harvey seems to have aimed.[44] But it clearly belongs to the same genus of literary devices and stems from the same effort to make visible the content and quality of a ver-

---

41. Venice, 1497; BN Paris Rés. V 318.

42. See M.J. Carruthers, *The Book of Memory* (Cambridge, 1992).

43. BN Paris MS grec 1638, fol. 67 recto, on 3.37.3.

44. The fullest studies to date of Budé's habits as an annotator rest on the practices exhibited in his copy of Pliny, a remarkable composite of printed and manuscript components now preserved in the Bodleian Library (Auct. L.4.3). See E.T. Merrill, "On the Bodleian Copy of Pliny's Letters," *Classical Philology* 2 (1907): 129–56, esp. 152–55; and Lowe and Rand, *A Sixth-Century Fragment,* esp. 59, where Rand writes, "Budaeus appears to have expressed his grades of interest rather elaborately—at least I can discover no other purpose for the different

bal form.[45] Though Erasmus did not lay much faith in the elaborate symbolic memory theaters of his contemporaries, he did urge students to annotate their texts systematically. He instructed them to use marks that not only called attention to all significant turns of speech, moral sentences, and exemplary actions but also indicated to which category the passage in question belonged. Such methods endured.[46] In the middle of the seventeenth century, Jan Amos Comenius included an image of a museum or study in his *Orbis sensualium pictus.* A reader inhabited this neat room, decorated only by shelves packed with thick books, fore-edges outward. Comenius describes with precision how he "readeth Books, which being within his reach, he layeth open upon a Desk," and marks the best things in them "with a dash, or a little star, in the Margent."[47]

Though the visual formed a natural and vital part of Budé's response to Homer, it was dominated, even overwhelmed, by the verbal. Whole pages of his text swarm with notes, most of them in Greek. When decoded, these give a rich sense of what Budé read and thought and used—of the emotional and intellectual weight that he assigned to each speech and combat, and of the help he received from other texts as he worked through a primary one. At the simplest level, Budé summarized what he read. Where a backward diagonal or a pointing hand was not explicit enough, a few words in Greek could convey the message or the relevance of a long section. Some of his Greek prose texts show only notes of this kind—the content of which natu-

---

signs employed. The simple obelus apparently denotes interest, the pointed obelus great interest, the doubly pointed obelus intense interest, and the pointing finger of a carefully drawn hand burning interest. He also adds catchwords." On the significance of the appearance of the obelus among the marks used by Budé, see later in this chapter. Cf. Budé, *L'étude des lettres,* ed. de la Garanderie, in which Budé's annotations in his working copy of *De studio litterarum* are typographically reproduced; Mme de la Garanderie refers explicitly to the unsolved problem of what the nonverbal notations mean.

45. On Harvey's coded annotations see L. Jardine and A. Grafton, "'Studied for Action': How Gabriel Harvey Read His Livy," *Past and Present* 129 (November 1990): 30–78.

46. Erasmus, *De ratione studii,* in *H. Grotii et aliorum dissertationes de studiis instituendis* (Amsterdam, 1645), 321: "His itaque rebus instructus, inter legendum auctores non oscitanter observabis, si quod incidat insigne verbum, si quid antique aut nove dictum, si quod argumentum aut inventum acute, aut tortum apte, si quod egregium orationis decus, si quod adagium, si quod exemplum, si qua sententia digna quae memoriae commendetur. Isque locus erit apta notula quapiam insigniendus. Notis enim non solum variis erit utendum, verum etiam accommodatis, quo protinus, quid rei sit, admoneant."

47. J.A. Comenius, *Orbis sensualium pictus,* trans. C. Hoole (London, 1672), 200–201. The Latin (ibid.) reads: "dum lectitat *Libros,* quos penes se super *Pluteum* exponit . . . aut [optima quaeque] in illis *Liturâ,* vel ad *marginem Asterisco,* notat." For a more detailed account see Comenius, *Opera didactica omnia* (Amsterdam, 1657; repr., Prague, 1957), 1: col. 288: "Lituris ne maculet: asteriscis ad marginem notatis, reminiscentiam nemo sublevare vetat: quin consultum est"; 3: col. 108.

rally varied with the texts by which they marched. For example, his manuscript of Xenophon and Polybius bears the signs of a reading attuned to political, constitutional, and military questions. It was only appropriate that the author of a treatise on the education of a king should mark his progress through Polybius 6 with simple but revealing summaries: "the constitution of the Romans"; "only the people can judge in a matter of life and death" (in darker ink than the rest), "of how many men a legion is composed"; "the superstition of the Romans" (emphasized with a pointing hand).[48] In Xenophon, by contrast, the *Symposium* attracted Budé's attention, with its account of Xanthippe, its "praise of poverty," and its evocation of that figure beloved of Renaissance Platonists, ἀφροδίτη διττὴ (the two Aphrodites), which also received a pointing hand and another of his coded marginal signs.[49] Homer, of course, wrote no prose. But the 1488 edition contained a number of prose introductions, in Greek. These, as we shall shortly see, Budé adorned with summaries and cross-references. The text also received key-words from time to time.

A second form of annotation—the one usually preferred by modern historians of reading and the book, who like it when their subjects find present relevance or powerful excitement in a classical text—moves farther from the text. In these cases summary gives way to reaction. Budé certainly read his texts to draw personal and intellectual lessons that he meant to use. Reading Polybius' analysis of the social importance of the Roman funeral ceremony, Budé was struck by the historian's comment on Roman δεισιδαιμονία (superstition).[50] The mixture of pragmatic admiration and religiously inspired distaste that he felt for this pagan ritual, so vividly described by Polybius, still inspired him when he wrote his will, many years later. Budé instructed his heirs to hold no "pagan" ceremonies of mourning and rear no memorials after his death—but he admitted that grand tombs were appropriate for kings and other grandees, whose memory needed preservation.[51]

---

48. BN Paris MS grec 1643, fols. 174 recto: ῥωμαίων πολιτεία; 175 verso: θανάτου κρίνει μόνος ὁ δῆμος; 178 verso: στρατόπεδον ἐκ πόσων ἀνδρῶν συνίσταται; 197 recto: ἡ δεισιδαιμονία τῶν ῥωμαίων.

49. Ibid., fols. 153 verso, 159 verso (ἐγκώμιον τῆς πενίας), 166 recto.

50. BN Paris MS grec 1643, fol. 197 recto (with a pointing hand as well as a note).

51. BN Paris MS Dupuy 581, fol. 171 recto–verso, at 171 verso: "Et si je ne veux qu'il y ait ceinture funebre ny autre representation à lentour du lieu où je seray enterré le long de lannée de mon trespas, parce que il me semble estre l'imitation des Cenotaphes, dont les Gentils anciennement ont usé, combien que j'estime les coustumes de ce faire à lentour des sepulchres des Princes, Prelats et autres grands personnages, dont la Memoire se doibt celebrer es lieux esquels ilz ont eu domination, prelature, ou magistrat eminent." On this text see Charton-Le Clech, *Chancellerie et culture au xvie siècle,* 220.

Homer was, of course, a preeminently provocative writer, whom later Greeks and Romans from Ion to Caligula cited in every imaginable connection and some unimaginable ones.[52] Christopher Comes van Manderscheit's Homer, for example, contains a neat political reading of a Homeric phrase: "Homer calls the prince ποιμένα λαῶν [shepherd of the people], for as the sheep must obey the shepherd, so the subjects must obey their prince. For ποιμήν properly means 'shepherd.'"[53] Budé's margin offers an even neater political application of Homer. Reading of the "twelve glorious kings" of the Phaeacian people in *Odyssey* 8.390, he drew a pointing hand and remarked, "note that this resembles our state, that is, the twelve peers of France."[54] Here one may see at least an inkling of the interest in the comparative study of institutions that would lead Budé to introduce a famous, elaborate digression on the Roman Senate, the Parisian Parlement and the Athenian Areopagus into his *Annotationes in Pandectas*.

Such reactions, however, are rare. Homer was too alien to Budé, and Budé himself was too committed to working his way into the hard detail of the text, for personal reactions and general opinions to play a large role in his notes. Budé stepped back from the text not while he chipped at the surface but afterward, when making the bright pebbles he had taken away with him into new mosaics. Like other Renaissance readers confronted by a massive classic—for example, Harvey, who did much the same with the copy of Livy, now also in Princeton, to which he devoted a lifetime's attention—Budé attacked the text again and again. The best way to begin, of course, was by surrounding such core works with a protective shell of collateral texts—texts that could help at every level, from the purely grammatical to the sublimely tropological. This both Harvey and Budé did. But where Harvey generously recorded in his notes the dates and titles of his collateral sources and even the names of those with whom he read them, Budé gave little information on his sources, none on his company. Only close attention to the content of his marginalia and to collateral evidence makes it possible to establish some basic points about what he knew and when he knew it.

Even the very simple notes from which we and he began are quite revealing: they eliminate certain possibilities and suggest others about what else lay on Budé's desk as he began to read. The synonyms he jotted down do not correspond, for example, with what he could have learned from a stan-

---

52. Cf. Plato's *Ion* and Suetonius *Caligula* 22.1, 22.4, 34.2.

53. BN Paris Rés Yb 151, fol. [Div] recto: "Principem Hom vocat ποιμένα λαῶν. Vt enim pastori oves, ita subditi principi parere debent. ποιμήν enim proprie opilionem significat."

54. II, sig. GGiii verso: "σημείωσαι hic instar nostrae reipublicae: id est xii patriciorum franciae."

dard reference book on Greek published by Aldo Manuzio in 1496, the *Thesaurus cornucopiae*. This did not supply the glosses that Budé deployed, and Budé's copy of it, now in Paris, shows little sign of use for Homeric purposes (by contrast, the section of the work that deals with Ionic Greek prose is elaborately annotated, since Budé used it systematically when he worked through the Greek text and Valla's Latin translation of Herodotus).[55] The beginning notes in the Homer came, in fact, not from any of the Greek books printed in Italy in the 1480s and 1490s but from a single, readily identifiable set of then unpublished Greek notes on the text: the so-called D scholia, or scholia Didymi, eventually printed by Janus Lascaris in Rome in 1517.

Scholia are the commentaries—made up of lemmas (words from the text to be explained) and short or long discussions—that adorned the margins of many of the classical Greek texts read in Greek schools of the imperial age and the Byzantine period. Hellenistic commentaries, often the work of a single, named author, filled rolls separate from those of the texts they dealt with, to which they might be keyed by a system of symbols. Along with lexica, *zetemata* (collections of discussions on particular problems), reference works on particular subjects, and treatises, they stood at the disposal of schoolmasters and readers in the Hellenistic age and after. Most such works have disappeared. Their contents are known in large part indirectly, through explanatory notes on texts, generally anonymous and often compilatory. These notes were entered in some papyri and then, with greater ease and system, in the margins of codices—the new form of book that came into being early in the Christian Era and soon established itself as standard for classical as well as Christian texts.[56] The central texts of Greek poetry—Homer, Pindar, and the tragedians—stood in special need of explanatory comment for students. Their language—when read in the third or second century A.D., to say nothing of the twelfth—was archaic, studded with unusual words and forms (Roman students, of course, found it entirely foreign and needed more elementary lexical help than Greeks). They referred to mythical characters that needed identification and embodied argumentative and literary structures that needed elucidation. The scholia met these needs, in a variety of ways. Compiled over a long period, from late antiquity until the first Byzantine Renaissance of the ninth and tenth century, they endured after more sophisticated Hellenistic monographs had dropped from sight. The scholars of Palaeologan Byzantium—who provided the Italian human-

---

55. BN Paris Rés. X 25.

56. For an up-to-date survey see H. Blanck, *Das Buch in der Antike* (Munich, 1992), 86–96.

ists with their Greek texts, their knowledge of the language, and their peda-
gogical methods—regularly used scholia (and often wrote their own).

When the Greek poets arrived in the West, their voices sometimes failed
to make much of an impression against the deafening chatter of their critical stowaways.[57] Yet the scholia that Western humanists confronted often
had excellent qualities. Some of them, for instance, contained not only
information but argument, giving (not to mention conflating) both sides
of ancient opinion on a disputed point. An alert humanist could find in a
single scholium not only what he considered the right answer to a learned
query but also a wrong answer, which he could have fun abusing.[58] Sometimes—as in the case of the scholia to Pindar, which misrepresented him as
an erudite, allusive writer, a *poeta doctus,* but which also laid due and heavy
emphasis on the rhetorical motivations that structured his poetry—they
pushed the Renaissance reader in useful directions.[59] Often the biographical
and literary suggestions of the scholia have proved surprisingly durable,
finding new applications through the centuries as philologists posed new
historical and literary questions.[60] These helpful assemblages of notes
seemed around 1500 to glitter with rare and valuable information. A friend
of Aldo Manuzio, so one story goes, warned him not to publish the scholia
on Euripides and Sophocles because the northern barbarians, once equipped
with them, would no longer have to come to Italy.[61] Budé used scholia regularly when reading prose texts: two copies of Demosthenes, one manu-

---

57. See in general *Realencyclopädie der classischen Altertumswissenschaft,* ed. A. Pauly, G.
Wissowa, and Kroll (1890–) s.v. "Scholien," by A. Gudeman; and N.G. Wilson's splendid
analysis, "Scoliasti e commentatori," *Studi classici e orientali* 33 (1983): 83–112.

58. See G. Valla to Johannes Placentinus, in J. Heiberg, *Beiträge zur Geschichte Georg
Valla's und seiner Bibliothek,* XVI. Beiheft zum Centralblatt für Bibliothekswesen (Leipzig,
1896), 87: "Quod autem exigis in epistolis Ovidii unde Paris Alexander quoque [so Heiberg, in
his note; MS Alexanderque] dictus, et utrum prius nomen habuerit, non dubium, quin primo
Paris dictus, non ut perversa Grammaticorum Graecorum fert opinio, ὅτι ἐν πήρᾳ ἐτράφη,
quod in detrimentum suae civitatis natus sit, sed παρὰ τὸ παριέναι τὸν θάνατον, id est, quod
destinatam sibi mortem praeterierit. Posterius autem Alexander nominatus, quod patriae suae
ἠλέξησεν, ὅ ἐστιν ἐβοήθησεν, id est opem tulerit, bello Graecorum ingruente: alexo enim arceo
prohibeoque significat, unde Alexander; quare Alexander posterius, Paris prius sine controver-
sia vocitatus." Heiberg shows (ibid., n. 4) that both the answer Valla ridicules and another version of the one he adopts appear in a single scholium to *Il.* 12.93.

59. See the elegant study of T. Schmitz, *Pindar in der französischen Renaissance* (Göttingen,
1993), esp. chap. 4; cf. G. Most, *The Measures of Praise* (Göttingen, 1985).

60. See the fine case study by G. Benedetto, *Il sogno e l'invettiva* (Florence, 1993), chap. 2.

61. Beatus Rhenanus to Charles V (preface to Erasmus, *Opera omnia* [Basel, 1540]), in
Opus epistolarum Des. Erasmi Roterodami, 1:67: "Hoc candore destituebatur ille, qui Venetiis
olim Aldo Manutio commentarios Graecos in Euripidem et Sophoclem aedere paranti dixit,
'Cave, cave hoc facias, ne barbari istis adiuti domi maneant et pauciores in Italiam ventitent.'"

script and one printed, and his manuscript of Plato's *Leges* all bear in their margins scholia that Budé entered with meticulous neatness.[62]

The D scholia on Homer—one set among many on Homer—were particularly helpful. They offered the newcomer a helping hand with Homeric vocabulary, for example, as it came up in the text, offering glosses, synonyms, and etymologies. Numerous parallels connect them with Budé's first, scattered efforts at marginal glossing, and Budé's occasional expansions would not have required the use of another source:

Budé's glosses	*Scholia Didymi*, ed. Lascaris
μῆνιν] χόλον ἐπίμονον, ἀπὸ τοῦ μένειν	μῆνιν] ὀργὴν χόλον
οὐλομένην] ὀλεθρίαν	οὐλομένην] ὀλεθρίαν
ἰφθίμους] ἰσχυρὰς, γενναίας,	ἰφθίμους] ἰσχυρὰς,
ἰσχυροψύχους	γενναίας
βουλῇ] Γνώμη	Βουλῇ] Γνώμη

Budé was by no means the only one to find these scholia most helpful. A copy of the printed text, now in Paris, bears the notes entered by no less an intellectual than the Florentine Republican Donato Giannotti (who recorded, for example, that ὀλεθρίαν, the word in the scholia that explains οὐλομένην, means *damnosam*).[63]

The question is not why Budé found these particular scholia so helpful but how he found them at all—given that he set to work some two decades before they reached print. Fortunately, the answer seems quite simple. Middle-aged in years by the 1490s, Budé was still young as a student. His experiment with Hermonymus, though it ended disastrously, was not an isolated one. When Budé needed to attack a hard text in a new field, he found himself a teacher. Fra Giovanni Giocondo, for example, provided him with both the verbal glosses and the numerous diagrams with which he

---

62. One of Budé's manuscripts of Demosthenes is Leiden University Library MS BPG 33, with scholia entered by the scribe, down to fol. 14 recto and at fols. 75 verso–81 verso. Budé enters scholia at fols. 17 recto, 23 recto, and 54 recto. His copy of the 1504 Aldine edition is Staatsbibliothek zu Berlin Preußischer Kulturbesitz, Haus 2, libri impressi cum notis manuscriptis folio 7, with content summaries and many scholia resembling the T scholia as reported by Dilts in his edition. (Budé's manuscript of the *Epitaphios logos*, written by Hermonymus, is Cambridge University Library MS Nn. 4.2, which later belonged to G. de Marnef; notes in his hand appear at fol. 5 verso.) His manuscript of Plato's *Leges*, Leiden University Library MS Voss. gr. fol. 74, has numerous notes, some of which are copied from the Platonic scholia: e.g., 102 recto, which corresponds to *Scholia Platonica* 715e Greene; 207 recto (817d Greene); 207 verso (818b Greene).

63. BN Paris Rés. Yb 23, sig. αii recto–verso.

decorated the margins of his Vitruvius.[64] Budé cheerfully advertised Giocondo's help in the *Annotationes in Pandectas,* in which he drew more than once on the textual and material evidence that the Italian architect had provided. In Greek, too, Budé eventually found more help than his claims of autodidacticism in the letter to Tunstall would suggest. In fact, he lavishly praised another Greek: "I specially cultivated Janus Lascaris, a Greek of high scholarship in both languages, whom the pope has now set in charge of a school for Greeks in Rome. While he wanted to do anything he could to help me, he could not help me greatly, since he was spending his time, for the most part, in the king's retinue, far from Paris, and I was generally in Paris, rarely at court. But this man of exquisite courtesy freely did whatever he could. Sometimes when he could be with me he gave me a direct lesson (but this did not come about twenty times); even when he was away he entrusted his chests of books to me and left them with me."[65] Lascaris must have tried out on his clever French pupil what he later offered a far larger audience of readers: the scholia that could give a student who already had some Greek a rapid entrée into the Homeric vocabulary and some explication of the content of the epic. When the printed edition of the scholia finally appeared, the papal privilege enthusiastically described them as the work "of very ancient and previously unpublished authors."[66] Not only books from Italy, then, helped Budé; his choice of what to read was dictated by a human intermediary. Two references in the *Commentarii linguae Graecae* confirm how much he owed to conversations with Lascaris about Greek texts.[67]

A book buyer, diplomat, and literary entrepreneur who came to France in 1495, Lascaris brought with him a massive library (parts of which he had bought for the Medici, in the course of two remarkable journeys to Greece,

---

64. See V. Juren, "Fra Giovanni Giocondo et le début des études vitruviennes en France," *Rinascimento,* ser. 2, 14 (1974): 101–15.

65. Budé, *Opera,* 1:363: "In quis praecipue colui Ioannem Lascarem, virum Graecum, utraque lingua pereruditum, qui nunc in urbe Graecorum scholae praefectus est a Pontifice. Is quum omnia causa mea cuperet, non magnopere iuvare me potuit, quum ageret fere in comitatu regis multis ab hac urbe milibus distractus, et ego frequens in urbe, rarissime in comitatu fuerim. Fecit libens id demum quod potuit, vir summa comitate praeditus, ut et nonnumquam praesens mihi aliquid praelegeret, id quod vicies non contigit, absens etiam librorum scrinia concrederet et penes me deponeret."

66. The fullest study of Lascaris, badly in need of replacement, is B. Knös, *Un ambassadeur de l'hellénisme—Janus Lascaris—et la tradition greco-byzantine dans l'humanisme français* (Uppsala, Stockholm, and Paris, 1945); for the passage quoted in text here, see 152. For further bibliography and important supplementary texts and materials see A. Pontani, "Per la biografia, le lettere, i codici, le versioni di Giano Lascari," in *Dotti bizantini e libri greci,* ed. Cortesi and Maltese, 363–433.

67. Knös, *Un ambassadeur de l'hellénisme,* 209–10.

as the Florentine Signoria reminded him in a sharply worded recall notice). He lent these books willingly to French intellectuals. Marginal notes in a list of them that has survived show that Budé had borrowed Syrianus, the commentaries of Sopatros and Marcellinus on Hermogenes, some speeches of Demosthenes, and the "Atticisms" of Moschopoulos. More interestingly still, the same notes show that Lascaris had a copy of the 1488 Homer, which he lent to the historian Paulus Emilius.[68] As late as 1510 Budé recalled his use of Lascaris' collection, while explaining why he had retained another of Lascaris' books that had reached him indirectly; still later, in 1526, Lascaris told a correspondent that he could not provide him with a given book until Budé had finished using it.[69] Budé's ability to gain access to the scholia, accordingly, poses no general difficulty. A collection that almost certainly included them was housed for a time among his books, and its owner was just the man to suggest how to use them.

Just at this point, sadly, as Budé's first competent Greek lessons come into focus, the scene dissolves again. A shared error provides strong evidence that Lascaris based his edition of the scholia on Vaticanus graecus 33.[70] But the list of Greek texts that Lascaris had in France does not include anything that looks like this (or a copy of it). And as we will see, this is by no means the only time, or the chief one, when the evidence on Budé's transactions with his Greek friend, intellectual and commercial, thins out to nonexistence. Only the Homer in Princeton fills in what would otherwise be a bare and frustrating narrative.

Once Budé had mastered the language, he turned first, and naturally enough, to the materials that came between the same covers as the Homeric epics. These were rich. When Homer became widely accessible again in the West, in the edition supervised by Demetrius Chalcondyles in 1488, the

---

68. The list is preserved in a famous manuscript, Vat. gr. 1412. See K.K. Müller, "Neue Mittheilungen über Janos Laskaris und die Mediceische Bibliothek," *Centralblatt für Bibliothekswesen* 1 (1884): 407, 408, 411, 410; for analysis of these materials and for Lascaris' activities as a book dealer see esp. J. Whittaker, "Parisinus Graecus 1962 and the Writings of Albinus," *Phoenix* 28 (1974): 320–54, 450–56; Whittaker, "Parisinus Graecus 1962 and Janus Lascaris," *Phoenix* 31 (1977): 239–44; and J.J. Keaney, "John Lascaris and Harpocration," *Greek, Roman, and Byzantine Studies* 23 (1982): 93–95. On Lascaris and the Medici collection see E.B. Fryde, *Humanism and Renaissance Historiography* (London, 1983) and S. Gentile, "Lorenzo e Giano Lascaris: Il fondo greco della biblioteca medicea privata," in *Lorenzo il Magnifico e il suo mondo*, ed. G.C. Garfagnini (Florence, 1994), 177–94.

69. Budé to Lascaris, 14 March 1510, in Budé, *Correspondance*, vol. 1, *Les lettres grecques*, trans. G. Lavoie, with the collaboration of R. Galibois (Quebec, 1977), 142–43; Lascaris to an unnamed correspondent, probably 1526, in Pontani, "Per la biografia," 389–90.

70. V. de Marco, "Sulla tradizona manoscritta degli 'Scholia minora' all' Iliade," *Atti della Reale Accademia Nazionale dei Lincei*, ser. 6, 4 (1932): 394–95.

smooth hulls of the epics were barnacled with substantial ancient parasites that affected their progress: the pseudo-Herodotean and Plutarchan lives of Homer and Dio's *Oratio* 53.[71] These texts, which until recently have provoked more scorn than interest from modern classicists, offered readers a set of differently polarized lenses, each of which produced a somewhat different-looking Homer. Pseudo-Plutarch evoked an ancient sage who had anticipated the positions of the main Greek philosophers; Herodotus described a witty improviser who had reacted to every confrontation with an elegant epigram; Dio praised a best-seller who had found enthusiastic readers north of the Crimea and (in translation) an audience in India. Poliziano—himself a poet as well as a scholar, and one who had translated and annotated four books of the *Iliad*—took these texts seriously enough to make them the basis of his introductory lecture on Homer in 1486.[72] Lascaris, who supposedly attended that lecture, reproached Poliziano—but for failing to reveal the sources of his learning, rather than for the content of his discourse.[73] Budé, who found the same three texts at the start of his printed Homer, thought they provided plenty of signposts for the serious reader to use in seeking the core of meaning concealed by the surface of the epics.

Pseudo-Plutarch's elaborate *Vita Homeri*, for example, argues, deploying many artful quotations, that the roots of every form of philosophy later professed in Greece could be found in Homer. Budé read this text with as much care as the epics themselves. He wreathed the text in summaries, calling attention to Plutarch's remark that Homer wished to describe manliness of body in the *Iliad* and strength of soul in the *Odyssey* (4; Budé adds a pointing hand and writes περὶ τῆς ἰλιάδος καὶ τῆς ὀδυσσ.); to Plutarch's insistence that Homer made the Gods interact with humans to show that they were concerned with human affairs (5: πεποίηκε τοὺς θεοὺς ὁμιλοῦντας τοῖς ἀνθρώποις; 117: ὁμιλοῦντας τοῖς ἀνθρώποις τοὺς θεοὺς ποιεῖ); to Plutarch's descriptions of Homer's language (8: ποικίλη τῇ λέξει κέχρηται

---

71. On the equipment that Renaissance readers of Homer could deploy see in general D.C. Allen, *Mysteriously Meant* (Baltimore, 1970); P. Ford, "Conrad Gesner et le fabuleux manteau," *Bibliothèque d'Humanisme et Renaissance* 47 (1985): 305–20; and A. Grafton, "Renaissance Readers of Homer's Ancient Readers," in *Homer's Ancient Readers*, ed. R. Lamberton and J.J. Keaney (Princeton, 1992), 149–72.

72. See A. Levine [Rubinstein], "The Notes to Poliziano's *Iliad*," *Italia Medioevale e Umanistica* 25 (1982): 205–39.

73. See N.G. Wilson, *From Byzantium to Italy* (London, 1992), 101–4. Wilson points out that the story exists in two versions. The one told by Budé makes Poliziano plagiarize Plutarch; that told by François Duaren, who claimed to have heard it from Budé, makes him plagiarize Herodotus and describes Lascaris' intervention. The only point that could be added to Wilson's analysis is that both critiques were true; Poliziano's encomium of Homer as father of medicine, for example (ibid., 102), came not from his mother wit but from Plutarch.

and pointing hand; 16: ὁμηρικὴ ὀνοματοποΐα and pointing hand; ὅμηρος ποικίλοις τοῖς εἴδεσιν ἐχρήσατο τῶν παραβολῶν); to Plutarch's assemblies of quotable quotations (151: ὁμήρου ἀποφθέγματα, two pointing hands, Γνῶμαι ὁμηρικαὶ); and to Plutarch's demonstration that Homer provided wholesome doctrine about the fact that a house will survive when its women obey (187: horizontal line with a dot above and one below, followed by σημείωσαι περὶ τοῦ διὸς καὶ ἥρας; pointing hand; περὶ τοῦ καθήκοντος τῆς συνοικούσας γυναικὸς; horizontal line with dot above and dot below).[74]

So far Budé did nothing terribly unusual; the other annotator in the Princeton volume took similar pains to identify the particular morals whose genealogy stretched back to Homer.[75] But as Budé worked, he began to find certain segments of the introductory text particularly exciting. In 92 Plutarch argues that the ancient sages had set out their deepest thoughts in poetic form because by doing so they both pleased the learned and baffled the ignorant, who could not despise what they did not understand. Budé marked the passage boldly, with a stylishly grim-looking profile of a humanist. He also used this device a number of times to single out important passages in one of his manuscripts of the Gospels—a clear sign of the value that he also ascribed to pseudo-Plutarch's discussion of allegorization.[76] More remarkably, he applied this principle systematically to the Homeric text, testing and embellishing Plutarch's own detailed allegories as he went.[77] At 129, for example, Plutarch explicates Athena's restraint of Achilles as a physical allegory of the bipartite soul and a moral one of the opposition between prudence and anger.[78] By this passage Budé entered what he must have seen as the most relevant bit of the Homeric text, *Iliad* 1.193: "So

---

74. I, sigs. BIII recto; ibid.; [CVII] verso; BIII verso; [BV] recto; CIII recto; [DVI] recto; EIII recto.

75. E.g., on Plutarch's treatment of Thales (ἡ ἀρχὴ τοῦ παντὸς); on Stoic doctrines in Homer: (ἀρχηγὸς ὁ ποιητὴς τοῦ τῶν στωϊκῶν δόγματος); and, more generally, πρῶτος ὅμηρος φιλοσοφεῖ.

76. Cambridge University Library MS Ll. 2.13, which Hermonymus described in his colophon as written for Budé in Paris (fol. 184 recto), has a number of faces in its margins: see fols. 33 verso, 39 verso, 59 verso, 115 verso, 117 recto, 120 recto, 123 recto. The first of these, at Matthew 19.23–24, singles out Christ's teaching that it will be easier for a camel to pass through the eye of a needle than for a rich man to enter the kingdom of heaven: recall that Budé was a rich man. Another Cambridge MS of the Gospels, also written by Hermonymus (MS Kk. 5.35), has no such marginalia.

77. Budé made something of a practice of this sort of systematic cross-referencing. For examples see his manuscript of Plutarch's *Moralia*, Leiden University Library MS Voss. gr. Q. 2, II, fols. 346 verso and 368 verso, where he uses the numbers of the gatherings; and his Aldine Demosthenes of 1504, Staatsbibliothek zu Berlin Preußischer Kulturbesitz, Haus 2, libri impressi cum notis manuscriptis folio 7, fols. 40 and 54.

78. I, fol. DI verso.

[Achilles] pondered in his mind and heart." At *Iliad* 1.193 Budé referred back to Plutarch in a marginal note: "vide Plut. supra [chart.] 23."[79]

Pseudo-Plutarch's interpretation of the passage fixed it once and forever in Budé's mind as an allegory of the prudence that the wise politician needs. In *De asse* he worked a restatement of this reading into a prominent position in his argument that even aristocrats must study. Budé there described the Homeric scene as "a notable fiction, one that should be continually kept in mind." He explicated the details of the text with passion and energy:

> Let us see how Homer, the wisest of poets, created his Achilles, so that we can learn from him if our state is properly constituted at present. . . . That very clever judge of human affairs had decided to make the character of Achilles stand for a strong, relentless soldier and leader. He then made the goddess Minerva stand over him repeatedly and, as it were, train him by warning him from behind, sometimes grasping him by the hair when she sees that he is being carried away headlong and boiling over with anger. He brings in his Achilles between anger and reason by turns, finally obeying Minerva and thrusting his drawn sword into his scabbard, suppressing and conquering his anger. One sees her imperiously forbidding, and him obediently repressing his anger. She threatens punishment if he does not obey the god; he puts away the impulse of his mind, so that he might not be described as disobedient.

Budé summed up what he took as Homer's message in terms that pseudo-Plutarch had not used but would almost certainly have accepted: "those who lack wisdom and prudence cannot carry out great deeds in war or in peace."[80]

---

79. I, fol. AIII verso. Budé also entered exegetical material in the margin: τῆς κόμης ἡ φρόνησις αὐτὸν κρατεῖ. ἔνθα ἵδρυται τὸ λογικὸν τῆς ψυχῆς μέρος . . .[by the hair. Prudence rules him; there dwells the reasonable part of the soul . . .].

80. Budé, *De asse* (Paris, 1514), fol. XII recto–verso, repr. with small changes, in *Opera*, 2:23 (I reproduce the latter): "memorabile figmentum ac memoria etiam atque etiam tenendum." "Videamus cuiusmodi Homerus poetarum sapientissimus Achillem suum finxerit, ut ex eo scire possimus an res nostra publica recte atque ordine hoc tempore constituta sit. . . . Ille igitur rerum humanarum perspicacissimus aestimator, quum sub Achillis persona fortem ac strenuum militem eundemque ducem formare statuisset, deam illi Minervam instantem identidem finxit, quasique condocefacientem monitione postica, nonnumquam caesarie reprehensantem cum praecipitem eum ferri atque ira excandescere sensit. Achillem autem suum inducit inter iram ratiocinationemque alternantes, Minervae tandem monitis obtemperantem, strictum ensem in vaginam ira suppressa edomitaque condentem. Videre est illam quidem imperiose

This case suggests that the package in which Homer came determined at least in some part the use Budé made of the contents. The episode in question, after all, shows two heroes violating every canon of decorum. Athena's intervention, though it prevented bloodshed, could not avert a massive loss of dignity on all sides. Erasmus, accordingly, explicitly rejected the idea that this text could provide good moral guidance. He agreed, and told young Latinists, that readers could find many wholesome myths to allegorize in Homer. But he also saw and evoked, in *Moriae encomium* and elsewhere, characteristics of Homer's gods and poetry for which traditional allegory could not, in his view, account.[81] In this case at least, the ancient introduction made Budé inattentive to particular features of the original text that his Dutch friend thought salient (even as it sharpened his attention to other features of the structure of the text).

Budé also read Dio, and he placed a wavy line in the margin at the passage in which Dio describes how hard he finds it to decide between those who explicate Homer's gods allegorically and those who condemn them as immoral.[82] He found pseudo-Herodotus even more compelling. This life treats Homer not as an inspired moralist but as a wandering bard. It offers biographical contexts for his compositions, usually by back-formation—a process nowadays much decried. Budé, however, accepted pseudo-Herodotus' method and results. Herodotus explains the name Homer as a reference to the poet's blindness, "since the Cymeans call blind men *homeroi* (13)."[83] Budé found similar information at the beginning of pseudo-Plutarch. He summarized it and added a specific reference to the text of the *Odyssey*: "ὅμηρος ἐπηρώθη τοὺς ὀφθαλμοὺς *vide odyss 8° ubi* τοῦ δημοδόκου *meminit. 47*" (Homer lost the use of his eyes. See book 8 of the *Odyssey*, where he mentions Demodocus [a blind bard]); then comes a pointing hand.[84] At the point in question (8.63–64) he referred backward, at the appropriate verses, to the relevant lines in pseudo-Plutarch, writing δημοδόκος and adding another point-

vetantem, hunc autem iram obsequiose prementem. Illa ni pareat ipse numini, vindictam interminatur: hic ponit vim animi, ne non paruisse dicatur . . . planum fit utique, qui sapientia et prudentia careant, res ab iis maximas nec bello nec pace geri posse."

81. Erasmus *Adagia* 2.1.1 ("Festina lente"). For his reading of Homer, and the tensions inherent in it, see the excellent treatment by T. Bleicher, *Homer in der deutschen Literatur (1450–1740)* (Stuttgart, 1972), 55–68.

82. Dio 53.3. Budé summarized the passage thus (sig. [EVIII] recto): περὶ τῶν ἀπομεμφομένων τὸν ὅμηρον ἕνεκα τῶν μυθολογημάτων.

83. I use the translation by M.R. Lefkowitz in *The Lives of the Greek Poets* (London, 1981).

84. I, sig. BI recto.

ing hand.[85] Budé thus showed that he had learned from ancient example to read the texts as autobiography as well as philosophy.

Yet Budé was hardly a docile reader. His own descriptions of reading, scattered in his works, cover a range of experiences, public and private—from his own deft impromptu translation of a Greek letter of Lascaris' at court (where, he remarked in discreet Greek of his own, no one could contest his interpretation) to the king's public discussion of the anti-Gallic prejudices he discovered in Livy when the text was read aloud at the royal table in French translation by the official *anagnostes,* or reader (his majesty preferred Josephus). Budé knew how to skim, and he described in some detail the rapid and superficial way in which he leafed through modern scholarly works by others. But he also knew how to scrutinize a text in detail, as when he set out to decide a vexed question in Cicero—and he let others know that he expected them to work in the latter mode if they hoped to decode his *De asse.* He made his own choices among commentators and translators—he found Themistius, for instance, especially handy for those books of Aristotle that, he held, had not been intended for a larger public.[86]

Hence one would not expect Budé always to use the ancient introductions to Homer in a single way. Indeed he did not. In his working copy he marked not only Plutarchan allegories but also literary judgments—like section 216, where Plutarch describes Homer as the master of painters as well as poets, because of his ability to represent every sort of animal from lions to pigs and to compare them appropriately to humans. Budé summarized the passage in Greek.[87] His interest was not casual. In his earliest published discussion of Homer, in the *Annotationes in Pandectas,* he quoted the passage. He did so, moreover, immediately after disparaging Poliziano's argument that the epics contained all important knowledge as a mere plagiarism of Plutarch, and he said nothing of substance in the *Annotationes* about Plutarch's allegorical exegesis of the text.[88] Budé thus excitingly suggested,

---

85. II, sig. [FFVII] recto.

86. Budé to Lascaris, 12.6.1521, in Budé, *Correspondance,* 1:154; Budé, *La philologie,* ed. and trans. M. Lebel (Quebec, 1989), 78–79; Budé to B. Rutilio, in M.-H. Laurent, "Guillaume Budé et le '*De oratore*' de Cicéron," *Mélanges d'Archéologie et d'Histoire* 64 (1952): 239–47; Budé to Lamy, 2.5.1510, in *Correspondance,* 1:126–27.

87. Budé wrote ὅμηρος ζωγραφίας διδάσκαλος and ἡ ποιητικὴ ζωγραφία λαλοῦσα by ps.-Plutarch 216; two pointing hands accompany the verbal notes (I, sig. [EVII] recto).

88. Budé, *Opera,* 3:212: "Plutarchus in eo libro quem de Homero composuit, qui liber nondum Latinus ex professo factus est, licet Politianus, vir ille quidem excellentis doctrinae, sed animi non satis ingenui, ex eo libro rerum summas ad verbum transcribens, quasique flores praecerpens, non erubuit id opus pro suo edere, in quo nullam praeterquam transcribendi ac vertendi operam navaverat, in eo igitur libro Plutarchus ad hunc prope modum inquit . . ." On Budé's use of marginal notes to identify ideas and texts that he would later use in his own written work, see also Merrill, "On a Bodleian Copy," 152–55.

to the well-informed reader, that Homer had set out to be a vivid writer rather than a profound thinker. At least one highly qualified reader plainly read Budé's remarks in this sense. They inspired Rabelais to insert into the prologue to *Gargantua* his still-controversial discussion of ancient and modern, classical and Christian, allegorization, in which he repeated the charge that Poliziano had committed plagiarism and mocked the notion that Homer had had complex abstract ideas in mind as he wrote.[89]

Evidently Budé viewed his interpretative equipment not as a permanent mounting for his text, which fixed its position and illumination, but rather as a set of temporary decorative frames, rather like those of an old-fashioned seaside photographer, in which he could make his text look moral or vivid, physical or theological, as the occasion seemed to require. Certainly one collateral piece of evidence suggests as much. Budé's copy of one of the most systematic of all Renaissance allegorical commentaries, Landino's *Disputationes Camaldulenses,* is preserved in the Bibliothèque Nationale. Its margins summarize Landino's explication of Virgil point by point, with single words, phrases, and occasional pointing hands—all normally signs of interest, and often of assent, as in the case of Landino's discussion of the two Aphrodites. But sometimes summary yields to dissent—and even contradiction. Landino explains that Mary does her work with the mind alone, which is immortal and incorruptible; Martha does hers with the senses, which humans share with animals. That is why Mary is told that she has chosen "the best part [*optimam partem*], which shall not be taken away from her." Budé's marginal note reads: "In the Greek text the reading is 'good,' not 'best.' Therefore your deduction is false."[90] Elsewhere he questions Landino's etymological explanation of the name *Gerion* as "terrae litem": "but there is an eternal struggle of the earth, that is, the body against the spirit." Budé writes, "The spelling conflicts with the interpretation, since *Geryon* is spelled γηρυόνης [from γηρύω, 'sing']."[91] Budé seems generally to

---

89. F. Rabelais, *Oeuvres complètes,* ed. J. Boulenger, revised by L. Scheler (Paris, 1955), 5: "Croiez-vous en vostre foy qu'oncques Homère, escrivent l'*Illiade* et *Odyssée,* pensast ès allégories lesquelles de luy ont calfreté Plutarche, Heraclides Ponticq, Eustatie, Phornute, et ce que d'iceulx Politien a desrobé?" (Do you honestly believe that Homer, as he wrote the *Iliad* and the *Odyssey,* had in mind the allegories that Plutarch, Heraclides Ponticus, Eustathius and Phornutus have foisted upon him, and that Politian filched from them?) For the interpretation of this difficult passage—which is by no means a straightforward attack on allegorical interpretation—see E.M. Duval, "Interpretation and the 'Doctrine Absconce' of Rabelais' Prologue to *Gargantua,*" *Etudes rabelaisiennes* 18 (1985): 195–216.

90. C. Landino, *Disputationes Camaldulenses* (Florence, 1480); BN Paris Rés. Z1059, sig. Ciii verso: "graece non optimam sed bonam legitur. quare tu falso argumentaris."

91. BN Paris Rés. Z1059, sig. h verso: "Cum hoc sensu pugnat orthographia. geryones enim scribitur γηρυόνης."

have regarded Landino's allegories as sensible and helpful, and they took shape in a culture not radically distant from his own. Nonetheless, they elicited a range of responses from him, some highly critical. Similarly, he did not simply accept and apply the far more richly varied Homeric readings that he encountered in treatises, scholia, and commentaries.

Budé never abandoned his engagement with the literal sense of particular Homeric lines. A great many of his notes and extracts, naturally enough, reflect a strictly technical interest in definition of terms. Often they draw on another reference work that reached print early, the Venetian edition of the *Etymologicum magnum* (1499). Budé had his copy of this, also now in Paris, at his side as he mastered the epics. Its margins swarm with precise references to the Homeric verses incompletely cited in the text and with passages from the Homeric commentary of Eustathius (who had also used the work).[92] But both the full command of the epics that these notes suggest and the form of their script indicate that they fall relatively late in the course of his Homeric work—and certainly well after he had mastered the text as a whole. Moreover, most of these notes relate less to problems of interpretation in any wide sense than to what Budé himself described, in his letters to Erasmus, as the ceaseless, necessary drudgery that went into his great lexicographical work. This apparently rested not on systematic files so much as on annotated books and notebooks, the connections among which were recorded only in his own capacious memory.[93]

Unfortunately, we lack at least one sort of record without which Budé's encounter with Homer cannot be reconstructed in every detail. From the fifteenth century, humanists had advised their pupils not only to annotate their books but also to compile systematic notebooks in which they entered the most useful and distinctive facts, myths, and metaphors they encoun-

---

92. BN Paris Rés. X 63. Budé's notes are keyed to books and page numbers in Homer and correspond to the 1488 edition. For a discussion of the sources and content of the *Etymologicum magnum* see K. Alpers, "Griechische Lexicographie in Antike und Mittelalter, dargestellt an ausgewählten Beispielen," in *Welt der Information,* ed. H.-A. Koch, with A. Krup-Ebert (Stuttgart, 1990), 14–38 at 28–29.

93. See *Opus epistolarum Des. Erasmi Roterodami,* ep. 1328, V, 153: "Caeterum quod Corradus tibi de Lexico Graeco, nec agnosco ipse nec inficior. Aliquando id in mentem mihi venerat; sed scribendi labor me deterruit. Nam ut institu.eram, res erat immensi laboris, nec tamen commentationis tam mihi iam intractabilis quam valde argumentosae, duntaxat post adnotandi laborem iamdiu exanclatum. Plurima enim ita orsa habeo, ut detexendis iis non magnopere fortasse assudandum mihi esset: sed sparsa, incondita et dissipata, et quae me defuncto parum adiumenti successoribus meis allatura sint"; cf. 1812, VII, 35.

tered.[94] Comenius described his ideal reader as one who "picketh all the best things out of [his books] into his own Manual" or notebook.[95] Budé, an ideal humanist reader if ever there was one, kept elaborate notebooks, seven of which survive in a private library in Geneva. In them he entered what he saw as the most useful results of his classical reading. For the most part, though by no means exclusively, he filled these small, closely written manuscripts with excerpts from texts, metaphors, and pithy sayings—chewy morsels of ancient texts, which he thought readily applicable to modern subjects. The meticulous, line-by- line scrutiny revealed by the marginal notes was thus accompanied, or followed, by a second sort of examination: reading as application, as compilation for use. Budé recorded and highlighted the results of these second readings with great care. For one text, the *Deipnosophistae* of Athenaeus, he even used a system of colored inks to record his extracts and comments.

The Genevan notebooks, however, represent no more than a fraction of Budé's original compilation, and the record of his preparations to use Homer consists of a few fragments only.[96] In each case, Budé's notes began from a Homeric passage that had caught his eye as he read the printed text. In each, he gave the word in question a twist that one could not have predicted from his original marginal note.

94. See, e.g., Guarino's detailed instructions, in E. Garin, *Il pensiero pedagogico dello umanesimo* (Florence, 1958), 382–83. For sympathetic treatments see R.R. Bolgar, *The Classical Tradition and Its Beneficiaries* (Cambridge, 1954); and M.M. Phillips, "Erasmus and the Art of Writing," in *Scrinium Erasmianum*, ed. J. Coppens (Leiden, 1969), 1:335–50.

95. Comenius, *Orbis sensualium pictus,* trans. Hoole, 200: "ex illis in *Manuale* suum optima quaeque excerpit." A more detailed account appears in *Opera didactica omnia*, 1: col. 288; 3: cols. 108–9. Comenius emphasizes the need to devise an information retrieval system as well as to compile notes: "Sed memento, *Diarium hoc instrui oportere Indice alphabetico:* qui tibi necessaria requirenti, ubi consignatum stet unum quodque, indicet, eoque inventioni promtae serviat."

96. In the dedicatory letter to what is described as Budé's *Lexicon Graeco-Latinum seu Thesaurus linguae Graecae* (Geneva, 1554), Claude Baduel describes Budé's practice of taking detailed lexical notes, including illustrations of usage, and claims that the dictionary he presents includes not only the material of Budé's already published in the imperfect lexicon of Jacques Toussain but also further information derived from "tres Budaei commentarii" made available to Baduel by Budé's son Jean. As Budé mentions Baduel twice, in the diary-like entries at the end of his seventh Genevan notebook, it is clear that he belonged to Budé's circle: there seems no reason to doubt that he had access to the notebooks he describes. But the actual content of the dictionary Baduel published matches none of the lexical materials in the seven surviving notebooks: strong evidence, if any is needed, that many more once existed. My thanks, again, to M. Reverdin, for calling Baduel's *Lexicon* to my attention and placing his own copy at my disposal.

At *Iliad* 1.231, Budé glossed the epithet Achilles applied to Agamenon, δημοβόρος, "devourer of the people," explaining that it referred to a devourer of τὰ δημόσια, "the public funds."[97] In his notebook he explained, in detail, in what rhetorical context this term and its Latin equivalent might prove useful in his own time.

> plebivorus dici potest δημοβόρος βασιλεὺς apud homerum in pri. iliad. 4. interpres plebivorax transtulit. angariator ut ipse inquit subditorum. quo nomine notari possunt qui quovis peculatus genere populi substantiam exedunt quique populi
> viscera
> loculos exterant. huic *plebicola* rex opponi potest.

[The δημοβόρος βασιλεὺς in book 1 of Homer's *Ilias* could be called "plebivorus" [in Latin]; the translator rendered it as "plebivorax," the one, as he says, who forces his subjects into service. This epithet can be used for those who consume the substance of the people by any form of embezzlement and who crush their strongboxes [or] entrails. The king who is "plebicola" can be contrasted with this sort.]

At *Iliad* 1.402–3 Budé noted that the hundred-handed Briareus was a marine *daimon* who had deprived his own father Poseidon of his rights.[98] In his Genevan notebooks he showed how the *daimon*'s name might serve as an appropriate epithet for a tyrant, or even for the Holy Father in Rome, given his possession of the power to bind and to loose.

> hecatoncher centimanus briareus cuius meminit homerus in primo iliados qui iovem a vinculis deorum liberavit: quinquaginta hominum vires habens. sic appellari potest quicunque potentia vel viribus excellit.
> ab immensa absolvendi potestate ligandique
> pontifex summus. Et rex praepotens qui copias suas in varia loca distribuere potest: et manus varias in provincias spargere ut dicitur: cuiusque manus nullibi distineri possunt prae copiarum multitudine.

[Homer mentions the hundred-handed Briareus, who freed Jove from the chains of the gods, in *Iliad* 1: he had the strength of fifty men. Anyone outstanding in power or strength can be called this—the pope,

---

97. I, sig. AIIII recto.
98. I, sig. [AVI] recto.

from his enormous power to bind and to loose; and a very powerful king who can send his forces out to various places and distribute various bands into the provinces, as the saying goes: "and his bands could not be held off anywhere because of the large numbers of his forces."]

At *Iliad* 5.60, Budé remarked that Harmonides, the builder of Paris' ships, was a τέκτων (a carpenter; his calling is given as his other name in 5.59).[99] In his notebook, however, Budé discussed not the builder but the ships themselves, or rather the adjective that Homer applied to them, ἀρχεκάκους, "the origins of evil," in 5.62–63, which Budé quoted:

archecacos, principium et causa malorum. homerus de harmonide ὃς καὶ ἀλεξάνδρω τεκτήνατο νῆας ἐΐσας ἀρχεκάκους, αἳ πᾶσι κακὸν τρώεσσι γένοντο

[Archecacos means the beginning and cause of evils. Homer says of Harmonides: "who crafted for Alexander the well-balanced ships, the origins of evil, which brought destruction on all the Trojans."]

Each entry in the notebook reveals more than the parallel notes in the margins of Budé's text; the first two show precisely how he intended to turn what he had gleaned from the text into raw materials for his own prose. Taken with Budé's marginal notes and his own finished prose, these notes make it possible to chart the general course of his Homeric reading, from the first contact with text and commentary to the reflection that preceded creative reuse—a vast recycling project, carried out on a grand scale, and always with meticulous attention to detail. But in the absence of further Homeric notebooks, a full reconstruction remains impossible.

Still, the margins of the Princeton Homer tell some instructive tales. They show, for instance, that pseudo-Plutarch was far from the only ancient reader who helped Budé penetrate between the lines, and some of the results he drew from his more recondite sources were hardly obvious. In 102 Plutarch explains that the battle of the gods in *Iliad* 21 teaches a lesson about natural oppositions. The combat of Athena and Ares, in particular, stands for the conflict of τὸ λογιστικὸν τῷ ἀλογίστῳ, τουτέστι τὸ ἀγαθὸν τῷ κακῷ [the rational against the irrational, that is, good against evil]. Budé here offered in the margin, as he often did, a brief summary in Greek: περὶ τῆς τῶν θεῶν παρατάξεως παρὰ τῷ ποιητῇ [on the poet's juxtaposition of

---

99. I, sig. EIII recto.

the gods for battle], as well as a reference to *Iliad* 21.[100] At the margin of 21.410 he repeated and expanded on Plutarch's allegorization: "recte autem Mars id est impetus a sapientia vincitur: et iniusta causa a iusta: mars denique ex faemina tantum natus: a pallade ex viro tantum nata et armata. vide plut supra char. 19" [Mars, that is, impulse, is rightly beaten by wisdom; and the unjust cause by the just one; and Mars, finally, who was born from a woman alone, by Pallas, who was born from and armed by a man alone. See Plutarch, fol. 19 above].[101] The curious point here is not that Budé found the passage striking. Any Renaissance reader would have done so, even if he did not have a fully formed interpretation to offer. One Erythraeus (Rossi), for example, who owned a copy of the 1488 edition now preserved in the Vatican Library, showed both his fascination and his consternation when he entered a summary of Monty Pythonish literalness in his margin at the same passage:

> Mars prosternitur a Minerva
> Pallas Martem vincit
> Pallas Marti insultat
> Venus manu ducit Martem a Minerva prostratum

> [Mars is laid out by Minerva.
> Pallas is victorious over Mars.
> Pallas taunts Mars.
> Venus leads Mars away after Minerva lays him out][102]

Neither is it surprising that Budé had more to say. But if the general tenor of Budé's note, which strains to domesticate the female's triumph over the male, seems predictable, one detail stands out as odd, even wild. To the interpretation given by Plutarch Budé adds the observation that the offspring of a man only, Athena, rightly defeated the offspring of a woman only, Ares. This is incorrect mythology, in the Greek tradition: Ares was hardly a wise child, but he knew his own father.[103] It does not come from pseudo-Plutarch. Where then did Budé find this doctrine? What—if anything—can it tell us about his reading of Homer?

---

100. I, sig. [CV] verso.

101. I, sig. ZI recto.

102. Biblioteca Apostolica Vaticana Inc. 2.17.

103. Ovid is the earliest source for the view Budé presents. But Budé does not cite parallel literary sources in his Homeric notes, here or elsewhere; hence I arrive at the analysis that follows in text.

A rich source that one would expect a pupil of Lascaris to consult when Homeric mysteries came up is the enormous Homeric commentary of Eustathius, deacon of Santa Sophia and later metropolitan of Thessalonica. This Byzantine scholar and churchman of the twelfth century assembled a vast amount of material on both the *Iliad* and the *Odyssey,* covering everything from history and myth to prosody and meter, and drawing on a version of the Homeric scholia richer than the one we now have, as well as on works now extant.[104] His work did not appear in print until 1542–50, but it established itself even in the age of manuscripts as an invaluable aid to the understanding of the Homeric poems. Erasmus, for example, recommended it as containing a large stock of allegorized myths for aspiring Latinists. Lascaris had copies of Eustathius' commentaries on *Iliad* 1–8 (Laur. 59, 2) and the *Odyssey* (Laur. 59, 6) with him in France, and we shall see that Budé cited Eustathius explicitly elsewhere.[105] Appositely enough, Eustathius provides what he calls a "mythical" explanation "according to the ancients" for Athena's victory. But this is not identical with Budé's: Athena, Eustathius says,"was born of a man alone, ἐξ ἀνδρὸς μόνου, and Ares of a woman *as well* [as a man], καὶ ἐκ γυναικός." Budé could hardly have misconstrued the passage.

The best explanation for Budé's deviant doctrine is that it comes from a deviant source. In fact, the error in question identifies the source precisely. One of the richest sets of scholia on the *Iliad,* known to philologists as B, concerns itself chiefly with exegetical questions and offers a great many allegorical and mythical explications of really or supposedly puzzling points. And one of the chief witnesses to this branch of the ancient scholarly tradition, a tenth-century manuscript now in Venice (Marc. gr. 453, or B), offers precisely the explication Budé copied out: ἔστι γὰρ ἡ μὲν ἐξ ἀνδρὸς μόνου, ὁ δὲ ἐκ γυναικός, [she is born of a man only, he of a woman]. Here and elsewhere, Budé drew on materials that would not come into general use by philologists until 1788—when the French philologist Villoison published the Venice scholia, making possible the radical new work of Friedrich August Wolf and others on the history of the Homeric text.[106] It was nat-

---

104. See R. Browning, "Homer in Byzantium," *Viator* 6 (1975): 15–33; Browning, "The Byzantines and Homer," in *Homer's Ancient Readers,* ed. Lamberton and Keaney, 141–44.

105. Müller, "Neue Mittheilungen über Janos Laskaris," 407.

106. For a similar use of bT material to flesh out the general outlines Budé brought away from pseudo-Plutarch, see his note on 2.372, I, sig. [BVI] recto: "homerus ubique pluris facit τῶν σωματικῶν τὰ ψυχικὰ. ut hic inducens agamemnonem optantem non decem aiaces sed decem nestores"; cf. bT ad loc.: δῆλός ἐστιν ὁ ποιητὴς τῶν σωματικῶν τὰ ψυχικὰ προτιμῶν.

ural that he found the forms of exegesis practiced by the scholia rather more convincing than his professional successors did in the Enlightenment.[107]

More surprisingly still, Budé also had a source of information about the material preserved in a second Venetian manuscript, Marc. gr. 454 (known to specialists as A). This splendid tenth-century codex bears in its margins and between its lines the richest surviving record of the textual criticism practiced by the scholars of Hellenistic Alexandria. Aristarchus and his colleagues—like Budé, so long afterward—used a shorthand to express their opinions about particular Homeric words and lines. They equipped the margins of their texts with so-called critical signs—for example, the obelus, or horizontal line, which indicated that a given line or passage should be omitted in reading, as inappropriate to a character or a situation. Longer notes sometimes gave the reasons why Aristarchus, Aristophanes of Byzantium, or Zenodotus thought a correction necessary. Many of these reasons, examined from a modern point of view, reflect literary criticism of an author rather than textual criticism of the manuscripts. Moreover, none of the Alexandrian material is directly transmitted; the Venice manuscript preserves material that had already been edited and epitomized by scholars of the first centuries B.C. and A.D. Nonetheless, the Venice A manuscript fully deserves the prominence it attained in 1795, when Wolf used its testimony to write the first modern history of an ancient text. It—or rather Hartmut Erbse's edition of its scholia—is the first place a modern scholar must go to listen to Alexandrian colleagues—the first scholars who insisted that difficulties in the Homeric text could be resolved by surgery, or even total excision, but not by allegorization—engaged in discussion.[108]

Until now, historians of scholarship have normally supposed that no modern philologist heard these ancestral voices until Villoison published the Venice A manuscript in 1788. True, the Venetian scholar Vettor Fausto, better known for his efforts to create a modern trireme than for his textual

---

107. In general, Renaissance scholars did not view scholia with the contempt of their modern successors, who seem to find many of them more exasperating than illuminating (a view that took root very early. See F.A. Wolf, *Prolegomena to Homer [1795]*, trans. A. Grafton, G.W. Most, and J.E.G. Zetzel, rev. ed. [Princeton, 1988], 13–14 and n. 29; and M. Schmidt, *Die Erklärungen zum Weltbild Homers und zur Kultur der Heroenzeit in den bT-Scholien zur Ilias* [Munich, 1976]). For an explicit early modern view see, e.g., C. Hornei's preface to his edition of the T(ownley) scholia, which are closely related to B, on *Iliad* 9 (Helmstedt, 1620), dedicatory letter: "totae enim occupatae fere sunt, non tam in vocum explanatione quam in observationibus et monitis rhetoricis, ethicis, et politicis ex poeta deducendis, quam opt. et tantum non unicam esse interpretandi poetas rationem nemo ignorat nisi et quid sit poetica ignoret."

108. *Scholia Graeca in Homeri Iliadem* (Berlin, 1969–83).

criticism, did enter some notes from A into a copy of the 1488 edition now in the Marciana.[109] But no scholar of the sixteenth through eighteenth centuries cited this material in print (some did cite material from the exegetical scholia).

The Princeton Homer shows that Budé knew a surprising amount about the material in A. He seems to have seen, in some form or other, the critical signs; the obelus, for example, appears as one of his coded marginal signs. More revealingly, he used information from the A scholia to describe at least one Alexandrian effort to correct the *Iliad* by eliminating material that did not live up to their canons of taste. Many scholars had read, as Budé did, in pseudo-Plutarch that the Alexandrian scholar Aristarchus had divided Homer's works into books.[110] But Budé also discovered specific evidence about the ways in which Aristarchus and others had tried to deal with aesthetically and logically problematic passages in Homer. The A scholia preserve many of these ancient critical discussions, several of which Budé brought to light for the first time in centuries. For example, Paris seemingly challenges all the best Greek champions at once at the start of *Iliad* 3. The two lines in question, Budé notes, "ἀθετοῦνται] quod nec arma habet monomachiae apta: et absurdum est hominem timidissimum omnes simul fortissimos provocasse" [are condemned, since Paris has no weapons suitable for single combat, and it is absurd for a man of such timidity to have challenged all the strongest at once.][111] Budé thus became, so far as I can tell, the first modern scholar to consider in detail the typical procedure of Alexandrian textual criticism.[112]

Naturally, Budé did not anticipate the conclusions that Wolf and his successors drew from this material. They have drawn strict distinctions, whenever possible, between the critical material in Venetus A and the exegetical efforts of B and T. Budé, by contrast, used the interpretation of Paris' challenge found in the exegetical scholia to show that the Alexandrians' criticism missed the point of the line. The other scholia explained that Paris

---

109. Ibid., 1:xv–xvi; *Scholia Graeca in Homeri Iliadem*, ed. W. Dindorf, vol. 1 (Oxford, 1875), xxiv–xxvi.

110. See Budé's note on ps.-Plutarch, 4: ἀρίσταρχος διήρηκεν τὴν τοῦ ὁμήρου ποίησιν (sig. BIII recto); and his development of this in the *Annotationes in Pandectas,* in *Opera,* 3:212: "Duas autem Homerus poeses reliquit, Iliadem et Odysseam, ab Aristarcho Grammatico in numerum librorum divisas, utramque secundum Alphabeti Graeci numerum et ordinem."

111. I, sig. [CV] verso.

112. See also Budé's remark, derived from A, at 23.405–6, I, sig. [ETviii] verso: "graeci ἀθετοῦσι hos versus duos . . ." For a modern discussion of this and other Alexandrian practices see L.D. Reynolds and N.G. Wilson, *Scribes and Scholars,* 3d ed. (Oxford, 1991), 10–16. Similar procedures appear in other traditions as well: see for one case in point M. Fishbane, *Biblical Interpretation in Ancient Israel* (Oxford, 1985).

challenged not the Greeks but his fellow Trojans to fight: "aliqui sic inter-
pretantur: προκαλίζετο πάντας ἀρίστους τῶν τρώων, ἀντίβιον μαχέσασθαι
τῶν ἀργείων [Some take the line in the following way: "He challenged all
the best of the Trojans, to fight against the Greeks"]. An additional note
records Budé's assent: "et recte sic accipiunt" [And they are right to read it
in this way]. In this case, exposure to Alexandrian methods did not prove
contagious.

It is hard to know exactly how much material Budé drew from any given
tradition, since they often overlap. At *Iliad* 23.531, for example, Homer
describes Meriones as ἥκιστος . . . ἐλαυνέμεν ἅρμ᾽ἐν ἀγῶνι [the slowest . . .
at driving a chariot in the race]. Not surprisingly, the word ἥκιστος caught
Budé's trained lexicographer's eye. He wrote "ἐλάχιστος semel apud
poetam legitur. apud oratores ἥκιστα pro οὐδαμῶς ponitur" [ἐλάχιστος is
found once in the poet. The orators use ἥκιστα for οὐδαμῶς].[113] Here, evidently, Budé translated (and added his own information to) the A scholium,
which read: <ὅτι> τὸ ἥκιστος τῶν ἅπαξ εἰρημένων ἐστί [<note that>
ἥκιστος is one of the words used only once]. But elsewhere the nature of his
sources for such information is less clear. On *Iliad* 3.54, for example, where
Hector tells the unwarlike Paris that his κίθαρις (lyre) will not help him
against Menelaus, Budé writes: "κιθάρα sunt qui pilei genus esse dicant.
Multa autem sunt semel dicta apud Homerum" [There are some who say
that a κιθάρα is a sort of cap. For there are many words that are used once
in Homer].[114] Budé could have taken this from the A scholia, parts of which
it resembles: "as some did not find Paris playing the lyre anywhere in the
poem, they changed κίθαρις to κίδαρις. They say this is a kind of cap. But
there are many words that are used once in Homer." But if Budé used A
here, he did not do so systematically (or see a complete text of the
scholium). For he omitted to explain that the second remark, that many
words are found only once in Homer, served to rebut the first, since it
showed that the correction of *kitharis* to *kidaris* was unnecessary. But he
could also have drawn on Eustathius, who comments that "some say that
the κίδαρις is a kind of cap mentioned once by the poet, and they say that
in Homer and others there are other words that are only used once."[115]
Though the A scholium resembles Budé's note more closely, the differences
do not prove that it was his source. That Budé used the A scholia is clear;
how he used it remains to be worked out, point by point.

---

113. I, sig.)I verso.
114. I, sig. [CVI] recto.
115. Eustathius 381.13.

In general, Budé—like a number of the later scholars who edited Greek scholia in the sixteenth century—seems to have worried less about preserving the point of view of some given kind of annotation or annotator than about cultivating the densest, richest hedge of notes he could around Homer. Sometimes he conflated interpretations that had originally contradicted one another. At 3.49, for example, Hector describes Helen as νυὸν ἀνδρῶν αἰχμητάων [a daughter-in-law of warriors]—that is, of the Greeks. Budé comments: "νυὸς proprie nurus dicitur. hic autem ἀντὶ τῆς νύμφης capitur. omnes autem graeciae principes ἐμνηστεύσαντο τὴν ἐλένην" [the proper sense of *nuos* is daughter- in-law. Here, however, it is taken instead of *numphe* [bride or young girl]. But all the princes of the Greeks wooed Helen].[116] In this case Eustathius had explained that one must take *nuos* as *numphe,* meaning that all the Greeks would fight for Helen boldly, ὡς ἀδελφοὺς ὑπὲρ νύμφης [as brothers for the sake of a virgin <sister>]. The exegetical scholia, by contrast, explained that Homer called Helen the collective daughter-in-law because πάντες . . . οἱ ἀριστοὶ ἐμνηστεύσαντο τὴν ἐλένην [all . . . the best of the Greeks wooed Helen], though she wound up with Menelaus. Here and elsewhere Budé seemingly preferred to synthesize rather than to discriminate—a tendency in which most users of scholia would follow him until Hemsterhusius and Valckenaer began, two centuries later, to divide the transmitted scholia up into their original strata and components.[117]

Sometimes Budé went still farther afield, enriching the tradition of Homeric exegesis with other scholarly materials originally alien to it. At *Iliad* 20.307–8, for example, Poseidon prophesies that Aeneas καὶ παῖδες παίδων [and the sons of his sons] will be kings one day among the Trojans. Budé writes: "poeta hic praesagit Romanum imperium. nam licet antiquior ipse roma fuerit: potuit tamen hoc praescivisse vaticiniis sibyllarum aut aliis oraculis. hunc autem versum καὶ παῖδες παίδων ferunt homerum ab orpheo accepisse, orpheum ab oraculo quodam apollinis. ab homero deinde virg. et nati natorum et qui nos ab il. [*Aeneid* 3.98]" [The poet here prophesies the Roman Empire. For though he was older than Rome, he could have known this in advance from the prophecies of the Sibyls or other oracles. But they say that Homer took this verse, "and his sons' sons" from Orpheus, and Orpheus from a certain oracle of Apollo, and Virgil, finally, from Homer: "and his sons's sons and those that will be born from them"].[118] Budé could

---

116. I, sig. [CV] verso.

117. See A. Grafton, *Defenders of the Text* (Cambridge, Mass., 1991), chap. 9; and Benedetto, *Il sogno e l'invettiva.*

118. I, sig. YI recto.

find a reference to a Homeric prophecy of Rome's future in the exegetical scholia, which also explained that the poet had derived this enlightenment "from the oracles of the Sibyl." But the remainder of the literary genealogy he offered came not from the Greek but from the late antique Latin scholarly tradition, as represented by Servius' comment on *Aeneid* 3.98: "sane hic versus Homeri est, quem et ipse de Orpheo sustulit, item Orpheus de oraculo Apollinis Hyperborei" [this verse certainly comes from Homer; he took it from Orpheus, and Orpheus in turn from an oracle of the Hyperborean Apollo]. Evidently Budé's ancient world, like that of Servius, had room for inspired pagan prophets—at least at the relatively early period, before 1508, when he compiled these notes. Here, and in other cases, Budé took off from unusual stations only to arrive at crowded, ordinary platforms.[119]

The permanent validity of Budé's conclusions matters less than the richness of his sources. The most erudite Renaissance Hellenists had their difficulties with the Greek of the scholia; Poliziano turned ἡ Δημώ, the name of a woman philospher quoted by a scholiast, into the name of a nonexistent man, *Hedemo*.[120] Students of Greek, quite reasonably, showed more inclination to preserve and integrate traditions than to distinguish among them. The Greek heritage was larger than the Latin, the texts were more alien, and the layers of their content were harder to separate. Whatever Budé's immediate sources, they glittered with interpretative gold and pyrites that did not become the public property of scholars until the eighteenth century.

A final judgment on Budé's work must await an edition of his notes (which I hope to provide) and the identification of his intermediate source (which has so far eluded me). Budé evidently used materials that were not in wide circulation in his time. Where he found them, as usual, he does not specify. Budé was a habitué of great libraries, private and public. In France he certainly knew the library of Saint Victor, whose catalog was brilliantly

---

119. Cf. the physical allegory that he offers at 15.21, where Zeus describes how indignant the gods became when he hung Hera up on high with anvils suspended from her feet (I, sig. [Pviii] recto): "physicum est quod dicit: nam aetheri subest aer, aeri autem aqua et terra duo gravia elementa: quae connexionem dii turbare non poterant." Such physical allegories—here as in the case of Hera's seduction of Zeus at the end of book 1—could be found even in the more common scholia and made their way rapidly into the classroom, for obvious reasons. See A. Grafton and L. Jardine, *From Humanism to the Humanities* (Cambridge, Mass., and London, 1986), chap. 5.

120. Levine [Rubinstein], "Notes to Poliziano's *Iliad*," 212. Her commentary shows that Poliziano, like Budé, drew material from scholia in a way that sometimes makes it impossible to determine his precise source. See further Cesarini Martinelli, "Grammatiche greche e bizantine."

parodied by Rabelais, and he probably frequented many of the other collections harbored in that most submerged of lost worlds of learning, the Paris of the old Colleges, which the Revolution demolished.[121] In Italy in 1505, he saw the private collection of Pietro Crinito, where he was not impressed by a manuscript of Poliziano's. In the Vatican he managed to inspect something more useful than the usual suspects, such as the Roman Virgil, that were always dragged out for visiting grandees: a "compendium iuris civilis . . . per indicis seriem ordine alphabeti sermone Graeco compositum" [a compendium of the civil law, laid out in alphabetical order, in Greek].[122] But the evidence suggests that he never reached, or at least never worked in, Bessarion's library of San Marco in Venice, where the Venice scholia themselves awaited discovery. In 1520 and 1521 Budé took a serious interest in the Marciana collection. He tried to induce Christophe de Longueil, who had permission to use the whole collection, to provide him with full information "de ista Bibliotheca Alexandrinae aemula" [about that library, which rivals that of Alexandria]. But the effort failed.[123] In 1521, when Lascaris found what he took as a new text, Diodorus 17, in Venice, Budé described the library both to other friends and to Lascaris himself as one "supposedly full of a vast quantity of remarkable texts"—and thus as one of which he had no personal and precise knowledge.[124]

It seems most likely, then, that Budé obtained his materials from an intermediary source or sources—more precisely, that he used materials belonging to Lascaris, who after all knew the Homeric scholia intimately and published the first edition of one set of them. Boivin and Villoison suggested that Budé used a glossed manuscript as his chief source. Matteo Devaris, after Lascaris' death, listed a glossed *Iliad* in an old script among the books that borrowers had not returned to Lascaris. But neither the manuscript Boivin had in mind nor any other I have inspected offers all the glosses Budé copied.[125] Two copies of the first edition of Homer with manuscript notes by Lascaris have been identified. One of them bears material from the B

121. Delaruelle, *Budé,* 165 n. 3.

122. Ibid., 104–5; for the standard visit see C. Bellièvre, *Souvenirs de voyages en Italie et en Orient, notes historiques, pièces de vers,* ed. C. Perrat (Geneva, 1956), 4–5. Admittedly Bellièvre also found something to boast about in his visit. He was allowed to examine the *vetustus codex* of Virgil, "quem non licet unicuique palpare," firsthand, to verify what Poliziano had said about it in the *Miscellanea.*

123. See L. Di Domenico, "Stralci da interfolgi e giunte inedite Morelliane sull'uso fatto di codici niceni," in *Miscellanea Marciana di Studi Bessarionei* (Padua, 1976), 37–38; and M. Zorzi, *La Libreria di San Marco* (Venice, 1987), 103.

124. Budé to de Brie, 19.6.1521, in Budé, *Opera,* 1:415 = Budé, *Correspondance,* 1:77; cf. Budé to Lascaris, 11.5.1521, *Opera,* 1:151.

125. For the Devaris inventory, from Vat. gr. 1412, see P. de Nolhac, "Inventaire des manuscrits grecs de Jean Lascaris," *Mélanges d'Archéologie et d'Histoire* 6 (1886): 260.

scholia in its margins. And Lascaris had a copy of the first edition with him in France.[126] But collation reveals that neither copy used by Lascaris contains the material from the A scholia that Budé entered in the volume now in Princeton.

In general, it seems likely that Lascaris, or his books, provided the channel by which Budé's information reached him. But I see no reason to assume that Budé simply copied one source, a preselected anthology of Homeric glosses already compiled by Lascaris. He could just as well have made his own, quite personal selection from the material offered by several books and manuscripts. This hypothesis fits the working methods attested by Budé's other books much better than does a simple effort to reduce his Homeric notes to a mere copy of something older. Until a source is produced, they should count as his own work.

For the rest of Budé's life, in any event, his thought and writing showed the deep imprint of his Homeric studies. This is true, first of all, in a literal sense; Homeric allegories, some of which he had demonstrably first considered in the margins of his working copy, came readily to mind and pen as he wrote his last essays on the liberal arts in the 1530s. At the end of *De philologia,* for example, the reader meets again two familar figures from *De asse:* the Homeric Athena, grasping Achilles by the hair to teach him wisdom, provides what Budé clearly still saw as the most moving figure of prudence that he could offer to François I.[127] The "most ancient . . . poets" still play the role, in *De studio litterarum,* of sages who did not wish the profane to understand their philosophical revelations and therefore cloaked them in integuments of myth and puzzle. These in turn gave rise to the licentious misunderstandings of later Greek mythology and orgiastic religion—the errors for which Plato wished to expel Homer and Hesiod from his just city.[128] Yet the poets—such as Hermes Trismegistus and Dionysius the Areopagite, in both of whom Budé warmly believed—had genuinely transmitted an ancient wisdom that matched the teachings of Christianity in part.[129] Budé's predisposition to believe that there had always been one truth, to which the best of the gentiles had enjoyed partial access (and of which they

---

126. Biblioteca Apostolica Vaticana Inc. 1.50 and BN Paris Rés. Yb 3–4. See Pontani, "Per la biografia," 431, for a recent discussion, emphasizing that Lascaris certainly wrote the glosses in the Parisian exemplar.

127. Budé, *L'étude des lettres,* ed. de la Garanderie, 218–21.

128. Budé, ibid., 110–13.

129. See ibid., 112–13, 88–91; for Dionysius cf. Budé's long notes from Bessarion's defense of Plato in his copy, BN Paris MS grec 447, fol. I recto.

had offered a partial revelation) surely reflected the long-lasting impact of his first encounter with classical allegorization. So perhaps did certain features of his prose—such as his tendency to conceal his precise meaning (only to take offense when misread) or his pervasive and eminently Homeric use of myths and similes (the extended simile between hunting and the pursuit of wisdom in *De philologia,* which was eventually pulled out and republished as a separate work, seems particularly Homeric in both scale and tone).

No text reveals Budé's lasting commitment to his early way of reading better than the *De transitu Hellenismi ad Christianismum*—the long, meditative, often troubled work of his last years, in which he tried to show how classical culture was both superseded by and enfolded in the Christian revelation.[130] In the margin of his working copy of the *Odyssey,* for example, he had copied out Eusthatius' explanation of the marvelous plant *moly,* given by the god Hermes: ἔστι δὲ θεόσδοτον ἀγαθὸν. ἀλληγορεῖται δὲ πρὸς τὴν παιδείαν. ὁ Ἑρμῆς ἐκφαίνει ταῖς λογικαῖς μεθόδοις [It is a divinely given good. Allegorically, it refers to education. Hermes reveals it by rational methods].[131]

But when Budé returned to the passage in *De transitu,* his assumptions about the validity of pagan culture—and about the inspiration and morality of pagan poets—had shifted. His reading of the text was not totally dissimilar in content from his original note, but he now pitched the old song in a different key. The greatest scholars, Budé said, had held that by the name *moly* Homer referred to philosophy: "This man, the most clever of mortals, thought wisdom so powerful that it could restore to themselves and to humanity the characters of men that had degenerated into brute and animal-like or bovine states."[132] But he himself refuted this traditional view as the inadequate one of mere pagans. Wisdom came, as the poet and his commentator both suggested, from above, from God. But that real wisdom did not lie in the culture of the Greeks, "which is dug up from the earth, and human inventions"; rather, it must be found "in the wells of celestial wis-

---

130. See esp. the *thèse,* itself impressively complex and meditative, of M.-M. de la Garanderie, *Christianisme et lettres profanes* (Lille and Paris, 1976).

131. II, sig. II I verso. Cf. Eustathius on *Odyssey* 10.306.

132. G. Budé, *Le passage de l'Hellénisme au Christianisme,* ed. and trans. M.-M. de la Garanderie and D.F. Penham (Paris, 1993), 191 (2.207): "Sub nomine autem *molyos* herbae Homerus philosophiae doctrinam significasse symbolice creditur a doctissimis. Cuius vim eam esse (ut volunt) arbitratus est ille vir mortalium ingeniosissimus, eamque facultatem, mores ut hominum degeneres et efferatos aut veterinarios factos, atque pecuarios, sibi tandem illa naturaeque humanae restitueret."

dom."[133] Homer and Eustathius, Budé now thought, had literally said more than they knew. Their allegory held true even though the content that they had meant it to express was false. Both in his acceptance of the image by which they had expressed the attaining of wisdom and in his assertion that it was incomplete, Budé displayed the freedom with which he could manipulate a tradition to which he remained, in complex ways, loyal.

One striking feature of Budé's response to Homer and his commentators, then, is its flexibility. Another, less expected, feature is its immediacy. Like many of the great sixteenth-century humanists, Budé won more respect than affection. The chilly formality for which he was known in some quarters emerges well from the famous remark that he allegedly made to the servant who came to tell him, at his wife's request, that their house was on fire: "Kindly inform your mistress that domestic matters are not my affair." Yet his responses to Homer—like his letters and treatises—show a more flexible and responsive personality than the anecdote leads one to expect. So do some of the curious sparks that the ancient readers and later scholiasts struck from Budé's imagination as he worked through them.

In chapter 30 of pseudo-Herodotus, for instance, Homer meets women sacrificing to a goddess. The priestess, annoyed, says, "Man, get away from our rites." Homer asks which god she is sacrificing to. When told it is the protectress of children, he utters an extemporaneous prayer in verse: "Hear me, as I pray, Protectress of Children, grant that this woman reject love and sex with young men, but let her delight in old men with grey brows whose strength has been blighted but whose hearts still feel desire."[134] Beside these verses Budé entered not a summary but an expression of strong interest: a pointing hand and the words σημείωσαι ταῦτα τὰ ἔπη [mark these verses].[135] The ancient anecdote evidently echoed his hopes—or fears?—about his own much younger wife, whom he married in his late thirties.

This fresh and serious response to a text that now seems comic may teach a moderately serious lesson. Budé did not need Paul Veyne to teach him to listen when the Greeks told stories about their heroes and traditions, however foolish an individual witness might seem. He knew that all branches of the ancient scholarly tradition had to be studied before any of them was cut

---

133. Ibid., 191–92 (2.208): "Id quod si de Hellenica philosophia dictum est, quae mortalium revera inventum fuit, quanto nos congruentius id tribuere divinae disciplinae potuimus? Inter *moly* enim nostrum atque illud Homericum, cum plurimum, tum hoc refert, quod illud e puteis sapientiae coelestis, hoc e terra effoditur, humanisque inventis. Quare plus est *oxymoriae* in vita et moribus Hellenismi philosophiae, quam verae solidaeque sapientiae."

134. Trans. Lefkowitz, *Lives*, 151.

135. I, sig. [AVII] verso.

off. He read Homer's ancient, late ancient, and Byzantine interpreters with the care, the attention, and the willingness to argue that he brought to any other important text.[136] And he found in them the same rewards and excitements that he found in the epics they dealt with. The excitements of reading, in the Renaissance, included that of wrapping oneself in the long, sticky threads of a millennial tradition.[137]

136. Cf. Schmidt, *Die Erklärungen zum Weltbild Homers.*

137. Cf. the wise words of L. Deitz, "Julius Caesar Scaliger's *Poetices libri septem* (1561) and His Sources," *Studi Umanistici Piceni* 14 (1994): 91–101, at 92.

5

Johannes Kepler: The New Astronomer Reads Ancient Texts

Johannes Kepler, like his intermittent correspondent Galileo Galilei, often rebelled against the cultural authority of old books. In 1599 Michael Maestlin, who had taught Kepler astronomy at the University of Tübingen, asked him to help another Tübingen professor, Martin Crusius, prepare an encyclopedic commentary on Homer. Crusius' commentary laid out at length, in a style that Budé would have found familiar and attractive, Homer's teachings on "ethics, domestic economy, politics, physics, etc." He meant to show "how great a poet Homer is, and of how great wisdom."[1] Maestlin wanted Kepler to make a particular technical contribution to this massive enterprise. Since Crusius interpreted the encounters of the gods in the *Iliad* and *Odyssey* as conjunctions and oppositions of the planets named after them, he wanted Kepler to compute their exact dates, providing a chronology (and perhaps an explanation) for the war. Kepler clearly rejected the notion that one could find precise astronomical data in the ancient epics. Diplomatically, however, he did not say so. Instead, he suggested that Maestlin compute the dates; then he, Kepler, would supply astrological interpretations. He thus neatly ensured that the project came to nothing.[2]

Kepler's refusal to collaborate in gilding a new frame of physical allegory around the epics seems natural, even inevitable. He had already broken with basic elements of traditional cosmology in his first major astronomical work, the *Mysterium cosmographicum* of 1596. Soon he would set out to create a new astronomy—one that broke, as Copernican astronomy had not, with the classical tradition that stretched from Ptolemy to his own

---

1. *Diarium Martini Crusii 1598–1599,* ed. W. Göz and E. Conrad (Tübingen, 1931), 201–2: "Posui ubique doctrinas Ethicas, Oeconomicas, Politicas, Physicas, etc. . . . Ex his commentariis demum intelligeretur: quantus sit Poëta Homerus, quantâ sapientia."

2. Johannes Kepler, *Gesammelte Werke,* ed. M. Caspar et al. (Munich, 1937–), 13:330, 14:45.

time.[3] Kepler admitted that he was only one little German working at what he expected to be the end of history, but he claimed the right to introduce new ideas into cosmology. He warned traditional philosophers not to try to repress "by the prescription of antiquity" those who hoped to change and improve natural philosophy. Aristotle's opinions could not and should not be maintained against the "new discoveries that are being made every day."[4] It seems altogether reasonable that Kepler, unlike more traditional humanists from Budé to his teachers in Tübingen, could see Homer as a poet, not a master of the sciences, and could draw the conclusion that mathematical and astronomical analysis of his work would only waste time, paper, and spirit.

This impression grows even stronger when one examines Kepler's later career. One of Kepler's masterpieces, the *Astronomia nova* of 1609, in which he presented his first two laws of planetary motion, began with a mythological flourish. Kepler described himself, in the preface, as leading to his earthly ruler a superhuman captive: the snarling, imprisoned god of war himself—Mars—whose motions he had conquered as all previous astronomers had failed to do.[5] But in the body of his work, Kepler distinguished himself, sharply and finally, from his classical predecessors. He made clear that his work rested on the uniquely precise data that Tycho Brahe had collected in his Danish island observatory of Uraniborg, using enormous measuring instruments to enhance the power of his naked eye. These data Tycho had brought with him to Prague, where Kepler joined him in 1600. Without this empirical foundation, something new in the world, Kepler could never have erected his own new structure by endless, meticulous computation. In a justly famous passage, Kepler described how by following Ptolemy one could arrive at a model for the motion of Mars that yielded results correct to within eight minutes of arc. This model, however, he cheerfully rejected, since Tycho's empirical evidence enabled him to reach a new level of precision: "Ptolemy states that he does not descend, in his observations, below ten minutes or one-sixth of a degree; the incertainty (or, as they say, the latitude) of the observations is therefore greater than this error in Ptolemy's computation. But since the kindness of heaven has granted us that most diligent observer Tycho Brahe, whose observations expose the error of eight minutes in Ptolemy's computation for Mars, it is

---

3. See B. Stephenson, *Kepler's Physical Astronomy* (New York, 1987). For Kepler's life see in general *Dictionary of Scientific Biography*, ed. C.C. Gillespie (New York, 1979–80), s.v. "Kepler, Johannes," by O. Gingerich, with bibliography.
4. Kepler, *Gesammelte Werke*, 8:225.
5. Cf. F. Saxl, "The Revival of Late Antique Astrology," in *Lectures* (London, 1957).

proper for us to recognize and cultivate this gift of God in gratitude. For we may thus work toward . . . at last finding out the true form of the motions of the heavens."[6] Here Kepler clearly stated that the world of scientific practice had changed. Only the vast array of data compiled by his noseless, arrogant patron, rather than any given quantity of ancient books, would enable the astronomer to read the book of nature. The voice of the Renaissance intellectual seldom sounds more modern than in Kepler's relentlessly precise and scrupulous delineation of the novelty of his work.

Kepler seems preeminently a man of the new world of the observatory, not of the old one of the library. He felt at home in many of the new habitats for inquirers into nature that reached their mature forms in the years around 1600. The environments that he frequented included Tycho Brahe's last workshop in Prague, where he lived from 1600 to 1612—admittedly a private, rather than a public, locus for work on nature, but also one where the tools and results of observation reached a unique refinement. But Kepler also knew and used the Kunstkammers at Dresden and Prague. Recent work has shown that these spectacular assemblies of natural and human antiquities—where twisted narwhal horns and multifaceted crystals invited inspection beside fine examples of every human craft from the flint axe to the glass lens—were centers of pointed inquiry into the mysteries of nature. Their visual presentation of the relation between natural materials and human industry, between precious metal and human craft, maintained a productive connection between natural and human history and offered Kepler—and others—much food for creative thought.[7]

Where the most advanced science of Kepler's time has a compellingly modern look, the most advanced scholarship could hardly seem more outlandish. Taken as a group, the specialist philologists of his day look rather frightening. And even when one encounters them as individuals, their learning seems more likely to oppress than to exalt the modern reader. Their favorite mode of publication—the thick Latin folio or quarto larded with quotations in Greek and Hebrew, in which Isaac Casaubon commented at

---

6. J. Kepler, *Astronomia nova*, chap. xix, in *Gesammelte Werke*, 3:177–8: "PTOLE-MAEVS vero profitetur se infra X minuta seu sextam partem gradus observando non descendere. Superat igitur observationum incertitudo seu (ut aiunt) latitudo huius calculi Ptolemaici errorem. Nobis cum divina benignitas TYCHONEM BRAHE observatorem diligentissimum concesserit, cuius ex observatis error huius calculi Ptolemaici VIII minutorum in Marte arguitur, aequum est, ut grata mente hoc Dei beneficium et agnoscamus et excolamus. In id nempe elaboremus, ut genuinam formam motuum coelestium . . . tandem indagemus."

7. See esp. H. Bredekamp, *Antikensensucht und Maschinenglauben* (Berlin, 1993), now available in English translation as *The Lure of Antiquity and the Cult of the Machine*, trans. A. Brown (Princeton, 1995); T.D. Kaufmann, *The Mastery of Nature* (Princeton, 1993), chaps. 5–7; and P.E. Findlen, *Possessing Nature* (Berkeley, Los Angeles, and Oxford, 1994).

Rabelaisian length on Strabo and Athenaeus, and in which John Selden investigated in diverting detail the marriage customs of the Jews—seems not only inaccessible but literally crushing.[8] And no subject has fewer obvious attractions than their favorite discipline: chronology, the bristlingly technical form of classical scholarship that concerned itself with the nature of ancient calendars and the precise dates of historical events, and that expressed its opinions in massive tables as well as impenetrable prose.[9] The scholars of Kepler's time took all knowledge as their enormous province. They insisted that the philologist could purify and interpret the ancient sources of every discipline in the encyclopedia. They read oriental languages as happily as Western, corrected the text of the Bible as boldly as that of Livy, and gossiped as agreeably about the deficiencies of their competitors' Arabic as about the excessive size of their salaries. It seems an alien world—as alien from the locales of Kepler's science in the 1590s as from the post-modern learning of the 1990s.[10]

Many scholars have held that the museums and laboratories fostered a new "culture of curiosity," one that grew up alongside the older culture of humanism.[11] Its adherents—the most famous, and eloquent, of whom was Francis Bacon—emphasized novelty over tradition, observation over interpretation, objects over books. Soon Descartes, who inhabited a still more advanced world, a lucid geometrical cosmos where even curiosity was abolished, would proclaim the death of the book, which could teach only taste and tolerance, not clear and distinct truths about the universe.

However, the two worlds of curiosity and erudition were not so separate as they have been made to seem. Relations between the book of nature and the books of men, the study of nature and that of antiquity, were tangled in

---

8. See, respectively, M. Pattison, *Isaac Casaubon* (London, 1875); and J. Selden, *Uxor Ebraica*, ed. and trans. J. Ziskind (Leiden, 1991), with valuable notes on Selden's use (and misuse) of the Hebrew sources—those that deal with western sources, classical and modern, need to be used with caution.

9. See A. Grafton, *Defenders of the Text* (Cambridge, Mass., 1991), chap. 4; and, for a fuller account, A. Grafton, *Joseph Scaliger*, vol. 2 (Oxford, 1993).

10. For general accounts see, e.g., E. Trunz, "Der deutsche Späthumanismus als Standeskultur," in *Deutsche Barockforschung*, ed. R. Alewyn (Cologne and Berlin, 1965), 147–81; and A. Grafton, "The World of the Polyhistors: Humanism and Encyclopedism," *Central European History* 18 (1985): 31–47. The intellectual origins and assumptions of this encyclopedic culture are best explored by W. Schmidt-Biggemann, *Topica universalis* (Hamburg, 1983). For its institutional basis in the Holy Roman Empire see G. Grimm, *Literatur und Gelehrtentum in Deutschland* (Tübingen, 1983), 15–114, modifying Trunz in important ways; but Grimm seems unduly reluctant to admit, even in the teeth of some of his own evidence (see, e.g., 101–3, 111), that many humanists pursued literary and mathematical studies together.

11. The notion of a culture of curiosity is owed to K. Pomian, *Collectionneurs, amateurs et curieux: Paris, Venise: xvie–xviiie siècles* (Paris, 1987).

the period 1550 to 1650. Humanist intellectuals sometimes insisted as firmly as Paracelsian reformers that modern inventions, practical and theoretical, had outdone the ancients. Such enthusiasms crossed all religious and political borders. In 1571–74 Conrad Dasypodius designed and erected a spectacular astronomical clock in the Strasbourg cathedral—a three-story structure of such complexity that it is a sort of miniature cathedral to time in its own right. In 1577 Paulus Fabritius adorned the entry of Rudolph II into Vienna with some spectacular devices of his own: rotating celestial and terrestrial globes and an elaborate clock that gave the time for many locations. Both Dasypodius and Fabritius used many traditional images and devices; but both men also displayed enthusiasm for that preeminently modern device, the mechanical clock, and respect for that preeminently revolutionary thinker Copernicus. Fabritius, who pointed out that Copernicus had not invented a new hypothesis but revived and documented an ancient one, challenged any effort to characterize relations between ancients and moderns with one simple formula.[12]

During the telescope wars of 1609 and after, Galileo artfully deployed an antischolarly rhetoric. He contrasted fertile reality to sterile books, the practical work of engineers and artisans to the tedious squabbling of pedants.[13] But in other texts, as Paolo Rossi and Eileen Reeves have shown, he took the books of men (and the written book of God) quite seriously. By the time he wrote the *Assayer,* he had steeped himself in Jesuit commentaries on the Book of Daniel. More surprisingly, he cast his own view of his enterprise in the language not of the practical man of vision but of the learned commentator on texts. He compared nature to a book written in the language of mathematics—a language, he insisted, that only experts could read. This second set of metaphors represented nature not as a user-friendly, unrolled scroll accessible to anyone with open eyes but as an encrypted text that only virtuous mathematicians—the prophets of Galileo's time—could decipher.[14]

At least once, moreover, Galileo showed how hard and how indepen-

---

12. For Dasypodius see Grafton, *Scaliger,* 2:1–2; for Fabritius see Kaufmann, *Mastery of Nature,* chap. 5.

13. See, e.g., Kepler, *Gesammelte Werke,* 16:329.

14. P. Rossi, *La scienza e la filosofia dei moderni* (Turin, 1989), chaps. 3–4; E. Reeves, "Daniel 5 and the *Assayer:* Galileo reads the Handwriting on the Wall," *Journal of Medieval and Renaissance Studies* 21 (1991): 1–27; Reeves, "Augustine and Galileo on Reading the Heavens," *Journal of the History of Ideas* 52 (1991): 563–79. Cf. B. R. Goldstein, "Galileo's Account of Astronomical Miracles in the Bible: A Confusion of Sources," *Nuncius* 5 (1990): 3–16. See more generally H. Blumenberg, *Die Lesbarkeit der Welt,* 2d ed. (Frankfurt a.M., 1983).

dently he had thought about the art of reading. Discussing the *Jerusalem Delivered* of Tasso, he wrote:

> It has always seemed to me, and seems, that this poet is indescribably stingy, poor, and wretched in his inventions. By contrast Ariosto is magnificent, rich, and admirable. And when I begin to consider the knights and their actions, along with all the other little stories in this poem, I feel as if I were entering the little private study of some little virtuoso, who has taken pleasure in decorating it with things that have some strange quality, either because they are ancient, or because they are rare, or for some other reason. But in fact they are just worthless little things. He would have, so to speak, a petrified crab, a dried chameleon, a fly, and a spider in gelatin, in a piece of amber, and some of those little figures made of clay that are said to be found in the ancient tombs of Egypt. Similarly, where painting is concerned, he would have some little sketch by Baccio Bandinelli or Parmigianino, and other, similar bric-a-brac. By contrast, when I enter the *Furioso,* I see opening before me a [royal] wardrobe, a great hall, a royal gallery, adorned by a hundred ancient statues by the most famous sculptors, with a great many complete history paintings, and the best ones, by famous painters, and a great number of vessels, crystals, agates, lapis lazulis, and other jewels, and finally full of rare, valuable, marvelous, and wholly excellent things.[15]

Here the museum—in two of its manifold forms—stands as a metaphor for the book. The precision and vividness of Galileo's imagery—and his choice of so modern a metaphor for this literary purpose—astonish. The bold

---

15. Galileo, *Considerazioni sul Tasso,* in *Opere,* ed. A. Favaro (repr. Florence, 1965), 9:69: "Mi è sempre parso e pare, che questo poeta sia nelle sue invenzioni oltre tutti i termini gretto, povero e miserabile: e all'opposito, l'Ariosto magnifico, ricco e mirabile: e quando mi volgo a considerare i cavalieri con le loro azioni e avvenimenti, come anche tutte l'altre favolette di questo poema, parmi giusto d'entrare in uno studietto di qualche ometto curioso, che si sia dilettato di adornarlo di cose che abbiano, o per antichità o per rarità o per altro, del pellegrino, ma che però sieno in effetto coseline, avendovi, come saria a dire, un granchio petrificato, un camaleonte secco, una mosca e un ragno in gelatina in un pezo d'ambra, alcuni di quei fantoccini di terra che dicono trovarsi ne i sepolcri antichi di Egitto, e così, in materia di pittura, qualche schizetto di Baccio Bandinelli o del Parmigiano, e simili altre cosette; ma all'incontro, quando entro nel *Furioso,* veggo aprirsi una guardaroba, una tribuna, una galleria regia, ornata di cento statue antiche de' più celebri scultori, con infinite storie intere, e le migliori, di pittori illustri, con un numero grande di vasi, di cristalli, d'agate, di lapislazari e d'altre gioie, e finalmente ripiena di cose rare, preziose, maravigliose, e di tutta eccellenza." See on this passage E. Panofsky's classic essay "Galileo as a Critic of the Arts," *Isis* 47 (1956): 9–10, from which I borrow some phrases in the translation given in the text.

mathematician who despised the study of texts devised what is perhaps the richest set of metaphors any early modern intellectual found to describe the act of critical reading.

Kepler's ideas about reading and its traditions were even deeper and more complex than Galileo's. In the specific case of Homer, he did not need his mastery of modern science to reject the notion that the *Iliad* and *Odyssey* encoded astrological messages. Ancient Greek writers had long since rejected the effort to read the conversations, battles, and sexual activities of the Homeric gods as literary horoscopes; Erasmus had showed himself skeptical in a more general way. Kepler simply revived the healthy skepticism of his predecessors. He did not reject the humanist tradition but recovered a critical element within it.[16] Sometimes he struck a similar pose in work that leveled ancient authority. When Kepler attacked Aristotle's views on comets, for example, following numerous precedents in fifteenth- and sixteenth-century astronomical thought, he described himself in strikingly ambivalent terms, as "creating new doctrines, or rather recovering the old ones of Anaxagoras and Democritus."[17]

Kepler devoted himself throughout his life to traditional forms of scholarship as well as modern forms of science. He was, after all, a product not only of the new world of the laboratory but also of an older (and long-lived) forcing-house of hermeneutical talents: the Tübinger Stift, the theological college where gifted boys, supported by meager scholarships, learned the central tenets of high Protestant humanism in an atmosphere of plain living and high reading. Kepler rapidly came to feel at home in the world of disciplined intellectual work that Tübingen students and their professor inhabited—a world in which Crusius, throughout the long years of his distinguished career, continued to record, day by day, his careful, repeated progresses through such demanding texts as the works of Aristotle and his commentators. On 16 August 1568 he began the *Analytica posteriora*, remembering as he did that "on this day seven years ago my first wife, Sibylla, died"; on 31 December 1572, finishing book 4 of the *Historia Animalium*, he remarked that "the day was very cold; perhaps the great and new star that arose in Cassiopeia last November and is still there, in the same place, is responsible for the extreme cold of this winter"; on 15 Octo-

---

16. See in general J. Seznec, *The Survival of the Pagan Gods*, trans. B.F. Sessions (New York, 1953); and T. Bleicher, *Homer in der deutschen Literatur (1450–1740)* (Stuttgart, 1972). For classical attacks on astronomical readings of Homer see Heraclitus *Problemata Homerica* 53 and Plutarch *De audiendis poetis* 19e.

17. Kepler, *Gesammelte Werke*, 8:225: "Ignoscant igitur Philosophi, antiqua dogmata tuentes, nova fabricanti dogmata, seu potius vetera illa ANAXAGORAE et DEMOCRITI revocanti . . ."

ber 1573 he finished another text "in my house, next to the city wall, below the main building of the University of Tübingen."[18] These scrupulously detailed subscriptions, which record Crusius' unflagging effort to render in full the moral accounting of his laborious days, adumbrate the confessional style of Kepler's science. Crusius' detailed marginal notes and drawings, in which he compared Aristotle's evidence about animals with the remarks of his late antique commentators and the illustrations of the modern naturalist Gesner, reveal a combination of philological and scientific preoccupations that the reader of Kepler will also find familiar. What scholars have long seen as Kepler's peculiar mixture of credulity and criticism, erudition and empiricism, derives to a considerable extent from the particular high style of Protestant humanist culture to which he had his first exposure as a malleable boy.[19]

Like any good Protestant, Kepler grew up listening to sermons and disputations. Long hours of practice gave him a discriminating ear for exegesis. At the age of twelve he already found it shocking when a preacher distorted the text of Paul's Epistles to make it support a sermon against the Calvinists.[20] Classical reading also occupied many hours of Kepler's young life. A consistently excellent student, he mastered the syntax and semantics of classical prose and poetry at least as well as the mysteries of Ptolemaic and Copernican astronomy. Kepler also engaged in the characteristic exercises of the young humanist: for example, he played the part of Mariamne in a Latin drama about John the Baptist, which was staged in the marketplace before an audience containing all the notables of Tübingen.[21]

---

18. Aristotle, *Opera*, ed. D. Erasmus (Basel, 1550); Tübingen University Library C.d.855.2, copy 2. The notes in question appear on *Opera*, 1:60: "Incepi 1568. die Aug. 16. ᾗ ἡμέρᾳ πρὸ ἑπταετίας ἡ πρώτη μου γυνὴ, σίβυλλα ῥωνηρίνη, ἀπέθανεν"; 1:461: "Absolvi 31 Decemb. 1572. die frigidissimo. Stella haec nova et magna, mense proximo Octobri in Cassiepea exorta et adhuc durans in eodem loco, fortassis tantum frigus hac hyeme efficit"; 2:425: "Absolvi die 15. Octob. 1573 die Iovis. domi mea, muro oppidi contiguae, infra Domum Vniversitatis Tybingae . . ."

19. For an eloquent profile of late humanism, which emphasizes its intellectual and scholarly seriousness and its escapist qualities and offers many parallels to the analysis offered here, see Bernd Roeck's case study of Augsburg in the years around 1600: *Als wollt die Welt schier brechen* (Munich, 1991), chap. 3.

20. Kepler, *Gesammelte Werke*, 12:49; see also Kepler's analysis of his horoscope, ibid., 19:329. For the development of Kepler's views on theology and biblical interpretation see J. Hübner, *Die Theologie Johannes Keplers zwischen Orthodoxie und Naturwissenschaft* (Tübingen, 1975), esp. 2–8, 160–65, 210–29.

21. See in general F. Seck, "Marginalien zum Thema 'Kepler und Tübingen,'" *Attempto* 41/42 (1971): 3–19. For the defects in Kepler's preparation as an astronomer see A. Grafton, "Michael Maestlin's Account of Copernican Planetary Theory," *Proceedings of the American Philosophical Society* 117 (1973): 523–50, at 524–32.

Kepler also produced quantities of another humanistic speciality, imitative occasional poetry in Latin. By 1590, when he set out to write an epithalamium for Johannes Huldenreich and Anna Gößlin, he could turn out a spectacularly clever pastiche of a challengingly clever ancient poem, the *Laus Pisonis*, rewriting line after line to fit new circumstances.[22] Allusions, metaphors, and similes, fitted with an embroiderer's dexterity to the fabric of the original, made it even richer. The author of the *Laus Pisonis* proclaimed his inability to sum up the virtues and achievements of his hero's family: "Nec si cuncta velim, breviter decurrere possim" [Not even if I wished could I give a brief summary of all these things] (18). To make his similar confession even more impressive—and to draw one line out into an elegiac distich—Kepler wove into the phrasing of the original, which he borrowed, a proverbial expression drawn from the story of the *Odyssey*. Very likely he found this not directly in Homer's Greek but already formulated in Latin by Erasmus, in his handbook of useful Latin expressions from the classics, the *Adagia*.[23] But the form in which Kepler cast the proverb became his own elegant pastiche:

Nam si cuncta velim brevibus pertexere telis,
    Tractarem telas, Penelopea, tuas

[For if I wished to weave all this together [even] with short threads,
I would be working on your web, Penelope]

                        (79–80)

Kepler showed, here and elsewhere, that he had mastered the techniques for expanding on a theme in peerlessly correct Latin that Erasmus laid out definitively in his well-titled textbook *De duplici rerum ac verborum copia*, with its list of 250 ways to say "Thank you for the letter" in good Latin.

Suitably revised and embellished, the neat ancient poem of praise to a brilliant lawyer became a still neater modern poem of praise to Huldenreich, a perpetual law student. Kepler, of course, made no effort to conceal his

---

22. I use the excellent edition and commentary by F. Seck, *Keplers Hochzeitsgedicht für Johannes Huldenreich (1590), Nova Kepleriana*, n.s., 6 (1976) = *Abhandlungen der Bayerischen Akademie der Wissenschaften*, Mathematisch-Naturwissenschaftliche Klasse, n.s., 155 (1976). Seck analyzes in detail Kepler's use of the *Laus Pisonis*. Cf. Seck's edition of and commentary on Kepler's Latin poems, in Kepler, *Gesammelte Werke*, vol. 12; cf. also Seck, "Johannes Kepler als Dichter," in *Internationales Kepler-Symposium: Weil der Stadt 1971: Referate und Diskussionen*, ed. F. Krafft (Hildesheim, 1973), 427–51.

23. Erasmus *Adagia* 1.4.42 ("Penelopes telam retexere"). Note that Kepler alludes to, rather than copies, Erasmus' formulation.

borrowings and would not have described his technique or his poem as unconventional. Presumably he hoped that a reader who knew both texts (and the other sources on which he drew) would admire and enjoy the meticulous attention to the verbal detail of the *Laus Pisonis* that his work revealed. Demonstrating one's learning and cleverness, rather than celebrating the occasion in question, was after all the object of such exercises. In the course of such emulative study of ancient texts, the distinction between reading and writing, exegesis and composition naturally blurred.

Kepler never abandoned these pursuits. The six stately volumes of his correspondence—those macaronic monuments (half Latin and half German, half mathematical and half unintelligible) to the folly and grandeur of the mind of the Holy Roman Empire, contain dozens of discussions of passages from the Bible and the classics. Several of his scientific works include detailed digressions about problems in the early history of the exact sciences. His *Apologia* for Tycho against Ursus, which has received two substantial editions and commentaries in the last decade, amounts to one of the earliest full-scale efforts to trace the history of ancient astronomy.[24]

Comments scattered throughout Kepler's work show how much the act of reading meant to him. He described his encounters with books with articulate interest, dating and describing the most important ones—like his reading, at the age of seventeen, of Julius Caesar Scaliger's *Exercitationes* against Cardano, which inspired him to study natural philosophy.[25] Kepler couched these descriptions of reading in a crisply precise terminology that enabled him to bring out even small nuances with great clarity. He evoked at different times not only the fashionable appeal of Scaliger but the horror with which he read the paranoid, weirdly argued pamphlet by Nicolas Ursus against Tycho, with its apparently deliberate misreadings of ancient and modern texts; the delight with which he savored Erasmus Reinhold's ruminations, "purissimo et suavissimo sermonis genere," on the general effects of the stars on the sublunary world; the microscopic attention with which he scrutinized Girolamo Cardano's detailed descriptions of comets, word by word. Kepler used Cardano's well-chosen adjectives to guide his own observations and compensate for the weakness of his own eyesight. The Italian magus' vivid prose made clear to Kepler what a comet's tail actually looked like (as it did to other observers who used Cardano's findings as a model even when theirs differed from his).[26]

---

24. N. Jardine, *The Birth of History and Philosophy of Science* (Cambridge, 1984; repr., with corrections, 1988); V. Bialas, in Kepler, *Gesammelte Werke,* vol. 20.

25. Kepler, *Gesammelte Werke,* 8:15.

26. Ibid., 8:344–45, 10:40 (Kepler describes Reinhold's text colorfully: "in ea namque flores halant ex hortis Philosophiae penitissimis, admirabilis fragrantiae, quae lectori veluti

Kepler's expertise in the world of the book was extensive and varied. He knew how to search for manuscripts of a classical text in the library catalogs that began to reach print in considerable numbers at the end of the century; how to evaluate the books that formed part of an estate, taking account of an ongoing fall in prices; and how to equip his own books with the special bindings and elegant inscriptions that would make them please university senates, patrons, and friends.[27] After Tycho's death, he worked through his former patron's published and unpublished works with the care of a professional philologist, establishing a meticulous list of the works that still awaited publication as well as those that had never reached completion. "He mentions the following passim," wrote Kepler in his draft of the list: "*De globo caelesti,* a work promised in his *Mechanica* and the description of the globe. A tabular exposition of the fixed [stars] separately promised in the appendix to the *Mechanica.* Certain astrological works, ibidem. He wanted to write a separate work on hypotheses and add a defense of his reputation against Ursus." A marginal note instructed: "Reread both his books and his letters and you will find many things promised and begun, partly new, partly connected with the books listed."[28] Kepler did not speak lightly when he described, in his horoscope, the almost obsessive care that he had always bestowed on his own collection of books and working papers.[29] He lived in a world of the book that Pico or Budé would have recognized.

Kepler, moreover, did not always read literally or resist the temptation to find hidden meanings in the classics. Annotating his *Somnium,* a rich, if strange account of a voyage to the moon, he stated, curiously, that Lucian had hinted that he meant his satirical *Verae historiae* as a profound account

---

mentem ipsam eripit"), 8:227–28 (on Cardano he says: "Propemodum ad vivum depinxit nostros Cometas, excepto colore").

27. For Kepler's hunt for manuscripts of Ptolemy's *Harmonica* see U. Klein, "Johannes Keplers Bemühungen um die Harmonieschriften des Ptolemaios und Porphyrios," *Johannes Kepler: Werk und Leistung* (Linz, 1971), 51–60. Cf. esp. Kepler to Herwart von Hohenburg, 12 July 1600, in *Gesammelte Werke,* 14:131; and Virdung to Kepler, 14 February 1604, ibid., 15:33. For his evaluation of the library of Hieronymus Megiser, done in collaboration with Tobias Zorer, in Linz, see *Gesammelte Werke,* 19:136–41; and for his use of his own books as well-wrapped gifts, see 19:343, 346, and passim.

28. Kepler, *Gesammelte Werke,* 20: pt. 1, 91: "Meminit passim et sequentium[:] De globo caelesti liber promissus in *Mechanicis* et descriptione globi.

Canonica fixarum expositio seorsum promissa in appendice ad *Mechanica.*

Astrologica aliqua. Ibidem.

De hypothesibus seorsim scribere voluit et adjungere assertionem famae contra Ursum." His marginal note reads: "Relege ipsius et libros et literas et multa invenies promissa et instituta partim nova partim ad recensitos libros pertinentia." Kepler himself, of course, wrote the desired work on hypotheses against Ursus.

29. Ibid., 19:329: "Sic etiam chartas exiguas a se scriptas asservavit, libros quoscunque oblatos, tanquam utiles olim futuros, mordicus retinuit."

of the physical world.[30] Evidently Kepler saw reading as a modulated activity—one that included a range of possible responses to an equally wide range of forms of writing. One might compare his sense of discrimination to the trained attention he presciently brought to bear on astronomical data and conditions of observation.

Sustained interest in older texts was only natural in someone of Kepler's time and place. Style interested him deeply—strange though that statement may seem to those who have enjoyed a bracing dip in the chill waters of his Latin. He had a humanist education, which gave him the normal sense that the ancients had said most things better than moderns could. And he wrote for courtly patrons, also expert humanists, who had a sharp and appreciative eye for striking turns of Latin phrase. Like most products of this system of training and patronage, Kepler never lost his desire to adorn his own style with gems and gewgaws filched from the best ancient writers. In pursuit of these he read and reread the classics. As a mature astronomer reprinting his *Mysterium cosmographicum,* he lamented that he had not yet read Seneca's *Quaestiones naturales* when he first wrote the book. Accordingly he had failed to quote Seneca in the preface, where he argued that nature retained plenty of secrets not yet explored. Kepler now provided the relevant sentence—"adorned," he said, "with the little flowers of Latin eloquence"—in a footnote.[31]

When Kepler deployed tags, moreover, he did so in the most approved humanist way, altering well-known ones just enough to show that he was citing them from memory and twisting them into a subtly new direction.[32] His declaration of independence from theological authority in the *Astronomia nova,* for example, has a powerful revolutionary ring to it: "In theology one must weigh the importance of authorities; in philosophy, however, that of arguments. Holy, then, is Lactantius, who denied that the earth is round; holy is Augustine, who granted the roundness, but still denied the Antipodes; Holy is the Office of those moderns, who grant the small size of the earth but still deny its motion. But more holy in my eyes is truth, as I use philosophy to show that the earth is round, inhabited on its other side in the Antipodes, and of the most contemptibly small size, and finally that it is car-

30. Ibid., 11: pt. 2, 332: "quae [sc. Lucian's *fabula*] tamen aliquid de totius universi natura innuebat; ut quidem ipse Lucianus monet in exordio." See the excellent analysis by J.S. Romm, "Lucian and Plutarch as Sources for Kepler's *Somnium,*" *Classical and Modern Literature* 9 (1989): 97–107.

31. Kepler, *Gesammelte Werke,* 8:22: "Non legeram SENECAM, qui pene eandem sententiam Eloquentiae Romanae flosculis sic exornavit, *Pusilla res mundus est, nisi in eo, quod quaerat, omnis mundus inveniat.*"

32. Cf. the analysis of Alberti's creative dealings with ancient texts in chapter 2.

ried through the stars, saving my respect for the doctors of the Church."[33] Unlike Kepler's modern editors, any contemporary would have known that he was deploying the best of ancient authority in favor of his revisionism. Aristotle argued, in the *Ethica Nicomachea* (1.4), that one should always prefer the rigorous claims of truth to those of friendship, even when assessing a friend's ideas. Cicero, among others, gave it a reverse twist in the *Tusculanae Disputationes:* "I would rather err with Plato . . . than be right with those people" [Errare mehercule malo cum Platone . . . quam cum istis vera sentire] (1.17.39). Alexandrian neoplatonists revised the saying, replacing Plato's name with that of Socrates, since they wanted to show that Aristotle had agreed with his teacher even when he ventured to disagree with him.

Renaissance writers of many kinds seized upon the phrase in both of its forms. Poliziano, for example, cited it in the later form, in which Socrates is mentioned, while defending Pliny against Leoniceno; the latter used it in turn, but in the original form, in his reply.[34] The Latin form of the aphorism that Kepler actually adapted, "Amicus Plato, sed magis amica veritas," appears in one of the Renaissance's great works on reading (and much else), *Don Quijote* (2.9.18). Closer to Kepler's home, Martin Luther had already used it in his work on the servitude of the will.[35] Like Luther, in short, Kepler built his revolution soundly on the wholesome doctrines of the best texts, and he stylishly proved as much to his contemporaries.

Kepler's interest in the substance of ancient texts was just as natural as, and even more sustained than, his concern for their style. For all the rhetoric of prefaces and manifestos, the substantive practice of natural philosophy in the late Renaissance changed sluggishly at best. As Charles Schmitt, Ian Maclean, and others have shown, most scientists of the sixteenth and early seventeenth century, resorted to books not only when explicating the natural world in university courses but also when writing about it for a mature

---

33. Kepler, *Astronomia nova*, introduction, in *Gesammelte Werke*, 3:33–34: "In theologia quidem authoritatum, in philosophia vero rationum esse momenta ponderanda. Sanctus igitur LACTANTIVS, qui Terram negavit esse rotundam; Sanctus AVGVSTINVS, qui rotunditate concessa, negavit tamen Antipodas; Sanctum Officium hodiernorum, qui exilitate Terrae concessa, negant tamen ejus motum: At magis mihi sancta veritas, qui Terram et rotundam, et Antipodibus circumhabitatam, et contemptissimae parvitatis esse, et denique per sidera ferri, salva Doctorum Ecclesiae respectu, ex Philosophia demonstro." Kepler implicitly sides with Copernicus here against Lactantius *Div. in.* 3.24 and Augustine *City of God* 16.9 (*Gesammelte Werke*, 3:456–57 n).

34. A. Poliziano *Epist.* 2.6, in *Opera* (Basel, 1553), 19: "De vestris enim illa sunt scholis, amicus Socrates, amicior veritas: et item, amici ambo, plus tamen habendum honoris veritati est"; 2.7, in *Opera*, 21: "Fateris enim vera esse, quae in scholis nostris lectitantur: amicus Plato, magis amica veritas. Sed cum ambo sint amici, pium esse veritatem in honore praeferre."

35. See L. Tarán, "Amicus Plato sed magis amica veritas," *Antike und Abendland* 30 (1984): 93–124.

public. Commentators by vocation, they saw their duty not as discovering facts never before seen and drawing inferences from them but as assembling facts from reliable sources in a new and revealing order. Most scientific research took the form of a search for *experientia litterata,* the written records of scientific facts, ancient or modern. Most scientific writing resulted not in reports on controlled situations but in commentary or bricolage—either the discussion of canonical texts, line by line, in marginal notes or the rearrangement of fragments from them into new treatises. The normal early modern scientist resembled a bookworm dragging its length down endless shelves rather than Cesi's lynx fiercely scrutinizing the secrets of nature.[36]

The young Kepler frequently mounted this sort of scientific expedition around the shelves of a library. When discussing magnetism and the compass with the learned madman Herwart von Hohenburg, chancellor of Bavaria, Kepler quoted lavishly. His sources included Cardano's *De subtilitate,* a rich compendium of anecdotes about seals and symbols, candles made from the fat of corpses, and the curative powers of saliva; Scaliger's *Exercitationes* on that work—at more than nine hundred pages perhaps the longest as well as the most venomous book review in literary history; and Theodor Zwinger's genuinely weighty *Theatrum humanae vitae,* with its thousands of pages of carefully indexed anecdotes and examples.[37] Every German university student and teacher knew these useful handbooks. Kepler's colleagues ransacked them for ideas and evidence when producing doctoral theses for debate. Such short treatises, normally written by professors for their students, for a fee, made no pretense to intellectual innovation. Rather, they reaffirmed the solvency of individual accounts in the vast, if increasingly fragile, central bank of bookish knowledge.[38] When Kepler produced comparable Mannerist assemblages of quotation and argument, he engaged in normal science of the bookish kind. And his results could be as unsurprising as his reading matter.

But Kepler read in many ways, some of them highly complex. Reading, as he knew well, was a learned art par excellence, one governed by complex, explicit rules. German Protestants shortly after Kepler's time wrote the first full-scale manuals that framed these rules and even devised the name of the

---

36. See C. Schmitt, *Studies in Renaissance Philosophy and Science* (London, 1981); and I. Maclean, "The Interpretation of Natural Signs: Cardano's *De subtilitate* versus Scaliger's *Exercitationes,*" in *Occult and Scientific Mentalities in the Renaissance,* ed. B. Vickers (Cambridge, 1984), 231–52.

37. Kepler, *Gesammelte Werke,* 13:188–97.

38. See Schmidt-Biggemann, *Topica universalis.*

art they defined: hermeneutics.[39] Their efforts, moreover, were not isolated. A number of developments—both in the world of the book and in the organization of knowledge itself—combined to make all learned readers of the late Renaissance self-conscious about their craft. A first problem—one about which readers had complained for centuries, since long before the invention of printing—lay in the frightening loss of control over the resources of learning experienced by sixteenth-century librarians, scholars, and teachers. The pullulation of available books that resulted from the rise of printing challenged the coherence of traditional orders of knowledge and the adequacy of traditional modes of reading. No single person could hope to command the vast range of titles that appeared at each Frankfurt and Leipzig book fair. No single library could continue to contain all the main publications in every significant branch of knowledge. The libraries of the late sixteenth and early seventeenth centuries, with their towering shelves, polyglot contents, and rickety ladders, looked like an emblem of the biblical verdict that "Of the making of many books there is no end." The death of the seventeenth-century polymath G.J. Vossius—whose library ladder collapsed under him—symbolizes almost too neatly the collapse of bookish wisdom under its own weight.

Intellectuals devised some impressive ways of damming and redirecting this flood of knowledge. Catalogs of individual libraries, from Augsburg to Oxford, revealed the contents of encyclopedic collections to distant readers and enabled researchers across Europe to find and obtain rare individual items. Treatises on individual subjects, from history to theology, listed titles field by field. Conrad Gesner, a Swiss natural philosopher and polymath, brought these and other localized finding aids together into a vast, alphabetized bibliography. He carefully distinguished between titles he had seen himself and those about which he had only read. Surpassing his medieval and Renaissance predecessors in both scope and precision, he ransacked libraries, corresponded with scholars across Europe, and studied publishers' catalogs. He established for readers a place to stand amid the tides of texts: a full and accurate body of data about both manuscripts, for which he gave the traditional incipits, and printed books, for which he gave details of publication. He also drew up, as an integral part of the same enterprise, elaborate instructions for making use of these materials. His *Pandectae* laid out systematically the structure of the arts and sciences, giving details of their subdivisions and their relation to one another. The reader who needed

---

39. See H.-E. Hasso Jaeger, "Studien zur Frühgeschichte der Hermeneutik," *Archiv für Begriffsgeschichte* 18 (1974): 35–84; 19 (1975): 89–90. See also W. Alexander, *Hermeneutica generalis* (Stuttgart, 1993); *Unzeitgemäße Hermeneutik,* ed. A. Bühler (Frankfurt a.M., 1994).

information on a given topic could search in the *Pandectae* for relevant loci, or subject headings. Under these the reader would find coded references to the bibliographical sections of the work, which would in turn point toward the precise materials needed. Gesner's many imitators created similar "libraries without walls," trying to list all the authors of one country or advising on how to create a single perfect library.[40]

But no method of cataloging, however elegant, could remedy the more fundamental problems. In the first place, the flood of literature that threatened to overwhelm Europe's scholars was far from homogeneous. Ancient philosophers, historians, orators, and poets disagreed on dozens of issues, from the constitution of the universe as a whole to the best life for humans within it. Modern experience revealed some wonders that the ancients apparently had not known—from the new technologies of the compass, gunpowder, and the printing press to the new worlds that these devices had enabled Europeans to find, conquer, and publicize. Lists and engravings of things newly discovered flanked equally potent catalogs of ancient inventions long since lost.[41] It seemed difficult to know where one should put one's trust—how far one should trust ancient authority and how far one should accept the claims of moderns to revise or subvert it. The apparently simple enterprise of finding one's information about nature in the proper books became more and more complex, as the mine of ancient authorities continued to sprout new veins; and new writers—some of whom used the ancients' own methods against them—claimed that traditional methods of stripping texts for facts and theories yielded no solid results.

As early as 1543, Georgius Agricola, himself a great authority on mines and metals, wrote a long letter to the doctor Wolfgang Meurer, then in Padua. Agricola made clear that he was a man of the book, an expert reader of Aristotle, and asked Meurer "to buy for me at Venice these Greek commentaries of the Greek interpreters of Aristotle, and take care that no page is missing, and that you bring them with you, complete, to Leipzig: I mean Simplicius on the *Physica, De caelo, De anima;* John the grammarian on the books *De ortu et interitu,* or, as they say, *De generatione et corruptione;* and the works of Themistius and of the others, who have explicated Aris-

---

40. H. Zedelmaier, *Bibliotheca universalis und bibliotheca selecta* (Cologne, Weimar, and Vienna, 1992), offers an original analysis of Gesner's work and its relation to that of his predecessors, which I follow. For later and more specialized enterprises see R. Chartier, *L'ordre des livres* (Aix-en-Provence, 1992), chap. 3. On the way that one reader annotated his copy of an epitome of Gesner, see *Gabriel Harvey's Marginalia,* ed. G.C. Moore Smith (Stratford-upon-Avon, 1913), 125–26.

41. See A. Grafton, A. Shelford, and N. Siraisi, *New Worlds, Ancient Texts* (Cambridge, Mass., and London, 1992), chap. 3.

totle's books on natural things in Greek—whether it is Alexander of Aphrodisias, or Michael of Ephesus, or Metochites, or Eustratius, or Ammonius."[42] But Agricola contemplated with equanimity the news that the brilliant anatomist Andreas Vesalius had just attacked the authority of Galen—a report that he could not verify or falisify, since he had been unable as yet to see or buy the book:

> I have not yet seen the books of Vesalius *De humani corporis fabrica*. For only a few copies of them were brought to Leipzig and they were sold before I had news of them. I will take good care to have them sent me from Frankfurt. I find it surprising that the Greeks did not exhaust this subject, especially since Galen, following Marinus and Lycus, worked very hard at it. If this brilliant young man has not set others' discoveries out for sale as his own, no good man will disapprove of his industry and effort, and he will win for himself true and solid praise. If he has rashly ventured into ground that belongs to others, anyone can see that Galen will not lack for supporters to throw him out again headlong. But I hope that our Vesalius—who, as they say, has entered into debate with many great intellects—has judiciously examined everything and carefully explained his own ideas. I hope this all the more, because I strongly desire that men exist in our time who can add something to the discoveries of the ancients.[43]

42. G. Agricola to W. Meurer, 1 January 1544, in *Virorum clarorum saeculi xvi et xvii epistolae selectae*, ed. E. Weber (Leipzig, 1894), 3: "Quoniam vero video te mihi, quacunque in re possis, gratificari velle, etiam atque etiam peto abs te, ut hos Graecorum Aristotelis interpretum Graecos commentarios mihi Venetiis emas et consideres, ne eis ulla pagina desit tecumque integros Lipsiam perferas: Simplicium dico in libros phys., de coelo, de animo [*sic*], et Ioannem grammaticum in libros de ortu et interitu sive, ut isti loquuntur, de generatione et corruptione, et Themistii opera caeterosque, qui libros Aristotelis de rebus naturalibus Graece explanarunt, sive Alexander Aphrodisiensis fuerit, sive Michael Ephesius, sive Metachytes, sive Eustratius, sive Ammonius . . ."
43. Ibid., 2: "Vuessalii autem libros de partibus corporis humani nondum vidi; nam et pauca eorum exempla Lipsiam allata fuerunt et antea, quam de iis certum haberem, divendita. Diligenter curabo, ut ex Francofordio ad me apportentur. Miror hoc argumentum a Graecis non satis esse explicatum, praesertim cum Galenus, post Marinum et Lycum atque alios, in eo multum operae studiique posuerit. Si iuvenis acerrimo ingenio aliena inventa pro suis non venditavit, et nemo vir bonus eius industriam et studium improbabit et laudem sibi pariet veram et solidam; sin in alienam possessionem temere pedem posuit, quis non videt Galeno non defore, qui praecipitem ex ea exturbent? Sed spero Vuessalium nostrum, quia cum multis et magnis ingeniis, ut audio, conflictatus est, omnia iudicio expendisse et sua diligenter explicasse, atque eo magis id spero, quod vehementer velim nostra aetate homines existere, qui aliquid ad veterum inventa addere possint."

Philologists and historians had to deal not only with disagreements but with actual fakes, such as the texts about the early history of Mesopotamia and Italy forged, with great aplomb, by a late fifteenth-century Dominican, Annius of Viterbo, which outsold and outinfluenced Herodotus and Diodorus Siculus in the sixteenth-century marketplace of invented traditions.[44] Readers like Kepler, who wished to interpret both the books of nature and those of men, found that their path to the truth looked increasingly crooked and overgrown as time went on. How could readers know whom they could trust about the past or the present, about historical events or natural phenomena? And how did the evident fact of cultural change, which had been apparent already to Valla, affect the value of ancient texts for the modern world?

One natural response to these questions lay in the creation of an art of reading: a set of rules and questions that, when systematically applied, would enable the reader to choose the right texts, extract their true contents, and apply them properly to the present. In the 1560s historical-minded jurists like François Baudouin and Jean Bodin drew up methodical treatises on how to read the whole range of historical texts, ancient and modern. Philosophers like J.H. Alsted described the various kinds of reading that they considered legitimate and useful. And a series of intellectuals, including the Catholic satirist Barclay as well as the Protestant philosopher Bacon, gradually developed a program for what came to be called a *historia litteraria* of humankind: a history of human thought that would collect all the philosophical, literary, historical, and technological achievements of humankind.[45] This history, so its theorists claimed, would reveal not only what the great advances had been but also how they had been made. Earlier humanists, such as Valla and Vives, had already argued that all the arts, from architecture to poetry, fell and rose together.[46] The new history would show how all these intellectual achievements of a given period were organically related to one another. All of them revealed the influence of a common cultural spirit, one that informed all the arts and changed from period to period: "every century," wrote Barclay, "has a 'genius,' which tends to turn the minds of mortal toward certain studies."[47] He proceeded to trace the

---

44. A. Grafton, *Defenders of the Text* (Cambridge, Mass., 1991), chap. 3.

45. See esp. E. Hassinger, *Empirisch-rationaler Historismus* (Bern and Munich, 1978; new ed., Freiburg, 1994); and Schmidt-Biggemann, *Topica universalis*.

46. See M. Baxandall, *Giotto and the Orators* (Oxford, 1971).

47. J. Barclay, *Icon animorum* [1614], 2, in Barclay, *Euphormionis Lusinini sive Jo. Barclaii Satyricon* (Leiden, 1674), 350: "Nam omnia secula genium habent, qui mortalium animos in certa studia solet inflectere."

"changeable spirits of all centuries" from period to period in the history of the Roman Empire, trying to explain how the rise of the soldier emperors and the barbarian invasions had destroyed Roman high culture and why habits of deference to authority had made the philosophy and jurisprudence of the Middle Ages so sterile.[48] Read in this spirit, texts became—as they had been for Pico, in the single case of astrology—not only the works of individuals but also the clues to the nature and potential of the wider culture in which their authors had participated.

Reading, in short, became a highly self-conscious activity, and readers brought to the task of determining the importance and utility of a text a self-critical and demanding attitude and an elaborate set of questions. Three case studies will identify some of the distinctive features of Kepler's practice as a reader and connect these both to the setting he worked in and to his practices as a natural scientist.

First, the reader as courtier. Political reading, in the Renaissance, meant above all the reading of history—the search, in classical and later texts, for examples of good and evil, prudent and imprudent conduct. This form of reading was of course anything but new: its assumptions and methods had been laid out in antiquity, by Thucydides and Polybius, among others; and its results lay plain to see not only in dozens of treatises on how to be a good prince but also in dozens of large- and small-scale historical paintings. When Albrecht Altdorfer portrayed Alexander's conquest of Darius, dressing the Macedonian and Persian troops in brilliant-colored modern armor, he gave a uniquely vivid expression to the normal view that modern rulers, like his patron, could best guide their conduct by directly imitating ancient models, which remained perfectly relevant in their time.[49]

From the early sixteenth century on, however, the new sensitivity to the complexities and difficulties of reading brought this enterprise into difficulties. After reading the *Discorsi sopra la prima deca di T. Livio* of his friend Machiavelli, Francesco Guicciardini warned, none too gently, that only experience of the unique present, not immersion in the alien past, could bring political wisdom: "How wrong it is to cite the Romans at every turn. For any comparison to be valid, it would be necessary to have a city like

---

48. *Satyricon*, 350–52.

49. See the classic studies of G. Nadel, "Philosophy of History before Historicism," *History and Theory* 3 (1964): 291–315; R. Koselleck, "Historia magistra vitae: Über die Auflösung des Topos im Horizont neuzeitlich bewegter Geschichte," in *Vergangene Zukunft* (Frankfurt, 1984), 38–66; and E. Keßler, "Das rhetorische Modell der Historiographie," in *Formen der Geschichtsschreibung*, ed. R. Koselleck et al. (Munich, 1982), 37–85.

theirs, and then to govern it according to their example."[50] Yet Machiavelli himself often cited classical examples in a way that made their modern relevance more problematic than Guicciardini suggests, and at times he seemed to question the very possibility of imitating the past.[51]

Scholars who wished to preserve the political relevance of classical historiography had to find arguments more precise than the old ones of the rhetorical tradition. The one most often invoked became known as the thesis of *similitudo temporum,* "similarity of periods." Those who accepted it argued that one could perfectly well continue to use classical texts to solve modern political and military problems—as long as one began by finding texts that originated in and addressed societies structurally like modern ones. The example of republican Rome, for example, seemed only dubiously relevant in the corrupt, sophisticated, monarchical world in which most sixteenth-century intellectuals worked. The empire, however, was another matter. No ancient author found more readers in early modern courts than Tacitus, the empire's grimly analytical historian. His mordant dissections of character and conflict revealed a world startlingly like that of the late sixteenth century, a chiaroscuro panorama of phosphorescent corruption in high places, its foreground crowded by the bodies of honorable dissenters foully murdered, its center dominated by scowling tyrants. Even Guicciardini was struck by the relevance of his work. He advised that "If you want to know what the thoughts of tyrants are, read in Cornelius Tacitus the last conversations of the dying Augustus with Tiberius."[52] Translations of the difficult text of Tacitus, commentaries on his political lessons, and rearrangements of his stories and lessons into more systematic order filled the shelves of the specialists called *politici,* "politicians," who swarmed the courts and universities of the day.[53] These men advised rulers and aristocrats, often disastrously, and taught university courses on the arts of empire and diplomacy. Practitioners of a fashionable trade, they lavished learning on the most pragmatic of projects.

The *politici* read less for private enlightenment than for public consump-

---

50. F. Guicciardini *Ricordi* 110, in *Opere,* ed. V. de Caprariis (Milan and Naples, 1961), 120 (trans. M. Domandi in *Maxims and Reflections of a Renaissance Statesmen* [New York, 1965], 69).

51. See T. Hampton, *Writing from History* (Ithaca, N.Y., and London, 1990), chap. 2.

52. Guicciardini *Ricordi* 13, in *Opere,* 99 (trans. Domandi, *Maxims and Reflections*). Cf. *Ricordi* Series C 18, in *Opere,* 100; and *Ricordi* 76, in *Opere,* 113.

53. See A. Momigliano, "The First Political Commentary on Tacitus," in *Essays in Ancient and Modern Historiography* (Oxford, 1977), 205–29; P. Burke, "Tacitism," in *Tacitus,* ed. T.A. Dorey (London, 1979); G. Oestreich, *Neostoicism and the Early Modern State,* trans. D. McClintock (Cambridge, 1982); and M. Morford, *Stoics and Neostoics* (Princeton, 1991).

tion, basing their authority and influence on their claim to make ancient texts teach modern lessons.[54] As cheerful in defeat as their stargazing counterparts, the astrologers, they disregarded not only the many occasions when events contradicted their predictions but also the dour warnings of the most learned humanists that their whole enterprise was doomed. Neither Joseph Scaliger, who warned that "neither I nor any other grammarian can say anything useful about politics," nor Isaac Casaubon, who explained the fall of Essex as the result of his having put too much faith in the teaching of a *politicus e libro,* could stem the tide of political exegesis that lapped around the grim imperial busts in Tacitus and Suetonius.[55]

Like the *politici,* Kepler assumed that one studied ancient historians to draw pragmatic lessons from them. His teachers at Tübingen probably initiated him into this black art. Another student's notes on Crusius' lectures on Thucydides, held from 1579 to 1581, deal mostly with grammatical and semantic points but also show a sharp interest in the text's political lessons. Explicating the Melian dialogue, Crusius took care to point out that the Athenians showed themselves prudent, as well as ruthless, when they advised the Melians not to confuse their wishes with the probabilities of their situation. A nice parallel from Herodotus drove home the value of Thucydides' *prudentiae gnome:* "The very act of wishing is always deceptive. Thus wishing fooled Croesus, who wished to gain a kingdom but overturned his own."[56] A second comment, this one dealing with a political term central to Thucydides, the πρόφασις ("pretext") used by a power for going to war, stimulated an even grimmer reflection: "Just as nowadays they undertake a war under the pretext of religion, but really to satisfy their greed."[57]

---

54. L. Jardine and A. Grafton, " 'Studied for Action': How Gabriel Harvey Read His Livy," *Past and Present* 129 (1990): 30–78. Many late sixteenth-century humanists in the Holy Roman Empire also adopted this new style of scholarship, which emphasized in commentary the drawing of pragmatic lessons from texts and in written and spoken Latin the use of wit and paradox to attract and dazzle. As in England, so in the empire the new fashion reflected a desire to prepare both one's students and oneself for life at court. See W. Kühlmann, *Gelehrtenrepublik und Fürstenstaat* (Tübingen, 1982), esp. pt. 1, chaps. 1–2 and 5; and the essays by Kühlmann, M. Warnke, K. Garber, and M. Beetz in *Res publica litteraria: Die Institutionen der Gelehrsamkeit in der frühen Neuzeit,* ed. S. Neumeister and C. Wiedemann (Wiesbaden, 1987).

55. For Scaliger on Lipsius see *Scaligerana II,* ed. P. Desmaizeaux (Amsterdam, 1740), s.v. "Lipsius"; for Casaubon see Jardine and Grafton, "How Gabriel Harvey Read His Livy."

56. Tübingen University Library, MS Mc 44, fol. 61 verso (from 1581): "ipsa βούλησις semper fallit. τὸ βούλεσθαι decepit Croesum, qui cupiebat regnum acquirere sed suum evertit."

57. Ibid., fol. 24 recto (a marginal note): "sicut hodie saepe sub praetextum religionis bella suscipiunt, revera autem ob avaritiam explendam." It is not clear whether Crusius or M.H., the student whose notes I cite, was the author of this reflection. On the manuscript in question see H. Röchelein et al., *Die lateinischen Handschriften der Universitätsbibliothek Tübingen,*

Like the *politici,* the adult Kepler read Tacitus in a public context—at the imperial court in Prague, where he collated the original text with translations into French, Italian, and German and made his own version of book 1 of the *Historiae.* Like the *politici,* he took an almost obsessive interest in the text. The brilliant Flemish humanist Justus Lipsius offered to recite all of Tacitus, word by word, with a dagger held to his throat, to be plunged in if he made one mistake. In something of the same spirit, Kepler made his fifth child, Ludwig, learn Latin partly by obsessive study of his own German Tacitus. Starting at the advanced age of six, the boy spent three years translating his father's German back into Latin and comparing his results with the original. Like the *politici,* Kepler commented at length on the problems and lessons of his text, in parenthetical remarks he inserted into the body of his translation rather than in a separate commentary.[58]

Normal interpreters—the most influential of whom was Lipsius—treated the text less as an organic whole than as a set of lessons to be memorized. Lipsius' own most famous book, the *Politica,* simply rearranged tags from Tacitus and others to fit the topics of a systematic treatment of politics. Arnold Clapmarius, the Helmstedt prodigy whose posthumous *De arcanis rerumpublicarum* made a great splash on its appearance in 1605, went even further in the same direction. He insisted that Tacitus offered his readers all the *arcana* of government, the secret principles that Roman emperors had employed to retain their power; and he diced the text into pill-sized axioms, topic by topic.[59] His readers would know, in detail, how to fool the public into believing that their loyalty should lie with a ruthless governor and government.

Kepler clearly shared the belief that Tacitus could provide instruction in prudence for modern *politici.* He also clearly shared the hope that his scholarship could help courtly readers to profit from reading the historian. When Ludwig published Kepler's translation, he described it as a sharply practical work on government and warfare, the reader of which could draw useful parallels between ancient and modern times. Ludwig dedicated it to Maria Salome, Gräfin von Hebersdorff, who had asked him for a copy of the text

---

(Wiesbaden, 1991), 1:137; consultation of the *Die Matrikeln der Universität Tübingen,* ed. H. Hermelink, vol. 1: *Die Matrikeln von 1477–1600* (Stuttgart, 1906), revealed several candidates for the role of M.H., without giving decisive support to any one.

58. See the excellent presentation of the text by F. Boockmann in Kepler, *Gesammelte Werke,* 12:367–75.

59. See in general M. Stolleis, *Arcana imperii und Ratio status* (Göttingen, 1980), repr. in Stolleis, *Staat und Staatsräson in der frühen Neuzeit* (Frankfurt a.M., 1990), chap. 2 (the rest of this collection is also relevant); and P.S. Donaldson, *Machiavelli and Mystery of State* (Cambridge, 1988), chap. 4.

for her son, later an officer in Wallenstein's army.[60] Kepler's Tacitus, with its general introductions and helpful, sometimes elementary glosses, was clearly intended to serve a public of rulers, not one of scholars.[61] It provided material for the collective discussions of politics, in which modern cases were referred to ancient examples, that made up so much of court life in the Latin-drenched courts of central Europe. Kepler's reading of Tacitus thus had a public and collective as well as a private dimension, amounted as much to performance as to meditation, and aimed at intervention rather than contemplation.[62]

Kepler's exegetical skills and training served him throughout his time at the Prague court, as Barbara Bauer has shown. They enabled him to avoid imitating the evil example of the Roman astrologers described by Tacitus, by offering his patron horoscopes carefully tailored to prevent political errors. More important still, they empowered Kepler, since they made it possible for him to perform more than one of the specialized jobs that the seventeenth-century court offered. He felt entirely capable of providing the pragmatic advice of a specialist *politicus*—which, he thought, would help a ruler far more than could astrological predictions.[63] The imperial astronomer, in short, did nothing out of the ordinary when he devoted so much time and imagination to the analysis of a Roman imperial history. All this was conventional.

But Kepler's actual analysis of his text contrasted sharply with the fashionable ones. He insisted on treating Tacitus' work as an organic whole, in both its content and its expression. He urged his reader to find in it not simple, ready-to-serve lessons but a complex, supple portrait of a moving target. Tacitus, he explained, had represented the Roman state at a time of strain, in a situation of civil war that had forced it to use all its sinews and muscles—a situation like that of the modern Holy Roman Empire. He had thus revealed its strengths and weaknesses in vivid detail—but in a way that the reader could capture only by working through his text as a whole, not by snipping it into bits and reassembling it like a jigsaw puzzle.[64]

---

60. Kepler, *Gesammelte Werke,* 12:103, 105–6.
61. Ibid., 12:377.
62. In a fascinating article, which I came across only after publishing the first version of the present study in 1992, B. Bauer offers a complementary discussion of Kepler's exegesis of Tacitus. Her conclusions agree with and add further support to those presented here: see "Die Rolle des Hofastrologen und Hofmathematicus als fürstlicher Berater," in *Hofischer Humanismus,* ed. A. Buck (Weinheim, 1989), 93–117, at 107–10.
63. Bauer, "Die Rolle des Hofastrologen," 103–17.
64. Kepler, *Gesammelte Werke,* 12:112.

Kepler also warned the reader not to look for simple maxims about political prudence. Tacitus wrote that Nero's death and Galba's rise to empire had revealed an *arcanum imperii*—that one could become an emperor without being at Rome. Clapmarius inferred that Tacitus was stating a formal, secret law of the Roman Empire, a principle consciously (if covertly) applied by Augustus and Tiberius. He dutifully wrote a chapter about the need for emperors to be crowned only in their capitals.[65] Kepler, by contrast, insisted that one should take the passage in a much more general way. Tacitus meant only that "the secret was out"; every "Obrister" and "Rathsherr" in the empire could hope to attain power in the provinces if he had sufficient military and political support. He had not stated a formal rule of empire but described a single political situation.[66] In this case the scientist clearly read the text with more penetration than the humanist. Kepler responded to the same needs and interests that the humanist commentators on Tacitus confronted. But he framed his response in a characteristically individual way. In his version of Tacitism, as in his aversion to allegorization, Kepler showed the density and intricacy of his involvement with textual knowledge. He also showed that though he aimed his work at a court audience, he did not feel he had to cut his cloth exactly as courtly fashion dictated.

Second, the scientist as skilled reader of classical imaginative literature. Kepler worked intermittently for some years on a literary project that his son published after his death: an account of the landscape and inhabitants of the moon, an eerie tale cast in the eerie form of a story told by a demon to the son of a witch. Kepler derived this fantasy, inspired by the new realization that the moon was a solid, irregular body like the earth rather than a perfect heavenly sphere, from his mother wit. No ancient writer could have anticipated his suggestion that each lunar day must be fifteen of our days long and scalding hot, or that the large, quick-moving creatures that inhabited the moon sheltered themselves from the sun in caves. Still, he eventually learned that he had not been the first to explore this imaginative extraterrestrial territory. Two classic texts, Plutarch's *De facie in orbe lunae* and Lucian's *Verae historiae*, had already described voyages to the moon.

---

65. A. Clapmarius, *De arcanis rerumpublicarum* (Amsterdam, 1644), 98–100 (2.20). Cf. his curious canon-law parallel on page 99: "Porro in Pontificio Imperio arcanum videtur, peregrinum, et qui in Hispania erat, creari posse pontificem. Id quod ex Iovio colligo in vita Hadriani."

66. Kepler, *Gesammelte Werke*, 12:126: "Nicht / daß es ein lang verschwiegener / unnd etlichen wenigen bekandter Griff gewest wäre: sondern weil sie jetzo an Käyser Galba ein Exempel hatten: da gedacht ein jeder Obrister unnd Röm: Rathsherr: halt still / wil es nun hinfort also zugehn / wil ich mir selber das beste gönnen."

Kepler insisted on the independence of his own inspiration: "Whenever I reread this book of Plutarch's, I find myself wondering, time and again, what coincidence brought it about that our dreams or fables corresponded so precisely. For I can go over with quite precise recall the occasions for the single parts of my invention, and not all of them arose from the reading of this book."[67] But he also recorded, with a humanist's loving total recall, every occasion on which he had later read his two forerunners: "At that time I had not yet seen Plutarch's works. Afterward I happened upon the two books of Lucian's *Verae historiae,* written in Greek; I chose these to learn the language, aided by the pleasure to be derived from his very bold fable. . . . At Graz in 1595 I obtained Plutarch's book for the first time . . . and in Prague in 1604 I copied many things from it into my *Astronomiae pars optica.*"[68] Evidently Kepler still saw his intellectual life as so many earlier humanists had: as a long, occasionally bumpy progress, punctuated by memorable meetings with great books.

Kepler's engagement with the Plutarch text, in particular, shows a remarkable energy and commitment—as well as a whole range of humanistic skills. He read the text in the Latin version by a hard-pressed and hard-working scholar, Wilhelm Xylander (originally Holzmann), which made clear that many corruptions confronted the reader. The text lacked an opening and was pocked with lacunae. In 1622, writing to Sebastian Tengnagel in Vienna, Kepler asked his correspondent for two bibliophilic favors: to gain entrance for the bearer of his letter to the archducal library and to find Kepler himself a Greek text of the *Moralia.* "Xylander's translation," Kepler wrote, "swarms both with lacunae and with obscurities of other sorts: I hope that the Greek text, however lacunose it may be, will shed more light for me." Accordingly he asked to see a manuscript, or at least the Basel edition, of the Greek original.[69] When this plea received no answer, Kepler

---

67. Kepler, *Somnium* (1634), in *Gesammelte Werke,* 11: pt. 2, 332: "Quem quidem Plutarchi librum quoties relego, toties impense soleo mirari, quo casu factum sit, ut nostra nobis somnia seu fabulae tam accurate congruerent. Nam ego quidem sat fida memoria repeto occasiones singularum commenti mei partium, quod eae mihi non omnes sint natae ex lectione huius libri. Extat apud me charta pervetus . . ."

68. Ibid.: "Quo quidem tempore Plutarchi opera mihi nondum visa erant. Postea incidi in Luciani libros duos historiae verae, graece scriptos, quos ego libellos mihi delegi, ut linguam addiscerem, adiutus iucunditate audacissimae fabulae. . . . Graetii primum anno 1595 Plutarchi libellum sum nactus . . . exque eo Pragae anno 1604 multa in Astronomiae Partem Opticam transtuli."

69. Kepler, *Gesammelte Werke,* 18:87–88, at 87: "Nascitur enim mihi libellus sub manibus, cui ex libello Plutarchi de facie Lunae subsidiis est opus; ubi versio latina Xylandri ut lacunarum ita et de caetero tenebrarum plena est: plus mihi lucis a Graeco textu, quantumvis lacunoso affulsurum spero."

sent another—this time carried by that strange figure, the Arab Orientalist Joseph Abudakan.[70] In December 1623 he wrote to his friend Bernegger in Strasbourg that he could make no progress on his *Lunaris astronomia* for want of the Greek text, which Tengnagel had promised but not sent. Without it, his reconstruction of Plutarch's full text must remain highly conjectural: "By reading Xylander's translation I think that I have sniffed out what the philosopher thought in the gaps, but I am stuck fast. I could finish up more properly if I could read in Greek the passages that precede and follow the gaps."[71] In February 1624 Bernegger finally declared himself able to supply Kepler with the text as given in the octavo edition of Plutarch by Henri Estienne. Bernegger also offered to obtain a collation of a manuscript in the Royal Library in Paris.[72] But Kepler asked only for a copy of the passages preceding and following the lacunae in Xylander's text.[73]

Despite the gaps in his text (and his library) and the practical difficulties of remedying them, Kepler attacked Plutarch exactly as Scaliger or Casaubon would have. He went through the work once to master the general argument and sequence of thought, jotting down summaries in the margins. These he assembled at the end, to form an index to the text as a whole.[74] Next he worked through the text again, sentence by sentence, filling the lacunae by conjecture—sometimes with supplements that retain their place to this day in the modern editions of Plutarch's *Moralia*.[75] Where Xylander remarked that the text lacked a beginning and that one character in it, Sulla, appeared in other works by Plutarch, Kepler reconstructed the lost passage and identified each speaker in Plutarch's dialogue.[76] In the end

---

70. Ibid., 18:88.

71. Ibid., 18:143: "Ex lectione versionis Xylandrinae videor subodorari, quid sibi voluerit Philosophus in lacunis, haereo tamen: quod si, quae lacunas proxime antecedunt et sequuntur, ea Graece legerem, rectius me expedirem."

72. Ibid., 18:155.

73. Ibid., 18:176.

74. Kepler's translation and notes appear in *Gesammelte Werke,* 11: pt. 2, 380–419. But his procedures are much clearer when followed in the first edition that accompanied his *Somnium seu opus posthumum de astronomia lunari* (Frankfurt a.M., 1634), 97–[184]; for his indexing see 183–[84]: "Catalogus plaerorumque thematum iuxta ordinem et numerum foliorum in editione Wecheliana, annotatum hic in marg."

75. Plutarch has Sulla explain at 920c that the appearance of the man in the moon cannot simply result from the moon's brightness affecting the viewer's vision, a process that, he incomprehensibly describes in Xylander's text as caused by "the weakness that we call" [δι' ἀσθένειαν, ὃ καλοῦμεν]. Kepler renders this as "quod [connivere] dicimus" [which we call dazzlement]—a better supplement than Xylander's "caecutire."

76. Xylander has only one page of *annotationes* on the whole book (Plutarch, *Moralia* [Frankfurt, 1620], *Annotationes,* 53–54). On the opening he remarks: "Carere initio librum, quod est esse ἀκέφαλον, non est obscurum. Syllae huius etiam in aliis libris est mentio nostri Plutarchi."

he produced a new Latin version of the entire text, with its holes plugged by his ingenious supplements, and with its textual and substantive errors corrected by his running commentary, which came out with his *Somnium* in 1634.[77] Kepler was thus perhaps the last great physical scientist to emend a classical literary text—impressive evidence for that unity of the scholarly encyclopedia that still, perhaps, existed in the time of Leibniz, almost a century later, but now can only be mourned.

Kepler did not confine himself to textual criticism. At times, he felt certain that Plutarch himself was in the wrong. In a strange passage near the end of the text, for example, Plutarch describes the moon's passage through the shadow cone of the earth. The souls carried on it cry as they lose sight of the harmonious universe in the dark, and the souls of the wicked try to approach the moon, only to be frightened away by the brasses beaten by the earth's inhabitants during the eclipse and by the moon's own Gorgon face. Plutarch uses this mythological excursus, in turn, as the basis for a critique of the astronomers: "As to her breadth or magnitude, it is not what the geometers say but many times greater. She measures off the earth's shadow with few of her own magnitudes not because it is small, but she more ardently hastens her motion so that she may quickly pass through the gloomy place bearing away <the souls> of the good that cry out and urge her on."[78] Kepler explicated the passage with elaborate notes. He pointed out, drily, that no one any longer believed it necessary to make noises during an eclipse—and that Plutarch might have done better not to pay attention, as he did here, to popular beliefs while trying to found a new theology.[79] He also remarked on Plutarch's confusion about the Caspian Sea, which he had taken as a gulf of the outer ocean, and on his strange decision

77. Kepler describes his procedures thus (*Gesammelte Werke*, 11: pt. 2, 380): "E Graeco lacunis plurimis deformato, Latine redditus, annotatis ad marginem lectionibus, interpretis iudicio emendatioribus et plerisque in lacunis suppletus, coniecturis ex materia et circumstantiis personarum loquentium ductis: passim etiam notis illustratus. Estque lacunarum, quas codices hiatibus indicant, impletionis signum []: quas vero coniectura sola arguebat, eae *scriptura diversa* curatae sunt."

78. Plutarch *De facie* (trans. Cherniss) 944a. Here is Xylander's Latin version: "Latitudinem autem eius et magnitudinem non quantam geometrae dicunt, sed multis modis maiorem. dimetitur autem umbram paululum suis magnitudinibus, non ob parvitatem, sed calidissime motum concitat, ut celeriter perambulet umbrosum locum, simul efferens animas bonorum festinantes et vociferantes. nam cum in umbra sunt, exaudire desinunt harmoniam caeli. simul etiam animae quae infra sunt supplicia luentium tunc per umbram lamentantes et conclamantes adferuntur."

79. Kepler, *Somnium*, 178 (*Gesammelte Werke*, 11: pt. 2, 434): "*c* Neminem hodie superesse puto in orbe terrarum, qui hac superstitione sit infectus. Ita non semper consensus plurimorum respiciendus in examinandis et recipiendis opinionibus, quod hic fecit Plutarchus, novam Theologiam extruens."

to locate on the moon both the place of reward for the souls of the virtuous and that of punishment for the souls of the wicked.[80] But he paid the closest attention to Plutarch's discussion of the size of the moon, which, he pointed out, was totally misguided: "Plutarch falls into a ridiculous confusion here. For if the earth's shadow cone were measured off by more lunar diameters, the moon would be shown to be still smaller. The speed of its motion does not make it appear small; rather, this explains the small length of time that the planet stays in the shadow."[81] The bigger the moon, the fewer—not the more—lunar diameters would measure the diameter of the earth's shadow cone. The content of Plutarch's lunar myth, not its wording, needed correction—if it was to match the strictly scientific content of other parts of the text.[82]

Yet Kepler did not simply want to exult over Plutarch's error. Instead, he tried to argue that Plutarch himself must have meant to say, correctly, that the moon's high velocity made it spend so little time in the shadow cone.[83] This effort to save Plutarch's credit was not a chance one. Kepler also noted that Plutarch remarked that the moon had depths and hollows like those of the earth. "The Belgian telescope," he pointed out, "has very clearly confirmed these conjectures of Plutarch's."[84] Plutarch, in short, might have had an uncertain grasp of mathematics—but his cosmological speculations had been highly prescient.

This point was not a minor one for Kepler. In 1610 he read Galileo's *Sidereus nuncius,* the incomparably exciting treatise that used the evidence of the telescope to transform the moon into a planet like the earth. With characteristic honesty Kepler pointed out that he had previously taken the opposite point of view. At the request of Wacker von Wagenfels he had per-

---

80. Ibid. (*Gesammelte Werke,* 11: pt. 2, 435): "*e* Caspium Plutarchus habet pro sinu Oceani exterioris. . . . *g* Eadem Luna Plutarcho et sedes beatis tribuit et carcerem damnatis torquendis."

81. Ibid. (*Gesammelte Werke,* 11: pt. 2, 434): "*a* Ridicule hallucinatur Plutarchus. Nam si pluribus dimetiretur, adhuc multo minor esse argueretur. Nec enim ei parvitatis speciem induit celeritas motus; sed bene horarum paucitatem haec causatur, quibus in umbra versatur sidus."

82. Cf. H. Cherniss, "Notes on Plutarch's *De facie in orbe lunae,*" *Classical Philology* 46 (1951): 137–58, at 152–53; Cherniss' edition of the *Somnium* (Cambridge, Mass., and London, 1984), 208 n. a; and P. Donini, "Science and Metaphysics: Platonism, Aristotelianism, and Stoicism in Plutarch's *On the Face in the Moon,*" in *The Question of "Eclecticism": Studies in Later Greek Philosophy,* ed. J.M. Dillon and A.A. Long (Cambridge, 1988), 126–44, for more modern explanations of the discrepancies between segments of the text.

83. Kepler, *Somnium,* 178 (*Gesammelte Werke,* 11: pt. 2, 434): "Hoc puto, erat in animo Plutarcho."

84. Ibid. (*Gesammelte Werke,* 11: pt. 2, 435): "*f* Has Plutarchi coniecturas confirmat Dioptron Belgicum clarissime." Kepler refers to *De facie* 944BC.

formed an "experimentum" to determine the nature of the bright and dark areas on the moon. Climbing a mountain in Styria, he had looked down and seen that the river below him seemed bright, the earth dark. Thus, in the "lunar geography" that he had inserted in the *Astronomia nova,* Kepler contradicted Plutarch, who took the bright areas of the moon as land masses and the dark ones as seas. Galileo, however, had shown that though made up of earth, the moon's solid portions gleamed in the light of the sun. Convinced, Kepler happily agreed "to listen to you [Galileo] disputing against me on Plutarch's behalf, with mathematical arguments."[85] Kepler thus took Galileo's brilliant, deliberately provocative book as an elegant confirmation of the ideas of an ancient author—a reading that Galileo may well have found provocative in his turn, and one that nicely reveals the diverse ways in which classical authorities affected the substance as well as the style of Kepler's work.

Third, the scientist proper. Kepler's astronomical work constantly refers and responds to earlier texts. In his first major book, the *Mysterium cosmographicum,* he argued at length that his thesis about the five regular solids both drew on and improved on Pythagoras and Plato. He also discussed Ptolemy's astronomy at length, comparing his models for planetary motion to the Copernican ones—though he owed the substance of his discussion not to mother wit but to his helpful teacher, Maestlin.[86] In later books, notably the *Tabulae Rudolphinae,* he sketched a full-scale history of astronomy from its ancient origins to his own day.

Kepler gradually developed a coherent story about the development of his science. It had come into being—here he agreed with such contemporaries as Henry Savile—in the ancient Near East, in the land of the Chaldeans, whose eclipse observations Ptolemy cited. But the Chaldean astronomers had not begun work at the fabulously early dates claimed by the "Chaldeans" mentioned in classical texts. The earliest observations referred to with any precision were those that Callisthenes, Aristotle's disciple, had supposedly turned up in Babylon. These began only 1,903 years before Babylon fell to Alexander the Great. As to the observations actually used by ancient astronomers, the earliest were the Babylonian eclipse

---

85. Kepler, *Dissertatio cum nuncio sidereo* (1610); in *Discussion avec le messager céleste,* ed. and trans. I. Pantin (Paris, 1993), 18: "Itaque nihil me liber meus impedit, quo minus te audiam, contra me, pro Plutarcho, mathematicis argumentis disserentem."

86. For the first edition of the *Mysterium* see Kepler, *Gesammelte Werke,* vol. 1; for the second, with his commentary, see *Gesammelte Werke,* vol. 8. See also the reprint of the second edition, ed. E.J. Aiton, trans. A.M. Duncan (New York, 1981).

records used by Ptolemy. These began only with the era of Nabonassar in 747 B.C. Astronomy, in short, was not as venerable as history or poetry.

The best of ancient astronomy, in fact, was quite recent. Kepler thought that Dionysius, an astronomer of the third century B.C. mentioned in the *Almagest,* had begun the systematic observation of planetary motions, with some help from the Chaldeans. Hipparchus produced the first rough tables in the second century B.C. And ancient planetary theory reached completion, in the double form of precise geometrical models and accurate predictive tables, only in the work of Ptolemy, in the second century A.D.[87]

Astronomy, moreover, was no pure science, even as Ptolemy practiced it. Its ancient students had been inspired less by the austere task of predicting the motions of the planets than by the profitable one of predicting events on earth, which they saw as controlled by the stars. Ptolemy himself wrote the standard manual of astrology, the *Tetrabiblos.* And all classical astronomy, before and after Ptolemy's time, retained the clear signs of its origin in superstition. As a tree could be traced unequivocally to its roots, so astronomy could be traced back to the divinatory beliefs that had spawned it. Its technical substance, like the tree's rings, bore the ineradicable evidence of its history.[88]

Kepler treated classical astrology in an especially insightful way—not as a bundle of implausible superstitions, but as a discipline with all the apparent order, rigor, and elaboration of a valid ancient science. Originally, to be sure, celestial divination had been nothing more than the normal superstition of the Chaldeans, a bundle of obvious *nugae.* But Ptolemy and other Greek astronomers had used the tools of logic and computation to make the *nugae* seem precise and coherent. They had thus made superstition look as rigorous as science—and ensured that their successors would continue to take both studies very seriously.[89]

Kepler's sketches of the history of astronomy differ sharply, as Nicholas Jardine has shown, from the ones that frequently provided a starting point for sixteenth-century university lecture courses on classical astronomy. These usually took the form of set pieces, like modern introductory lectures; they were designed to enhance the lecturer's prestige and bolster his enrollments. To make the genealogy of his discipline as noble as possible, the lecturer would push its beginning to the earliest possible date and identify as its

---

87. Kepler, *Gesammelte Werke,* 10:37–8.
88. Ibid., 10:36: "ut in arborum fibris anni, sic in tota divinissimae artis compositione lineamenta quaedam apparent ortus hujus: ut Matrem et Nutricem Astrologiam abnegare non possit Astronomia filia et alumna."
89. Ibid., 10:38.

inventors the most famous possible individuals. He could attain both ends, and often did, by making Adam and Noah the inventor and the transmitter, respectively, of real astronomy. The teacher wanted his field to be glamorous as well as ancient. So he usually insisted that astronomy had been cultivated above all in the mysterious Near East, by sage Chaldeans, Magi, and Egyptians. Zoroaster and Hermes might receive as much space, attention, and praise as Hipparchus and Ptolemy. Miraculous feats—like Thales' famous eclipse prediction—bulked larger than humble accumulation of data and drawing up of tables. The enterprise, finally, was not analyzed in technical detail but apotheosized in the adjectival clouds of epideictic rhetoric. Astronomy's past, so evoked, gave it legitimacy and prestige. The real details of parentage and the like were—as happens so often—prudently left unexamined.[90]

Kepler's history, by contrast, rested on close examination of primary sources. He portrayed astronomy as the result of human effort, carried out by boring Greeks, rather than that of divine revelation, freely offered to exciting Orientals. He had well-developed ideas about how to study and edit the scientific texts of the ancient world. When Bernegger collated for him in Heidelberg a manuscript of Porphyry's commentary on Ptolemy's *Harmonica,* he remarked that "there is less need to collate exemplars [in the case of such technical works] than in philological and historical texts and others of that kind. For the subject matter itself sufficiently reveals what the reading should be in any doubtful passage"[91]—a precept that, for all its exaggeration, still has more than a small measure of truth to it. And he insisted on the flawed and contingent nature even of the science of Ptolemy, Copernicus, and of Johannes Kepler himself.

This history had a genealogy of its own, as Kepler scrupulously stated. Pico, as we have seen, had already dismantled the Chaldeans' claims as dextrously as Kepler would, using the same evidence. Kepler repeatedly said that he took Pico's work very seriously, even if he did not accept all of its conclusions.[92] But Kepler did not simply copy his predecessor. Pico strictly distinguished between astronomy, which he praised as rigorous science, and astrology, which he dismissed as worthless superstition. Moreover, he inserted astrology into a single, constricted position in his family tree of the mathematical sciences. He described it not as the wicked stepmother of the

90. See Jardine, *Birth of History.*

91. Kepler to Bernegger, 23 March 1615, in *Gesammelte Werke,* 17:139: "Collatione exemplarium minus est opus, quam in Philologis et Historiis, caeterisque huiusmodi. Nam ipsa materia, quid quolibet loco dubio legendum sit, satis indicat."

92. See, e.g., Kepler, *Gesammelte Werke,* 6:266, 14:285.

other art but only as its worthless daughter. Kepler, by contrast, insisted that science had sprung from superstition in the first place. In its final form astrology embodied the sophisticated mathematics of Ptolemy; but in its origins, the belief in divination from the stars had preceded and inspired the growth of astronomy. The desire to know the human future gave rise to the science of planetary motions, and the two were intertwined throughout history. Kepler's attack on myth was even more radical than Pico's; he extended it to the mythical autonomy of science.

Kepler addressed his history, like his German Tacitus, to patrons at court—a court, moreover, where scientists and artists alike actively discussed the relation of ancient to modern wisdom, the scale of the knowledge that had been lost over time, and the brilliance of modern technical and scientific innovations. Such subjects were widely debated throughout the Holy Roman Empire. Prague, as a center of magical and alchemical researches, naturally played a special role in the generation and preservation of tales about ancient wisdom. The prominent alchemist Oswald Croll, for example, had his base of operations in Rudolf's court. In 1608 he explicitly claimed that his researches would enable him to reveal to incredulous modern eyes the lost secrets of Egyptian chemistry—a thesis that soon received a sharp rebuttal from Andreas Libavius, who agreed that ancient and medieval alchemical texts contained valuable, now-forgotten information, but denied the existence of a perfect Eastern science, in antiquity or in his own day.[93] But many forms and colors appeared in the rich tapestry of Rudolf's court. One characteristic figure in it was Johannes Pistorius, an expert student of the cabbalistic tradition. He edited such writers as Paulus Riccius and Johannes Reuchlin, who had dedicated themselves to recovering the lost, oral wisdom of ancient Judaism.[94] Kepler described Pistorius as a man of encyclopedic learning ("Polyhistor ille omnium scientiarum"). And

---

93. See O. Croll, *Basilica Chymica* (Frankfurt, n.d.) and A. Libavius, "Prodromus vitalis philosophiae Paracelsistarum," in *Examen philosophiae novae, quae veteri abrogandae opponitur* (Frankfurt, 1615), 3–12; Libavius, *Syntagmatis selectorum undiquaque et perspicue traditorum alchymiae arcanorum, tomus primus [-secundus]* (Frankfurt, 1615) 13; Libavius, *Appendix necessaria syntagmatis arcanorum chymicorum* (Frankfurt, 1615), dedicatory letter, sig.):(3 verso. On these debates see O. Hannaway, *The Chemists and the Word* (Baltimore and London, 1975); and, more generally, R. Evans, *Rudolf II and His World* (Oxford, 1973); H. Trevor-Roper, *Princes and Artists* (London, 1976), chap. 3; and E. Trunz, *Weltbild und Dichtung im deutschen Barock* (Munich, 1992), chap. 2. Some artists and intellectuals at Rudolf's court nourished a real appreciation for technological and artistic progress; see T.D. Kaufmann, *The School of Prague* (Chicago and London, 1988), 96–99. Courts, like other early modern institutions, were highly complex organizations—as Kepler's case itself clearly shows.

94. Cf., however, H.C.E. Midelfort, *Mad Princes of Renaissance Germany* (Charlottesville and London, 1994), 133.

the questions that Pistorius put to Kepler show, in fact, that he took an informed interest in the astronomical advances of his own time as well as in the ancient theology of the Jewish patriarchs. Was it really true, he asked more than once, that Tycho's astronomical observations had reached the highest possible level of precision? Or could one somehow improve on them? Kepler maintained that no one could improve on Tycho—though after he received news of Galileo's telescope, he had to admit that he had been wrong.[95] Kepler's dismissal of horoscopic astrology, his downgrading of Near Eastern sages, and his downplaying of the rigor of astronomy contradicted positions that some alchemists and astrologers of the Habsburg court loved to maintain. His reading of early astronomy produced critical history, not fluffy genealogy.[96] But he found sympathizers as well as opponents in advancing his arguments, and some humanists, such as Pistorius, saw more potential in modern culture than he did. The public character and high quality of these discussions show once again that the erudite, humanistic court of Prague (which historians of an older generation deplored as a bookish, backward-looking milieu) offered a stage for lively debates about the most up-to-date intellectual issues—debates in which contemporary authors and their readers could still play an active and unpredictable part.[97]

Kepler's case shows that not all the bookish science of the years around 1600 led into dead ends or labyrinths with no centers. The work of late sixteenth-century readers was as varied as it was profuse, and some of it had organic connections to the most powerful empirical and mathematical science of the time. Advanced natural philosophy and advanced textual scholarship had been pursued together in Byzantium, especially in the last two hundred years of the empire's existence. They were brought together again by Regiomontanus, Poliziano, Pico, and others in late fifteenth-century Italy. More than a century later, science and scholarship were still tightly connected in many sectors. The nature of their bonds awaits full exploration.[98]

---

95. Kepler, *Dissertatio cum nuncio sidereo,* in *Discussion avec le Messager céleste,* ed. and trans. Pantin, 14 and 76–77 nn. 76–78.

96. For a more critical assessment of Kepler's philological attainments, see B. Eastwood, "Kepler as Historian of Science: Precursors of Copernican Heliocentrism according to *De revolutionibus* I, 10," *Proceedings of the American Philosophical Society* 126 (1982): 367–94. W.N. Stevenson has undertaken a detailed study of Kepler's work on Lucan, which promises to offer the fullest and most precise assessment yet of Kepler's Latin scholarship.

97. For a parallel argument based on quite different evidence see Kaufmann, *Mastery of Nature,* chap. 6.

98. See the classic work of P.L. Rose, *The Italian Renaissance of Mathematics* (Geneva, 1976).

Kepler distinguished between mathematics and philology, and he strongly preferred the former to the latter.[99] But he insisted that astronomers had to use history and philology as well as computation and observation. Otherwise they could not assess their oldest data—those preserved by ancient writers. Problems of interpretation were not confined to the early history of astronomy: they also affected its vital substance, the precise astronomical observations recorded by Ptolemy that even the iconoclastic Tycho had had to use as a baseline in trying to establish the long-term motions of the planets. In the course of the sixteenth century, however, doubts had arisen about the value of these data. G.J. Rheticus, the astronomer who published the first report on Copernicus' system, later decided that Greek astronomers had gone down the wrong path when they started creating elaborate mathematical hypotheses about the stars. The Egyptians had simply observed the heavens, using their infallible instrument, the obelisk, to guide them. So doing, they had created a far solider form of astronomy than the Greek, which Rheticus proposed to revive. He tried to show that Copernicus himself had taken his side. The old astronomer, Rheticus recalled, had pointed out to his young friend that the sources Ptolemy had used, the astronomical texts of the Chaldeans and of Hipparchus, were lost. He had also claimed that "the ancients" (presumably Ptolemy) had deliberately altered certain observations that they did transmit, to make them fit their own theories.[100] Herwart and other speculative astronomers in Kepler's time revived this thesis, which had some prima facie support in the *Almagest* itself. Only close scrutiny of the surviving sources, rigorously conducted, enabled Kepler to reject their critique.[101] Direct study of classical texts thus formed an integral part of Kepler's astronomy, as it had formed part of Copernicus' before him.

Most important, attention to Kepler's precise ways of reading, his meticulous scrutiny of the grain and texture of past science, ancient and modern, helps to explain a crucial feature of his scientific writing. Historians have long wondered why Kepler included so much information in his works

---

99. Kepler, *Gesammelte Werke*, 14:165; see Jardine, *Birth of History*, 27, for the circumstances.

100. Kepler, *Gesammelte Werke*, 8:102–3 (from Rheticus' report). Copernicus supposedly remarked that "plerasque observationes veterum synceras non esse, sed accommodatas ad eam doctrinam motuum, quam sibiipsi vnusquisque peculiariter constituisset"; he also lamented, showing his own high degree of philological insight, that "Non habere nos tales auctores, quales PTOLEMAEVS habuisset post Babylonios et Chaldaeos, illa lumina artis, HIPPARCHVM, TIMOCHAREM, MENELAVM, et caeteros, quorum et nos observationibus ac praeceptis niti ac confidere possemus."

101. See, e.g., Kepler, *Gesammelte Werke*, 14:285.

about his own trials and failures. It seems likely that he did so precisely because he had a particular, late-humanist sense of his own position in history. After spending a lifetime reading the ancients, Petrarch imitated Ovid and wrote a formal letter, *Posteritati,* to answer his future readers' questions. After spending a later lifetime working through a much richer canon, one that included Greek as well as Latin texts, Erasmus imitated Galen and wrote a *Compendium vitae* to shed light on the origins of his own writings. Though Kepler wrote no formal autobiography, he drew up a rich set of historical glosses on his own past.

The various strategies Kepler adopted in presenting his own development clearly reveal the sophistication of his historical sense. Like Petrarch, he saw himself as addressing not only his own contemporaries but a future reading public—one living perhaps hundreds, or thousands, of years after his own time. He suspected, moreover, that later readers might well have an advantage over contemporary ones. Kepler had discovered true implications of Pythagorean and Platonic ideas that the ancients had misunderstood and failed to exploit. Similarly, his own books might have to wait a long time before a new Kepler recognized the justice of their theses: "If you accept my views," he wrote in the *Harmonice mundi,* "I will be delighted; if you find them irritating, I will put up with it. I cast it out as a bet, and I write a book to be read either by my contemporaries or by later readers, it does not matter. Let it await its reader for a hundred years, if God himself had to await a real contemplator of the universe for six thousand years."[102]

Kepler knew, from his classical training, just what sort of historical facts later readers would both need and lack. Accordingly, he set out to provide them. In his second edition of the *Mysterium cosmographicum,* he identified the sources and weaknesses of the data he had used, explained his assumptions, and corrected his own slips and errors. But he left his early text intact, using a method that, as he admitted, "is usually followed when one must reprint someone else's work, where one changes nothing, and comes to the aid of those passages that need correction, explication, or supplementation, in commentaries printed in a different typeface."[103] Only thus could he deal with a work that, as he admitted, time had made into a sort of public prop-

---

102. Kepler, *Harmonice Mundi,* quoted by H. Günther, *Zeit der Geschichte* (Frankfurt a.M., 1993), 170: "Si agnoscitis, gaudebo; si succensetis feram: jacio in aleam, librumque scribo, seu praesentibus, seu posteris legendum, nihil interest: expectet ille suum lectorem per annos centum, si Deus ipse per annorum sex milia, contemplatorem praestolatus est."

103. Kepler, *Gesammelte Werke,* 8:10: ". . . formam editionis talem elegi, quae solet observari in libris alienis recudendis, ubi nihil mutamus; quae vero loca emendatione egent, aut explicatione, aut integratione, ea commentariis adiuvamus, differenti typo exaratis."

erty in its original form. It could not be brought up to date, but it could be equipped with an apparatus that would show the reader "where my contemplations of the universe began, and to what point I developed them"[104]—an apparatus that would, in short, illuminate Kepler's heroic role in the recent history of science. Kepler's use of that preeminent literary genre of the scholarly humanist, the commentary, is revealing. So, even more, is his insistence on laying out the twisted paths of his own development.

This same effort informs the *Astronomia nova,* in which, as Kepler explicitly said, he adopted not a logical but a "historical" mode of exposition, laying out his mistakes as well as his correct conjectures in full detail. He nicely mixed the classical and the modern, comparing his work to those of the "Argonauts" Columbus and Magellan. Their accounts of their wanderings, like his, delighted the reader because they described many false trails as well as the few dramatic correct ones.[105] Kepler made quite clear that in choosing the literary form he did, he drew on the rhetorical, rather than the scientific, tradition. It seems clear that in melding the two, he set out to give his future readers just the sort of material he himself did not have about Pythagoras and Ptolemy.

Kepler's strategy of self-presentation, warts and all, seems humble, but it was in fact extremely radical. With few exceptions, ancient practitioners of the exact sciences cast their work in forms so impersonal as to discourage—or perhaps prevent—any sort of biographical analysis.[106] Histories of earlier arguments or pieces of research rarely appeared in their work, and those that did were selective and polemical. Ptolemy, for example, offered his

---

104. Ibid.: ". . . ut intelligat [sc. lector], a quibus initiis, quousque perductae a me fuerint contemplationes mundanae."

105. Kepler, *Astronomia nova,* in *Gesammelte Werke,* 3:36: "Nil igitur mirum, si methodis superioribus admisceam tertiam Oratoribus familiarem, hoc est, historicam mearum inventionum: ubi non de hoc solo agitur, quo pacto lector in cognitionem tradendorum perducatur via compendiosissima: sed de hoc potissimum, quibus Ego author seu argumentis seu ambagibus seu fortuitis etiam occasionibus primitus eodem devenerim. Quod si CHRISTOPHORO COLVMBO, si MAGELLANO, si Lusitanis, non tantum ignoscimus, errores suos narrantibus, quibus ille Americam, iste Oceanum Sinensem, hi Africae Periplum aperuerunt; sed ne vellemus quidem omissos, quippe ingenti lectionis jucunditate carituri: nec igitur mihi vitio vertetur, quod idem eodem lectoris studio per hoc Opus sum secutus. Nam etsi Argonauticorum illorum laborum nequaquam legendo reddimur participes; mearum vero inventionum difficultates et spinae ipsam etiam lectionem infestant: at communis haec fortuna est omnium librorum Mathematicorum: existentque nihilominus, ut sumus homines quorum alios alia delectant, qui superatis perceptionis difficultatibus, hac integra inventionum serie simul ob oculos posita, ingenti voluptate perfundantur."

106. The prefatory letters of Archimedes are a partial exception; but they offer no enlightenment about his errors and false starts.

reader not accounts of how he had actually studied the stars but data and demonstrations carefully selected to support the towering final structure of his theories. The nature, extent, and style of the lost written sources he used are impossible to reconstruct in detail. Only one or two late and secondary works, like Proclus' commentary on book 1 of Euclid and Simplicius' commentary on book 2 of Aristotle's *De caelo*, fill in some of the missing history of debate and some of the theories of the writers whose works are lost. But the great scientists themselves wrote in such a way as to conceal the prehistory of their own work. This tradition persists, and violations of it—like those carried out by James Watson and Edwin Chargaff—still have the power to shock. But Kepler already saw it as harmful. The austere, finished literary form adopted by Ptolemy and imitated by Copernicus made it impossible to see exactly where and how they had gone wrong. By adopting an open, even labyrinthine, form of exposition, and by making his texts into open-ended dialogues with his earlier selves, Kepler provided his future readers with exactly the information that his own sources denied him.[107]

This initiative did not have a long future before it; but it did have a particular and revealing past. In a general sense, it came from the humanists. No humanist would have made the mistake of Kingsley Amis' protagonist in *Lucky Jim,* who abused a work written under the direction of his professor, because he had not bothered to read the preface, which recorded that useful fact. Obsessed as they were with the lives of the ancients whose works they read, most humanists framed their own works for future counterparts whose similar curiosity they hoped to gratify.

But Kepler's ruminative, discursive, and philological form of exposition also had a more precise historical origin. Kepler himself identified the works that formed his sensibility, the fashionable books of his youth, whose theses and content shaped his early work, and whose failings it took him many years to see: the natural magic and astrology of Cardano and the Aristotelian critique of Cardano by the elder Scaliger.[108] These works that differ so radically from Kepler's in content have a profound kinship with them in form. They pullulate with autobiographical and personal detail, from the trivial—like Scaliger's careful note that one of his sons could not stand cab-

---

107. A recent study makes insightful use of Kepler's comments on his own work and sheds a new light on his debt to a number of ancient works (notably Plato's *Timaeus* and Proclus' commentary on book 1 of Euclid): see J.V. Field, *Kepler's Geometrical Cosmology* (Chicago, 1988).

108. In a note to the second edition of the *Mysterium cosmographicum* Kepler describes his younger self as "imbutus dogmatibus I.C. SCALIGERI de Motricibus intelligentiis" (*Gesammelte Werke*, 8:113).

bage—to the spectacular—like Cardano's careful accounts of how he had spoken with spirits, dreamed strange dreams, and drawn up horoscopes.[109] They seem, in fact, to take every possible opportunity to offer such information, and they make clear that any substantial scientific treatise took shape over years of work and drew on experiences of many sorts—including the correction of one's own errors.

It is not hard to explain why Scaliger and Cardano, who loathed one another's ideas, expounded them so similarly. Both were medical men. In the Renaissance, of course, two ancient authorities ruled in the medical schools: Galen and Aristotle. Cardano saw Galen as a vital, central figure in the history and culture of his craft, and he emulated both Galen's philological approach to earlier authors and his systematic effort to place his own work in the history of his field.[110] His first autobiographical works directly imitated Galen's *De libris propriis* as well as Erasmus' *Compendium vitae* in form; his chatty self-revelations also reveal a subtler but pervasive Galenic impress. Scaliger also respected Galen, but he devoted himself to Aristotle, which meant that he mixed a good bit of Aristotelian history of doctrine and some interesting reports of particular observations in with his multiple Galenic anecdotes.

Cardano's approach often closely resembled Kepler's. He made clear from the start of his career as a writer that his perpetual efforts at a precocious autobiography had a double purpose. He would enable his readers both to see how he himself had developed and to learn how they could master many subjects, make many discoveries, and write many books, perhaps as quickly and effectively as had Cardano himself.[111] He explained in detail that he had undertaken some projects to please a particular patron, others to obey warnings received in dreams.[112] He extended his approach to the study of other scientists—above all Galen, whose biography he set out at one point to write, on the basis of an impressively systematic collection of evidence.[113] And in the second version of his *De libris propriis*, he made

---

109. For the fact that one of Scaliger's children could not abide cabbage see J.C. Scaliger, *Exotericarum exercitationum liber quintus decimus, de subtilitate, ad Hieronymum Cardanum* (Paris, 1557), fol. 213 verso; Joseph identifies himself as the child in question in his copy, BN Paris Rés. R 1531.

110. See V. Nutton, "Galen and Medical Autobiography," *Publications of the Cambridge Philological Society*, 198 (n.s., 18) (1972): 50–62.

111. See, e.g., Cardano's *Libellus de libris propriis, cui titulus est Ephemerus*, first published with his *De sapientia* (Nuremberg, 1543), 419: ". . . accedit his singularis quaedam utilitas intelligendi, quonam pacto facile, quis multa et discere et invenire ac scribere queat . . ."

112. Ibid., 425, 426, 429–30.

113. Ibid., 430: "Coepi et Galeni vitam texere, opus Celso non minus, si ex ungue leonem, adsunt comparationes, opera, vitae, sententiae: collegi et fragmenta quaedam . . ."

even clearer how the desire to develop his work as a scientist and the desire to document his own development, how the methods of Greek medicine and those of modern humanism, interacted in him:

> I wrote at the same time a book on my own books—really not a book but rather a table; then I enlarged it and changed it again, until it was refashioned to its present size and order. The book underwent all these changes not so much because of the things that were added regularly [to my writings] as by a certain judgment. In it I set out for myself a sort of image of everything I had written—not only to aid my memory and choose the books that I should finish and correct first, but to show from what causes, at what times, and in what order I wrote such things and to attest to the power of the divinity in the proper place. In this literary genre I imitated Galen and Erasmus, both of whom wrote catalogs of their books.[114]

Even Kepler did not document his errors and discoveries quite so precisely.

The style of exposition Kepler applied with hesitation to the exact sciences was the fashionable one of his youth: that of humanistic science, derived from the ancient medical tradition. Once more, in short, ancient books proved capable of teaching moderns some crucial, shocking lessons— at least when read in the light of what ingenious modern commentators and adaptors had done with them. They taught Kepler that his texts, like all others, should be understood and presented as the product of a specific time, place, and experience. When Kepler treated his own work as contingent, not absolute, he showed how powerful a lesson this could be. It meant that he presented himself as the object, as well as the subject, of the history of science.

Like Galileo's brilliant, polished rhetoric, Kepler's devoted self-scrutiny belongs to a period style of intellectual inquiry. Newton and others would soon restore decorum in the writing, if not the practice, of natural philosophy. Yet Kepler's experience and achievement were neither isolated nor

---

114. Cardano, *De libris propriis* [1554], in *Opera omnia* (Lyons, 1663), 1:69: "Conscripsi et eodem tempore librum de libris propriis, imo non librum, sed potius tabulam; deinde auxi iterumque mutavi, donec ad hanc magnitudinem huncque ordinem redigeretur. Non tam necessitate eorum quae adiiciebantur in dies, quam etiam certo iudicio liber hic tam saepe mutatus est. Iconem ergo quandam mihi in eo proposui omnium eorum quae a me conscripta sunt, non solum ad memoriam confirmandam, eligendosque mihi libros quos prius absolverem et castigarem: sed ut doceam quibus causis, temporibus, quoque ordine talia conscripserim, et ut vim numinis suo loco testarer. Imitatus sum in hoc scribendi genere Galenum et Erasmum, qui ambo catalogum librorum suorum scripserunt."

unimportant. Bacon and Descartes used autobiography in much the same way, exposing their own early errors, in a fashion that they probably adapted from Montaigne, to map the fault lines in the received philosophical systems of their day. Without the particular reading of ancient texts and fusion of previously incompatible classical styles that made it possible for these men to play their modern roles, the scientific revolution would have taken a radically different form. The laboratory could not exist without the library.

Epilogue

The case studies offered in this book yield no single, radical thesis. But they do suggest two modest, tentative conclusions. The first is simply that any effort to identify a single, narrowly defined way of reading the classics as characteristic of the intellectuals of the Renaissance does violence to the intricacies of the evidence. Radically different styles of reading both competed and coexisted, in the same library and even in the same intellectual. Budé, for example, read his texts both as a philologist seeking to correct the errors of scribes and printers and as a philosopher searching for moral lessons.[1] Kepler read his as a scientist collecting data, a historian reconstructing the past, a political adviser looking for pragmatic guidance, and a rhetorician forming an elegant style. Pico read his as both a syncretic philosopher and a critical philologist—though he, unlike Budé and Kepler, seems to have experienced considerable conflict as he changed hermeneutical styles. Only an approach that gives due space to the survival of medieval traditions and the revival of ancient models as well as to the forging and honing of the tools of humanistic philology can do justice to the richness of the primary evidence preserved in library lists, marginal notes, and formal treatises.

The second conclusion is that the humanists of the Renaissance created a particular style of bookish but unblinkered intellectual life that would endure for centuries. Whatever their differences, humanists shared the belief that a new culture could be constructed on classical foundations—a faith in the unique value of their favorite texts and of what the serious reader could learn from them. In subsequent centuries, this conviction underwent many changes but never disappeared. From Edward Gibbon—meditating about ruins, emperors, and barbarians in his well-stocked London library—to Walter Benjamin and Ernst Junger—two radically different Germans who met radically different fates but both found in bookstores and book-based

---

1. Cf. M. Lowry, "The Arrival and Use of Continental Printed Books in Yorkist England," in *Le Livre dans l'Europe de la Renaissance*, ed. P. Aquilon, H.-J. Martin, and F. Dupuigrenet Desrousilles (Paris, 1988), 449–59.

friendships some solace for the horrors of the twentieth century—humanistically educated readers have seen reception and creativity, reading and writing, as intimately connected. Like the humanists of the Renaissance, later ones have made the finding and buying of their books into vividly dramatic processes, literary odysseys. Like the humanists of the Renaissance, later ones have transformed printed books, the uniform products of a modern process of manufacturing, into highly individual possessions, decorated, bound, and annotated in as many different ways as there were readers to customize them. Like the humanists of the Renaissance, modern ones have transformed their notes on what they read into vast Watts towers of materials apparently unconnected by origin or purpose, leaving their heirs to decode and establish the connections they left undefined. Warburg and Benjamin recall Budé and Harvey in their characteristic, desperate effort to collect and assess past worlds on paper. Like the humanists of the Renaissance, later ones have often owed as much to the reading of modern commentaries as to that of the original texts. And like the humanists of the Renaissance, later ones have often transformed their readings in wholly unpredictable as well as fruitful ways, making scholarly commentaries as well as classical texts serve ends that their authors could never have anticipated.

No modern scientist has shown more devotion to ancient texts and systematic reading than Sigmund Freud. His dealings with books began with Heinrich Brugsch's description of his voyage to the ancient land of Persia, lavishly illustrated with color plates, which Freud dismantled "like an artichoke," page by page, with the help of his sister. His conscious intellectual life began with the great illustrated bilingual Bible that his father taught him to read. The erotics of books, their texture and fragrance, exerted a compelling attraction on him: "La chose écrite est une chose sexuelle."[2] As a teenager and a student, he read precociously and eagerly in a vast range of texts and subjects. He saw the myth of Oedipus and other products of Greek culture as offering insight into a basic humanity precisely because he had been trained in his gymnasium to make this assumption as he read classical texts. And as Ilse Grubrich-Simitis has shown in a fascinating recent work, some of Freud's most imaginative writing was inspired by his systematic reading. The study of Salomon Reinach on ancient religion, not resentment of his disciples' falling away, seems to have led Freud to compose *Totem and Taboo*. He found in Jacob Burckhardt's *Greek Cultural History* not only much fascinating information on a past civilization that he deeply cared about but also the core of his own method of interpreting what

---

2. L. Flem, *L'homme Freud* (Paris, 1991), 119–47 (the quotation in the text is from 122).

patients told him in the present. The "gleichschwebende Aufmerksamkeit" (closely hovering attention) of the ideal analyst described by Freud—one who listens on principle to all testimony, even the apparently trivial, and refuses to decide in advance which points merit close attention—reproduces the hermeneutical attentiveness of the ideal cultural historian as described by Burckhardt. Freud revealed this not only in the note of 1899 in which he recorded what he had learned but also in an enthusiastic letter to Fliess.[3] A hundred years ago, classical reading still had much to offer the boldest of modernists—as Eliot, Pound, Joyce, and De Chirico would have agreed.

At the end of the twentieth century, prophets denounce—and applaud—the impending death of all traditional forms of reading. All printed texts may drown in the endlessly attractive vortex of the computer, attentive reading may turn into trancelike scanning, and the smells, tastes, and human details of the individual book may be replaced by the uniform shapes and colors of the computer monitor. Whether modern humanism, now grown old, will survive this excess of new forms of access, as it has survived four centuries of other calamities and triumphs, a historian cannot and should not predict.[4]

When the Baal Shem Tov had to do an important thing, he went out into the woods, lit a fire, said a prayer—and the thing was done. In successive generations, his disciples ceased to light the fire, to go out into the woods, even to say the prayer. Yet the thing was still done, time after time, generation after generation: what could be done was enough. The Baal Shem's last heir could carry out none of the rites that were called for. But he could recall, as he sat in his palace, on his golden throne, how these things had once been done. And the magic of his words achieved what his predecessors had had to accomplish through elaborate rituals.[5] *Forsan et haec olim meminisse iuvabit.*

---

3. I. Grubrich-Simitis, *Zurück zu Freuds Texten* (Frankfurt a.M., 1993).

4. Cf. S. Birkerts, *The Gutenberg Elegies* (Boston and London, 1994).

5. Cf. J. Levenson, *Confucian China and Its Modern Fate* (Berkeley, 1958–65); but I am indebted to Moshe Idel for the interpretation of the story given here.

A Note on Further Reading

History of the Book and of Reading

The history of the book in early modern Europe began as a French special-ity and concerned itself at first with quantitative, rather than qualitative, data and problems—in particular, with statistical analysis of the contents of libraries, as revealed by postmortem inventories. For useful introductions to and critiques of these pioneer efforts, see R. Chartier, *The Cultural Uses of Print in Early Modern France*, trans. L.G. Cochrane (Princeton, N.J., 1987), esp. chaps. 5–7; and R. Darnton, *The Literary Underground of the Old Regime* (Cambridge, Mass., and London, 1982), chap. 6. Gradually, how-ever, the central interest of historians of the book has shifted from recon-structing patterns of distribution and possession to uncovering what the experience of reading meant at a given time and place. Carlo Ginzburg's monograph *The Cheese and the Worms*, trans. J. Tedeschi and A. Tedeschi (Baltimore and London, 1980), which set out to show how a particular heretic, a miller interrogated at length by the Inquisition, had read Sir John Mandeville and other texts, remains one of the most ingenious efforts in this line; see also R. Darnton's study of readers' responses to Rousseau, in *The Great Cat Massacre and Other Episodes in French Cultural History* (New York, 1984), chap. 6. A very recent monograph, which helpfully surveys various methods of studying reading, both historical and literary, and then applies them in a rich case study of an Elizabethan intellectual, is W. Sher-man's *John Dee* (Amherst, Mass., 1995). More anthropological approaches can be sampled in *Ethnographies of Reading*, ed. J. Boyarin (Berkeley, Los Angeles, and Oxford, 1993).

Renaissance Humanism and the Book

The best introduction to Renaissance humanism and its larger context is provided by the collected general essays of P.O. Kristeller, *Renaissance Thought and Its Sources*, ed. M. Mooney (New York, 1979). On the development of new forms of manuscript book in the fifteenth and sixteenth centuries, see B.L. Ullman, *The Origin and Development of Humanistic Script* (Rome, 1960); J. Wardrop, *The Script of Humanism* (Oxford, 1963); and A.C. de la Mare, "New Research on Humanistic Scribes in Florence," in *Miniatura fiorentina del Rinascimento,* ed. A. Garzelli (Florence, 1985). Though there is no comprehensive study of the printing of classical texts, M. Lowry's elegant monograph *The World of Aldus Manutius* (Oxford, 1979) offers an informative introduction to the world of the humanistic printers. The development of bindings—which, in the Renaissance, were taken very seriously as an expression of the owners' tastes and interests, and which rapidly assumed a classicizing style—is studied by A. Hobson in *Humanists and Bookbinders* (Cambridge, 1989). For the growth of the most important humanistic libraries, one may consult B.L. Ullman and P.A. Stadter, *The Public Library of Renaissance Florence: Niccolò Niccoli, Cosimo de' Medici, and the Library of San Marco* (Padua, 1972); and *Rome Reborn: The Vatican Library and Renaissance Culture,* ed. A. Grafton (Washington, D.C., Vatican City, New Haven, and London, 1993). On earlier and later collections the best place to begin is A. Hobson's *Great Libraries* (New York, 1970), which offers a well-informed introduction to the history and architecture of more than thirty great libraries, several of them formed in the Renaissance. See also the informative and stimulating essay of R. Chartier, *L'ordre des livres* (Aix-en-Provence, 1992).

The Study and Interpretation of Classical Texts in the Renaissance

L.D. Reynolds and N.G. Wilson survey the development of classical scholarship from antiquity onward in their concise and stimulating *Scribes and Scholars,* 3d ed. (Oxford, 1991), with an up-to-date bibliography. A general introduction to Renaissance approaches to the study of classical texts appears in A. Grafton, *Defenders of the Text* (Cambridge, Mass., and London, 1991), chap. 1; see also *Der Kommentar in der Renaissance,* ed. A. Buck (Boppard, 1975). Some of the fullest studies as yet available of the history of textual criticism and interpretation take the form of monographs on individuals: P. de Nolhac's old but vital *Pétrarque et l'humanisme,* 2d ed. (Paris, 1907); B.L. Ullman, *The Humanism of Coluccio Salutati* (Padua, 1963)—see also R.G. Witt, *Hercules at the Crossroads* (Durham, N.C., 1983); J.F. d'Amico, *Theory and Practice in Renaissance Textual Criticism: Beatus Rhenanus between Conjecture and History* (Berkeley, Los Angeles, and London, 1988); W. McCuaig, *Carlo Sigonio* (Princeton, N.J., 1989); and A. Grafton, *Joseph Scaliger* (Oxford, 1983–93). W. Schwarz, *Principles and Problems of Biblical Translation* (Cambridge, 1955), and J. Bentley, *Humanists and Holy Writ* (Princeton, 1983), are informative, complementary introductions to the study of the Bible in the same period. On the continued taste for allegorical interpretation, much of it classical in origin, see J. Seznec, *The Survival of the Pagan Gods,* trans. B.F. Sessions (New York, 1953); and D.C. Allen, *Mysteriously Meant* (Baltimore and London, 1970). Renaissance intellectuals believed that the classics had not only the highest scholarly and literary qualities but also immense practical value: they considered them the primary sources for instruction in government leadership and in warfare, and they thought mature men should continue to study them throughout their lives. This pragmatic form of humanism was given its most popular formulation by Justus Lipsius, whose work and world can now be best approached through M. Morford's *Stoics and Neo-Stoics* (Princeton, 1991). On the role of the classics in forming high policy see in general G. Oestreich, *Neo-Stoicism and the Early Modern State* (Cambridge, 1982): for a case study see L.A. Jardine and A. Grafton, " 'Studied for Action': How Gabriel Harvey Read His Livy," *Past and Present* 129 (1990): 30–78.

Index

Abraham, 118
Achilles, 163–65, 170, 180
Aeneas, 35, 48, 177–78
Agamemnon, 170
Agricola, Georgius, 200–201
Ailly, Pierre d', 124
Alberti, Leon Battista, 53–92, 113, 116, 130
Albumasar, 124
Alcibiades, 110, 137
Alexander of Hales, 129
Alfonso of Aragon, 50
Allegory, 109–11, 163–65, 167–68, 172–74, 178n. 119, 180–82, 185, 191, 195–96
Alsted, J.H., 6
Amaseo, Girolamo, 145–46
Anaxagoras, 67
Aphrodite, 167
Apollo, 178
Archytas, 67
Ares (Mars), 171–72, 186
Aristarchus, 175
Aristophanes, 145
Aristotle, 13, 16–18, 97, 106, 108, 120–21, 122, 125–26, 128, 131, 186, 197
Astrology, 111–34, 185, 214–16
Astronomy, 117–18, 129, 185–87, 189, 194–95, 208–21
Athena, 163–65, 171–72, 180
Athenaeus, 169
Augustine, 112, 114, 131, 196
Aurispa, Giovanni, 42
Averroës, 106

Bacon, Francis, 97, 202
Bacon, Roger, 105
Barbaro, Ermolao, 96, 109
Barbaro, Francesco, 47
Barclay, J., 202–3
Barzizza, Gasparino, 55, 62, 83–84
Bate, Henry, 105
Bellanti, Luca, 113, 123
Benivieni, Girolamo, 98, 107, 127
Bernegger, Matthias, 210, 215
Beroaldo, Filippo, 103
Berosus, 29
Bessarion, Cardinal, 12, 28
Biondo, Flavio, 72
Bisticci, Vespasiano da, 14, 25, 26, 38, 41
Boethius, 137
Boiardo, Feltrino, 41, 44
Brahe, Tycho, 186–87, 195, 217, 218
Briareus, 170
Brunelleschi, Filippo, 87
Bruni, Leonardo, 11, 14, 18, 40, 57, 84, 88
Budé, Guillaume, 135–83
Budé, Jean, 148–49
Burchard, Franz, 108
Burckhardt, Jacob, 53–55, 226–27
Bussi, Giovanni Andrea de', 25, 25n. 48
Bussoni, Biagio, 33–34

Caesar, 22, 33, 39
Callimachus, 104, 127
Callisthenes, 213
Camerte, Varino Favorino, 145–46

Campanella, Tommaso, 101
Cardano, Girolamo, 15, 194, 221–23
Casaubon, Isaac, 205
Chalcondyles, Demetrius, 161
Chambellan, David, 149–50
Chrysippus, 2, 67, 86
Chrysoloras, Manuel, 12, 89
Cicero, 24, 33, 39, 43, 59, 62, 67, 68n.
    52, 73, 77, 79–83, 85–86, 89, 112,
    114, 115, 166
Clapmarius, Arnold, 206, 208
Comenius, Jan Amos, 6, 154, 169
Crinito, Pietro, 43, 100, 106, 132,
    179
Croll, Oswald, 216
Crotus Rubeanus, Johannes, 139–40
Crusius, Martin, 185, 191–92, 205

Dante Alighieri, 86, 109
Dasypodius, Conrad, 189
Dati, Leonardo, 57, 62–63, 66, 68
Decembrio, Angelo, 19–49
Decembrio, Pier Candido, 21, 26
Demo, 178
Demodocus, 165
Demosthenes, 141
Devaris, Matteo, 179
Dio Chrysostom, 162, 165
Diodorus Siculus, 11, 29, 71, 179
Diogenes Laertius, 115
Dionysius, 214
ps.-Dionysius the Areopagite, 14
Donatus, 33
Dondi, Giovanni, 89–91

Elia del Medigo, 105, 106
Epictetus, 2–3, 5
Epicurus, 109
Erasmus, Desiderius, 4–5, 45, 110,
    136–38, 140, 141, 144, 154, 165,
    168, 173, 191, 193, 223
Este, Leonello d', 20–48, 56
Este, Niccolò d', 20, 44
Eudoxus, 118
Eugenius IV, 26, 32, 71
Eusebius, 63–64
Eustathius, 168, 173, 176, 177, 181–82

Fabritius, Paulus, 189
Facio, Bartolomeo, 50–52
Fausto, Vettor, 174–75
Ferdinand of Aragon, 50
Ficino, Marsilio, 85, 94, 96, 97–98,
    106, 113, 116, 116n. 74, 118,
    122–23, 127
Flaminio, Giovanni Antonio, 102–3
Francis I, 141, 180
Freud, Sigmund, 226–27

Galen, 201, 222–23
Galilei, Galileo, 185, 189–91, 212–13
Gaza, Theodore, 150
Gellius, Aulus, 22, 112
Geryon, 167
Gesner, Conrad, 199–200
Ghiberti, Lorenzo, 77
Giannotti, Donato, 159
Giocondo, Giovanni, 159–60
Gonzaga, Francesco, 38
Gratius, Ortwin, 139
Gualengo, Giovanni, 32–33
Guarini, Guarino, 12, 20, 21, 22, 45,
    46, 64, 96
Guarino, Battista, 96, 103
Guicciardini, Francesco, 113, 203–4

Hannibal, 32, 44
Harmonides, 171
Harvey, Gabriel, 153, 156
Hector, 177
Helen, 48, 177
Henry of Hesse, 112
Hermeneutics, 1–7, 202–3
Hermes Trismegistus, 91–92, 93–95,
    102, 115, 116, 117, 132, 215
Hermonymus, George, 146–47, 149–50
Herodotus, 29, 71, 157, 205
ps.-Herodotus, 162, 165, 182
Hesiod, 130–31
Hipparchus, 117, 214, 218
Hippocrates, 17
Homer, 110, 135–83, 185–86, 191
Horace, 70, 97
Horapollo, 104
Hutten, Ulrich von, 139–40

Iamblichus, 116, 117
Imitation, 79–91

Jerome, 30, 129
Josephus, 108–9, 166
Junius, Franciscus, 143
Justin, 33
Juvenal, 31n. 68, 45

Kepler, Johannes, 123–24, 185–224

Lactantius, 196
Lamola, Giovanni, 22, 39
Lamperti, Ioannes, 11
Landino, Cristoforo, 85–86, 167–68
Lascaris, Janus, 105, 157, 160–61, 162,
    179–80
Laus Pisonis, 193–94
Lazzarelli, Ludovico, 95
Leoni, Pietro, 129
Leoniceno, Nicolò, 102, 105, 197
Libavius, Andreas, 216
Libraries
    Alexandria, 25–26
    Giovanni Aurispa, 42
    Guillaume Budé, 143–45, 148–52
    Jean Budé, 148–49
    David Chambellan, 149–50
    Leonello d'Este, 19–49
    Sigmund Freud, 226–27
    Francesco Gonzaga, 38
    Giovanni Gualengo, 32–34
    Janus Lascaris, 160–61, 179–
        80
    Lucullus, 24
    Cosimo de' Medici, 26
    Lorenzo de' Medici, 105–6, 129,
        160–61
    Marciana, 173–74, 179
    San Marco, 43, 106, 132
    Hieronymus Megiser, 195n. 27
    Pico della Mirandola, 100–
        108
    Federigo da Montefeltro, 38
    Rome, 24
    Joseph Scaliger, 37
    University of Leiden, 24–25

Vatican, 1, 15–16, 21–26, 70–72, 93,
    95, 105, 179
Saint Victor, 178–79
Linacre, Thomas, 138
Lipsius, Justus, 206
Livy, 32, 33, 40, 44, 84
Longueil, Christophe de, 179
Lucian, 64, 92, 195–96, 208–9
Luther, Martin, 113, 197

Machiavelli, Niccolò, 122, 133, 203–4
Maestlin, Michael, 185
Mainardi, Giovanni, 111
Malatesta, Sigismondo, 56
Manderscheit, Christopher Comes van,
    156
Manetho, 29
Manilius, 129, 143
Manuzio, Aldo, 45, 157, 158
Marsuppini, Carlo, 41
Mascarini, Giovanni, 100
Medici, Cosimo de', 94
Medici, Lorenzo de', 96, 109, 113, 128
Melchior, 107
Menelaus, 176
Mercurio, Giovanni, 94, 95
Meriones, 176
Mithridates, Flavius, 94, 106–7
Montefeltro, Federigo de', 38
More, Thomas, 136, 140
Moses, 132

Nabonassar, 118, 214
Nabuchodonosor, 118
Narcissus, 78
Naudé, Gabriel, 34
Nechepso, 128
Niccoli, Niccolò, 37, 39
Nicholas V, 11, 14–16, 23, 25, 26, 56,
    71
Ninus, 118
Notebooks, 6, 168–71
Numa, 124

Oresme, Nicole, 112, 124–25
Orpheus, 115, 131, 177, 178
Ovid, 79, 219

Paris, 175, 176
Pericles, 15, 18
Petrarch, F., 36, 82–83, 90, 109, 219
Pico della Mirandola, Gianfrancesco,
    111
Pico della Mirandola, Giovanni, 43,
    93–134
"Pico Master," 101
Pisani, Ugolino, 27
Pistorius, Johannes, 216–17
Pius II, 19, 20n. 32, 56
Plato, 47, 67, 68, 97, 98–99, 104, 110,
    111, 115, 117, 118, 122, 128, 131,
    197
Plautus, 25, 42, 62
Pletho, George Gemisthus, 115, 118
Pliny the Elder, 7, 77, 79, 81, 197
Pliny the Younger, 30, 89
Plotinus, 78, 97–98, 122–23
Plutarch, 39, 70, 208–13
ps.-Plutarch, 162–66, 171–72
Poggio Bracciolini, 12, 15, 36–37, 39
Poliziano, Angelo, 43, 96, 100, 103,
    105–6, 122–23, 126–31, 134, 162,
    178, 179, 197
Polybius, 155
Pompeius Trogus, 118
Pontano, Giovanni Gioviano, 62
Porphyry, 116, 122, 215
Poseidon, 170, 177
Posidonius, 90
Proclus, 108, 110, 130, 221
Propertius, 103–4, 103–4n. 34
Protagoras, 68
Ptolemy, 65–66, 104, 108, 112–13,
    117, 118, 124, 125, 186, 214, 215,
    218, 220–21
Ptolemy Philadelphus, 16n. 16, 23, 25,
    36
Pythagoras, 64, 124, 128, 132
Pythagoreans, 115, 119, 125–26

Quintilian, 17, 18, 51, 59

Rabelais, François, 167
Reuchlin, Johannes, 138–39, 150
Rheatinus, Thomas, 45

Rheticus, G.J., 218
Ricci, Matteo, 1–4
Rucellai, Giovanni, 56, 67

Sadoleto, Jacopo, 150–51
Sallust, 17, 33
Salutati, Coluccio, 11, 22–23, 36
Savile, Henry, 213
Savonarola, Girolamo, 96, 131–32
Scala, Bartolomeo, 59–60
Scaliger, Joseph, 37, 123, 143, 205
Scaliger, Julius Caesar, 194, 221–22
Scholia Demosthenica, 158–59
Scholia Homerica, 157–61, 173–77
Scholia Pindarica, 158
Scholium Plautinum, 25, 25n. 48
Scipio Africanus, 32
Seneca, 3, 24, 27, 76–77, 83, 90, 196
Serenus Sammonicus, 23–24
Servius, 47–48, 178
Severianus, 129
Sibyls, 177–78
Silber, Eucharius, 93
Simplicius, 221
Socrates, 110, 197
Solon, 132
Strozzi, Tito Vespasiano, 27, 42, 44

Tacitus, 204–8
Tengnagel, Sebastian, 209
Terence, 23, 33, 42, 48
Themistius, 166
Theophrastus, 72n. 65
ps.-Thomas Aquinas, 137
Thucydides, 12–19, 49–52, 70–71, 73,
    153, 205
Tortelli, Giovanni, 50
Toscanelli, Paolo, 113
Traversari, Ambrogio, 14
Tunstall, Cuthbert, 146
Tura, Cosimo, 101

Valla, Giorgio, 103, 104
Valla, Lorenzo, 11–19, 23, 39, 49–52,
    71, 88, 157
Vegio, Maffeo, 46, 84
Vesalius, Andreas, 201

Victorinus, 82
Villoison, J.B.G. d'Ansse de, 173
Virgil, 4–5, 20, 44, 45, 46, 47–48, 84,
    177
Vitruvius, 74–75, 159–60
Vives, Juan Luis, 136
Voigt, Georg, 57
Vopiscus, 24

Wolf, Friedrich August, 173–74

Xenophon, 155
Xylander, Wilhelm, 209–11

Zeuxis, 79–83
Zoroaster, 93, 101, 102, 107, 115,
    117, 125, 132, 215

Plates

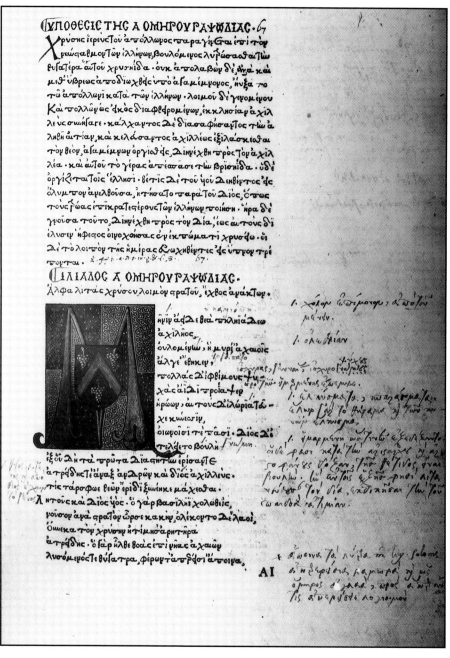

Fig. 1. The beginning of the *Iliad*, from Guillaume Budé's copy of the first printed edition of Homer. An illuminator has added the first letter of the text, a capital mu, splendidly adorned with the arms of the Budé family. Guillaume's marginal notes reveal the beginnings of his Homeric studies. (Courtesy Department of Rare Books and Special Collections, Princeton University.)

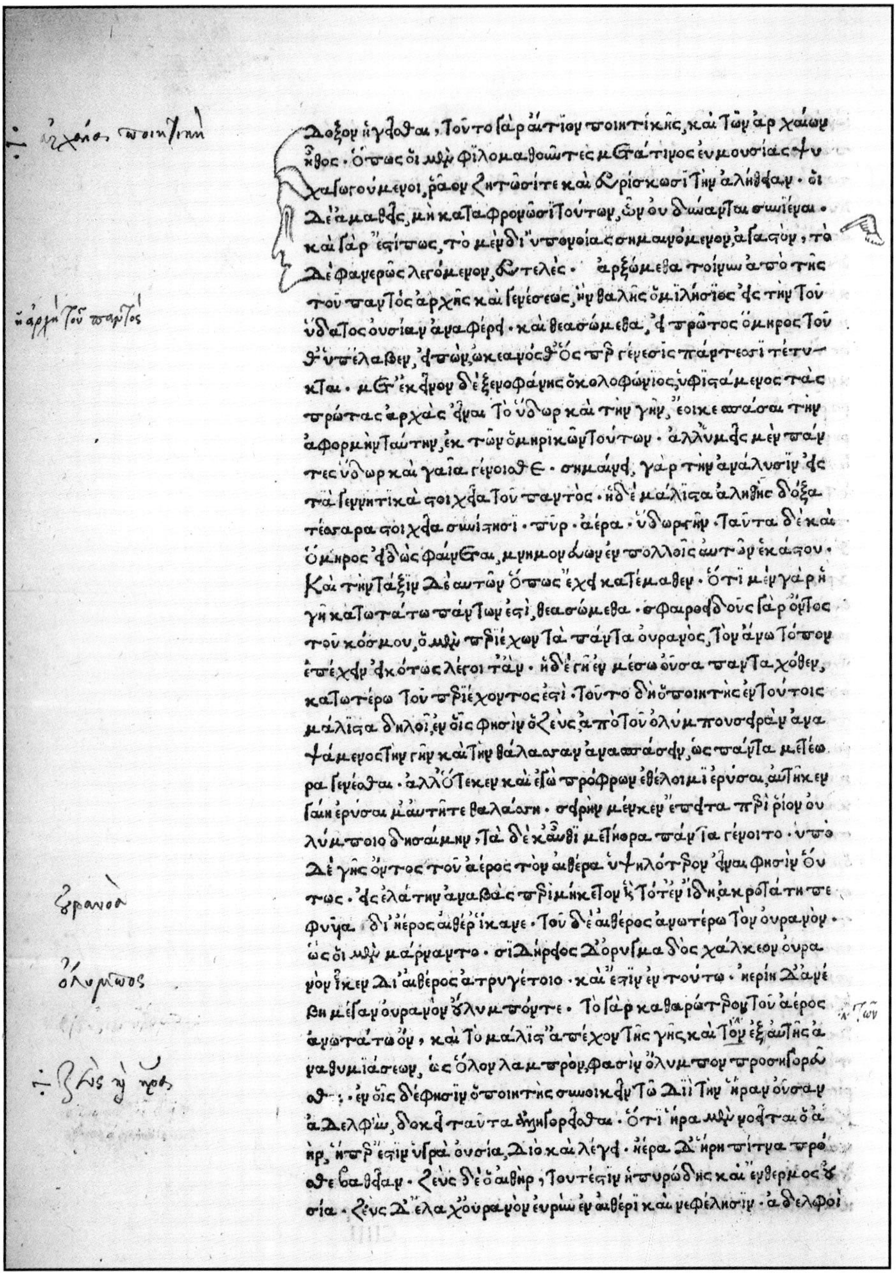

Fig. 2. Budé drew the slightly gloomy profile in the left margin—a visually as well as substantively memorable device—to make a statement about the text—the *Vita Homeri* by pseudo-Plutarch. (Courtesy Department of Rare Books and Special Collections, Princeton University.)

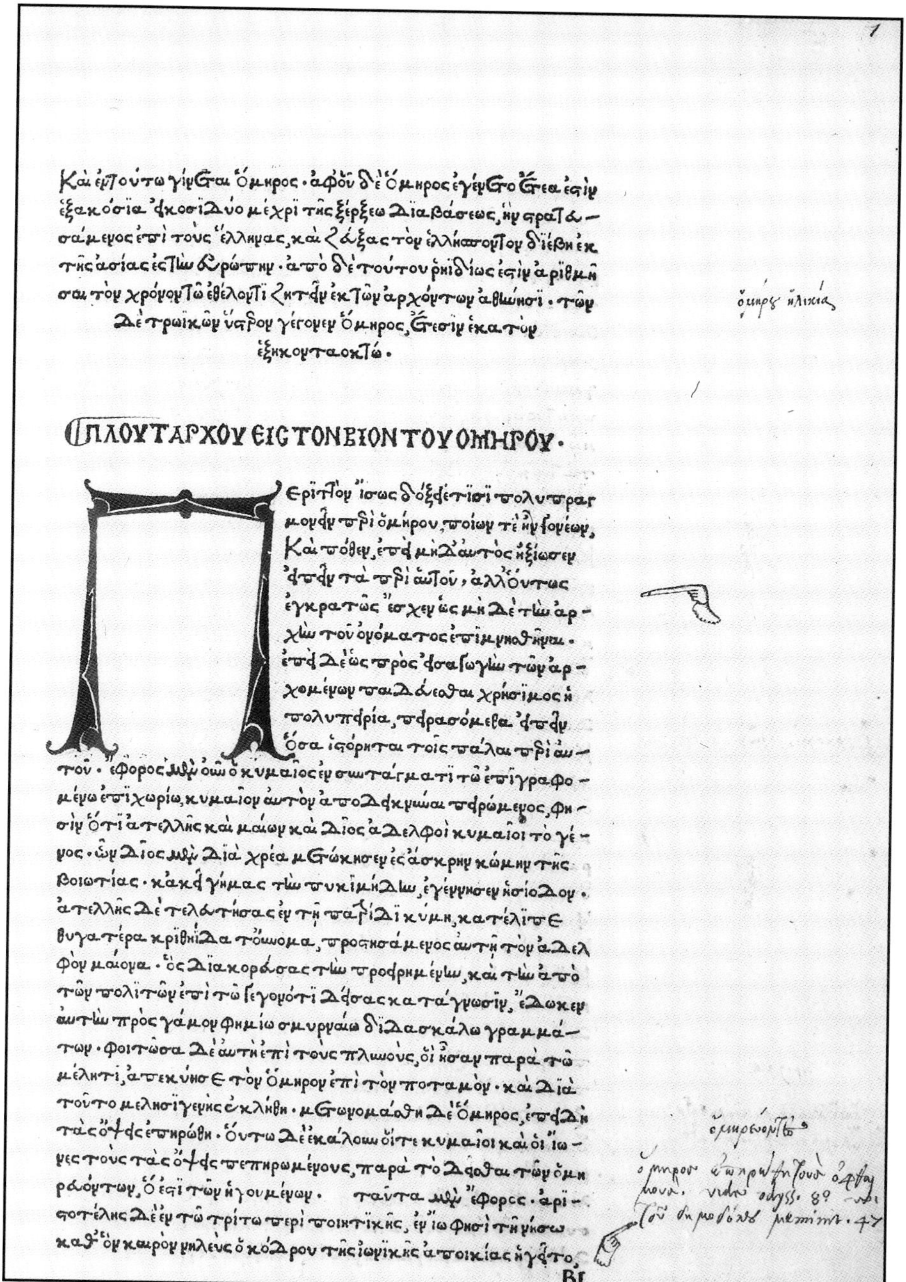

ΠΛΟΥΤΑΡΧΟΥ ΕΙΣ ΤΟΝ ΒΙΟΝ ΤΟΥ ΟΜΗΡΟΥ.

Fig. 3. Budé's marginal notation summarizes a passage in pseudo-Plutarch's *Vita Homeri* that describes Homer as blind. Budé also adds a cross-reference to the appearance of the blind bard Demodokos in book 8 of the *Odyssey*. (Courtesy Department of Rare Books and Special Collections, Princeton University.)

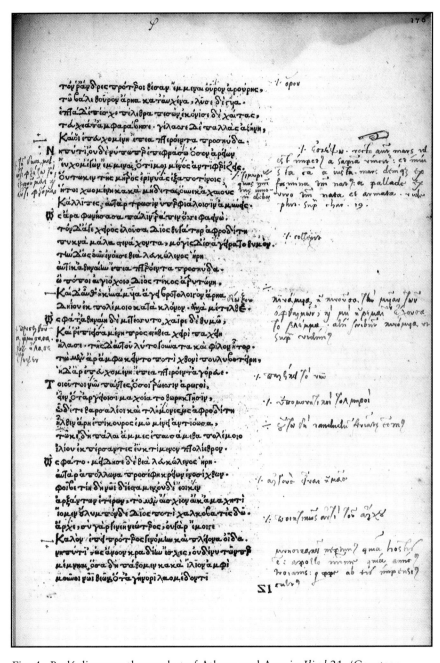

Fig. 4. Budé discusses the combat of Athena and Ares in *Iliad* 21. (Courtesy Department of Rare Books and Special Collections, Princeton University.)

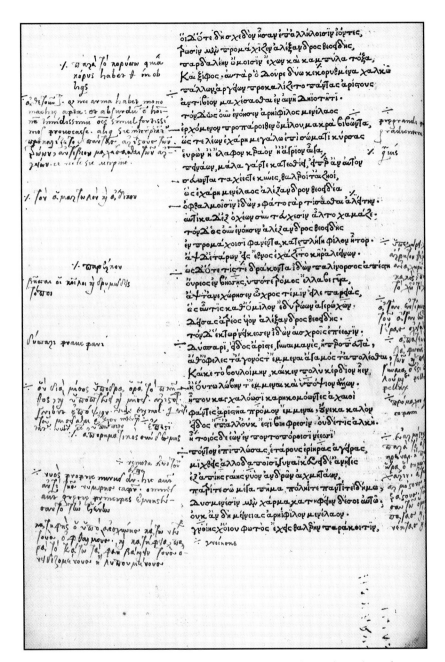

Fig. 5. Budé points out that ancient scholars had condemned two lines from
the beginning of *Iliad* 3 as illogical. (Courtesy Department of Rare Books and
Special Collections, Princeton University.)

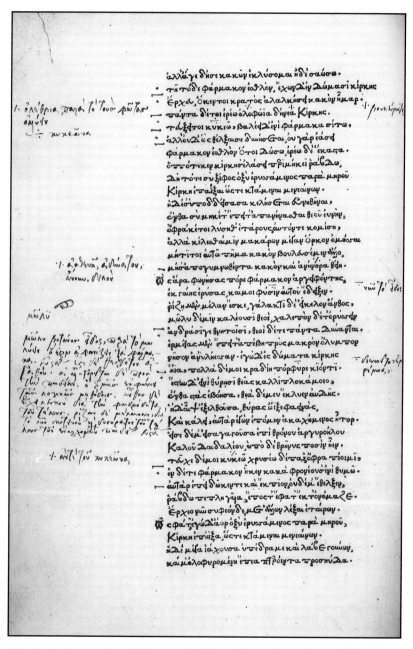

Fig. 6. In the margins of this page, Budé copies out from the twelfth-century Homeric commentary of Eustathius of Thessalonica, one of his favorite sources, a note on the allegorical meaning of the magical plant moly, mentioned in the *Odyssey*. (Courtesy Department of Rare Books and Special Collections, Princeton University.)